JEWISH RELIGIOUS MUSIC IN NINETEENTH-CENTURY AMERICA

JEWISH RELIGIOUS MUSIC IN NINETEENTH-CENTURY AMERICA

Restoring the Synagogue Soundtrack

Judah M. Cohen

INDIANA UNIVERSITY PRESS

This book is a publication of

Indiana University Press
Office of Scholarly Publishing
Herman B Wells Library 350
1320 East 10th Street
Bloomington, Indiana 47405 USA

iupress.indiana.edu

© 2019 by Judah M. Cohen

All rights reserved

No part of this book may be reproduced or utilized in any form or by any means, electronic or mechanical, including photocopying and recording, or by any information storage and retrieval system, without permission in writing from the publisher. The paper used in this publication meets the minimum requirements of the American National Standard for Information Sciences—Permanence of Paper for Printed Library Materials, ANSI Z39.48-1992.

Manufactured in the United States of America

Cataloging information is available from the Library of Congress.

ISBN 978-0-253-04020-6 (cloth)
ISBN 978-0-253-04021-3 (paperback)
ISBN 978-0-253-04024-4 (ebook)

1 2 3 4 5   24 23 22 21 20 19

The [new] Minhag America [prayer book] will be introduced
in the Synagogue, as soon as the choir and the pupils of
the Talmid Yelodim Institute will be sufficiently prepared,
which we hope will be the case
Sabbath next.

—*THE ISRAELITE* (NOTICE, LIKELY ADDED BY ISAAC MAYER WISE), OCTOBER 2, 1857.

Minhag America premiered two weeks later.

CONTENTS

Acknowledgments ix

Accessing Supplemental Materials xiii

Introduction *1*

1 Early Strata: Of Choirs and Reform through the Mid-Nineteenth Century 19

2 The Sound of German Jewry: Hymnals and Singing Societies in Wilhelm Fischer's *Zemirot Yisrael* 55

3 *Bildungsmusik*: G. M. Cohen, B'nai B'rith, and the Voices of American Jewish Cultivation 76

4 Musical Populists: G. S. Ensel, Simon Hecht, and the Quest for the Singing Congregation 117

5 The 1866 *Sulzerfeier*: The Viennese Model and the Grandeur of the Urban Worship 174

6 A New Cantor, a New Repertoire: *Zimrath Yah* 185

7 The Path to the *Union Hymnal* 217

Conclusion: Restoring the Soundtrack of Jewish Life in Nineteenth-Century America 267

Works Cited 277

Index 295

ACKNOWLEDGMENTS

ON DECEMBER 8, 1999, AS PART OF MY dissertation fieldwork, I attended a weekly cantorial practicum at New York's Hebrew Union College School of Sacred Music.[1] That day, the program comprised excerpts from cantor Gershon Ephros's six-volume *Cantorial Anthology* (published 1929–69), a classic foundational work for cantorial education.[2] The students' meticulously prepared presentations received public plaudits. In the private discussion that followed, however, Ephros's material became the subject of vigorous debate. Cantorial faculty described the *Cantorial Anthology* as Ephros's attempt to link choral music traditions from the nineteenth century with Eastern European chant styles that emerged in the twentieth-century synagogue. One senior student cut to the quick, though, by describing the day's presented compositions as "second rate" and recommending that they "be thrown out." Students and faculty alike responded by defending the *Anthology*'s place as part of the cantorial legacy, while quietly avoiding discussions of quality.[3] Their subsequent comments characterized musical practice in the nineteenth-century synagogue as a formative era that paved the way for a superior understanding of Jewish music in the twentieth century.

That view of the time period, I found, extended beyond the practicum discussion to the classroom. Except for a few canonical composers such as Salomon Sulzer, Samuel Naumbourg, and Louis Lewandowski, the era held a largely transitional character, focusing on Jewish musical authorities who shifted Jewish music from reliance on "oral tradition" to a score-based written tradition. Assuming that tradition to lie mainly with Eastern European Jewish populations, moreover, instructors gave American synagogue composers from this time especially harsh treatment: often excluding them from the repertoire, and regularly dismissing them as uninformed, overly commercial, or (for non-Jewish composers) unconnected to Judaism.

As a graduate student in ethnomusicology who interpreted critiques of musical quality as revealing commentaries on the boundaries of identity, I marked such discussions for further consideration. During spare moments, I explored the open music shelves of the Hebrew Union College library for overlooked works that pushed back through layers of history. A few years later, via an invitation to write the musical history of Manhattan's Central Synagogue, I took my first opportunity to research the 1800s in detail. I am grateful to the students and faculty of the (now) Debbie Friedman School of Sacred Music, as well as Ann Mininberg, Cantor Elizabeth Sacks, and the clergy and staff at Central Synagogue for showing me how much more I needed to learn.

By the time I could dive into the nineteenth century in earnest, a broad swath of out-of-print and out-of-copyright works had appeared on both curated and noncurated internet sites, including Google Books, Hathi Trust, the Goethe University Library's Compact Memory site, Ancestry.com, and ProQuest online newspapers. These digitized versions of obscure works made the era suddenly and easily accessible, benefiting my research immensely. But as with most archives, they also left many holes that only archival research could fill. Fortunately, most of the archives I approached had deeply knowledgeable staff who fulfilled requests with extraordinary speed, while providing their own helpful ideas. A Bernard and Audre Rapoport Fellowship allowed me to dive deeply into the immense offerings of Cincinnati's American Jewish Archives in summer 2014, with constant generous support from Kevin Proffitt, Elisa Ho, Dana Herman, Joe Weber, the fantastic staff, and director Gary Zola. Warren Klein, curator of the Herbert and Eileen Bernard Museum of Judaica at Congregation Emanu-El of the City of New York, provided me access to early congregational minutes of its affiliated synagogues. Curtis Mann of the Sangamon Historical Society generously provided materials pertaining to Springfield, Illinois; Jay Hyland of the Jewish Museum Milwaukee and Diane Everman of the St. Louis Jewish Community Archives did similarly with materials from their respective cities. Outside of the United States, Noam Silberberg at the Jewish Genealogy and Family Heritage Center of Warsaw's Emanuel Ringelblum Jewish Historical Institute parsed key Polish records with me; and Gila Flam, curator of the immense music collection at the National Library of Israel, speedily provided digital copies of materials not available anywhere else. A spring 2016 sabbatical semester as a fellow of Indiana University's Institute for Advanced Study allowed me the space and encouragement to put the balance of my manuscript together, along with the enthusiastic support of Suzanne Ingalsbe and Eileen Julien. A year devoting three hours per week with Indiana University's Faculty Writing

Group, led by Laura Plummer and facilitated by Alisha Jones and Tessa Bent, allowed me to finish it up.

The current form of this narrative has benefited from a number of opportunities to present work in progress. In addition to papers at meetings of the Society for Ethnomusicology, Association for Jewish Studies, and World Congress of Jewish Studies, I am grateful for invitations to try out my ideas at Cincinnati's Hebrew Union College and American Jewish Archives, the Indiana University Musicology Colloquium Series, and a conference convened by Jascha Nemtsov in the German-Polish border town of Görlitz/Zgorzelec. A shorter version of my chapter on G. S. Ensel appears in the *American Jewish Archives Journal*; I am grateful to two anonymous reviewers for their deeply thoughtful comments and to editors Dana Herman and Gary Zola for their permission to include a substantial portion of that essay here.[4]

Profound thanks also go to a community of colleagues who encouraged me and offered valuable critique, giving of their time amid often crushing administrative and teaching loads. Mark Kligman's generous close reading of the entire manuscript helped my ideas immensely, as did insights from Francesco Spagnolo, Mark Slobin, and Diana Matut. My Indiana University colleagues in the Department of Folklore and Ethnomusicology and Jacobs School of Music's Department of Musicology have been a constant source of support, especially nineteenth-century specialists Halina Goldberg and Kristina Muxfeldt. My dear colleagues in the Borns Jewish Studies Program provided stability and confidence throughout, and I particularly thank Steve Weitzman, Jeff Veidlinger, and Mark Roseman for their calming stewardship of the program, Sarah Imhoff for her thoughts, and all of the program's faculty and staff for maintaining a warm and productive environment. Adah Hetko, Jaime Carini, and Meredith Rigby, my graduate assistants during the manuscript's final steps, provided crucial help with research, proofreading, and bibliography. Thank you also to Dana Herman, Michael R. Cohen, Sharon Mintz, Laurel Wolfson, and Chana Wolfson for their help in obtaining images. Writing can only happen once most other needs are met, a rare and coveted condition in today's academic scene; I am grateful for everyone's efforts to grant me the professional support and space to make such conditions possible.

At Indiana University Press, I am grateful for the professional, devoted, and efficient stewardship of Janice Frisch, Rachel Rosolina, and Kate Schramm, who transformed the normally glacial slog of academic publishing into a swift process while maintaining its academic vigor. Thank you also to Mary Jo Rhodes for her professional production work, and to Eileen Allen for compiling the index.

Most importantly, I could not have written this book without the support of my wife and life partner, Rebecca, and the enthusiasm of my children, Rena and Gabriel. They have been with me throughout this project, regularly insisting that I disengage from my computer to join in family activities (board games, escape rooms, baseball, soccer, volleyball, and plenty of carpools…), and ensuring a meaningful work-life balance. Perhaps at some point they'll have the chance to read this book to see if it was worth all the fuss. My parents, Richard and Treasure Cohen, imbued in me the curiosity to turn strange and obscure questions into perhaps equally strange and obscure answers; and my father-in-law, Stanley Nash, provided constant encouragement as a fellow academic citizen.

Finally, I dedicate this book to the memories of two relatives and a dear friend who died during its writing. My mother-in-law, Edna (Hirsch) Nash, came with her family on the journey from Central Europe to the United States almost a century after the events in this book but under different and dire circumstances. My nephew Andrew Levy's journey was far briefer. Both found music nourishing and fulfilling, helping them transcend the limitations they faced. Both also leave music as part of their lasting legacy: in Edna's descendants and in Andrew's music therapy fund. Lou Mervis, meanwhile, made my position at Indiana University possible, and with his wife, Sybil, and their wonderful extended family welcomed my own family to Bloomington with enthusiastic support and lasting friendship.

May their memories be a blessing.

Notes

1. In 2011, shortly after the passing of songleader/songwriter/liturgist Debbie Friedman, the school changed its name to the Debbie Friedman School of Sacred Music.

2. Gershon Ephros, ed. *The Cantorial Anthology of Traditional and Modern Music*. 6 vv. New York: Bloch, 1929–69. Ephros (1890–1978), a student of A. Z. Idelsohn in Jerusalem during the 1910s, served as a prominent cantor in Perth Amboy, NJ, and taught at the Hebrew Union College School of Sacred Music.

3. Post-practicum discussion, Hebrew Union College–School of Sacred Music, New York City, December 8, 1999.

4. Judah M. Cohen, "Interwoven Voices of the Religious Landscape: G. S. Ensel and Musical Populism in the Nineteenth Century American Synagogue," *American Jewish Archives Journal* 69, no. 1 (2017): 1–40.

ACCESSING SUPPLEMENTAL MATERIALS

Supplemental materials are available for this volume and can be viewed online at http://jewishreligiousmusic.com.

JEWISH RELIGIOUS MUSIC IN NINETEENTH-CENTURY AMERICA

INTRODUCTION

On May 9, 1798, as the United States anticipated war with post-revolution France, New York synagogue Shearith Israel joined other houses of worship to observe a "Day of Public Humiliation" declared by President Thomas Jefferson. Its service that day, partly preserved in a pamphlet issued two months later, featured an English-language sermon by presiding reverend Gershom Seixas.[1] Music, however, framed the oration: after an opening prayer, the attendees intoned Psalms 46 and 51, "chaunted verse by verse; first by the Reader, and repeated by the Congregation"; and after the sermon, the sanctuary resonated with Psalms 120, 121, 130, and 20, all "chaunted jointly by the Reader and the Congregation."[2] The ritual appeared consistent with public services at Shearith Israel dating back to at least 1760 (when "the Reader gave out the psalms" for singing on either end of the sermon). But the 1798 pamphlet highlighted two distinct musical strategies: short tunes repeated responsively for lengthier psalms (twelve verses for Psalm 46, twenty-one for Psalm 51), a practice often described as "lining out," and a suggestion of longer compound melodies for the shorter concluding psalms (eight to ten verses each).[3] The pamphlet lacks information on specific tunes, harmonic and instrumental conventions, language choice, and even the worshipers' existing musical knowledge. Specific clues emerge, however, when seen within the American context: the emphasis on psalmody reflected a popular congregational practice that inspired a number of contemporary versified English translations. While Seixas led the assemblage by singing single-voiced (monophonic) chants, congregational responses likely included voluntary harmony, a practice consistent with contemporary understandings of the term *chaunting* (as seen in the works of numerous contemporary American composers including Andrew Law and William Billings). The tunes, moreover, probably came from a small corpus of known melodies that could apply flexibly to a variety of texts. Two of the psalms (46 and 121) had been chanted at Shearith Israel's first Thanksgiving service in 1789, but their appearance in 1798 alongside other less common psalms suggested few, if any, special tunes.[4] While Seixas had Hebrew facility, moreover, most of the American Jews who sang that day had little practical knowledge of the language and likely preferred English.[5]

These clues hardly lead to definitive descriptions, but offer a glimpse at the complex role that music held in engaging a congregation, focusing them on a communal message, and giving them a public voice in America's active political and religious landscape. Seixas and Shearith Israel used these conventions to shape their approach to civic worship, thereby balancing a sense of Jewish identity with the needs of the day.

Assembling these clues contradicts a number of assumptions long held in the study of music in Jewish life. Rather than seeing local practices as an even playing field upon which various denominations negotiated musical terms, the few scholars who have written on this period have presented an exceptionalist paradigm, treating Jewish musical customs as an extension of "tradition," a shorthand term for communal efforts to preserve and control a body of cherished knowledge. Neil Levin, in the most detailed discussion of music of New York's Shearith Israel congregation at this time, bases his discussion in a European parent population, Amsterdam's Spanish-Portuguese ("Sephardic") synagogue, which he claims was "known for its meticulous preservation and the continuity of its musical heritage and practice." While allowing for "a degree of variation and adaptation" in American synagogue music practice, Levin asserts, such change "was somewhat minimal in this case, owing to the care taken by learned Sephardi *hazzanim* from Europe in teaching this repertoire and keeping it intact as much as possible."[6] In this view, the psalm singing for the 1798 event emphasized Jewish identity by staying true to a long-standing, transatlantic melodic corpus.

Perhaps regular religious services hewed more closely to this traditionalist point of view. But the psalms invoked at the May 1798 service appeared to serve a broader American mode of expression. The same presidentially decreed observance generated at least nineteen other such sermon-focused pamphlets across New England alone, and while Seixas's sermon may have differed politically from many of them, the uniformity of the underlying ritual presented Jews as participants in a nation-defining act, ideologically, spiritually, and musically continuous with their non-Jewish neighbors.[7] At a Wednesday service, which presented no specifically Jewish musical restrictions for the small group of worshipers, invention and adoption may have been considered in equal measure.

Seen as a creative and participatory act rather than one reliant on European precedent, this moment can offer a more expansive—and, perhaps, more realistic—portrait of what it meant for Jews in America to sound out their religious identity. The May 1798 service also offers a useful starting point for this book, which seeks to define more clearly the sound of nineteenth-century American Jewry: a time and a place that scholarship on "Jewish musical tradition" renders "infirm and characterless" at best, and invisible at worst.[8] In Europe, as Philip Bohlman has described, the very idea of "Jewish music" came into existence during this era, as Jews worked to match their hosts' religious, ethnic, and national values of the time by creating their own compatible, systematically constructed, vision of the musical past.[9] Geoffrey Goldberg, Tina Frühauf, and others have contributed significantly to this line of thinking, exploring Jewish debates over synagogue music, organs, choirs, and the nature of identity in both urban and rural settings.[10] In the following chapters, I hope to bring the United States more fully into the conversation through discussions of its musical personnel, negotiations over leadership roles, and plans of action during a period of rapid growth.

Compared to Europe, antebellum America might seem at first like a quiet musical backwater. The young nation lacked widely recognized music academies. Music publishing, which required its own specialized processes, remained costly, laborious, and technologically demanding. Relatively few performance venues could accommodate large-scale public performances. The era of recordings and cheap sheet music that accompanied the nation's late-nineteenth-century population explosion remained decades away.

Yet what America lacked in infrastructure, it balanced with an active and exploratory cultural and religious landscape. Jewish populations, like other minority religious denominations, began small but grew in number and resources. About 2,500 Jews lived in the United States by 1800, steadily growing to about 15,000 in 1840. In 1848, however, nationalist upheavals in Central Europe caused migration to jump dramatically, and between 200,000 and 250,000 Jews came to the United States as part of a total post-1848 exodus comprising about 3.8 million German immigrants.[11] These Central European arrivals changed the face of American Judaism in ways that mirrored their non-Jewish counterparts, establishing institutions in their new environment that both recalled their lives across the Atlantic and addressed America's new realities. Abuzz with musical activity and experimentation, the new country had different rules and a different character. Europe continued to exhibit an influence as an arbiter of taste, a center of musical training, and a supporter of new compositions. But America held its own as a dynamic voice in a transatlantic musical conversation, both reflective and critical of European exports. Those who stayed in Europe, moreover, looked to America as a lucrative, welcoming, and more liberal market, open to innovation as it laid the groundwork for its own musical establishments.[12]

The view from America also illuminates new aspects of modern Jewish musical history, further nuancing distinctions between musical change as a broad form of theological experimentation and change attributed to the specific rhetoric of Jewish "reform." Greater attention to this era gives a clearer view of the parameters of musical debates, which took zigzag paths through musical genres and practices rather than progressing evolution-like from simple solo chant to more complex choir-organ arrangements, as often romantically imagined. Different congregations altered their musical practices depending on such factors as finances, spiritual leadership, demographics, and communal cohesiveness—revealing, for example, a tendency to treat congregational singing, choral singing, instrumentation, and solo chant as separate items. This level of detail also opens a window onto the interactions between institutional structures, scholarship, and personnel that began to build up the cantor as a musical counterpart to the rabbi, while developing a repertoire that both inspired and was inspired by the beginnings of musicological research. Among other things, this book rebuts the all-too-frequently held view of this era as a time when Jews aimed to bring "Christian" forms of music into worship in efforts to create a "listening" congregation.[13] To the contrary: Jewish communities, just like the Christian communities around them, engaged in wide-ranging discussions about the effectiveness of a variety of musical strategies to foster an active and dynamic congregational life, and made numerous efforts to adopt popular musical ideas to Judaism's unique sound and spirit. A "silent" congregation, then as today, offered little benefit to synagogues that depended heavily on an active and prosperous membership.

"Jewish Music": Shifting the Narrative

I gain inspiration in this project from the larger field of American music, a discipline that since the 1970s has worked to include the United States in musical history narratives by skillfully challenging and complementing Eurocentric scholarship. In this spirit, I follow John Graziano's meticulously researched assertion that the Eurocentric perception of nineteenth century American cities (especially New York) as undeveloped proves more imaginary than real.¹⁴ Complementing this perspective, scholars of American Jewish history over the past century have compiled a considerable literature amid a Jewish studies discipline that increasingly interrogates the purpose and organization of Jewish historical narratives.¹⁵ Yet the field of "Jewish music"—a term that only gained relevance late in the period covered in this book—has yet to take up this complexity with sufficient rigor.

Part of the dilemma with Jewish music research lies in both scholarly and lay efforts to approach music as a product of a linear and definable "tradition," thereby heightening its symbolic capital. Two of the most prominent Jewish music researchers of the mid-twentieth-century, Abraham Z. Idelsohn and Eric Werner, frequently couched their meticulous scholarship in romantic notions of Jewish musical essences and origins, thereby turning music into a metaphor for passionate adherence to spiritual survival.¹⁶ Music's indeterminacy, its reputation for emotional immediacy, and its near-magical treatment as a deeply held source of heritage consequently reinforced Werner and Idelsohn's scholarly authority. Concepts such as "oral tradition," which minimized lacunae in the documentary record by appealing to a sense of existential conservatism, thereby gave music the power to "prove" such unprovables as cultural continuity, religious longevity, and common origin.

The field consequently developed as an artistic parallel to twentieth-century rabbinic training and practice. Idelsohn, in his position at Hebrew Union College from 1924 to 1935, brought music into the institution's rabbinic curriculum alongside Hebrew and liturgy. Austrian émigré and music scholar Eric Werner, Idelsohn's successor, cofounded New York's Hebrew Union College School of Sacred Music in 1948, (re)establishing music's physical embodiment in the cantor—a move that led other Jewish denominations to do similarly.¹⁷ Werner's 1959 opus *The Sacred Bridge* gave music a role in Jewish-Catholic postwar reconciliation projects, his biography of composer Felix Mendelssohn thrust claims about Jewish identity into the trajectory of Western music history, and his 1976 book *A Voice Still Heard* promoted Central and Eastern European (Ashkenazic) Jewish culture as a crucial but endangered font of Jewish musical authenticity.¹⁸ Balanced between these intellectual and practical objectives, Jewish music took an active part in twentieth-century discussions linking the Jewish past with communal efforts to shape the future of Jewish life in America and beyond.

Yet ironically, American scholars of synagogue/"Jewish" music looked past America to reinforce their ideas: selecting Zionist, Eastern European, or Central European narratives to anchor grand historical arcs befitting the Jewish people, while treating the United States as a fertile yet fragile ground. This strategy allowed scholars to imbue their work with a moral weight that confronted American Jews with a classic ethical conundrum: as inheritors of a (now) clearly delineated musical "heritage" in a new land, they could respect the burden of history, embrace the tradition, and build on it—or reject it at their peril.

I come to this study at a time when the veracity of these scholars' broad claims comes under scrutiny.[19] During my years of fieldwork at the Hebrew Union College School of Sacred Music (1999–2003), I learned how American cantorial students gained their identities as long-standing vessels of Jewish sound; yet nineteenth-century America rarely received any attention, save the occasional derisive remark that synagogue musicians of the time lacked knowledge and artistry and produced little of lasting value. At the same time, when I conducted historical research to bring depth to my ethnographic work, I found frustrating gaps in the history of cantorial music and leadership: inherited fact began fading into implication and reverse engineering based on the *assumption* of continuity. Mark Slobin attempted to address these issues by considering the cantor as a synagogue worker who gained increasing musical specialization into the late nineteenth century.[20] Slobin's concepts, in turn, began to point to an idea of synagogue musical leadership that developed its view of tradition through engagement with contemporary problems. Reappraised this way, Idelsohn, Werner, and their contemporaries came into focus as public intellectuals whose efforts to give Jewish life a musical "usable past" cemented their contributions to larger Jewish communal agendas.[21] Their pragmatic attempts to link sound, concept and context usefully opened the door to the nineteenth century, where I found counterparts who made similar efforts to bring music and worship into the national conversation about American Jewish identity and culture. Ultimately, this approach also led me to see strong structural and intellectual continuities between the nineteenth century and the "dawning" of Jewish music research in the twentieth century—with rising leaders of each time constructing a history, legacy, and theory for the new age of Jewish sound.

This book contains the first fruits of that search.

Synagogue, School, and Home

Current research on nineteenth-century Jewish musical practice tends to focus on ideas of religious "reform," most prominently by championing synagogue musicians such as Salomon Sulzer (Vienna, 1804–1890), Samuel Naumbourg (Paris, 1817–80), Hirsch Weintraub (Königsberg, 1811–81), and Louis Lewandowski (Berlin, 1821–94)—figures that further reinforce European primacy as stewards of tradition and champions of modernity.[22] The larger narrative attempts to lay claim on these composers' careers as a function of that transition, with the move into the modern requiring negotiation between lives devoted to artistry and Judaism. Yet a closer look at communities in the United States reveals a broader canvas upon which musical figures and congregants acted, that ranged well beyond the sanctuary. David Conway's recent work provides comparative insight into the European relationship between music and Jewish identity during the eighteenth and nineteenth centuries as a career choice, a form of leisure, and a mode of patronage.[23] A somewhat different topography, perhaps imported from smaller Central European towns, emerged in the United States, with many nineteenth-century Jewish populations developing a community model that intertwined the synagogue, the school, and the home in an expansive musical topography. Each of these realms connected intimately with the others, with its own forms of activity and accompanying music. The synagogue represented the community's public life as a place of gathering, ritual, and social events throughout the Jewish year. The school served as a place for transmitting religious, civic, and intellectual values to the community's children, while preparing them for Jewish adulthood. And the home provided a private, intergenerational, (ideally) stable unit that modeled both personal and public behavior across the life cycle. Isaac Mayer Wise promoted this arrangement as the pretense for his *Minhag America* liturgy and treated the synagogue sanctuary as a gathering site for each unit to mark its progress on Sabbaths and Jewish holidays. Many other congregations pursued similar programs, emphasizing in the process both internal coherence and continuity with the rest of American society.

Such an arrangement also allowed American Jewish populations to connect deeply with a musical culture that pervaded the national landscape. Family singing, often from communal songbooks, became a mark of the cultured household; a repertoire of educational hymns promoted order and achievement in the classroom; and prayer brought the whole community together—with adults, children, and seniors contributing in kind to a ritual overseen by clergy, with choir and (sometimes) keyboard accompaniment. Jewish communal leaders embraced this form of musical circulation as its own cohesive force, as musical literacy became a necessary skill for middle-class adulthood, especially for women. And these leaders took steps to promote their musical practices to other communities through publications and positive publicity—because to many communal leaders, facility with musical repertoire potentially comprised an important indicator of American Jewish accomplishment. The works that emerged toward this end only occasionally aspired to the "greatness" or "majesty" often attributed to Sulzer, Naumbourg, and (later) Lewandowski. Rather, they more often emphasized enculturation and intergenerational communication in an effort to strengthen community amid changing linguistic, religious, economic, and social conditions.

Seeing music in this configuration also presents a clearer and more effective context for encountering the works of synagogue "art" music for which the nineteenth century has become known. In America, the trend toward domestic art music composition as a point of prestige became increasingly prominent by the late 1860s. Such initiatives brought attention to the synagogue; however, the other two domains hardly stopped developing—especially in congregations that had neither the resources nor the personnel (nor perhaps the desire) to follow such ambitions. Art music served mainly to clarify and promote the role of increasingly professionalized musical specialists—organists, choir directors, and especially the cantor—as a complement to the intellectual leadership of the rabbi. In particular, the cantor's rising prominence during this time as an embodiment of musical "tradition"—unique among church personnel—also increased tensions between the urge toward artistic achievement and the enfranchisement of amateur congregational participation. In many ways, then, this time period laid out the terms of the "worship wars" that continue to roil in our own time.

Nineteenth-Century Synagogue Music: A Study of Sources

To view this era in greater depth, I aim to weave together individual, communal, musical, historiographic, and intellectual histories around a central core of published musical compendia—and in one notable case, a gold medallion. This source-based approach offers a set of landmarks for navigating a largely unmapped landscape, while at the same time acknowledging the works themselves as part of a material musical culture that measured success through production, circulation, and adoption. These sources also serve as point of entry for understanding the lives and journeys of their creators, who like their rabbinic colleagues traveled regularly and frequently crossed paths. I also attempt to provide enough context to place these efforts locally within the synagogue–school–home continuum that surrounded them, nationally via the competing spheres of New York and Cincinnati, and internationally among the intellectual music centers of London, Berlin, Paris, Prague, Odessa, and especially Vienna. Organizing this narrative as a progressive "essential library" of sorts thus gives the complex richness of this story, with its overlapping and concurrent narratives, a place from which to emerge. To this effect, I conclude each chapter with a future projection, to address the fate of each work and its creator(s) as others superseded them.

This perspective deepens the existing literature on the complex relationship between Europe and the United States during the "German" era that Zev Eleff, Tobias Brinkmann, Cornelia Wilhelm, Shari Rabin, and a host of others have so ably brought to light.[24] Eleff's nuanced work on religious authority in nineteenth-century American Jewish communities, which he describes as developing "through *gradual* transformation helped along by rough-and-tumble conflict and critical determinants of change," offers perhaps the most direct historical parallel to the discussions here.[25] Chronicling this era in musical terms, however—with its own authorities, its own rules of engagement and education, and its own modes of forging community and practice—offers a useful counterpoint to Eleff's examination of rabbinical leaders.[26] Rabbis recognized the need to harness music in order to give their rituals character and uniformity, even as they warily eyed attempts to elevate musical leadership in the form of the cantor as potential challenges to their own power. Musical figures, in turn, followed rabbinical strategies of professionalization, publication, and scholarship to enhance their own positions, sometimes through mutually beneficial partnerships with leading rabbis themselves. Both figures recognized that music had the flexibility to provide meaning for any theological or cultural configuration, in essence illuminating the dynamic range of local and national approaches to American Jewish life. Thus framed, music generated unique debates about the status of sound as a symbol of Jewish identity that changed depending on who created, controlled, and presented it; where it came from; how it was used; and how it was interpreted.

Restoring the Soundtrack

The epigraph to this book highlights the critical role that music held to prominent liturgists such as Isaac Mayer Wise—to the point that Wise felt his foundational prayer book *Minhag America* could only succeed with well-prepared music—and offers an entry into the deep integration of musical activity in nineteenth-century American Judaism. The implications of this quote run in progressive layers throughout the rest of the book.

I begin in the 1840s, chronicling the shift from British musical paradigms to Central European ones during a time when instituting a choir could reinforce *either* reform *or* traditional/orthodox identities. While Salomon Sulzer, the best known of the new-wave European synagogue composers today, had already built his reputation during the previous decade in Vienna, his music had not yet become a regular part of American Jewish worship. Building off trends toward choral singing set by Sephardic populations in the early nineteenth century (which I address only briefly), some American congregations looked to England for their music, hoping to adopt models of choral singing and English-language hymns similar to those just sanctioned by Chief Rabbi Nathan Adler. This activity, particularly in the mid-Atlantic states, established early strata upon which German American synagogues could define their own musical prayer leaders and build their own music programs. Thus, through the work of Ansel Leo (1806–78, arrived from London c. 1846), Henry A. Henry (1800–79, arrived from London in 1849), Leon Sternberger (1819–97, arrived from Bavaria in 1849), Isaac Ritterman (1820–90, born in Kraków, arrived from Bavaria in 1855), and Louis Naumburg (1813–1902, arrived from Bavaria in 1850), among others, a nascent class of synagogue music figures emerged. Their portfolios incorporated an array of official and unofficial roles as musicians, educators, and liturgical leaders as they negotiated energetic rabbinic discussions about religious ritual in American Jewish life. However, when Sulzer's paradigm-shifting music spread across North America during the late 1840s, spearheaded in part by Sternberger and Ritterman in addition to Isaac Mayer Wise, they had new decisions to make.

In contrast to these figures, I offer at the end of chapter 1 a possible counternarrative exploring what may have been lost in the move to new forms of musical identity. As many congregations trended toward family pews and mixed choirs, they began to shift away from other practices, including possible musical leadership roles for women in synagogues with gender-separated prayer through the end of the nineteenth century. While largely overlooked today, the presence of figures such as the *sagerin* in sources from this period destabilize assumptions of linear development and bring into question reform's own role as a herald of gender parity.

In the next section of the book, I explore the efforts of several religious leaders to treat music as a medium for ecumenical community building. These figures promoted a rich sonic overlap between German American and German Jewish identity, following a philosophy of civic harmony that viewed Jews and other subgroups as meaningful contributors to a culturally rich and diverse society. In their worldviews, music linked the synagogue with the institutions and discourses of the public square, with each sonic space reinforcing the others.

Chapter 2 opens with a discussion of hymn singing and singing societies, popular forms of music making among German populations on both sides of the Atlantic during this time. Developed as modes of national identity in the years before the 1848 unrest, group singing enacted a sense of liberal progressivism that envisioned an open, pluralistic society. In the United States, this environment offered an opportunity for Wilhelm Fischer, a respected (non-Jewish) organist and choral director, to publish one of the first notated Jewish hymnals for Philadelphia's Keneseth Israel congregation in 1863. Fischer received plaudits for channeling Jewish music effectively in his idiomatic four-part settings of psalms and prayer texts. His work, however, faced problems translating to broader Jewish America due to his alliance with ultra-Reform figure David Einhorn and the centrality of the German language to his philosophical goals. Combined with a greater concern for synagogue composers' Jewish identity as a test of musical authenticity, Fischer's work fell out of favor. While the singing society retained its social and liturgical relevance in American synagogue music for several decades, critics' reconfiguration of the practice as a borrowing from Christians—and therefore inappropriate for the synagogue—eventually took hold as a persistent narrative.

The career of Gustav M. Cohen, the focus of the next chapter, presents an alternative pathway for Jewish progressivism. Cohen understood choral singing as a symbol of liturgical reform, a barometer of cultural advancement, and a means of American acculturation. Serving a succession of communities as both spiritual leader and Jewish music specialist, however, he often faced a paradox in defining his portfolio. On one hand, he saw music as a public and immediate manifestation of ideology, through which Jews could connect with the broader community's musical practices. On the other hand, he sympathized with architects of both religious reform and *Bildung* (self-cultivation), who sought to integrate music into a larger program of Jewish cultural sophistication. Cohen attempted to balance these two goals in compendia such as *The Sacred Harp of Judah* (1864), which placed music education and development into the hands of the people. In parallel with his work in B'nai B'rith, a Jewish fraternal organization created in the 1840s, he hoped that such musical education could become a self-renewing resource that transcended denominationalism, even as he ultimately achieved mixed results.

The development of a distinct Jewish musical repertoire also called for the development of a matching scholarly rationale. In chapter 4, I explore the intersecting lives of Gustav S. Ensel and Simon Hecht, two German-born musician-teachers whose public debates over music started in Europe and continued as they relocated to smaller congregations in the American Midwest. Ensel, with his extensive musical background, produced the nation's first substantial scholarly treatise on music in Judaism, significantly predating—and predicting—twentieth-century developments by the likes of Idelsohn and Werner. Hecht, in contrast, applied his scholarly ideas to synagogue song, and in 1868 produced a widely used hymnal that nonetheless failed to meet the standards of a nationwide search committee. Ensel and Hecht's stories point to the musical pragmatism needed for a tiny Jewish minority to establish itself in the church-based ecosystem of America's small towns. Opening Judaism to broad-based scholarly discussions of ancient musical origins not only created an intellectual basis for worship, but also allowed Jews to assert their historical relevance in environments where musical resources needed to be shared among houses of worship.

In contrast to Fischer, Cohen, Ensel, and Hecht, who sought to empower congregants' voices by having them sing in harmony, a series of other figures emerged after 1865 who emphasized musical and compositional artistry in the synagogue, marking the ascent of a cantorial culture.

Postbellum America developed a critical mass of more than a dozen cantors trained or inspired by Vienna obercantor Salomon Sulzer. Although many synagogues sought musical expertise of some sort, usually connected to education, communities that could afford a full Vienna-style model rose to the status of flagships. Offering job security in return for musical prominence, these congregations partnered with individual "Sulzer-cantors" to develop music's potential as a symbol of Jewish cultural excellence. Their voices complemented well-trained choirs—of men and boys or men and women depending on religious leaning—and often organs as well, swelling synagogue music budgets and generating new controversies. The growing urban economic centers of Baltimore, Philadelphia, and New York, for example, had the resources to foot the bill, even as they increasingly turned to non-Jewish choristers to maintain the quality of their sound.

As I present in chapter 5, by 1866 the United States had developed the musical infrastructure to join an international celebration of Sulzer's fortieth year in his Vienna pulpit. His American disciples marked the occasion by sending a nice gift. But more importantly, they approached the anniversary as an opportunity to reinforce their connection to Sulzer and his spreading cantorial network, raising their own standing in the process.

Through Sulzer, cantors used their pulpits to reconfigure the idea of "Jewish music" into its own tradition that paralleled rabbinic textual interpretation, with far-reaching implications. While several prominent works of synagogue music saw publication during this time, none proved as central or significant as *Zimrath Yah*, a four-volume compendium of Jewish liturgical music published from 1871 to 1886, edited and distributed chiefly by cantors Samuel Welsch of New York City and Alois Kaiser of Baltimore, with the assistance of then–New York cantor Morris Goldstein and pianist-turned-industrialist/polymath Isaac L. Rice. *Zimrath Yah* reflected a major effort to establish a national synagogue-based musical repertoire of the highest quality. Created in the same spirit of American unification that led others to found the Union of American Hebrew Congregations (1873) and Hebrew Union College (1875), the compendium exemplified a maturing American Jewish population's ambition to stand alongside its European siblings. As with several of the other publications addressed here, *Zimrath Yah* eventually gave way to new liturgical and musical paradigms. In its time, however, the collection's critical engagement with European synagogue music, and its effort to cover all the country's major prayer books, solidified the cantor's position as a guardian of American Jewish sonic heritage.

In the 1880s, the idea of "Jewish music" took on an ethnic tinge inspired by ideas of ancientness and the developing field of musicology—including the codification of a series of modes, the increasing popularity of the augmented second interval, and the start of a timbral shift in cantorial singing from the refined *bel canto* style to a more exotic "cry in the voice" idiom.[27] Central European cantors in America, seeing the populations changing around them while also dealing with populist trends toward empowering congregational singing, had to negotiate these changes carefully. Chapter 6 consequently tracks the path of American synagogue music through three key works of the period. William Sparger and Alois Kaiser's 1893 compendium *A Collection of the Principal Melodies of the Synagogue from the Earliest*

Times to the Present gave contemporary synagogue music a public historical narrative that cohered with the American spirit of the Chicago World's Fair. The following year, the same two cantors led the recently formed Cantors' Association of America to produce an interim synagogue music manual for the *Union Prayer Book*, a long-anticipated liturgy that rabbinical leaders hoped would unify the nation's Jewish communities. Kaiser's continued work with these rabbis led to a more permanent (if problematic) solution in 1897 with the *Union Hymnal*. Exploring the stories behind these related publications and their attendant controversies reveals the complex terrain that cantors navigated as they tried, and often failed, to make music an equal player in Jewish liturgical discussions.

In the concluding chapter, I reflect on these interconnected narratives to comment on the way that we see, and especially hear, history. The nineteenth century, I argue, set the terms that we still use to look at music in Jewish life, defining music as a worthy bearer of tradition with its own history, philosophy, and spiritual import. At the same time, by reintroducing a complex view of sound to an era long buried in Jewish history, we can understand better how Jews of the "German period" curated music as part of a larger national dialogue on American identity. I offer here a way to parse the deep cultural and historical conversations embedded in their music-related materials, while arguing that sound must factor into any study of this era: in doing so, I contribute to a growing number of studies of American religious musical life and music.[28] Adding American Judaism to this mix, I hope, will add a few more strands to our understanding of the American musical tapestry.

I have relied on a raft of primary materials—available through new digital databases in addition to standard archival and microfilm sources—to give this era greater scholarly focus. Yet I make no claims at a comprehensive overview. Rather, I ask the reader to see this book as an attempt to create a structure for further correction, critique, and detail. My case studies mainly highlight the shifting ground between the Midwest and the East Coast as different Jewish populations, economic conditions, and migration patterns changed over more than half a century. In taking this approach, however, I give less attention to the early nineteenth century, as well as developments in the Southern and Western United States. Each area stands ready for deeper investigation.

Moreover, because of the nature of the available materials, the main musical figures I address in this book are all male. Although I present few women's stories, I urge the reader to look below the surface of these narratives to see hints of a significant, if still fragmentary, chronicle of women's involvement in synagogue music. Music, after all, served as a meeting point of philosophy and practice, emphasizing Elisheva Baumgarten's assertion about the medieval period that "despite the authority held by rabbinic leadership... rabbis alone did not determine practice."[29] When translated to the nineteenth century, Baumgarten's claim suggests that women's participation both buoyed musical practices in many Jewish communities, and often made male musicians' careers feasible. In some cases, women's synagogue attendance (more consistent than men) may have ensured a uniformity of congregational responses and hymn recitations that enabled new musical practices; in other cases, women lent their voices to both volunteer and paid choirs. Women often served as conduits for musical culture and instruction in the home, a crucial setting for learning synagogue melodies. Publications directed toward women, especially *Die Deborah* (a German-language companion to Cincinnati's *Israelite*), included extensive discussions of music as part of a broader interest in culture and the arts. Later in the century, Jewish women's organizations frequently took responsibility for sustaining musical activities and promoting musical scholarship as a social good. While few women receive mention by name in these pages, in other words, their audible contributions to musical practice and authority during this time made possible the rise of specialized musical forms and their (male) figureheads.

The period I address here also bears some responsibility for historians' continued tendency to relegate music to "specialists," because that very concept became a pretext for cantors' professionalization campaigns (as it did on a different level with the field of musicology). Widening the circle, however, shows music's more appropriate place during this time as a subject of enthusiastic general knowledge and discussion. By shifting the angles of the stories that we already tell, in other words, we can learn much about how we have come to define ourselves, and how we can see ourselves differently if only we trusted our historical "ears" a bit more.

A Note on Language

This book introduces a wide range of previously undiscussed materials from contemporaneous periodicals and synagogue records, including many German-language sources. In order to satisfy an English-language readership, I present these sources in English translation—nearly always my own. Although academic transparency encourages the inclusion of original texts in footnotes or an appendix, the volume of referenced sources makes that approach impractical here. Interested readers can follow the citations I provide for verification, often in publicly available databases; I can only hope for some indulgence that my translations are usable, or at least not deceptively incorrect.

As with many multilingual and transnational studies, moreover, proper names of synagogues, institutions, and people appear with multiple spellings in the available sources. While I maintain my sources' orthographic variety in quoted materials, I regularize spelling in the main text to conform to local conventions.

One crucial term, however, stands out: that of the musical prayer leader, which occupies a central place in this narrative. While twenty-first-century discussions of the "cantor" or "hazan" typically agree on at least the basics of the figure's overall portfolio and history, no such agreement existed in the nineteenth century. As Mark Slobin notes, even Salomon Sulzer's revered status as a model "modern cantor" in many circles traded in neologism rather than convention. Many others used alternate terms, including "reader" and even "rabbi," to indicate a range of community roles (musical and otherwise), or to present an idealistic, if blurred, desire for musical change.[30] In this one instance, then, I present a spectrum of terms in all of its diversity, and I ask the reader to interpret their inconsistent usage as the open and shifting signifiers they were during this age.

Beyond the Book

This book serves as part of a larger web-based project aimed to bring the sound of nineteenth-century American Jewish life to life through recordings, mapping projects, and extended analyses. In that regard, what you read here offers a first step, one way into an era with many overlapping musical ideas and sonic identities. Hopefully, before long, those interested in visiting this world can access a rich array of sources, past documents and scores, and ideally, musical interpretations.

Notes

1. For a more detailed analysis of Seixas's sermon, see Morris Schappes, "Anti-Semitism and Reaction, 1795–1800," *Publications of the American Jewish Historical Society* 38, no. 2 (1948): 119–28; Frederic Cople Jaher, *The Jews and the Nation: Revolution, Emancipation, State*

Formation, and the Liberal Paradigm in America and France (Princeton, NJ: Princeton University Press, 2009), 155–56; Howard Rock, *Haven of Liberty: New York Jews in the New World, 1654–1865* (New York: New York University Press, 2012), 100–3. None of these accounts address the psalmody around Seixas's discourse.

2. Rev. G. Seixas, "Discourse Delivered in the Synagogue in New York, on the Ninth of May, 1798. . . ." (New York: William A. Davis & Co., 1798).

3. "The Form of Prayer which Was Performed at the Jews Synagogue in the City of New York on October 23, 1760" (New York: W. Wyman, 1760); "Religious Discourse Delivered in the Synagogue in This City" (New York: Archibald McLean, 1789). An English-language prayer book printed in 1765/6 provides detailed information on alternating text recitation between reader and congregation but gives no overt discussions of music or singing (Isaac Pinto, trans., *Prayers for the Sabbath, Rosh-Hashanah, and Kippur . . .* [New York: John Holt, 1765/6]).

4. Richard Crawford, *American's Musical Life: A History* (New York: Norton, 2001), 15–55.

5. Jacob Kabakoff, "The Use of Hebrew by American Jews during the Colonial Period," in Shalom Goldman, ed., *Hebrew and the Bible in America: The First Two Centuries* (Hanover, NH: Brandeis University Press, 1993), 190–97.

6. Neil W. Levin, "Introduction to Vol. 1: Jewish Voices in the New World," http://www.milkenarchive.org/articles/view/introduction-to-volume-1.

7. William DeLoss Love, *The Fast and Thanksgiving Days of New England* (New York: Houghton, Mifflin/Riverside Press, 1895), 565–67.

8. Albert Weisser, "The 'Prologue' to Jewish Music in Twentieth-Century America: Four Representative Figures," *Musica Judaica* 6, no. 1 (1983/84): 60.

9. Philip Bohlman, *Jewish Music and Modernity* (New York: Oxford University Press, 2008).

10. See, inter alia, Tina Frühauf, *The Organ and Its Music in German-Jewish Culture* (New York: Oxford University Press, 2009); Tina Frühauf, *German-Jewish Organ Music: An Anthology of Works from the 1820s to the 1960s* (Middleton, WI: A&R Editions, 2013); Geoffrey Goldberg, "Continuity and Change in Frankfurt Liturgical-Musical Customs: Text and Sub-Text in Salomon Geiger's 'Divrey Kehillot,'" in Fritz Backhaus, ed., *Die Frankfurter judengasse: jüdisches Leben in der frühen Neuzeit* (London: Valentine Mitchell, 2008), 124–42; Geoffrey Goldberg, "Mahzor ha-hayyim: Lifecycle Celebration in the Song of the Ashkenazic Synagogue," *AJS Review* 33, no. 2 (2009): 305–39.

11. Jonathan Sarna, *American Judaism: A History* (New Haven, CT: Yale University Press, 2004), 375.

12. See the introductions to John Baron, *Concert Life in Nineteenth Century New Orleans: A Comprehensive Reference* (Baton Rouge: Louisiana State University Press, 2013) and John Graziano, ed., *European Music and Musicians in New York City, 1840–1900* (Rochester, NY: University of Rochester Press, 2006).

13. See, for example, Idelsohn, *Jewish Music*, 241–43.

14. Graziano, *European Music and Musicians in New York City*, 1–9.

15. David Biale, "Preface: Toward a Culture History of the Jews," in *The Culture of the Jews: A History* (New York: Schocken, 2002), vii–xxxiii; Moshe Rosman, *How Jewish Is Jewish History?* (Portland, OR: Littman Library, 2009).

16. Judah M. Cohen, "Whither Jewish Music? Jewish Studies, Music Scholarship, and the Tilt between Seminary and University," *AJS Review* 32, no. 1 (2008): 29–48; Abraham Z. Idelsohn, *Jewish Music in Its Historical Development* (New York: Henry Holt, 1929); Eric

Werner, *The Sacred Bridge: The Interdependence of Music and Liturgy in Synagogue and Church during the First Millennium* (New York: Columbia University Press, 1959).

17. Judah M. Cohen, "Becoming a Reform Jewish Cantor: A Study in Cultural Investment" (PhD diss., Harvard University, 2002), 62–64, 82–108.

18. Werner, *The Sacred Bridge*; Eric Werner, *Mendelssohn: A New Image of the Composer and His Age* (Glencoe, IL: Free Press, 1963); Eric Werner, *A Voice Still Heard: The Sacred Songs of the Ashkenazic Jews* (University Park: Pennsylvania State University Press, 1976).

19. Cohen, "Whither Jewish Music?"

20. Mark Slobin, *Chosen Voices: The Story of the American Cantorate* (Urbana: University of Illinois Press, 2002), 5–13.

21. See David Roskies, *The Jewish Search for a Usable Past* (Bloomington: Indiana University Press, 1999).

22. See, inter alia, Jascha Nemtsov and Herman Simon, *Louis Lewandowski: "Love Makes the Melody Immortal,"* Jewish Miniatures vol. 114A (Berlin: Hentrich & Hentrich, 2011); Tina Frühauf, *Salomon Sulzer: Composer, Cantor, Icon*, Jewish Miniatures vol. 133A (Berlin: Hentrich & Hentrich, 2012); Eliyahu Schleifer, *Samuel Naumbourg: The Cantor of French Jewish Emancipation*, Jewish Miniatures vol. 136A (Berlin: Hentrich & Hentrich, 2012).

23. David Conway, *Jews in Music: Entry into the Profession from the Enlightenment to Richard Wagner* (Cambridge, UK: Cambridge University Press, 2012).

24. Zev Eleff, *Who Rules the Synagogue? Religious Authority and the Formation of American Judaism* (New York: Oxford University Press, 2016); Tobias Brinkmann, *Sundays at Sinai: A Jewish Congregation in Chicago* (Chicago: University of Chicago Press, 2012); Cornelia Wilhelm, *The Independent Orders of B'nai B'rith and True Sisters: Pioneers of a New Jewish Identity, 1843–1914* (Detroit, MI: Wayne State University Press, 2011); Shari Rabin, *Jews on the Frontier: Religion and Mobility in Nineteenth-Century America* (New York: New York University Press, 2017); see also chapters 6–11 in Christian Wiese and Cornelia Wilhelm, eds., *American Jewry: Transcending the European Experience?* (New York: Bloomsbury, 2017), 103–211.

25. Eleff, *Who Rules*, 2.

26. Eliyahu Schleifer, "Jewish Liturgical Music from the Bible to Hasidism," in Lawrence A. Hoffman and Janet Walton, eds., *Sacred Sound and Social Change* (Notre Dame, IN: University of Notre Dame Press, 1992), 13–58.

27. Kimmy Caplan identifies American congregations' comparatively better treatment of Eastern European cantors compared to rabbis ("In God We Trust," 1998). See also J. D. Eisenstein, "The History of the First Russian-American Jewish Congregation: The Beth Hamedrosh Hagodol," *Publications of the American Jewish Historical Society* 9 (1901): 72–74.

28. Robert R. Grimes, *How Shall We Sing in a Foreign Land? Music of Irish Catholic Immigrants in the Antebellum United States* (South Bend, IN: University of Notre Dame Press, 1996); David M. Tripoli, *Sing to the Lord a New Song: Choirs in the Worship and Culture of the Dutch Reformed Church in America, 1785–1860* (Grand Rapids, MI: Eerdmans, 2012); Otto Holzapfel, *Religiöse Identität und Gesangbuch: Zur Ideologiegeschichte deutschsprachiger Einwanderer in den USA und die Auseinandersetzung um das 'richtige' Gesangbuch* (New York: Peter Lang, 1998). These works complement institutional histories of music sponsored by individual religious movements and organizations.

29. Elisheva Baumgarten, *Practicing Piety in Medieval Ashkenaz: Men, Women, and Everyday Religious Observance* (Philadelphia: University of Pennsylvania Press, 2014), 218. I am grateful to Diana Matut for directing me to this reference.

30. Slobin, *Chosen Voices*, 29–50.

1

EARLY STRATA

Of Choirs and Reform through the Mid-Nineteenth Century

> Are we to have German, English, French, or Italian songs introduced into the service in the place of the Psalms, like the Christie Street Temple [Emanu-El] in New York, or are the old and time-honoured forms to be continued? What are we to have in the place of our present beautiful ritual? Is it the present silent, musical style of the St. Helen's Place [i.e., Great] Synagogue, of London, or the two hour *recreation* on Kippur, of the Hamburg Temple? Is it the "British" improved system of Burton Street['s West London Synagogue], of London, or the more accommodating (to business men) style of Berlin, and that on a Sunday, and for forty minutes? or, perhaps, the present or former form of [Temple Beth-El,] Albany, where two years since they had about a dozen singing girls and boys on the reading desk, with three men to assist, the table full of loose sheets of music; the whole resembling the study of some music mad "amateur," much more than a place from which was to be read the law of the living God of Israel? The truth of the matter is, that for the last few years we have had too much talk about *reform* . . . for, notwithstanding all the *improvements* of music and English, the seats on each Sabbath present a most meagre appearance, and the improver, as if ashamed of what he has done, has already a strong desire of quitting the wreck (now in its most improved condition).
>
> —Simeon Abrahams, letter to *The Occident and American Jewish Advocate*, June 1849

WRITING NEAR THE MIDPOINT OF THE NINETEENTH CENTURY, New York–born Simeon Abrahams (1810–67) derided not so much the idea of Jewish reform as its patchwork of haphazard applications—a perspective shared by other concerned observers including *Occident* publisher Isaac

Leeser. Much of the blame for this attenuated state, Abrahams implied, lay in the willingness of leadership to concede "old and time-honoured forms" to popular sentiment. "We have too many agrarians, or levellers, among us," he warned, rhetorically calling out "those who would rather bring things *down* to their standard, than take the time and trouble of *raising* themselves, and becoming acquainted with the why and wherefore of the different parts of our system of public worship."[1] Music, misapplied, could erode the integrity of worship—a claim that followed an editorial two years earlier, where he railed against unreliable and poorly prepared "hazanim" whose "chief qualifications" were the "ability to favour the congregation with some operatic tunes (tunes generally fit for any other place than one of religious worship)."[2] The solution, according to Abrahams, involved a more rigorous and uniform clerical education that gave religious leaders a deep knowledge befitting Judaism's distinctive "nationality."[3] Music could give that education shape and significance during religious rituals, thus imbuing Jewish populations with a distinct spiritual consciousness as they sought to inure themselves to the modern age.

Abrahams's concerns emphasized music's immediacy in transmitting and reinforcing Jewish identity in a pluralistic society. At a time when synagogue doors became open portals to broad civic discourse, prayer leaders faced the challenge of making Jewish liturgy distinct and orderly, unique, and yet understandable to outsiders. Synagogue boards of trustees, regardless of reform leanings, made regular adjustments to their congregations' musical vocabularies, frequently considering new solo, ensemble, and/or instrumental presentations of texts as a way to make prayer culturally relevant and aesthetically conversant with other local practices. Jewish musical change hardly began in this era; however, these years marked a period of musical elaboration that allowed Jewish populations to engage reasonably with their time and environment.[4]

Isaac Leeser's Philadelphia-based journal, *The Occident and American Jewish Advocate*, had contributed to this conversation from its early issues, producing one of the first published pieces of American Jewish liturgical music in its June 1843 issue: a simple setting of the hymn "Adon Olam" for "the voice, with piano accompaniment" (see fig. 1.1).[5] Dedicated to "The Portuguese Congregation of Philadelphia [Mikve Israel]," the adaptation by local musician Edward Roget used a "Favourite Air" by Italian composer Ferdinando Bertoni (1725–1813) titled, "*La verginella come la rosa*" ("Where, dear maid, should'st thou forsake me") as its melody.[6] The journal probably found preparing the score a pricey but worthwhile experiment, with the special movable type used to make the printing plate significantly more work intensive than setting a page of text: the creators' decision to syllabify every note in the vocal line, even if simply extending a vowel ("'o-la-a-a-a-am"), implied a level of inexperience. Yet in printing the piece, *The Occident* broadcast the extent to which Jewish musical practices linked public and private worlds. Roget, one of *The Occident*'s original subscribers, had achieved some local renown as a music instructor to the Jewish population; and two months earlier, he had coordinated a choir with soloists and an instrumental ensemble for the consecration of the German congregation Rodeph Shalom, leading a reviewer (presumably Leeser) to comment, "it is but seldom that sacred music was better given or had a more soothing effect on the audience."[7] His contribution to Mikve Israel's soundtrack, moreover, may have reflected an intimacy with the community's existing practices, or at least a tacit recognition that the opera singer who premiered the original tune in London was also "a favorite singer at the [Bevis Marks] Synagogue."[8] When presented in an arrangement that encouraged lay performance from *The Occident*'s pages, therefore, "Adon Olam" appeared to address knowingly the balance that American Jewish communities struck between local knowledge and musical cosmopolitanism.

As Abrahams hinted, the era also inched toward an acceptance of musical professionalism. Congregations typically elected their first service readers from within their ranks, expecting little more than musical competence from them in intoning the prayers. Institutional developments in Europe, however, led to new paradigms that demanded more distinct musical skills. Vienna's Salomon Sulzer, for example, had been developing his choral program since the late 1820s and published the first volume of his opus *Schir Zion* in 1840; yet that work and its proponents gained a meaningful place in America's religious musical landscape only after 1850 (partly spurred by Sulzer himself).[9] Before then, religious leaders in England and the Netherlands provided early nineteenth-century America with most of its musical ideas, coming up through the Caribbean, the American South, and the East Coast.[10]

Prevailing narratives tend to favor these musical changes as symptoms of "reform." The most closely chronicled case—that of congregation Beth Elohim in Charleston, South Carolina—portrays choral singing as a liberal leap forward by a "Reformed Society of Israelites," established in the mid-1820s. When Beth Elohim's members voted in 1840 to install an organ

Figure 1.1. E. Roget, "Adon Olam," based on the mid-eighteenth-century air *"La verginella"* by Ferdinando Bertoni. Printed in *The Occident and American Jewish Advocate* 1, no. 3 (June 1843), 143–44.

Continued

NOTE.—If sufficiently encouraged we intend giving occasionally some of the hymns sung in our worship, and we hope that this arrangement will be pleasing to our readers.

Figure 1.1. *continued*

to accompany its liturgy, approved by Prussian-born minister Gustavus Poznanski, music migrated to the center of the congregation's agenda.[11] A broader view of this era, however, offers a contrasting portrayal that sees choral music as a development adopted across the Jewish religious spectrum, with each congregation seeing the form as a way to further its own theological perspectives. Far less attention has been paid to music's specific contextual considerations, including its pathways, its instrumental forces, and the physical layout of the service.[12] Such topics often incorporated the choir and notions of "reform" into broader debates over leadership hierarchies, sophistication and cultural development, and matters of cultural knowledge. In chronicling that development in America, I begin with a small but influential group of ministers who arrived from England during the 1840s, and I progress just into the post-1848 era, when more specialized Bavarian émigrés joined them (introducing Sulzer's music in the process). Cultivating choral music during this time allowed musically adept ministers to present themselves as agents of religious orthodoxy for at least part of their careers, while often casting themselves as more conservative than many of their constituents.[13] Following in the spirit of Abrahams's push toward uniformity, however, rabbinic figures such as Isaac Mayer Wise and David Einhorn began to tie choral music to progressive ideologies that supported their national visions of American Judaism. Thus politicized, choirs transformed from a general practice to a point of division that rhetorically distinguished reform from an orthodoxy increasingly characterized as premodern.

From London to America: Translating British Practices Westward

In the first part of the 1800s, the religious and musical path of Jewish authority in the United States often tracked through London—whether through its influential synagogues, the powerful Chief Rabbinate, or the tens of thousands of mainly secular/progressive German Jews who had immigrated to England since the late eighteenth century.[14] Britain shared a language and heritage with its former colonies and maintained an organized religious structure that often led the British Jewish religious establishment to treat America's Jews paternalistically well into the 1850s. Many American communities in turn looked to British Jewish authorities for resolving disputes about Jewish practice, and others relied on Great Britain as its source of prayer books and religious paraphernalia.[15] Whether acquired as part of a turn to the West London Reform liturgy of David Woolf Marks or through the hiring of traditionalist British-born ministers, then, the sounds and organization of the early nineteenth-century American Jewish synagogue service owed much to British Jewish conventions.

British synagogues of all stripes began to introduce all-male choirs starting around 1841, justified as "an aid to . . . the imposition of elegance and decorum, which qualities acquired the attributes of moral virtue in themselves in the context of the self-consciously Anglo-Jewish synagogal service."[16] The choir's ability to maintain that decorum elevated its status as a spiritual body "expressly trained" to shun aesthetic achievement in favor of congregational devotion. An all-male choir marked Chief Rabbi Nathan Adler's 1845 installation service, and the innovation gained institutional status when Adler included it in section three of his 1847 "Laws and Regulations for All the Synagogues in the British Empire."[17] In America, Philadelphia's Isaac Leeser welcomed Adler's pamphlet and particularly highlighted a passage addressing music's role in clarifying relationships between reader, choir, and congregation: "The reader shall at all times recite the prayers with becoming dignity and solemnity; he shall avoid all profane melodies; reduce the customary modes of chanting to simplicity, and so arrange them as to produce harmony whenever the congregation has to join him."[18] Thus phrased, the regulations essentially transformed the choir into an idealized model congregation, adding fullness to the performed ritual while educating and empowering uninformed attendees. The regulations also codified a distinction between "profane" music and music appropriate to the synagogue, presumably excluding popular genres such as opera and parlor song. Rooted theologically in Adler's missive, then, choirs gained a carefully delineated, organic place in Jewish ritual, disarming claims of aesthetic overreach or Christian influence. The same regulations, moreover, expanded the portfolio of synagogue leadership to include musical refinement, placing new pressures on the education and skills of the "modern" minister to provide a meaningful harmonic accompaniment, while refining his singing voice to blend effectively with the choristers.

While Simeon Abrahams complained openly about unqualified ministers, he almost certainly considered recent British arrivals Ansel Leo (c. 1806–78) and Henry A. Henry (1800–79) part of the competent minority. Both figures had worked at London's Western Synagogue, a major force in defining the values of British Jewry at the time. Both came to the United

States with substantial experience. Both subsequently worked as theological and musical functionaries of their respective American congregations. And both displayed skill as musical leaders before being displaced by new, more elaborate musical paradigms.

Ansel Leo was born into a musical family, the oldest of seven children to Simon Leo (c. 1767–1837), hazan of the Western Synagogue from 1804 to 1830. Ansel and his siblings became fixtures of London's Jewish musical scene. He and his three younger brothers accompanied his father on the pulpit in the style of *meshorerim*, boy singers whose semi-improvisational adornment of the cantor's melodies resembled a protochoir.[19] Contemporary observers described the group as the "Mannheimer Kinder," highlighting their German background and possibly hinting at their stylistic provenance.[20] The family also gained recognition as Jewish musicians outside of the sanctuary. Most of the siblings made their livings as music teachers, and in more general venues Ansel performed paraliturgical "Hebrew melodies" alongside his sisters. His brother Louis became a recognized composer of synagogue music, with creations that spanned *meshorer*-style accompaniment through full choral compositions. When the patriarch Simon Leo died, Ansel succeeded him as the Western Synagogue's cantor from at least 1835 through the early 1840s.[21]

Leo presided during a period of early intellectual inquiry into the nature and content of "Jewish" music. To this end, he joined forces with his brother Louis and an unnamed sister to help renowned Jewish singer Henry Phillips deliver a celebrated two-part lecture series on "Hebrew Melodies."[22] Phillips promoted Jewish musical identity in these lectures as based in longstanding conservative melodic practices, claiming that "the chants and melodies now in use in the various Synagogues had descended, in all their original purity, to the existing race of Jews from the period that the chosen people rejoiced in the splendors of their sovereignty [i.e., from the Second Temple period]."[23] To support this claim, Phillips relied on the Leos to present his chosen melodies convincingly in solo and multipart choral settings, with Louis Leo accompanying. Linking into a larger sociohistorical interest in music's relationship to human character, the lectures received a great deal of press coverage and established parameters for connecting narratives of Jewish ancientness with contemporary musical sophistication.[24]

In February 1846, the trustees of New York synagogue B'nai Jeshurun wrote to Henry Levy of London for a suitable candidate to serve as its hazan. The congregation had started with local leadership in 1825 but shifted to a more dedicated pulpit leader in 1839 when it brought gentleman preacher Samuel M. Isaacs over from London. Although Isaacs lacked ordination, he served the congregation well for two three-year terms.[25] When he departed with a group of seceders to form the new congregation Shaarey Tefilah, B'nai Jeshurun looked to London a second time. Simeon Abrahams assisted in the search, which resulted in Ansel Leo's journey to the United States. Leo spent "six weeks on trial" with the congregation "including both days of [Shavuot]," and impressed its members with a "most beautiful voice" and engaging sermons.[26] Together with one of his brothers, who apparently accompanied him to New York, he also organized a protochoir with some local boys for the Shavuot holiday; congregants found "the effect" of the ensemble "not only pleasing, but it gave us an idea of what it will be when a full choir shall once be trained." B'nai Jeshurun elected Leo to the position on June 2 for one year at $1,000 and predicted that his hire "will be a great improvement in the service of our Synagogue, and will no doubt tend to more decorum and devotion than at present exists."[27] The reduction from Isaacs's previous salary of $1,200 may have resulted from Leo's inability to read from the Torah competently, a skill the trustees had required of the hazan in its most recent bylaws. Leo's musical talents, however, made him an attractive candidate, and despite repeatedly missing congregationally imposed deadlines to improve his Torah reading he continued to receive contract extensions.[28]

At least one event during Leo's tenure suggests the extent to which he served as a surrogate for the British chief rabbi in the United States. In 1847, Leo took it upon himself to query Nathan Adler about the appropriateness of permitting "ladies to assist with their vocal powers at the [upcoming] consecration of a Synagogue"—coincidentally S. M. Isaacs's congregation Shaarey Tefilah, comprising seceders from B'nai Jeshurun. Leo then publicized Adler's negative response in hopes that it would prevent "in future any innovation on our established religious ceremonies by professedly orthodox organizations."[29] That Shaarey Tefilah included women in its consecration choir anyway spoke to the limits of such influence, while also pointing to an ongoing feud between the two congregations.[30] But it also showed who had the chief rabbi's ear.

B'nai Jeshurun's continued appreciation of Leo's contributions led its trustees to tender him a three-year $3,000 contract in February 1849, the maximum duration allowed by the congregational bylaws.[31] While Leo deposed his responsibilities by presenting the prayers mostly solo, evidence suggests that he attempted to form a kind of choir during this time, perhaps in the style of the Mannheimer Kinder (that is, a small group of males surrounding the reader).[32] Leo's description of the musical program he oversaw for the 1851 dedication of B'nai Jeshurun's new synagogue building, while obviously more extravagant than a standard service, offers a useful window into the different forms of practice available, including all-male choir, solo chanting, a cantor–bass–boy singer trio, and an "old-style" practice of alternating lines between solo cantor and choir/congregation. The ceremony's reuse of music composed by Louis Leo for the 1836 rededication of London's Western Synagogue also indicates the extent to which London's practices remained in his sights:

> The orchestra which were composed of the most eminent Professional men in the city was truly beautiful. The opening symphony or overture called *Joseph* [French opera, 1807] composed by [Étienne] Méhul was most splendidly performed. The chorus composed of Boys & men numbering 25 were exceedingly well drilled and performed their parts admirably—The six first *mizmorim* [psalms] were all chaunted by me which was not according to my original intention as each *hazan* had been presented with a *mizmor* [psalm, singular] but as they were not present I was obliged to undertake the whole. The chaunting was in the old style by verse by *hazan* and verse next by chorus accompanied by the organ until the few concluding verses which were sang by the *hazan* to original music composed by my Brother Louis Leo of London—accompanied either by the organ or the Band. The 7th *Mizmor* was arranged as a Trio—sang by Mr. Lichtenstein, Master Hecht and myself—*Mizmor L'David* ["A Psalm of David"] was sang by myself and chorus accompanied by the full band. [After a long sermon and a recited hymn came] the *Noten T'shua* [a prayer for the government[33]] sung by me accompanied by the full orchestra, and the Finale *Hallelujah* [Psalm 150, probably composed by Louis Leo] by the chorus and the full orchestra.[34]

Although Isaac Ritterman unseated him in 1855, in a move that likely reflected an increased expectation of refinement in the hazan's position, Leo remained a member of B'nai Jeshurun. He fulfilled the role of "second" hazan during the High Holidays and continued to raise his voice in favor of the congregation's self-identified orthodox faction.[35]

Henry Abraham (H. A.) Henry, born in 1800, embodied a similar extension of the British Empire's musical influence into its former colonies, this time starting in the Midwest. By 1840 Henry had become a well-known educator and editorialist in London's Jewish circles, author of a popular textbook and an English translation of the Jewish religious service. His education and knowledge earned him a position as headmaster of the Jews'

Free School in the city.³⁶ Shortly after Ansel Leo's departure in 1842, the Western Synagogue elected him hazan, where he served for seven years. Henry likely had a good musical knowledge, possibly allowing him to lead a group of male *meshorerim* in a manner similar to Leo's.

At Simeon Abrahams's urging, Henry came to the United States in 1849, where he conducted a service (perhaps with Leo) at New York's B'nai Jeshurun before heading west.³⁷ Originally intending to audition for a position in Louisville, he disembarked the Erie Line at Cincinnati only to learn from some in the local Jewish population that the Louisville position had been filled. They urged him instead to seek the hazan position at the city's Bene Yeshurun congregation (KKBY), where current minister James K. Gutheim had announced plans to leave the ministry.³⁸ Acceding to their requests, Henry made himself available for the pulpit, and in September, the congregation elected him over Gutheim by a vote of 62 to 50.³⁹

The hire transformed the congregation's musical fortunes. Under Gutheim's ministry, a mixed choir had been organized in 1847–48 to accompany the consecration of KKBY's new synagogue building, trained by flutist Henry Sofge (who would later help found the Cincinnati Conservatory). Gutheim successfully submitted a plan to integrate the choir into regular worship under the hazan's charge, "for the purpose of leading the Congregation in making the responses."⁴⁰ Henry's election abruptly halted progress, frustrating congregants involved in the initiative. In December 1849, two months after Henry took the pulpit, the Committee on Synagogue, which oversaw major congregational affairs, reasserted its intentions to organize a choir; and the following March, at the urging of the congregation's president, the School Committee was "empowered to engage a Teacher on Vocal Music" for the congregational school (the Talmid Yelodim Institute).⁴¹ Henry by that time faced pressure to conform with the congregation's previous practices, including a directive to "say the prayers in the same form like Revd. J. K. Gutheim did," but his most contentious relationship remained with the choir.⁴² Working in clear counterpoint to the reverend's wishes, the synagogue trustees formed a Committee on Choir that June, which promptly hired a choral instructor (Mr. Nusbaum) and imported music from New York. On August 11, 1850, however, the committee reported that "Revd. Mr. Henry does not cooperate with them and they cannot succeed."⁴³ Henry submitted his resignation at the same meeting and looked again to Louisville, possibly to found a Jewish school. However, KKBY, after brief failed negotiations with another minister, reengaged him for another year at twice his previous salary.[44] Weeks later, the congregation's Committee on Religious Rules and Regulations secured Henry's support of a (probably) volunteer boys' choir.[45] Continued difficulties on other fronts, including the congregation's refusal to provide "cloak and hat" to hazan or choristers, led Henry and KKBY to part ways amicably for good in summer 1851.[46] Henry's successor, Jacob Rosenfeld, gave the choir far more latitude, allowing the committee to hire a non-Jewish choral instructor (William Klausmeyer) and to acquire a copy of Sulzer's *Schir Zion*.

How did Henry's choral differences with KKBY resolve? A clue appears in an account of the consecration of Syracuse congregation Knesses Shalom's new synagogue building in September 1851. On that occasion, Reverend Henry presided over the service with "his sons assisting him as choir," in a manner strongly reminiscent of Ansel Leo's extended *meshorer*-based practice.[47] Extrapolated, Henry's approach to choral music suggested an elaborated harmonic expression that reflected contemporary practices but also emphasized that all singers remain fully visible from the pulpit; in doing so, Henry reinforced the pulpit as an "orthodox," male Jewish domain. While continuing his ministry into New York, where he presided at congregation Shaare Zedek from 1853 to 1856 and then Rodeph Sholem from 1856 to 1857, he retained his standards as a proponent of orthodox Judaism. His eventual move to San Francisco, where he became hazan of the city's Polish-rite congregation Sherith Israel, set him as an icon of Jewish traditionalism and intellectualism in the developing west.[48] During his time in Sherith Israel's pulpit from 1857 to 1869, he appeared to condone alternate practices by nonorthodox congregations: he officiated at synagogue consecrations that included mixed choirs, sometimes accompanied by small keyboard instruments (such as the seraphine); and in at least one case, the mixed choir sang music arranged by fellow British émigré M. N. Jacobs, who reportedly had worked in London's (orthodox) Great Synagogue in the late 1840s.[49] Sherith Israel, in contrast, retained a reputation of maintaining the "strictest piety," presumably in music as with its other observances—and Henry made little mention of musical aesthetics in his writings.[50] His congregation, however, sought other experiences; in 1870, when Sherith Israel consecrated its new building, a recently deposed Henry led the procession to the structure on Friday afternoon, accompanied by a (likely all-male) choir and melodeon in a ceremony that ended before the Sabbath began.[51]

Leo and Henry, among other British émigrés, brought a conservative choral baseline to American synagogues. While acknowledging the slow separation of music and pastoral leadership, they retained the conventions of the unified pulpit figure in their congregations, adding a modicum of musical training to the preacher's expanding portfolio. The next generation similarly sought choral modes that preserved orthodox Jewish expression but from a different place of origin—Central Europe—and according to a different set of theological and aesthetic values.

German American Orthodoxy in Harmony: Isaac Ritterman

When Isaac/Ignatz Ritterman applied for the hazan position at New York's B'nai Jeshurun, he had all of the right qualifications. Born in Kraków around 1820, Ritterman pursued sacred music studies in Vienna during Salomon Sulzer's ascendancy.[52] He first formalized his musical education in 1844–45, completing an October-to-June course at Vienna's premier music school, the Konservatorium der Gesellschaft der Musikfreunde.[53] Graduating just before the school formally began to employ Sulzer as an instructor, Ritterman likely maintained some kind of informal connection to the obercantor, gaining facility with the master's music in the process.[54] Ritterman soon found a pulpit with Posen's progressive Brüderverein (Brotherhood/Fellowship) congregation, leading the choir in a style "based on Sulzer's famous work" during services held in Hebrew and German.[55] While celebrated for "deporting his office to the full satisfaction of his congregation," his overreliance on choral music, particularly during times such as the closing prayer ("Adon Olam") when the congregation wished to join in, likely created some friction.[56] Yet the Posen congregation proved too progressive for him; by the start of 1850, its members sought a new cantor because, as one writer wryly put it, the congregants "didn't like the old melodies."[57] For the next few years, Ritterman attempted to conduct his own services in London and Paris before returning to Vienna to take up a second course of study.[58] This time he sharpened his skills through a general sacred music course sponsored by the Institute for the Promotion of Real Sacred Music (Verein zur Beförderung und Verbreitung echter Kirchenmusik). Completing his studies "with great diligence and advantage," he moved to the United States in 1854 to seek a more permanent position.[59]

Ritterman began his American tour in Syracuse, New York, where by September 1854, he had been recognized as the hazan of the city's Temple Knesses Shalom/Society of Concord.[60] Founded in 1839, the group dedicated its first building in 1851, likely giving shape to its musical ambitions. Isaac Leeser, admiring the completed building in the lead-up to the dedication, described the "upper" gallery of the sanctuary as a space "for the choir, whenever they shall have it."[61] As previously noted, the consecration itself featured Henry A. Henry and his sons in a more modest choral configuration; and Leeser's account of the music's positive reception offered optimism for musical expansion moving forward.[62] Ritterman thus began his work as hazan by appearing to offer a balance between innovation and conservatism, and promoting a German-style musical agenda: he initiated regular musical study with a group of boys "from eight to twelve years of age," who premiered as a choir during the congregation's December 9 Sabbath morning service.[63] Reports to the *Israelite*, clearly embracing a progressive agenda, provided hopeful updates, highlighting the (likely unrealized) prospect of adding an organ the following month, and in February 1855 noting with delight the choir's regular addition of new music in a manner that attracted more than one hundred people to each week's service.[64] Although the writer mentioned some opposition, he nonetheless hoped that Ritterman's efforts could help attract a preacher on the order of Max Lillienthal to provide a strong intellectual complement.[65] Such a balance of emotion and scholarship could fulfill a congregational paradigm advocated by leading Cincinnati rabbi Isaac Mayer Wise.

While Ritterman enhanced the aesthetics of prayer in Syracuse, New York City's congregation B'nai Jeshurun made its own enhancements, adopting a new set of bylaws with a revised, progressive vision of the hazan's role: "No person shall be elected to the position of Hazan of this Congregation, unless he possesses the following qualifications: 1st he shall be a good reader and 2nd he shall have a sufficient knowledge of music to organize and conduct a Choir; and lastly he shall possess a sufficient knowledge of the Hebrew Language to understand the prayers he has to read."[66] These changes marked a significant upgrade from the responsibilities of current cantor Ansel Leo, effectively ending his nine-year tenure; the search for his replacement, however, mainly led to applications from European cantors, whom the trustees could not properly evaluate without importing from across the ocean.[67] Only Ritterman, living upstate, could step in without incurring substantial travel costs; and it appears, despite a lacuna in the records, that he took the position on spec. By March 1856, an active choir of a dozen men and boys at the synagogue received mention in the *New York Daily Times* as exemplifying a "novel feature of religious services of the Jews in this City."⁶⁸ Directed by "a new man, fresh from Germany," who qualified for the job through "his musical ability," the choir inspired the *Times* writer to note that "this addition to the services will be generally conceded to be an improvement and advance upon the past." Perhaps in a nod to the unfamiliar sound in the sanctuary, however, the writer also bemusedly thought he heard the choir singing "the air, 'I know that my Redeemer liveth,'" presumably from Handel's *Messiah*, to one of the Hebrew prayers.⁶⁹

In an April 11, 1856 meeting, after nearly a year of dragging its feet, the cantorial search committee declared Ritterman "the only person possessing the necessary qualifications required by our laws."⁷⁰ Yet the minutes of B'nai Jeshurun's congregational meetings continued to show ambivalence, likely seeking a compromise between conservative and progressive factions: at the same meeting the trustees agreed to engage Ritterman provisionally for twelve months, to see if his choral program was viable.⁷¹ B'nai Jeshurun supported the effort by purchasing a small reed organ (a melodeon) for rehearsals and committing a $500 annual budget.⁷²

For the next three years, Ritterman officiated from B'nai Jeshurun's pulpit, regularly performing compositions by Sulzer and others during Sabbath services with a choir that appeared to range from twelve to twenty-four members depending on the occasion.⁷³ Concerns persisted, however: when the congregation decided to give Ritterman an official year-long contract in spring 1857, the former hazan, Ansel Leo, and another member of the board vocally dissented, adding a "minority" opinion to the record. Finally, on June 15, 1858, the congregation concluded its choral experiment, hiring newly arrived European cantor Judah Kramer in Ritterman's place.⁷⁴ Two years later, the congregation changed its bylaws to make choral music far less central, striking the requirement of the cantor to direct a choir and noting instead, "In the event of a choir being established by the Congregation the *hazan* must possess sufficient knowledge of music to sing in time and tune with the Choir."⁷⁵

Ritterman turned to the Midwest for additional opportunities. In March 1859, St. Louis's United Hebrew Congregation, anticipating the opening of a major new building, advertised for a hazan who could introduce music to match its grandeur, yet maintain a conservative "orthodox" mien. From its founding in 1841, the congregation sought to follow the "Polish rite" synonymous with traditionalist practice. Resisting German innovations in its first fifteen years, the congregation instead employed a combined reader/hazan and shochet/slaughterer.⁷⁶ By the late 1850s, however, its growth and increased prominence opened the need for a grander service, albeit without organ accompaniment; and the group consequently switched to a more contemporary model for its hazan that combined musical ability and educational acumen. The advertisement that came from these discussions fit naturally into contemporary Jewish-interest papers across the nation.

After reviewing its options, the board looked favorably on Ritterman's application and offered to pay half of his expenses if he could come out for an interview. As recorded by the congregation's secretary, Ritterman stood before the board and answered a series of terse questions from the president with equally terse answers. Their exchange offered a vision of the roles the hazan would occupy as educator, music director, and minister:

> Are you able to organize and conduct a choir?
>
> [RITTERMAN:] "I am."
>
> Can you speak English?
>
> [RITTERMAN:] "Not very well but will try to learn."
>
> Are you able to officiate a wedding?
>
> [RITTERMAN:] "I am."
>
> Are you able to superintend a [sic] Elementary school?
>
> [RITTERMAN:] "I am."[77]

The board then asked Ritterman to chant "a prayer"; and, fending off a request to "continue with business" (i.e., table the matter), the board invited him to conduct Sabbath services that coming Friday night and Saturday morning. The congregation liked what it saw, and on April 3, its members elected Ritterman to a three-year contract by a vote of forty-one to three.[78]

Similar to B'nai Jeshurun, United Hebrew Congregation took to choral music as a way to beautify practices associated with "orthodox" Judaism, particularly in response to musical developments among reformers. Yet the congregation differed in its long-term acceptance of the choir. Using the building dedication as its major test, the congregation found Ritterman's services as both preacher and choir instructor impressive. Shortly afterward, they honored Ritterman with a resolution:

> Resolved, That this congregation feels pleasure in expressing its high sense for the services and abilities of their minister, the Rev. J. Ritterman, and while thanks are respectfully due and tendered to him for his efficient ministration on the day of the consecration, they fully confide in his zeal, abilities, and pious intentions.

> Resolved, that strongly impressed with the great good that must result to themselves and their children, by persevering and advancing in the path of orthodox Judaism, which has already produced such satisfactory results; the members of this congregation will strive to the utmost of their ability to uphold the purity of their faith as they have received it from their own fathers.[79]

At the same meeting, the congregation "also moved that 3 more voices be added to the choir and payed [sic] by the congregation."[80] These decisions reinforced the choir's place as a natural part the congregation's orthodox identity.

As with B'nai Jeshurun, however, United Hebrew Congregation's relationship with Ritterman and the choir faced significant adjustment over the next couple of years. As the congregation's only spiritual leader, Ritterman occasionally overstepped his bounds by attempting to "deliver [unsolicited] discourses" during weddings, leading to more than one warning from the board.[81] The choir, which started with promise, faced reductions due to the congregation's nearly constant financial problems and concomitant ideological squabbles. Months after the consecration, a faction of the congregation challenged the need to include a choir and argued "that all the singing and prayers shall be left to Mr. Ritterman."[82] Congregants also aired concerns about hiring non-Jewish singers and passed a motion in March 1861 to ban them from the choir altogether.[83] At the end of Ritterman's first year with the United Hebrew Congregation, he found himself working with an occasional quartet fully dependent on private donations, suggesting differences among the membership deep enough to supplant institutional support.[84] As the situation become untenable, both sides negotiated an early end to his contract, which released him in July.[85]

Ritterman largely remained in St. Louis through the 1860s, while maintaining an extended long-distance relationship with Memphis and initiating at least one more flirtation with New York. Memphis's new liberal-minded Children of Israel/Bene Israel congregation briefly named Ritterman its hazan in late 1862. The *Jewish Messenger* snipped that Ritterman would eventually slide down the liberal slope by adding a choir, non-Jewish choristers, and even an organ; yet liberal reports from Memphis noted such a successful debut of the congregation's amateur mixed choir during Passover 1863 "that even our orthodox brethren are anxious to have a choir" with no objection to including women's voices.[86] But Ritterman continued to move. In August 1863, "expelled from his [Memphis] office as Hazan . . . for violation of his contract," he reapplied for the United Hebrew Congregation hazan position.⁸⁷ His first attempt fell short: the St. Louis congregation sought additional applications and then appeared to drop the matter altogether.⁸⁸ Ritterman seems to have moved back to St. Louis anyway; and in 1864, he turned down a call to the pulpit of New York's congregation Ahawath Chesed, rejecting a provision that required him to lead weekday services as "inconsistent with the principles of Reform," and subsequently refusing the congregation's counteroffer to hire a weekday service reader for a 20 percent salary reduction (from $1,000 to $800).⁸⁹ Instead, he took a position in Albany where he "introduced a good choir and conduct[ed] divine service in the Sulzer style."⁹⁰ He reapplied to the United Hebrew Congregation in 1865, but the congregation chose a Mr. Heimbach over him in an arrangement that lasted less than a year.⁹¹ Ritterman then returned to Memphis, where he led the Polish (orthodox) congregation, helped local rabbi Simon Tuska consecrate Beth El Emeth's new (Reform) synagogue, and likely became familiar with the synagogue music of Württemberg-born German teacher/composer Sigmund Schlesinger.⁹² A more permanent position, however, remained elusive.⁹³

Finally, in a July 1867 swing toward liberalism possibly facilitated by a move to a new building, the St. Louis United Hebrew Congregation rehired Ritterman at a salary of $1,200 and purchased a melodeon, clearly expecting to reintroduce a paid choir.⁹⁴ Ritterman took over choir director duties and sought to place the choir next to him on an enlarged pulpit in the new building.⁹⁵ His reelection for another year at a salary of $1,500 suggested a positive outcome; however, the congregation's expenditures on the new structure apparently required him to take a salary cut in 1869, likely leading to his July 1870 resignation.⁹⁶ Whereas consternation over a choir led him to leave the first time, the pendulum may have swung the other way by 1870: after Ritterman's departure, the congregation rehired Henry Kuttner as its rabbi and intellectual leader, and instead of a cantor added an organ and choir director to provide music for the service.⁹⁷ Five years later, with the congregation once again purporting to represent orthodoxy, a cantor-choir director team (Reichenberg and Abbath, respectively) officiated; and in 1877, Ritterman again joined the congregation, this time as an assistant for High Holiday services.⁹⁸

In later years, Ritterman went back east, shifting roles once again. An Isaac Ritterman appears as the rabbi of Boston's Temple Mishkan Israel during the late 1870s, officiating at weddings and founding the short-lived Independent Order of Patriarchs of Israel (a fraternal organization parallel to B'nai B'rith) among other groups.⁹⁹ Ritterman returned to New York before his death in 1890; his grave, in Queens's Bayside Cemetery, memorializes him as a "minister and teacher."¹⁰⁰

Isaac Ritterman's specialized knowledge and training contributed to his shifting, often liminal status in mid-nineteenth-century America, alternately praised or criticized based on which constituents dominated which congregation. Musically, his championing of Sulzerian choral music in the name of traditional Judaism contributed to his status. During decades of activity, Ritterman used music optimistically as a counterweight to party politics in an era when many congregations included self-described followers of both "orthodox" and "reform" ideologies. His specialized skills, moreover, allowed him flexibility to negotiate rapidly shifting ideas of American Jewish religion and community before they gained their own opposing soundtracks.

(Lazarus) Louis Naumburg (1813–1902)

In Philadelphia, meanwhile, a well-known cantorial family expanded its influence. Samuel Naumbourg's first cousin Lazarus (Louis) was born in the Bavarian town of Treuchtlingen in 1813. Part of the German branch of the family that spelled its name without the *o*, Naumburg likely learned his cantorial skills at the feet of his father, Lazar. In 1850, shortly after the German upheavals of 1848, he became part of the large Central European Jewish migration to America that would soon sweep up other members of his family.¹⁰¹ After some months, likely looking through advertisements in the local Jewish newspapers, Naumburg found a position at Philadelphia's Keneseth Israel congregation, where the congregants had decided to take the leap from a combined reader/slaughterer position to a skilled reader and teacher, gathering his initial $500 salary by hiking seat costs by $2 per person.¹⁰² Following a successful yearlong probationary period, the congregation awarded him a three-year contract at the same salary.

Naumburg's first few years at Keneseth Israel saw an accelerating set of changes in the synagogue service. Although he likely sang solo in the pulpit initially, he also organized a children's choir, presumably from among his students; he appeared also to give occasional German-language sermons.¹⁰³ The congregation looked to Germany for other modifications as well, including adopting the rules of decorum associated with the Württemberg synagogue, and arranging Saturday's schedule to begin with services, hold a religious school session, and then have "a ½ hour lecture on the bible or Talmud" before the afternoon Mincha service.[104] By the end of 1852, the cantor's directive "to chant in a dignified manner" literally hushed the congregation, which could now only pray "softly after" Naumburg or whoever led.[105]

When the congregation moved to a larger building on New Market Street in April 1854, Naumburg hired local musician Wilhelm Fischer to direct a fifteen-person choir, acquired a loaner melodeon, hired an orchestra led by local musician M. Scherzer, and gave his own dedication in German.[106] The repertoire for the consecration, comprising hymns and psalm settings, included compositions by [Samuel?] Naumbourg, "[Wilhelm] Fischer, Kohen, [Louis] Waldteufel [1801–1884], [Jacques Fromenthal] Halevi, Sulzer, and [probably neighboring cantor Jacob] Fraenkel"—all of which had associations with conservative models of musical change.[107] This elaborate event modeled the congregation's musical fortunes as well. Pleased with Fischer's choral direction at the dedication, the congregation engaged him with a $250 contract, renewed annually. Fischer subsequently hired eight choristers on renewing three-month contracts; and the congregation contracted with the Baltimore firm of Pomplitz and Bodewald for an $800 pipe organ.[108]

In 1855, Naumburg secured his position as cantor/educator by assuming the role of headmaster for Keneseth Israel's new school.[109] Yet when the congregation absorbed a society of Jews seeking to institute reforms in March 1856, he initially chafed despite an offered salary increase to $800.[110] "After long reflection," noted the synagogue secretary in the minutes, "Mr. Naumburg answered the board that he would consider it if they would not go 'ultra-reform.'"[111] When he was immediately asked to shorten the liturgy and add "a few German songs," however, he demurred and "declared that under the circumstances he does not feel strong enough to be Temple Chasan."[112] Pushed to adopt reforms, Naumburg reconsidered his commitment.

Three days later, Naumburg returned to the board and agreed to its requests, justifying his decision by distinguishing the synagogue's intentions from his own preferences: "After long consideration," he wrote, "I decided to continue my post as chasen and religious teacher in your congregation. I will do my utmost to help with the enhancement of culture and help hand in hand with the board to reach the goal as you set for yourself."[113] Naumburg donned a full cantorial robe; he worked with Fischer to create a new music book for choral and congregational singing (addressed in chap. 2); and he accepted numerous changes in the liturgy, recommending the Hamburg prayer book for use in services and eagerly meeting ultra-reform rabbi David Einhorn during his occasional trips to Philadelphia to lecture.[114]

In 1857, the congregation hired Solomon Deutsch from Posen, sight unseen, as its first rabbi.[115] While good for the congregation's reputation as an intellectual center of radical reform, the rejostling of pulpit roles caused friction. Coming from one of Europe's most progressive congregations, Deutsch soon began to institute his own changes: seeking unsuccessfully to remove the readings from the prophets (haftarah) and the Aleinu prayer, but changing Torah reading to a triennial cycle; keeping the Hamburg prayer book but making cuts and alterations; and seeking to rectify "the fact that the German influence is missing" in the service by, among other things, replacing the final hymn ("Adon olam" or "Yigdal") with "a German song."[116] Additional updates affected Naumburg directly, such as the elimination of his standard robe once it became threadbare, the decision that "in front of the ark should be a place for the chasen to stand up and say his prayers," and eventually the elimination of the cantor's prayer shawl.[117] The content of the choir began to change as well, from paid (presumably non-Jewish) singers to at least an attempt by Fischer to train the congregation's young women for participation.[118] By summer 1858, however, as the congregation debated whether to eliminate second days of holidays except for the Jewish New Year, tensions between Naumburg and Deutsch became noticeable. By early 1860, the two had begun to clash publicly, and Deutsch presented an ultimatum to the congregation: either buy out his own contract or release the cantor.[119] Convinced that the two could no longer work together, the congregation weighed its options carefully and raised a fund to pay off Deutsch. Yet Naumburg blinked first: during a dispute with the rabbi in late February, he walked out of the service, leading to his prompt dismissal.[120]

Naumburg subsequently found work in Pittsburgh at the city's moderate reform congregation Rodef Shalom, where he officiated through 1870, overseeing the congregation's transition to Isaac Mayer Wise's organ- and choir-friendly liturgy *Minhag America*.[121] Wise, upon visiting the congregation in 1867, contrasted Rodef Shalom with the city's other ("Polish") synagogue, which he characterized as "men who labor under peculiar delusion that religion signifies an immutable form of worship."[122] Rodef Shalom, Wise observed comparatively, had an integrated program that linked the sacred and the everyday. A twenty-person mixed choir with organ accompaniment sang music by Naumbourg, Sulzer, and, of lesser quality in

Wise's eyes, Fischer. Naumburg oversaw both the sacred music program and the school and introduced a confirmation ceremony for the congregation's young men and women.[123]

Naumburg died in New York in 1902, as his (much) younger brother Elkan was building a reputation as a well-regarded businessman and music patron.[124] While not self-professedly orthodox, Louis Naumburg nonetheless retained a level of conservatism comparable to his more famous Parisian cousin. Wary of the most radical forms of German progressivism, he tended toward a middle ground, willing to move with his congregations gradually as they explored new aesthetic paradigms.

Leon Sternberger, Herald of the Sulzer Cantors

A new era in American synagogue music quietly took root in July 1849, when Leon Sternberger completed the month-long boat trip from Liverpool, England, to New York City. Born a cantor's son in Deggingen, Bavaria, on May 9, 1819, Sternberger became a prominent member of the first wave of "Sulzer cantors," training with the Viennese religious leader from around 1840 to disseminate the musical system institutionalized at Sulzer's Stadttempel.[125] By 1843, Sulzer had placed Sternberger with Warsaw's progressive Jewish community, where a correspondent with the *Allgemeine Zeitung des Judenthums* reported with delight how his services with choir and melodikon (small organ) impressed a visiting delegation of imperial Russian dignitaries looking to evaluate the community's level of organization and enlightenment.[126] Sternberger's six-year tour in Warsaw also included a position as cantor and educator in the city's short-lived liberal Jewish seminary.[127] As with other civic trends in Germany, France, and elsewhere, however, successive rounds of government regulation intended to accelerate Jewish assimilation took their toll, posing hardships for heterogeneous Jewish populations seeking to move at their own pace.[128] These impositions may have led Sternberger to depart for the United States, willing to take his chances in a freer musical and religious marketplace.

Shortly after his 1849 arrival, prospects indeed started to perk up, particularly from New York congregation Anshe Chesed. Since its founding in 1836, this community had entrusted its liturgical responsibilities to a competent member/layman, who led services, conducted weddings, and did other small jobs for the synagogue in return for a salary. During Sternberger's time in Warsaw, Jonas Hecht occupied this role. Synagogue minutes of the time showed Hecht's relationship with the congregation as both intimate and contentious. The board of trustees regularly chided him about his behavior: whether to address allegations of late-night gambling and carousing (1844), public conflicts with other synagogue officials (1845), skipping his service-leading responsibilities without a good excuse (July 1846), or attending an official Jewish function without a proper head covering (November 1846). Despite these lapses, however, the congregation renewed Hecht's contract annually, even nominally increasing his salary (from $400 to $420) in 1845.[129]

Perhaps inspired by similar developments at Emanu-El, Anshe Chesed made efforts to beautify its services in the years before Sternberger's arrival. In 1845, the congregation engaged a Mr. Ketter to organize a choir of children, men, and women but achieved little success.[130] Four years later, with a new building impending, the synagogue began a more involved effort, establishing a Committee for the Beautification of the Service, passing and posting a set of regulations for service decorum, and openly advertising for a musically skilled cantor. On the last two items, the congregation sent letters of inquiry to Sulzer in Vienna, Naumbourg in Paris, and Hirsch Weintraub in Königsberg. Sulzer, the only one of the three to respond, recommended his son Julius. Rather than move on this (reasonably?) nepotistic suggestion, the congregation hired local musician Levy Cohn to organize, train, and lead a mixed choir of adults and children.[131] Sternberger, meanwhile, responded to the hazan ad, and received an invitation to lead parts of the High Holiday services as a kind of audition.[132]

Jonas Hecht at first bristled at sharing services with Sternberger; however, the board overruled him.[133] Then, in a promising gesture, the board began to consult with Sternberger on the choir's progress.[134] Sternberger in turn warned that the group could not perform effectively under the current plan and offered to take over the choir from Cohn, proposing what was likely a Sulzerian model with a choir and a separate quartet for cantorial accompaniment.

> In Mr. Sternberg[er]'s opinion, 24 singers half adults half children would for the present be sufficient, and that of the 12 adults[,] 4 should stand near him to form a Quartet, further that in case the funds of the Congregation would allow it, then it would be advisable to pay 8 of the adult singers, so as to secure some good singers, as the advantages of free seats [a typical in-kind gesture for synagogue member-choristers], may not be sufficiently tempting to some and most likely that about $3 a month would be a fair remuneration. Mr. Sternberg[er] remarked further, that if he should be charged with the

teaching either gratuitously or for a certain salary, then he would manage it to the satisfaction of the Congregation, but that another teacher in such a case would be more in the way than of any use.[135]

At the following meeting, Sternberger recommended the purchase of music notebooks and a violin for teaching choral parts and suggested further that the congregation purchase *Schir Zion* and two other books for repertoire. The board agreed, but rather than send away to Vienna for a copy of Sulzer's work, it purchased Sternberger's copy directly for $11 (c. $333 2016 dollars).[136] Three days later, after tallying the number of qualified children and adults, the trustees released Cohn from his contract and asked Sternberger to move forward with his plan. Voted hazan at the start of October, Sternberger by the end of the month had passed tests of character and musical ability, the latter of which was conducted by the director of the Broadway Theater orchestra, and formally began his job at an $800 salary.[137]

Sternberger and Hecht faced their first major challenge in Anshe Chesed's May 1850 synagogue consecration, planning musical forces likely far more elaborate than standard rituals while seeking to raise the congregation's long-term aesthetic norms. Outlining a proposed twenty-person instrumental ensemble, the two also set the terms for the choir: with half of the sixteen named adults paid outright, half granted free synagogue seats, and eleven children, "two of whom have offered to sing for free seats for their parents."[138] Sternberger sought additional women (or strong-voiced children) for balance; and it appears that the synagogue took the request seriously enough to accept Hyman Frank's offer to commit his two sons to the choir in return for membership on the board of trustees (*Baal HaBayit*).[139] Two additional singers with musical skills—a woman and a young man—became salaried employees in January.[140] A month before the consecration of the new building on Norfolk Street, as the cloaks for the hazanim neared completion, the trustees further emulated the Vienna aesthetic by deciding that the hazan face the congregation from the pulpit, taking advice from both clergy partner Max Lilienthal and synagogue school teacher Herman Felsenheld.[141] While *The Asmonean*'s (commissioned) account of Anshe Chesed's consecration in late May made note of the choir's significant contribution (idiomatic of consecrations of the time), however, Sternberger received no mention, suggesting that he was either indisposed or overlooked by the writer in favor of Hecht.[142]

Over the next few years, the Anshe Chesed choir remained perhaps the most visible among the nation's synagogue choral programs. In 1852, under

Sternberger's leadership, it added Samuel Naumbourg's works to its library and gained its own synagogue committee, which added regular discussions of personnel and practice to board meetings.[143] Sternberger's choir also appeared unique in publicly advertising for both male and female soloists in the local *Asmonean* in order to satisfy the synagogue's continued policy to employ only Jewish singers: he sought a "solo bass" in July 1850, a tenor and bass in 1853, and a tenor, soprano, and alto in 1856.[144] Comparable only to Emanu-El in both scale and composition, the group remained a remarkably stable component of Anshe Chesed's worship for several years and a meaningful tribute to both Sternberger and his teacher, Sulzer.

By the mid-1860s, joined by more recent Sulzer students such as Adolph Rubin (Emanu-El, arrived 1852) and Samuel Welsch (Ahawath Chesed, 1865), Sternberger had become the senior statesman of a small but growing group of cantor/music-specialists, with an increasing slant toward reform-minded congregations. Sternberger signed a five-year contract at a $2,000 salary in 1865, and officiated alongside recently imported minister Moses Mielziner.[145] The following year, after Sternberger headed an American effort to honor Sulzer's fortieth year in the pulpit (see chap. 5), David Einhorn's newly founded congregation, Adas Jeshurun, attracted him with a more lucrative $3,000-per-year contract, thus allying the cantor with German reform's staunchest American advocate.[146] Adas Jeshurun and Anshe Chesed merged in 1873 to form Beth-El, agreeing to keep the Einhorn-Sternberger clergy team, and in 1876, Sternberger's salary rose to $3,600 with a $5,000 life insurance policy.[147] A respected and dependable long-term presence alongside the controversial rhetoric of Einhorn and his successor Kaufman Kohler, Sternberger received recognition at his 1886 retirement as a "quiet clergyman, whose adherence to new-school forms has not been at the expense of old-school modesty and sense."[148]

Isaac Mayer Wise and the Reforming of the Synagogue Choir

Sternberger's story—which continues later in this book—exemplifies a period of transition in mid-nineteenth-century America that saw choral music morph from a flexible theological practice into a political symbol of Jewish reform. Much of the credit for this transformation goes to Isaac Mayer Wise, who embedded music deeply into his vision of American Judaism and disseminated his ideas forcefully. Wise had gained his own experience with

Sulzer in Vienna, and he brought musical facility and violin competence to his American pulpits in Albany (1848–54) and Cincinnati (1854–1900). Over the second half of the nineteenth century, Wise looked to music as an outward sign of spiritual progress in a strenuous battle against religious lay complacency. He acquired the first volume of Sulzer's *Schir Zion* from New York's Max Lilienthal shortly after his arrival in America, when Lilienthal's congregation forbade him from using it: he described the episode decades later as a moment of realization about the entrenched power of the nation's Jewish lay leaders.[149] Shortly after assuming the pulpit of Cincinnati's Bene Yeshurun synagogue, Wise included music in his description of "the Second Period of American Jewish History," which drew a sharp difference between the "conservatives" who had set up the existing Jewish structures, and the "progressives" of the age to come. "In ten years hence," Wise claimed, "the conservatives will be no more opposed to an organ in the synagogue, to the abolition of the second [days of] holidays, and the Machsor [high holy day prayer book] and other reforms, than they are to-day opposed to a choir ... to all of which they once were opposed."[150] That same month, Wise premiered his choir of twenty to twenty-five men and women in the KKBY sanctuary, which sang five selections by Sulzer and two by Naumbourg after a summer of training by Wise and his violin. G. F. Junkerman, music supervisor for the Cincinnati public schools, took over the congregation's choir the following month. Wise's philosophical ambition to make music a fully congregation-based activity, however, became increasingly difficult to reconcile with his own synagogue leadership: an 1855 sanctuary expansion to include an organ, combined with greater demand for a polished musical aesthetic, eventually led KKBY to start paying its best singers, while struggling to recruit voices from within the congregation.[151] Even so, Wise remained a consistent champion for the choir as a progressive institution, claiming ultimately that "No reform of the Jewish service was possible until the Jewish ear had again become accustomed to harmony and beauty."[152]

Wise's progressivist narrative shifted the meanings of earlier strata of synagogue musicianship irrevocably, even as the musical figures themselves continued to work well into the 1880s. For Leo and Henry and their British contemporaries in America (qualified or less so), music remained an organic part of the liturgy, bundled with the ability to lead prayers, teach young people, and (perhaps) deliver sermons even as it began to gain its own specialized identity. Even Ritterman, whose training included choral instruction from Europe's most prominent music conservatories, treated music as a part of a broader ministry, emphasizing a meaningful service over musical refinement in association with the values of his various orthodox-leaning communities. Naumburg represented moderation, with the musical skills to address congregational desires as they transitioned into a more elaborate, reform-identified musical program, but drawing the line at the more radical reforms of Deutsch and David Einhorn. Sternberger took matters a step further, initiating a period of increased attention to music as a separate and significant element of Jewish identity, not just at its most publicly visible time during the ritual but also as part of Jewish home and school life. Sulzer's work realized music's potential as a sign of modernity. However, Wise and other rabbinical figures associated with reform actively politicized that space within American congregations, promoting organ- and choir-based musical resources and personnel to support their own vocabulary of liberal expression.

Postscript: Professionalizing the Cantorate—and Masculinizing It?

This era also presents a cogent yet overlooked matter, perhaps born of the current assumption that the cantorate had always been an exclusively male profession. Scattered reports from this time mention female liturgical singers leading other women in orthodox-leaning synagogues that separated the sexes, under the various titles of *sagerin* or *vorsagerin*. Late-nineteenth-century rabbi and music scholar Francis L. Cohen, for example, noted in 1887 that "on a smaller scale," the *sagerin* "still obtains in many Polish congregations, and may even be observed in London."[153] In 1892, during a discussion of synagogue music traditions, Cohen added greater sonic detail, albeit in condescending terms that undercut the figure's modern musicality and religious authority: "in Polish synagogues even now you will not fail to come across the aged person who acts as 'sagerin' (readeress) for a select circle of associates less profoundly versed in the Hebrew tongue, crooning forth the prayers in a dove-like lament, and usually weeping most bitterly at the most joyous passages of the ritual."[154] After the turn of the twentieth century, Cohen noted in his entry on the *sagerin* for the *Jewish Encyclopedia* that "the custom . . . is still followed in eastern Europe."[155] Subsequent scholarly literature in Jewish liturgy, history, and gender studies gave female liturgical leaders consistent if glancing mention, noting their prevalence throughout Central and Eastern Europe between the Middle Ages and the nineteenth century.[156] In music scholarship, however, the *sagerin*'s presence regressed as scholarship on the (male) cantor increasingly promoted longevity and tradition. Abraham Z. Idelsohn made no mention of the *sagerin* in his foundational 1929 text *Jewish History in Its Historical Development*. Forty-three years later, when Leo Landman's 1972 study of the cantorate appeared to reintroduce women into the narrative, he relegated such figures to Central Europe, no later than the thirteenth century.[157] Later music studies used Landman as their point of reference, remanding female liturgical leaders to the Middle Ages while reinforcing the modern cantor-as-male-tradition narrative.[158]

The gradual erasure of women from the narrative of Jewish musical leadership roughly coincides with the rise of the "modern" cantor beginning in the nineteenth century—even while women continued to officiate in gender-separated congregations—bringing an uncomfortable yet intriguing commentary about the implicit gendering of religious reform. For now, existing sources offer only hints of this transition—currently leaving it an addendum to this study rather than a full-throated claim. Yet compelling signposts reinforce further the complexities of this era of change and the difficulties in framing progress as a journey from orthodoxy to reform. Looking more closely suggests a different story of male and female liturgical leadership in which the supersession of reform actually marginalized women's active co-officiation of prayer on both sides of the Atlantic. In its place, historians of the cantorate paved the way for an incomplete, if convenient, argument for male cantor's continuous dominance of musical leadership well into the twenty-first century.

Viewed together, these years laid the groundwork for the cantor's development as an elite and well-compensated musical (male) artist, valued for his ability to harness the power of music in both presentation and writing—and developing as an analogue to similar (and more effectively documented) rabbinical efforts. *Artistic* cantors, however, proved only one of the paradigms that later took root in the United States. As I illustrate in the next chapters, cantor-*teachers* also integrated into American towns, working in concert with Isaac Mayer Wise's ideas of music as a medium for community building and teaching, and seeking in the process to foster a distinct genre of "Jewish" music consistent with broader American educational and cultural developments. Their stories often coincided with stories of moderate reform in the American Midwest, and set their own distinct soundtrack for the area's liturgical developments.

Notes

1. Simeon Abrahams, letter to *The Occident and American Jewish Advocate* 7, no. 3 (June 1849), 144–45.
2. Simeon Abrahams, "The Ministry," *The Occident and American Jewish Advocate* 5, no. 2 (May 1847), 87–90.
3. Abrahams, Letter to *The Occident*, 1849.
4. Philip Bohlman, *Jewish Music and Modernity* (New York: Oxford University Press, 2008).
5. E. Roget, adapter, "Adon Olam," *The Occident and American Jewish Advocate* 1, no. 3 (June 1843), 143–44.
6. Bertoni's air, which first appeared in the 1779 staging of the opera *La governante*, appears in books of popular Italian airs for several decades afterward. It remains in use today as a student flute piece titled, *Canzona*.
7. "Consecration of the New Synagogue Rodef Sholem of Philadelphia," *The Occident and American Jewish Advocate* 1, no. 2 (May 1843), 99.
8. Audrey T. Carpenter, *Giovanna Sestini: An Italian Opera Singer in Eighteenth-Century London* (Leicester, UK: Troubador, 2017), 53–54.
9. Hanoch Avenary, *Kantor Salomon Sulzer und seine Zeit: eine Dokumentation* (Sigmaringen: Jan Thornbeck, 1985), 254–55. (Citing a letter from Sulzer recommending Abraham Fischer for a position in New York during the early 1850s.)
10. Judah M. Cohen, *Through the Sands of Time: A History of the Jewish Community of St. Thomas, US Virgin Islands* (Hanover, NH: Brandeis University Press, 2004), 51–86; Edwin Seroussi, liner notes to *Judeo-Caribbean Currents: Music of the Mikvé Israel-Emanuel Synagogue in Curaçao*, Anthology of Music Traditions in Israel 22 (Jerusalem: Jewish Music Research Centre, 2009).
11. Robert Liberles, "Conflict over Reforms: The Case of Congregation Beth Elohim, Charleston, South Carolina," in *The American Synagogue: A Sanctuary Transformed*, ed. Jack Wertheimer (Hanover, NH: Brandeis University Press, 1995), 274–96; Gary P. Zola, "The Ascendancy of Reform Judaism in the American South during the Nineteenth Century," in *Jewish Roots in Southern Soil*, ed. Marcie Cohen Ferris and Mark Greenberg (Hanover, NH: University Press of New England, 2006), 160–65.
12. Sharona Wachs, *American Jewish Liturgies* (Cincinnati: Hebrew Union College Press, 1997); Jeff Janeczko, curator, "Jewish Voices in the New World," virtual exhibit, accessed March 23, 2017, http://www.milkenarchive.org/articles/virtual-exhibits/view/jewish-voices-new-world-sacred-music.
13. J. Jacob Neusner, "Anglo-Jewry and the Development of American Jewish Life, 1775–1850," *Transactions* (Jewish Historical Society of England) 18 (1953–55), 231–42.
14. Haim Sperber notes that by the mid-1800s, "many of the Jewish elite . . . rabbinical as well as secular, were from Germany." Haim Sperber, "Rabbi Nathan Adler and the Chief Rabbinate in Britain, 1845–1890," *European Judaism: A Journal for the New Europe* 45, no. 2 (2012): 10. See also Todd M. Endelman, "German-Jewish Settlement in Victorian England," in *Second Chance: Two Centuries of German-Speaking Jews in the United Kingdom*, ed. Julius Carlebach et al. (Tübingen, Germany: J. C. B. Mohr [Paul Siebeck], 1991), 37–56.
15. Israel Finestein, *Anglo-Jewry in Changing Times: Studies in Diversity, 1840–1914* (London: Valentine Mitchell, 1999), 59–61.

16. Ibid., 62–63.

17. Ibid., 62.

18. [Isaac Leeser], "English News," *The Occident and American Jewish Advocate* 5, no. 1 (September 1847), 53.

19. See Cecil Roth, *Records of the Western Synagogue 1761–1932* (London: Edward Goldstone, 1932), 123–25.

20. Arthur Barnett, *The Western Synagogue through Two Centuries (1761–1961)* (London: Valentine Mitchell, 1961), 64–66.

21. For earliest date, see *The Metropolitan Ecclesiastical Directory* (London: Hurst, 1835), 190, where Leo is described as "Principal Reader" for the Western ("Saint Albans Place") Synagogue. The cited account views both the Western and Duke Street synagogues as places where "the visitor will be highly delighted with the singing" (191).

22. On Louis Leo's solo songs, see "The Concerts, &c," *Sunday Times*, April 7, 1844, 5; "Theatricals and Music," *Sunday Times*, June 30, 1844, 2.

23. "Hebrew Melodies," *The Era*, January 21, 1844, 6.

24. See also "Lecture on Hebrew Music," *The Standard*, January 18, 1844; "Hebrew Melodies," *The Standard*, February 26, 1844.

25. B'nai Jeshurun minutes, February 8, 1846; October 27, 1839 (including proposal of new bylaws for the hazan); October 16, 1842.

26. "Elm Street Synagogue," *The Occident and American Jewish Advocate* 4, no. 4 (July 1846), 214–15.

27. Ibid. See also B'nai Jeshurun minutes, June 2, 1846. The reduction may also have resulted from the congregational split the previous year, which strained resources.

28. Ibid. Reading from the Torah seemed a lower priority for a hazan, although still valued by the congregation. The congregation's first reader, Phineas A. Hart, also could not read from the Torah despite the congregation's request that he learn. Admittedly, the stakes were lower in this case because Hart had volunteered for the position for several years before. At his request, the trustees introduced a $200 salary for the position.

29. "Letter from Rev. Mr. Leo," *The Occident and American Jewish Advocate* 5, no. 5 (August 1847). The letter was also reproduced in the London *Jewish Chronicle*. See also Adam Mendelsohn, "Great Britain, the Commonwealth, and Anglophone Jewry," in *The Cambridge History of Judaism, Volume 8, The Modern World, 1815–2000*, ed. Mitchell B. Hart and Tony Michels (New York: Cambridge University Press, 2017), 144–45.

30. Karla Goldman, *Beyond the Synagogue Gallery: Finding a Place for Women* (Cambridge, MA: Harvard University Press, 2000), 85. Further illustrating the ongoing feud between B'nai Jeshurun and Shaarey Tefilah was Leo's allegation that Isaac Leeser favored Shaarey Tefilah minister S. M. Isaacs over other *hazanim* when reporting on activities of the Bachelors' Hebrew Benevolent Association. See letter from Ansel Leo to Isaac Leeser, February 6, 5608 [1848]. Gerschwind-Bennett Isaac Leeser Digital Repository (http://leeser.library.upenn.edu).

31. B'nai Jeshurun minutes, February 11, 1849.

32. Hyman Grinstein, *The Rise of the Jewish Community of New York, 1654–1860* (Philadelphia: Jewish Publication Society, 1945), 570n46.

33. Dalia Marx, "The Prayer for the State of Israel: Universalism and Particularism," in *All the World: Universalism, Particularism, and the High Holy Days*, ed. Lawrence A. Hoffman (Woodstock, VT: Jewish Lights, 2014), 50–54.

34. Letter from Ansel Leo to Isaac Leeser, October 13, 5612 [1851]. Gerschwind-Bennett Isaac Leeser Digital Repository. The Hebrew words that Leo inserted into the text, a common practice of the time, are here presented in transliteration. In an interesting semantic turn, Leo crossed out the word *answer* when referring to the "old-style" practice of cantor–choir line alternation, seemingly rejecting the description of this practice as "call and response." Leeser paraphrased Leo's letter in *The Occident and American Jewish Advocate* 9, no. 8 (November 1851), 426–28.

35. Leo retired to a house in Yonkers from about 1860 until his death in 1878. "Rev. Ansel Leo," *The Jewish Messenger*, December 13, 1878, 2; see also "Congregation Gates of Prayer," *The Jewish Messenger*, October 12, 1859, 117, which details Leo's agreement to fill in for the ailing minister of congregation Shaarey Tefilah during Yom Kippur.

36. Barnett, The *Western Synagogue*, 149–50.

37. "Reverend H. A. Henry of Cincinnati," *The Occident and American Jewish Advocate* 9, no. 5 (August 1851), 269–71. Abrahams is not mentioned by name in the *Occident* report, but he seems to fit the bill as a "gentleman of New York (well known for the interest he takes in supplying vacant congregations, or those about becoming so, with suitable ministers)" (269).

38. "Changes in Minsters," *The Occident and American Jewish Advocate* 7, no. 8 (November 1849), 424–25; "Reverend H. A. Henry of Cincinnati." Gutheim moved on to become minister of New Orleans Congregations Shaarei Chesed (1850–53) and Nefutzot Yehudah, as well as a host of others.

39. "Reverend H. A. Henry of Cincinnati"; Israel J. Benjamin, *Drei Jahre in America, 1859–1862* (Hanover, 1862), 212; Bene Yeshurun Minutes Book (September 1849; Coll. 62, American Jewish Archives, Cincinnati, OH); herein KKBY Minutes Book.

40. KKBY Minutes Book, December 12, 1847–December 3, 1848. Discussion of the specific regulation of the choir took place at the meeting on February 27, 1848.

41. Ibid., January 20, March 18 and 31, 1850.

42. Ibid., June 16, 1850.

43. Ibid., June 19, July 14, August 11, 1850.

44. Ibid., August 14, September 30, 1850; "Louisville Congregation," *The Occident and American Jewish Advocate* 9, no. 6 (September 1851), 322–24. The president of Louisville's congregation viewed Henry's arrival with suspicion, which temporarily turned *Occident* editor Isaac Leeser against Henry.

45. KKBY Minute Book, November 11, 1850; March 9, 1851. There is no indication that the choir included adults.

46. Ibid., March 9, June 6, July 20, 1851; "The Rev. H. A. Henry," *The Occident and American Jewish Advocate* 9, no. 8 (November 1851), 416–17.

47. "Consecration of the New Synagogue, Kenesseth Shalom, at Syracuse, New York." *The Occident and American Jewish Advocate* 9, no. 7 (October 1851), 376.

48. Benjamin, *Drei Jahre*, 208–12.

49. "Consecration of the New Jewish Synagogue," *Sacramento Daily Union*, June 6, 1859, 2; "Dedication of the Synagogue Ohabai Shalome," *The Daily Alta California*, September 16, 1865, 1; "Consecration of the Synagogue," *Sacramento Daily* Union, May 23, 1864, 3.

50. "The Day of Atonement," *The Daily Alta California*, October 13, 1867, 2.

51. "Synagogue Dedication," *The Daily Alta California*, August 27, 1870, 1; see also Fred Rosenbaum, *Cosmopolitans: A Social and Cultural History of Jews of the San Francisco Bay Area* (Berkeley: University of California Press, 2009), 22–24.

52. Ritterman's age and birth date are confounded somewhat by the 1860 and 1870 censuses, which provide significantly different ages.

53. "Greene Street Synagogue," *The Asmonean*, August 24, 1855, 148. The *Asmonean* article describes the institution as the "Imperial School of Music," perhaps because the state provided funding at the time (even though it was precarious).

54. Avenary, *Kantor Salomon Sulzer*, 206. Sulzer's appointment began the month after Ritterman graduated, in July 1845.

55. G., "Posen," *Allgemeine Zeitung des Judenthum* 3, no. 47 (November 19, 1849), 666.

56. Ibid.

57. L. W., "Aus der Provinz Posen," *Der Orient* 11, no. 12 (March 23, 1850), 417.

58. *Jewish Chronicle* 6, no. 46 (August 23, 1850), 368; "Greene Street Synagogue."

59. The dates of Ritterman's course of study are likely a misprint, because the *Asmonean* article announcing his qualifications notes his attendance at the institute in 1854–55, when he was already in the United States ("Greene Street Synagogue").

60. *The Israelite* 1, no. 13 (October 6, 1854), 99.

61. [Isaac Leeser,] "Consecration of the New Synagogue, Kenesseth Shalom, at Syracuse, New York," *The Occident and American Jewish Advocate* 9, no. 7 (October 1851), 373.

62. Ibid., 376.

63. S. H[amburger], Letter to the Editor, *The Israelite* 1, no. 24, 190. See also B. G. Rudolph, *From a Minyan to a Community: A History of the Jews of Syracuse* (Syracuse, NY: Syracuse University Press, 1970), 43–49. Ritterman instituted his musical program at a time when the city's British and Eastern European Jews were establishing their own synagogues, hinting at the possibility that each congregation also honed its own musical identity.

64. "Syracuse," *The Israelite* 1, no. 28, 222; S. Hamburger, Letter to the Editor, *The Israelite* 1, no. 35, 277–78. Hamburger made reference specifically to musical settings of "Mizmor David" and a "Uv'nucho Yomar," which he assumed to be original compositions by Ritterman; there is a good chance, however, that these were Sulzer's settings from *Schir Zion*.

65. Ibid.

66. B'nai Jeshurun Bylaws, adopted January 28, 1855, article 6, section 7.

67. B'nai Jeshurun Minutes, May 27, 1855.

68. "A Choir in a Synagogue," *New York Daily Times*, March 12, 1856, 3. See also *Asmonean*, March 21, 1856, 182.

69. Ibid.

70. B'nai Jeshurun Minutes, April 11, 1856.

71. Ibid.

72. Ibid.

73. Grinstein, *Rise*, 95, 282; see also Israel Goldstein, *A Century of Judaism in New York: B'nai Jeshurun 1825–1925, New York's Oldest Ashkenazic Congregation* (New York: Congregation B'nai Jeshurun, 1930), 128.

74. "The Rev. Mr. Ritterman," *Jewish Messenger* 4, no. 2 (July 16, 1858), 13.

75. B'nai Jeshurun Bylaws, 1860, article 6, section 6. I have rendered the Hebrew characters in transliteration.

76. United Hebrew Congregation, Minutes, 1841–59 (American Jewish Archives, SC-10634).

77. Ibid., March 27, 1859.

78. Ibid., April 3 and 5, 1859.

79. Ibid., July 17, 1859.
80. Ibid.
81. United Hebrew Congregation Board of Trustees Minutes, October 21, 1859; April 15, 1860 (St. Louis Jewish Community Archives). I am grateful to Diane Everman for making these notes available.
82. United Hebrew Congregation Minutes (American Jewish Archives), September 14, 1859.
83. United Hebrew Congregation Minutes (St. Louis Jewish Community Archives), November 21, 1860; March 14, 1861.
84. Ibid., March 14, 1861.
85. Ibid., May 26 and July 6, 1861.
86. "Tennessee," *Jewish Messenger*, December 19, 1862, 187; Progress, Letter to the Editor, *The Israelite*, April 24, 1863, 331; Miarhpe, Letter to the Editor, *The Israelite*, June 5, 1863, 378. The initial choir of "Children of Israel" consisted of six sopranos, four altos, two tenors, and two basses.
87. *The Israelite*, August 14, 1863, 50. The exact nature of Ritterman's violation is unclear.
88. United Hebrew Congregation Minutes (St. Louis Jewish Community Archives), October 18, 1863.
89. *Die Deborah*, March 25, 1864, 155; Ahawath Chesed Minutes, vol. 1, March 1 and 6, 1864.
90. *The Israelite*, March 24, 1865, 309. An "Isaac Reiterman" appears as a "clergyman" in Albany as part of the 1865 New York State census (source: Ancestry.com). His wife Catrina does not appear with him, suggesting the unstable nature of the position.
91. United Hebrew Congregation Minutes (St. Louis Jewish Community Archives), July 12 and 30, 1865; United Hebrew Congregation Board of Trustees Minutes (St. Louis Jewish Community Archives), April 19, 1866.
92. *The Israelite*, July 21, 1865, 21; Selma S. Lewis, *A Biblical People in the Bible Belt: The Jewish Community of Memphis, Tennessee, 1840s–1960s* (Macon, GA: Mercer University Press, 1998), 37. Schlesinger would move to Mobile, Alabama, in 1866, where he served as the organist of the local synagogue from about 1870 until his death in 1906.
93. "Consecration Ceremony," *Memphis Daily Avalanche* 8, no. 49 (February 23, 1866), 3; "Memphis," *Jewish Messenger*, March 9, 1866, 4; *Public Ledger* (Memphis), October 31, 1867, 2.
94. United Hebrew Congregation Minutes (St. Louis Jewish Community Archives), July 8, 1867; United Hebrew Congregation Board of Trustees Minutes (St. Louis Jewish Community Archives), December 11, 1867, and March 2, 1868.
95. United Hebrew Congregation Minutes (St. Louis Jewish Community Archives), February 2, 1868.
96. United Hebrew Congregation Board of Trustees Minutes (St. Louis Jewish Community Archives), November 30, 1869, and July 7, 1870.
97. United Hebrew Congregation Minutes (St. Louis Jewish Community Archives), July 6, 1870; United Hebrew Congregation Board of Trustees Minutes (St. Louis Jewish Community Archives), July 17, 1870.
98. "The Hebrew New Year," *St. Louis Globe-Democrat*, October 1, 1875, 5.
99. *Boston Almanac and Directory*, vol. 40 (1874/5–1877/8), 102; "A Jewish Wedding," *Boston Daily Advertiser*, April 3, 1873, 1; *Boston Daily Advertiser*, July 27, 1878; *Boston Evening Journal*, August 28, 1874, 4.

100. "Isaac Ritterman," Find a Grave, last modified July 12, 2016, https://www.findagrave.com/cgi-bin/fg.cgi?page=gr&GSln=Ritterman&GSbyrel=in&GSdyrel=in&GSob=n&GRid=166900212.

101. Naumburg arrived in New York on the ship *Cummings* on May 30, 1850. *Registers of Vessels Arriving at the Port of New York from Foreign Ports, 1789–1919.* Microfilm Publication M237, rolls 1–95. Washington, DC: National Archives (accessed via Ancestry.com).

102. Keneseth Israel Board of Trustees Minutes, September 24, 1850 (American Jewish Archives, MS-551, Box 5, Folder 1). Keneseth Israel had started its cantorial search the previous year, dangling a salary of $350; however, after a negative experience with a minister named Davidson, the trustees appeared to raise the salary in hopes of competing with its New York counterparts.

103. Keneseth Israel Board of Trustees Minutes, August 1, 1852 (American Jewish Archives, MS-551, Box 5, Folder 1).

104. Ibid., October 3 and 10, 1852.

105. Ibid., October 3, 1852.

106. Ibid., February 5, 12, and 19, 1854. Possibly the minutes pointed to prominent Philadelphia musician Adolph Scherzer or the significantly less prominent "W. Scherzer," whose name appears on a couple of published compositions of the time. Nothing else is currently known about an "M. Scherzer."

107. [Isaac Leeser], "Philadelphia Consecration of the Synagogue Kenesseth Israel," *The Occident* 12, no. 2 (May 1854), 114–15.

108. Keneseth Israel Board of Trustees Minutes, September 30, 1855, March 30, 1856, May 7, 11, 12, 18, 25, and 28, 1856; [Isaac Leeser], "Philadelphia Consecration of the Synagogue Kenesseth Israel," *The Occident* 12, no. 2 (May 1854), 114–15; Letter from Weidnitzer to Isaac Leeser, c. April 17, 1854, http://leeser.library.upenn.edu/documentDisplay.php?id=LSTCAT_item72.

109. Keneseth Israel Board of Trustees Minutes, May 6 and June 3, 1855.

110. Shelley Kapneck Rosenberg, *Reform Congregation Keneseth Israel: 150 Years* (Philadelphia: Keneseth Israel, 1997), 2. Rosenberg describes the absorbed group as the "Reform Society," though a transcript of the minutes gives the group the name Temple Association Society.

111. Keneseth Israel Board of Trustees Minutes, May 25, 1856.

112. Ibid.

113. Ibid., June 8, 1856.

114. Ibid., July 6, 27, and 30, 1856.

115. Ibid., June 7, 1857. The extended contract, eight years at a salary of $1,000, shows the confidence with which the congregation greeted him.

116. Ibid., October 18, December 6 and 13, 1857; January 17, 1858.

117. Ibid., March 17 and August 24, 1858.

118. Ibid., March 24 and June 6, 1858.

119. Ibid., February 2, 1860.

120. Ibid., February 14, 1860. Deutsch was paid off shortly afterward.

121. Naumburg was such a beloved figure at Rodef Shalom that the community held a service marking his centennial in 1913.

122. Occasional, "Pittsburgh, PA," *The American Israelite*, April 5, 1867, 2.

123. Ibid.

124. In addition to serving as a founder of the New York series now known as the Naumburg concerts in 1905, Elkan Naumburg later donated the funds to create the Central Park band shell that now holds his name.

125. Records diverge on Sternberger's birth town. Obituaries note his birth in Wallerstein, while Sternberger's American passport application from May 23, 1894, notes his birthplace as Deggingen, confirmed by his 1846 marriage record (*American Hebrew*, January 22, 1897; National Archives and Records Administration [NARA], Washington, DC, NARA Series: *Passport Applications, 1795–1905*, roll no. 421—May 16, 1894–May 24, 1894).

126. "Warschau," *Allgemeine Zeitung des Judenthums*, August 7, 1843, 477.

127. Sternberger also married Matylde Sandzer in 1845–46. For both, see marriage record in Warsaw marriage records, no. 44, 231 (September 4, 1846), in the Jewish Records Indexing–Poland database (http://jri-poland.org). I am grateful to Noam Silberberg at the Jewish Historical Institute, Warsaw, Poland, for his assistance in locating this record.

128. See, for example, Geoffrey Goldberg, "The Training of *Hazzanim* in Nineteenth Century Germany," *Yuval* 7 (2002): 307–14.

129. Anshe Chesed Minute Book, in the Archives of Temple Emanu-El, New York. July 28, 1844; January 6, 1845; July 12 and 16, 1846; November 15 and December 3, 1846.

130. Ibid., May 11 and 18, 1845.

131. Ibid., August 19, 1849. Anshe Chesed Board of Trustees Minutes, July–September, 1849.

132. Ibid., September 19, 1849.

133. Ibid., September 9, 1849.

134. Ibid., October 14, 18, and 24, 1849.

135. Ibid., October 14, 1849.

136. Ibid., October 18, 1849.

137. Ibid., October 28, 1849.

138. Ibid., December 9, 1849.

139. Ibid.

140. Ibid., January 6 and 27, 1850.

141. Ibid., April 28, 1850; a rabbi Schwartz also agreed on the Vienna rite, though with the hazan facing away from the congregation.

142. "The New Synagogue," *The Asmonean* 2, no. 5 (May 23, 1850), 38–39. See also Grinstein, *Rise*, 177–78.

143. Grinstein, *Rise*, 276–78.

144. *The Asmonean*, 2, no. 11 (July 5, 1850), 84; 9, no. 7 (December 2, 1853), 56; 15, no. 6 (November 21, 1856), 41.

145. An Israelite, Letter to the Editor, *The Israelite*, November 3, 1865, 141.

146. "Domestic Record, New York," *The Israelite*, November 30, 1866, 4.

147. *Jewish Messenger*, May 19, 1876, 2.

148. *Jewish Messenger*, February 12, 1886, 5.

149. Isaac Mayer Wise, *Reminiscences*, trans. David Philipson (Cincinnati: Leo Wise, 1901), 50–51.

150. [Isaac Mayer Wise,] "The Second Period of American Jewish History," *The Israelite*, August 4, 1854, 28.

151. KKBY Board Minutes, 1855–57.

152. Wise, *Reminiscences*, 260.

153. Francis L. Cohen, "The Rise and Development of Synagogue Music," in *Papers Read at the Anglo-Jewish Historical Exhibition, Royal Albert Hall, London, 1887* (London: Jewish Chronicle, 1888), 84.

154. Francis L. Cohen, "Ancient Musical Traditions of the Synagogue," *Proceedings of the Musical Association for the Investigation and Discussion of Subjects Connected with the Art and Science of Music, Nineteenth Session, 1892–93* (London: Novello, 1893), 138 (talk given June 13, 1893).

155. Francis L. Cohen, "Sagerin," *Jewish Encyclopedia*.

156. See, for example, Emily Taitz, "Woman's Voices, Woman's Prayers: Women in the European Synagogues of the Middle Ages," in *Daughters of the King: Women and the Synagogue*, ed. Susan Grossman and Rivka Haut (Philadelphia: Jewish Publication Society, 1992), 65–68; Karla Goldman, *Beyond the Synagogue Gallery: Finding a Place for Women in American Judaism* (Cambridge, MA: Harvard University Press, 2000), 4.

157. Leo Landman, *The Cantor: An Historical Perspective* (New York: Yeshiva University, 1927), 68.

158. A 2007 issue of the *Journal of Synagogue Music* devoted to women in the cantorate, for example, repeats this information that "the only [post-Temple] historical information recorded on women's participation in what later developed into the professional cantorate, is in the European communities of Nuremberg and Worms of the 13th century" (Pamela Kordan Trimble, "Kol Ḥazzanit: Alternatives for Women Cantors to the Vocal Requirements and Expression of Traditional Ḥazzanut," *Journal of Synagogue Music* 32 [2007]: 101). Joseph A. Levine's introduction to the same issue sports a similar citation (p. 6).

2

THE SOUND OF GERMAN JEWRY

Hymnals and Singing Societies in Wilhelm Fischer's Zemirot Yisrael

> As this great Sængerfest [has] united here German and American, by the power of music, in fraternal feelings and harmonious sentiments, the victories of humanity must finally unite and harmonize the whole family of man to one grand oratorio, in which no discord shall disturb the harmony.... The world must become our fatherland, the human family our people, freedom, justice and truth our law and government. The world, I say, must become one great sængerhalle, and every human being an indispensable character in the universal Sængerbund.
>
> —Isaac Mayer Wise, Cincinnati Sängerfest celebratory picnic, June 19, 1870

Isaac Mayer Wise delivered these lofty words to a thirty thousand–strong crowd toward the close of one of the nation's premier amateur musical events. As an annual summit for a large Midwestern network of German American community choirs that had emerged since the late 1840s, the Sängerfest gave German Americans a powerful venue for "put[ting] their [own] assessment of American society into action," in Karen Ahlquist's words. "Distinguishing themselves from English-speaking community leaders who aspired to a sacralized concert life," Ahlquist continues, German Americans in the second half of the nineteenth century "used music to shape, assert, defend, and celebrate cultural difference on their own terms."[1] Wise's speech brought this worldview to full flower, transforming the specific vocabulary of this German American event—the Sängerbund as a collective of singing societies, the Sängerhalle as the Sängerfest performance venue—into a universalist, utopian metaphor.

Wise's celebration of the German men's choir (Männerchor) and its affiliates hinted at their significance as a meeting ground for Jewish, German, and American identities, described by Stanley Nadel during this period as "overlapping and inextricable."[2] A view of the Sängerfest organization itself, however, made this view even clearer. Wise's Cincinnati colleague Rabbi Max Lilienthal served as president of the 1870 festival committee; another member of the city's Jewish population designed the Sängerhalle; others sat on various organizing subcommittees; and still more sang in the different performing societies.[3] Just as German Americans cultivated musicality as an ethnic trait during this time, in other words, Wise viewed Jews' extensive participation in the Sängerfest as a full embrace of their fellow émigrés' values.

Amateur choral singing, after all, invoked the progressive spirit that spoke to the essence of German identity, especially when the post-1848 fatherland itself failed to live up to such ideals. Choral singing symbolically enacted full participation in a democratic process in America, sidestepping religious discrimination in favor of a comprehensive civic vision. Wise had elaborated on this idea in a June 1856 *Israelite* editorial, in which he recounted Cincinnati's interconnected "excitement" in hosting the Democratic National Convention, the North American Sängerfest, and Bene Yeshurun's confirmation service. Musically, Wise left no ambiguity about Jews' organic presence in German American culture, crowing, "No wonder that [significant Jewish participation] is the case in the German *Saengerbund*, as the Jew is almost THE representative of music emphatically"; and he closed his article with an appeal to the progressive spirit as the *real* seat of German (Jewish) identity: "Sing, sing, ye ill-fated sons of Germania! . . . Wherever liberty pours forth its glorious rays there is the fatherland of song; wherever song and music enrapture the bosom, there is your fatherland!"[4] Amateur ensembles and their music embodied this progressive ideology, locally enfranchising them and offering an ecumenical solution for integrating Judaism into a broad spiritual vision of American life.

Histories of synagogue music often credit hymn singing—with little nuance—as a crucial part of synagogue reform. Current (frequently anecdotal) histories too easily turn this practice into a morally fraught narrative that asserts Jews' adoption of hymn singing from the Christian church, thus abandoning their own traditions. In this chapter, I seek to restore a greater balance by portraying part singing as a coterritorial repertoire that played an important role in German, and later German American, identity—regardless of religious or political affiliation. In this setting, hymn singing offered a basic model for community building that filtered as readily into the synagogue as it did into other houses of prayer. From this same spirit, especially in the wake of 1848, the *Gesangverein*, or singing society, came to supplement and supersede hymn singing as a civic lingua franca among progressive Germans.[5] These practices cultivated able singers and expanded communal repertoires. They also inspired liberal-minded congregations, who viewed singing societies as models for creating and supporting their choirs, building their musical repertoires and styles, and hiring their music personnel.

Synagogues regularly employed musicians—especially organists and choral directors—who had built regional and/or national reputations through singing society networks.[6] Cincinnati's Carl Barus (1823–1908), music director and composer at Bene Yeshurun for more than two decades under Isaac Mayer Wise, played a major role in the region's Sängerfests, including directing the North American premiere of Verdi's *Requiem* at Cincinnati's 1879 Sängerfest.[7] Sigmund Schlesinger (1835–1906), who served the Sha'arai Shomayim congregation in Mobile, Alabama, from 1870 through 1906, led the city's Frohsinn Society; and in New York, Max Spicker (1858–1912) conducted the city's Beethoven Männerchor in the early 1880s while serving as organist and liturgical composer for Temple Emanu-El. These figures, who complemented their synagogue income with Sunday church work and broader musical activity, provided the nourishment that Jewish populations valued for growing healthy, singing congregations.

The clearest extant view of the connections between German part singing and the synagogue, however, can be seen in Philadelphia organist Wilhelm Fischer's 1863 book *Zemirot Yisrael*. As organist and choir director of Philadelphia congregation Keneseth Israel for twenty years (1856–76), Fischer helped shape the American Jewish musical landscape, influencing the sound and content of the service while supporting the work of three contrasting service leaders. Jewish hymnals had appeared before 1863, but *Zemirot Yisrael* represented its first full musical manifestation in America: a midcareer importation of German hymn conventions into American Jewish life, a dogged embrace of progress as a German cultural outcropping, and a uniquely detailed look into the sound of David Einhorn's mid-nineteenth-century agenda of radical Jewish reform.

The First Layer of Part Singing: Early Hymnals

Hymns, with their relatively simple harmonies, homophonic rhythm, uniform metric texts, community building properties, cultural ubiquity, and easy adaptability, led the way for Jewish musical change in the early nineteenth century. The middlebrow art form allowed educated populations semi-democratic opportunities for religious creativity. Writers with facility in verse could create their own hymns to idiomatic metric schemas, and anyone with basic musical training could similarly create a tune or chorale from their choice of texts. Collecting and disseminating new materials held a comparable simplicity: individuals or communities could produce inexpensive pamphlets of original hymn texts, using a limited number of hymn tunes that minimized the need for more expensive musical printing. The relative convenience of this ecosystem allowed hymns to take root and grow quickly among willing Jewish populations. With new hymns, however, came questions of boundaries: how could Jewish populations engage with hymn singing while avoiding accusations of emulating Christianity?

For Jewish communities in Central Europe, the answer lay in hymns' role as a medium for promoting integrative social agendas. With a relatively straightforward procedure for inclusion and a mostly clean slate, Jewish leaders could accompany a new body of materials with carefully considered arguments that treated hymns as a conduit for Judaism-specific relevance and feeling. Hymns reinforced the larger projects of reform advocates, who claimed a basis for such developments in the German philosophical tradition they aspired to join. Early European proponents such as schoolmaster Israel Jacobson (Westphalia, 1810; later Berlin, 1815) included hymn singing as part of a plan to foster a civic Jewish life at his school, expressing Jewish values in the vernacular language while rehearsing students in a long-standing communal form of music making; occasionally, the chapel services at his school also included idiomatic instrumental accompaniment.[8] By 1833, Hamburg hymnal coeditor J. Wohlwill viewed the development of the form genealogically, with each city (and its liberal religious leaders) establishing its own hymn-based character and repertoire as part of a network of different community practices:[9]

> The introduction of choral song belongs . . . rightly to the first improver, the blessed Israel Jacobson, recognized author of most of our worship reforms, to have a new necessary revival of prayer in our houses of God. Little by little, this example was followed in Kassel, Berlin and Hamburg. Great success beyond

expectations was achieved through attempts by poet, composer and teacher Mr. Dr. J[ohann] A[ugust] G[ünther] Heinroth [1780–1846], now academic Music Director in Göttingen. The songs drawn up by him and set to music were first sung and incorporated into both the Heinemann and Kley hymnals.

Dr. [Jeremias] Heinemann organized the first song collection in Kassel in 1810.[10] It contained only some twenty songs. The second edition appeared in 1815, the third in 1817, the fourth in 1821, and the fifth edition in 1825.[11] The last bears the title: German devotional book for Israelites to awaken and revive religious sentiment; In songs and prayers. . . .[12] It contains 101 songs, the first part mostly comprising what was created in Seesen, while the other is in great part borrowed from Christian hymnals.

In 1815 the first hymnbook of Mr. J. Johlson in Frankfurt a[m] M[ain] came out; the second edition in 1819, and the third edition in 1829.[13] This collection has grown to 540 pieces, almost all of which come from known German poets. The focus of the publisher was directed preferably at school usage, particularly in the teaching of Religion. Hence the inclusion of some poems which probably are not suitable as church songs: Schiller's "Three Words of Faith," Krummacher's Allegory of conscience ("In deep curvature of the breast," and so forth), etc.[14] In 1818 the "religious songs and chants for the Israelites, for home and public worship" of Hr. Dr. E[duard] Kley appeared.[15] These have been used so far in the New Temple at Hamburg in the first and then in the second edition (Hamburg 1821).[16] From them a third edition came out under the title: Hamburg Israelite Hymns for domestic and public worship (Hamburg 1827, 150 entries).[17] The songs in this collection are—with the exception of those by Heinroth—only by Jewish authors.

From these works, and the "General Song Books from [George Frederick] Seiler" Hr. Dr. M. Büdinger has written a new compilation, entitled: "Songs for revival of worship and of religious feeling in the Israelite children, with three and four-part set melodies." First collection, containing 68 hymns and 20 school songs.[18] (In the meeting of the Israelite head office of the province of Lower Hesse [Niederhessen].) Among these chorales are three in rhyming Hebrew stanzas.[19]

Leaders of Jewish religious reform across Central Europe, such as Jacobson, Heinemann (Württemberg), Eduard Kley (Hamburg), Josef Johlson (Frankfurt), and Leopold Stein (also Frankfurt), contributed new and adapted verses with each hymnal issue. These verses in turn became source material for new *Gesangbücher*, expanding repertoire and coverage, often even beyond designated hymns to the liturgy itself. Some communities also took the step of providing the music itself. In Frankfurt and Hamburg, for example, separately published *Melodienbücher* (books of melodies) provided musical settings to *Gesangbuch* texts; and in the 1836 Württemberg hymnal, texts introducing new melodies received their own four-part settings. Even when not openly published, manuscript-based musical settings survive for hymns in Braunschweig, Leipzig, and Hamburg, likely as an aid for musical personnel.[20] Proliferating Central European hymn-based practices eventually spread to the United States, where they joined the English hymn traditions that earlier synagogues, such as the Sephardic Beth Elohim congregation of Charleston, South Carolina, included from the 1820s.[21]

Music's presence, however, remained subservient to text as a point of concern. Wohlwill, introducing his hymnal in 1833, gave musical content only tangential mention, anticipating little controversy. When it came to the form itself, Wohlwill defended choral singing as derived from biblical psalm singing: apolitical, uplifting, meaningful, populist (as opposed to artistically elite), "completely corresponding to our religious sentiment," and conducive to building community with non-Jews.[22] He wrote, "Certainly it is not the task of our time, to increase separation and opposition in religious matters, but rather to promote rapprochement among the various parties where it is compatible with either honesty and truthfulness. Indeed, the whole practice of choral singing may not exactly have been raised from Israelite soil; but do you know a more dignified and uplifting form? Are the opera melodies that are often heard in the synagogues edifying? Or will it do [instead] to recall the temple singing of the old Levites?"[23] Three years later, the Württemberg hymnal's editor would similarly assert hymn singing's ancient derivation, noting that "religious song in and of itself, that is, the manifestation of religious feeling through words and music, is to Israel as old as the worship of one God."[24]

The greatest public challenge to the hymnal's broad acceptance lay in convincing community members that the authorship and content of the mainly German lyrics (alongside the Hebrew retained in the prayer settings) sufficiently reflected a Jewish religious worldview. Wohlwill answered this potential broadside with claims that a well-made repertoire displayed a comparable depth of learning and devotion: "A glance at the table of contents [of my coedited collection] shows that all the major principles and teachings have been considered."[25] Psalms remained an important part of the hymnal, as an ancient prosodic form and a useful meeting point of Jewish and Christian traditions. Even biblical passages, which Wohlwill claimed "are hardly suitable to poetic rendering," had been versified effectively. To keep the growing repertoire manageable, most hymnals appended an index of topics and first lines, recognizing that such a structure comprised a standard organization of knowledge to most people. Once the texts gained approval, musical competence could come through repetition, specialized publications, and trained personnel.

The considerations presented by Wohlwill and the other European editors remained central to hymn singing as the practice took root in the United States. Even those American synagogues that promoted choral singing faced external charges of snobbery, perhaps as a result of Sulzer's work: in 1860, for example, premier American hymnody scholar Daniel Furber likened the artifice of synagogue choirs to the priestly elite of the Jerusalem temple, a position he contrasted to the congregational humanism of Protestant singing.[26] Synagogues wishing to announce themselves publicly as Reform institutions thus promoted hymns as a form of populism, encouraging congregations to sing en masse while highlighting the patriotic/civic angle of democratic worship as a vehicle for their modernist ambitions. Hymnals from Temple Emanu-El and other congregations in the 1840s and 1850s sought this balance by selectively joining European materials with new works from local religious leaders, all of which emphasized the low threshold of musicality needed to participate.[27]

Singing Societies: Delivering German American Identity

Mid-nineteenth-century hymnody movements received a boost from the explosion of singing societies, which reinvigorated part singing under a new banner and a renewed aesthetic.[28] Developed in Central Europe shortly after the start of the nineteenth century to address liberal educational and patriotic efforts, they came to full form with the Württemberg (Germany) Sängerfest of 1845. Under classical Teutonic names such as Liedertafel (song table), Liederkranz (wreath of song), Germania, and Arion, or ideologically rhapsodic labels such as Frohsinn ("Glee," roughly) and Harmonia, these groups developed as social clubs, with their own constitutions, membership, associated activities, and repertoires. Although often started as all male (using the genre label *Männerchor*), in reality singing societies regularly included women when singing mixed choral works or staging popular operas; and sometimes women organized themselves into separate *Damenchöre*.

Singing societies offered Jews a way to participate in mainstream culture and activity, allowing them to cultivate specific civic expressions of Jewishness on their own terms. Records indicate the existence of specifically

Jewish singing societies as early as 1839, when a collective of Jewish teachers and service leaders in Sinsheim (Baden-Württemberg) convened a "gesangverein" that the local Jewish council embraced as a mechanism for introducing choral music to synagogue services.[29] By 1845, at least two different Jewish singing societies—one in Bernburg (Saxony) and another in Frankfurt—were giving public concerts to mainstream audiences while enhancing the sound of prayer in their local congregations.[30] The Frankfurt group in particular, called the Frohsinn society and directed by the Hecht brothers, sported eighty voices according to one report, including admirable "high tenors"; in concert, it performed popular works from the Männerchor repertoire including the Hunting Chorus from Carl Maria von Weber's 1823 opera *Euryanthe*, Carl Mangold's "Heiterer Lebenslauf" ("Mein Lebenslauf ist Lieb und Lust"), and Zöllner's "Schneiderlied," along with interludes that showcased some of the group's solo voices.[31] A decade later, in Swabia (southwestern Germany), Laupheim's Israelite Frohsinn society spurred Jewish newspapers to celebration when its rendition of Albert Methfessel's "Deutsche Sängergruß," earned it first place among rural groups in the annual Swabian Sängerfest, symbolically marking an important moment of Jewish cultural compatibility; the Frohsinn society hosted its own Sängerfests in subsequent years.[32] In 1859, Vienna's Jewish community established its Israelitische Gesangverein "Zion," with Sulzer's son Julius directing sixty to seventy singers of both genders (including one of his sisters), and nearly two hundred "supporting members" underwriting its cost; while the group sang secular music, its Jewish specialization amid the city's broad ecosystem of singing groups sought to improve the quality of choral song in the synagogue, perhaps even facilitating the second volume of Salomon Sulzer's *Schir Zion*.[33] Empowered by the flexibility of the four-voice, largely but not exclusively male singing format, these groups fluidly mixed their performances of German nationalist repertoire with ample synagogue work, reinforcing both identities in the process.

Similar principles applied to *Gesangvereine* in America, although German Jewish immigrants generally sought to manifest their progressive national-musical identities through general-interest groups rather than specific Jewish-identified ones. Only slightly behind their European counterparts, American singing societies sprouted during the 1830s and held their first *Sängerfest* in 1849; by the 1850s, the form had established a wide-ranging, regionalized network across the United States. Festivals, many held in late spring, mobilized thousands of singers and their followers to commune in Midwestern, Southern, and Northeastern cities, exchanging musical works and reinforcing cultural and political alliances. Repertoire centralized over time as well, with publishers in New York and other major cities producing compendia for these groups on a large scale.[34] Singing societies maintained their amateur status throughout, but as they grew, many hired professional directors and contracted with instrumentalists to perform increasingly involved works. In so doing, American *Gesangvereine* came to balance refinement with populism, while introducing a unique and entertaining body of art music by both European and American contemporary composers. Most central to the public square, moreover, the groups' religious ecumenicism appealed to liberal-leaning churches and synagogues, where they would appear regularly. In 1851, to cite one of many examples, the newly formed choir of Philadelphia's German Hebrew Congregation Rodeph Shalom invited members of the similarly new Harmonia Sacred Music Society to bolster its ranks during the High Holidays.[35] Although the Civil War put a damper on *Sängerfest* culture due to travel disruptions and difficulties sustaining membership, the immediate resumption of singing festivals right after war's end emphasized the form's continued strength.[36]

Amid these broader activities, Wilhelm Fischer's 1863 book *Zemirot Yisrael* represented perhaps the fullest form of German Gesangverein culture as imported into American Jewish life. Compiled at a time of considerable discussion about the appropriate representation of sound in Reform Jewish services, *Zemirot Yisrael* was geared for a population conversant in European and American Protestant hymn traditions and familiar with German singing society culture. The book ranges from simple chorales to a full cantata, presenting the refined technique of the composer and the progressive sound of the synagogue service. Its polished appearance and adherence to the German vernacular led some Jewish leaders to welcome it as a pioneering American musical publication. But the international public stage also invited scrutiny of the work as the product of a non-Jewish musician, testing the extent to which music for Jewish worship should require Jewish musical hands and voices to bring it fully into the American landscape.

Wilhelm Fischer: Musician and Progressive Activist

Wilhelm Fischer embodied the connections between religion, politics, and music that motivated many German American immigrants. According to Isaac Leeser, the Prussian-born Fischer arrived in the United States from Breslau around 1850 "with a well-earned reputation" as a musician and organist, and soon enhanced his credentials by publishing a singing instruction book.[37] He began his relationship with Jewish institutions in 1851, becoming the first music teacher and choir director for Philadelphia congregation Rodeph Shalom, where he worked through successive six-month contracts alongside musically talented reader Jacob Frankel (himself an 1849 émigré); by 1855, Fischer oversaw a Gesangverein-style choir, with trained, paid "assistants" leading a select group of the congregation's men and women on Sabbaths and major holidays.[38] Fischer also occasionally served the neighboring liberal congregation Keneseth Israel during this time, assisting with the music at its 1854 building dedication.

As with many in his post-1848 immigrant cohort, Fischer promoted a progressive religious and political agenda. Musically, this stance placed him at the center of several local singing societies. In 1855, while still serving Rodeph Shalom, Fischer became the founding director of the Liedertafel, a singing society that regularly enhanced the services of the city's liberal-minded (Christian) Independent German Congregation.[39] When the (then progressive) Republican Party met in Philadelphia for its first presidential convention in 1856, Fischer led the attendees in a series of four-part German-language songs, published as anthems for the occasion and intended to liven subsequent meetings.[40] In 1857, when the Liedertafel elected a different director, Fischer led a group of seceders to form the independent Arion singing society.[41] The members of the city's congregation Keneseth Israel undoubtedly knew of both Fischer's activism and choral experience when they hired him as their full-time organist and choir director in 1856.[42]

At Keneseth Israel, Fischer worked with Louis Naumburg to direct and create music for the Hamburg prayer book, and he continued his work with Julius Salinger following Naumburg's dismissal in 1860. Navigating the choir and its repertoire through difficult financial times, Fischer likely felt comfortable working within a German-speaking progressive population that, as Christian Wiese describes, "continued the religious modernization process begun in Germany within an imported German context."[43] When David Einhorn became the congregation's rabbi in 1861, Fischer and Salinger found themselves working with perhaps the foremost advocate of German Jewish cultural life in America. Together they helped Einhorn begin a vaunted transition from the Hamburg liturgy to Einhorn's ultra-Reform 1859 prayer book *Olat Tamid*.

Einhorn, recognizing that his philosophy could only work if it encompassed a complete ritual experience, turned his attention to congregational singing. Seeking to bolster the congregation's liturgical complement, he sent a letter to the synagogue board in May 1862 identifying a "decided shortage of hymn books not only in our reform congregation but in all the others in America."[44] To remedy this lacuna, Einhorn offered to compile a work of "eighty or ninety pages," combining his own verses with material from other hymnals. With the board's support, he printed a thousand copies, binding one hundred for use at Keneseth Israel and anticipating the prospect of shipping the book to synagogues across the country for twenty-five cents apiece.[45] Fischer had likely already created a repertoire of original music for several of the hymns in circulation and had music in use for key parts of the liturgy. Once Einhorn's chosen hymn texts found a more fixed form through the hymnal, however, the music could be similarly codified for regular use.

At the start of January 1863, the board of Keneseth Israel asked the choir committee to compile all of Fischer's original music into its own book, presumably for congregational consumption.[46] Fischer took this work upon himself, announcing a subscription for "the original compositions that are introduced by the local Israelitish Reform congregation, sung according to the prayer book."[47] By August of that year, moreover, he anticipated the publication of "a book of songs which corresponded to the hymnal of the congregation."[48] Board minutes showed neither a request nor a grant for production costs. Rather, Fischer collaborated on the book with Philadelphia-based publisher Schaefer & Koradi, a major nineteenth-century producer of German American intellectual, educational, and religious materials, that maintained an additional office in Leipzig. Professionally produced through the rather laborious plate-based music engraving processes of the day and appearing with a frontispiece by well-known Philadelphia lithographer Louis N. Rosenthal, the book's title *Zemirot Yisrael* (Songs of Israel) evinced Fischer's familiarity with existing synagogue music publications: sharing its name with the widely disseminated Württemberg hymnal and Paris cantor Samuel Naumbourg's celebrated original collection, both of which also combined text with musical notation (see fig. 2.1). Its specialized audience limited sales to music personnel and patrons. Keneseth Israel, for example, acquired twelve copies at $2.00 each, possibly to supply the choir and keep an extra few of copies in reserve—far less than the hundred copies of Einhorn's hymnal on which it was based.[49]

Figure 2.1. Wilhelm Fischer, *Zemirot Yisrael* (1863, here shown in the 1865 second edition), Title Page. (Source: Klau Library, Hebrew Union College)

Fischer framed his work as a step forward in Jewish musical creativity: "A contribution to the culture of the German Israelite religious song," he wrote in his introduction, that should "lead the way for its independence in regard to appropriate original melodies."[50] Criticizing previous synagogue hymnals as heavily dependent on "Christian chorale melodies," Fischer cited liberal German rabbi and *Allgemeine Zeitung des Judenthums* editor Ludwig Philippson's claim that hymns alone could not "connect intimately with the full musical rite of the Israelite religious service." Part of the issue, according to Fischer, was a recent transformation in hymn singing from an "original rhythmic, spiritually lively form" into a "sluggish, painfully dragging response" that "is not even so well liked in the Christian church." Christian attempts to revitalize the hymn repertoire, Fischer noted from his vantage point as a non-Jewish musician, suffered from the careless insinuation of popular songs (*Gassenhauer*). "The Israelites," Fischer noted in contrast, "have been protected from such abuses" through "the fine works for Hebrew song by Sulzer, Naumbourg, and others." In writing *Zemirot Yisrael*, then, Fischer aimed to add a parallel volume for German-language song that carried the same purpose and relevance as its Hebrew models, and thereby satisfy the emerging needs of Jewish religious observance.

In particular, Fischer attempted to create a musical bridge between home and sanctuary that remained musically true to the uniqueness of the Jewish religious spirit and corresponded closely to the values of the singing society. To do so, he determined to set original, "unfalsified" (*unverfälschte*) melodies to simple arrangements with straightforward voice leading, allowing amateur singers and keyboardists to access the repertoire. Those uninitiated in the practices of hymn accompaniment could instead play the "short introductions and endings" that he added to each piece in the collection. Fischer also offered suggestions for adapting the organ-focused keyboard parts to piano playing, compensating for both widely spaced chords and the organ's idiomatic pedalboard.

Fischer thought big, characterizing his work as a German American variant of Sulzer's and Naumbourg's projects, and presenting *Zemirot Yisrael* as the first of three volumes containing the full musical complement for Einhorn's German Jewish ritual. In this schema, the second volume would include "all of the liturgical chants belonging to the [Einhorn] prayer book" and the third would contain "mostly melodies, psalms, hymns, and cantatas for the holidays and other observances." The result, Fischer hoped, would foster an organic mode of worship for progressive Jews that remained both participatory and musically refined, while harnessing the cultural forms of the time into a meaningful ritual that stayed true to Jewish identity.

Inside *Zemirot Yisrael*

A perusal of *Zemirot Israel* revealed Fischer's strategies for issuing a musical helpmate to the liturgy. In addition to including a standard index of hymns by topic and holiday, Fischer added a concordance linking each piece to its counterpart in Einhorn's hymnal and indicated which melodies could apply to multiple texts (Fischer called them *Parallelmelodien*). Such a connection proved important, because the music contained within the book only set the first lines of each hymn text; even members of the choir had to refer to Einhorn's pamphlet to see all of the verses.[51]

The selections themselves followed Fischer and Einhorn's vision of the German Jewish ritual. Sixty German hymns of varying textures and mostly in major keys composed the first part of the book; two of these hymns pushed the form by including a solo between choral verses (nos. 40 and 52). The second part of the book presented a window into the choral conventions of the synagogue service, with eighteen selections for Sabbath morning, short entries for Sabbath evening and the minor festivals, and a cantata written for the Ninth of Av. While many of the prayers remained in German, Fischer's book also showed interaction between the cantor and congregation during a number of structurally important Hebrew prayers: the call to prayer (*Borchu*), the *Shema*, the *Kedusha*, responses to the half *Kaddish*, and sections of the *Hallel* service, as well as a number of generic "Amen" cadences and "Hallelujahs." Each of these entries, as written out by Fischer, either took place after a hazan solo, or clearly notated the interplay between the service leader and attendees.

Fischer's coherent amalgam of styles, moreover, closely followed singing society conventions, particularly in their emphasis on giving the text meaning, expression, and life. Fischer moved his settings along at a good clip: only thirty of the eighty-five selections primarily employed slow tempi (*larghetto, andante, adagio*, or *con gravita*). Instead, Fischer relied heavily on speedier tempi ranging from *moderato* to *andantino*, and *maestoso con brio* to *lebhaft*. Each piece featured numerous changes in dynamics and speed, with frequent notations of *espressivo* or *ausdrucksvoll* alerting congregants to lend feeling to their songs (see fig. 2.2). A pair of settings

Figure 2.2. Wilhelm Fischer, "Du meine Seele schwinge," *Zemirot Yisrael*, no. 54. (Source: Klau Library, Hebrew Union College). Note the marking "espress[ivo]," organ designations ("man[ual]" and "ped[al]"), and changes in dynamics, including two crescendos.

that used popular hymn tunes from sixteenth-century Lutheran minister Philipp Nicolai (no. 49, based on "Wachet auf," and no. 52, based on "Wie schön leuchtet der Morgenstern") further showed the collection's overlap with general singing conventions of the time.

Taken together, *Zemirot Yisrael* showcased an attempt to present the musical service holistically to congregants, defining a "German" style while hinting at a range of modal, linguistic, and ideological effects for different sections and occasions of the ritual. In effect illustrating (and perhaps updating) Einhorn's hymnal, Fischer's book painted and packaged a varied sonic landscape to accompany new developments in the liturgy, both for local use and for meaningful export.

Receiving the Hymnal

Fischer's book reached both sides of the Atlantic. In Berlin, *Zemirot Yisrael* received mention in 1864 in the same article that introduced Naumbourg's new book *Chants Religieux/Shirei Kodesh*. Although the reviewer, music pedagogue Emil Breslaur, noted that Fischer's reliance on the Einhorn liturgy reduced "the usefulness of this work" in Europe, he nonetheless described Fischer's "diligent and skillful" work as "very worthy of attention."[52] Breslaur also commented on Fischer's own identity as a non-Jewish musician, implicitly expanding on the composer's claims: "While work after work is appearing which arranges the old Hebrew texts anew, or sets new compositions to these [Hebrew] texts, the German song is all but neglected, and we must still rely on strangers [i.e., non-Jews] for temporary assistance. The few works of [Louis] Lewandowsky, Breslau and others constitute a notable exception, but that alone is not enough to address the need."[53] As a popular form still developing on American soil, German Jewish song gained acknowledgment as a medium with such a meager repertoire that composers' identities proved secondary simply to supplying enough material.

Locally, meanwhile, Philadelphia's Isaac Leeser repeated Fischer's claims about the work's versatility in his journal *The Occident and American Jewish Advocate*, understanding "from the author that the pieces can be sung with or without musical accompaniment and may be used for domestic as well as public devotion."[54] Leeser claimed that a lack of musical literacy released him from casting aesthetic judgment on Fischer's work, even as his voice as a respected, conservative-leaning liturgist and intellectual carried weight in the transatlantic Jewish world. Leeser's claim that Fischer had been "long in intimate intercourse with our people" thus constituted a qualified endorsement and supported Fischer's legitimacy. And he backed Fischer's eagerness to expand his audience by adding that "he also promises to issue the work with English words, to make it generally acceptable, and to add hereafter pieces for the various holy days."

Isaac Mayer Wise, in contrast, appears to have ignored the first printing, perhaps to protest Einhorn's theological and linguistic positions. Neither *The Israelite* nor *Die Deborah* acknowledged the work, indicating its relatively narrow adoption even among American liberal Jews.

Fischer's book endured, at least in the short term, as the sound of German American Jewry. Salinger died in January 1865, and a few months later, Keneseth Israel called William Armhold to its pulpit from Pittsburgh. Armhold appeared to endorse Fischer's collection, leading to its renewed interest within the congregation. Shortly afterward, following what Fischer described as "rapid sales" and "urgent and frequent requests," a second (musically identical) edition of *Zemirot Yisrael* was printed, and Fischer proudly expressed plans to prepare the promised follow-up volume.[55] While Fischer continued as Keneseth Israel's organist and choir director for a decade, however, that additional volume never materialized. He remained a prominent liturgical composer and presenter, writing music for other rabbis' new hymn texts; his former pulpit partner, Louis Naumburg, introduced Fischer's German hymns at his new pulpit in Pittsburgh in 1867; and emphasizing the centrality of the *Gesangvereine* to his musical/political views, that same year Fischer published a new edition of his singing method dedicated to the Philadelphia singing societies that had arisen under his watch.[56] Yet Jewish interest in Fischer's Germanic hymns remained limited to materials that congregants could use in the pews. While a figure such as Salomon Sulzer could succeed in a similar project by partnering with Isaac Noah Mannheimer and his celebrated moderate reform liturgy, Fischer's more idealistic political outlook allowed him to latch on to a far more controversial text in *Olat Tamid*, which resulted in limited distribution. Einhorn's Philadelphia congregants could accept Fisher's authority as a synagogue music composer through his deeply held dedication to the singing society and its spiritual universalism. Fischer likely faced resistance from moderate American reformers, however, who began to privilege Jewish identity as a pretense for musical authenticity. Singing societies began to fade, too. When Cincinnati hosted its next *Sängerfest* in 1879, Wise reiterated his assertions of the overlap between German Jews and Germans in America, while Lilienthal presented a "masterly oration on the history of *Gesangvereine* and *Sängerfest*" at the festival's concluding picnic. However, the genre as a whole, in Wise's view, had overleaped its aspirations to high art, pressuring amateur singers to perform ever-more sophisticated concert works with disappointing results.[57] "Jewish music," breaking off as its own genre, needed a new paradigm.

Later scholars largely forgot Fischer's collection. Convinced of Jewish music's uniqueness, they dismissed similar efforts from other non-Jewish synagogue organist/composers as pandering to pop culture or Christian practices. The values and practices of the singing society remained central to synagogue music, as subsequent chapters will show. Yet Fischer's hymnal remained stuck in its niche as a sonic manifestation of American Germanophone Judaism: reflecting the progressive civic spirituality of the era, while musically imprinting a major rabbinic figure's philosophy of German cultural preservation during a crucial period of American Jewish transition.

Notes

1. Karen Ahlquist, "Musical Assimilation and 'the German Element' at the Cincinnati Sängerfest, 1879," *The Musical Quarterly* 94, no. 3 (2011): 383.
2. Stanley Nadel, "Jewish Race and German Soul in Nineteenth-Century America," *American Jewish History* 77, no. 1 (1987): 6–26, esp. 12–14, 23, 25 (describing singing societies).
3. "The Saengerfest," *The Israelite*, June 24, 1870, 8–9; "Das Sängerfest," *Die Deborah*, June 24, 1870, 2.
4. Ibid.
5. See Mary Sue Morrow, "Somewhere between Beer and Wagner: The Cultural and Musical Impact of German Männerchöre in New York and New Orleans," in *Music and Culture in America, 1861–1918*, ed. Michael Saffle (New York: Garland, 1998), 79–109; Suzanne G. Snyder, "The Indianapolis Männerchor: Contributions to a New Musicality in Midwestern Life," in *Music and Culture in America, 1861–1918*, ed. Michael Saffle (New York: Garland, 1998), 111–40. See also Christopher G. Ogburn, "Brews, Brotherhood and Beethoven: The 1865 New York City Sängerfest and the Fostering of German American Identity," *American Music* 33, no. 4 (2015), 405–40.
6. Another non-Jewish synagogue organist, the West London Synagogue's Charles Verrinder, adds an international angle to this practice. See Susan Wollenberg, "Charles Garland Verrinder and Music at the West London Synagogue, 1859–1904," in *Music and Performance Culture in Nineteenth-Century Britain*, ed. Bennett Zon (New York: Ashgate, 2012), 59–82.
7. Ahlquist, "Musical Assimilation"; Barus's son, physicist Carl Barus Jr., operated the bellows of the organ at Bene Yeshurun for a time and remembered Wise "as a familiar guest in the organ loft, often in his vestments and discussing music and texts with father who had acquired considerable Hebrew verbiage by this time" (Axel W.-O. Schmidt, ed., *One of the 999 about to Be Forgotten: Memoirs of Carl Barus 1865–1935* [New York: AWOS, 2005], 41).
8. Tina Frühauf, *The Organ and Its Music in German-Jewish Culture* (New York: Oxford University Press, 2009), 29.
9. Wohlwill's book was the *Allgemeine israelitisches Gesangbuch eingeführt in dem Neuen Israelitischen Tempel zu Hamburg* (Hamburg: Perthes & Besser, 1833).
10. *Religiöse Gesänge für Israeliten, insbesondere das weibliche Geschlecht und die Jugend* (Cassel, 1810). Where contemporary bibliographic information is unavailable, I have included information from T. O. Weigl, *Vollständiges Bucher-Lexicon*, vol. 3 (Leipzig: Ludwig Schuman, 1835), 85.
11. *Religiöse Gesänge für Israeliten, insbesondere das weibliche Geschlecht und die Jugend* (Berlin: 1812, 1815, 1817 [97 pp.]); 4th ed. (Berlin: E. H. G. Christiani, 1821; 151 pp.).
12. *Deutsches Andachtsbuch für Israeliten zur Erweckung und Belebung religiöser Gefühle. In Gesängen und Gebeten* (Berlin: Bureau für Literatur und Kunst, 1825).
13. J. Johlson, ed. *Deutsches Gesangbuch für Israeliten: Zur Beförderung öffentliche und häuslicher Andacht* (Frankfurt, 1816); 2nd ed. (Frankfurt: Wilmans, 1819); 3rd ed.: *Shire Yeshurun: Israelitisches Gesangbuch zur Andacht und zum Religionsunterricht* (Frankfurt: Andreas, 1829); 4th ed., 1840.
14. Wohlwill here probably refers to Schiller's poem "Die Worte des Glaubens" and Krummacher's "Das Flämmchen," both from the early nineteenth century.
15. Eduard Kley, ed. *Religiöse Lieder und Gesänge für Israeliten zum häuslicher und öffentlicher Gottes-Verehrung* (Hamburg: Otto, 1818).

16. Eduard Kley, ed. *Hamburgisches Israelitisches Gesangbuch für hausliche und öffentliche Gottesverehung* (Hamburg, 1821).

17. Eduard Kley, ed. *Israelitisches Gesangbuch für hausliche und öffentliche Gottesverehung* (Hamburg: Johann Philipp Erie, 1827/8) [235 pp.].

18. Moses Büdinger, *Kol Zimra: oder, Gesänge zur Erweckung der Andacht und der religiösen Gefühls bei der israelitischen Jugend, mit drei- und vierstimmig Gesetzten Melodieen* (Cassel: n.p., 1832).

19. J. Wohlwill, "Literarische," *Der Jude* 2, no. 21 (October 18, 1833), 166–67.

20. *Melodien zu J. Johlson's Deutschen Gesangbuch für Israelitische Schulen* ([Frankfurt]: [n.p.]: [n.d.]); *Melodien zu J. Johlson Israelitische Gesange, Zweite Berbesserte und vermehrte Auflage, mit unterlegten Textworten* (Frankfurt: Benjamin Krebs, 1842), Eduard Birnbaum Collection Music Add., nos. 12, 14, and 16 (Klau Library, HUC, Cincinnati, OH).

21. Beth Elohim produced its own hymnal in 1842, with Penina Moïse as a notable major contributor. See *Hymns Written for the Service of the Hebrew Congregation, Beth Elohim, Charleston, S.C.* (Charleston, SC: Levin & Tavel, 1842).

22. J. Wohlwill, "Literarische," 168–69.

23. Ibid.

24. *Sefer Zemirot Yisrael. Gesang-Buch, zum Gebrauch be idem Unterichte in der mosaischen Religion und zur öffentlichen und häuslichen Gottesverehrung der Israeliten* (Stuttgart: Hallberger, 1836), III.

25. J. Wohlwill, "Literarische," 168.

26. Daniel Furber, "Choir-Singing Appropriately Jewish," in *Hymns and Choirs: or, the Matter and the Manner of the Service of Song in the House of the Lord*, ed. Austin Phelps, Edwards A. Park, and Daniel J. Furber (Andover, MA: Warren F. Draper, 1860), 320–23.

27. *Auswahl deutscher Gesänge zum Gebrauche im Tempel der Imanu-El Congregation in New York: nebst Anhang* (New York: Mühlhäuser, [1848]).

28. I here acknowledge Philip Bohlman's (*Jewish Music and Modernity*, 10) earlier, though very brief, mention of singing societies as a motivator of Jewish musical modernism.

29. *Israelitische Annalen* 31 (July 31, 1840), 267–68.

30. *Gemeinnützige Blätter zur Belehrung und Unterhaltung* 34, no. 13 (February 11, 1844), 52.

31. *Didaskalia* 355 (December 25, 1845), [4]; *Allgemeine musikalische Zeitung* 48, no. 9 (March 1846), col. 164.

32. *Allgemeine Zeitung des Judenthums* 19, no. 24 (June 11, 1855), 310–11; *Der Israelitische Volkslehrer* 9 (1859–60), 306. (In these reports, the winning song is described as "Sängergruß an Deutschland" with text by Otto and music by Methfessel. The local *Schwäbische Kronik*'s account of the Sängerbundfest (May 31, 1855, 898), notably, did not distinguish the *Frohsinn* society as Jewish, emphasizing the medium's homogenizing, nationalist properties.)

33. G. Wolf, *Geschichte der Israelitischen Cultusgemeinde in Wien (1820–1860)* (Vienna: Wilhelm & Braumüller, 1860), 190–92; *Neue Zeitschrift der Musik* 51, no. 26 (December 23, 1859), 231; *Allgemeine illustrierte Zeitung*, pilot issue ("Programm und Probenummer"), c. June 1860, 7; *Monatschrift für Theater und Musik* 6, no. 5 (February 1, 1860), 80; *Die Neuzeit* 2, no. 17 (April 25, 1862), 198; *Der Israelit* 8, no. 40 (October 2, 1867), 693; Avenary, *Kantor Salomon Sulzer*, 44, 123–27 (which notes that the "Zion" singing society eventually became all-male). Wolf (*Geschichte der Israelitischen Cultusgemeinde in Wien*, 191) openly challenged Sulzer, in his account, to write for the people: "the regenerator of synagogue song, Mr. Ober-Cantor S. Sulzer, would increase his merits if he wanted to compose more popular religious songs in which the public could take part."

34. Suzanne G. Snyder, "The Männerchor Tradition in the United States: A Historical Analysis of its Contribution to American Musical Culture," PhD diss., University of Iowa, 1991, 20–143.

35. Rodeph Shalom Meeting Minutes, July 20, 1851 (American Jewish Archives, MS-517, Box 2).

36. Snyder, "The Männerchor Tradition in the United States," 60, 143–44.

37. Leeser, review of *Zemirot Yisrael, Occident*, October 1, 1863, 330; Wilhelm Fischer, *Leitfaden für die Kunst des Gesanges* (Philadelphia: Schäfer, 1851) (this publication, not currently extant, appears in E. G. Gersdorf, ed., *Leipziger Repertorium den deutschen und ausländischen Literatur* 10, no. 1 [Leipzig: T. O. Weigel, 1852], 312). This Wilhelm Fischer, born in Bavaria in 1805 and listed as a music teacher in the 1860 and 1880 censuses, appears to be different from Baltimore-born musician and hymn composer William G. Fischer (1835–1912), who also spent much of his career in Philadelphia but focused on Welsh repertoire (http://cyberhymnal.org/bio/f/i/fischer_wg.htm).

38. Rodeph Shalom Minutes, 1851–55, especially January 7, 1851; December 21, 1853; January 18 and February 7, 1854 and ff. Congregation Rodeph Shalom Records (MS-517 Box 1, American Jewish Archives, Cincinnati, OH). By 1855, Fischer had the use of paid singers at Rodeph Shalom, suggesting a hierarchal system similar to that of the *Singverein*.

39. Violet Lutz, Finding Aid for "Harmonie Singing Society Records," Ms. Coll. 54, PACSCL Finding Aids, http://dla.library.upenn.edu/dla/pacscl/ead.html?id=PACSCL_GSP_MsColl54&fq=top_repository_facet%3A%22German%20Society%20of%20Pennsylvania%22&#ref5.

40. "Deutsche Republische Kampflieder," *Mittheilungen des Deutsch Pionier-Vereins in Philadelphia* 2 (1906), 22.

41. Lutz, Finding Aid.

42. Leeser, review of *Zemirot Yisrael*.

43. Christian Wiese, "Inventing a New Language of Jewish Scholarship," in *Speaking Jewish—Jewish Speak: Multilingualism in Western Ashkenazic Culture*, ed. Shlomo Berger, Audrey Pomerance, Andrea Schatz, and Emile Schrijver (Dudley, MA: Peeters, 2003), 283.

44. Keneseth Israel Minutes, May 4, 1862.

45. Ibid., through October 1862. The hymnal appeared under the title *Gesänge für den öffentlichen jüdischen Gottesdienst: aus verschiedenen Liedersämmlungen zusammengetragen* (Philadelphia: Stein & Jones, 1862). Philip Bohlman, in his treatment of Einhorn, does not mention this publication (Philip Bohlman, "Ethnic Musics/Religious Identities: Toward an Historiography of German-American Sacred Music," in *Land without Nightingales: Music in the Making of German-America*, ed. Philip Bohlman and Otto Holzapfel [Madison, WI: Max Kade Institute, 2002], 146, 148–51).

46. Keneseth Israel Minutes, January 4, 1863.

47. *Sinai* 7, no. 12, 347.

48. Keneseth Israel Minutes, August 16, 1863.

49. Keneseth Israel Minutes, December 6, 1863. Notably, the board disallowed Fischer's contemporaneous purchase of a melodeon for choir rehearsals, claiming the charge was unauthorized.

50. Preface to the first edition of *Zemirot Yisrael*.

51. The choir had received fifteen copies of Einhorn's booklet (April 4, 1864). The one exception to the single-line text setting was no. 59 ("O Tag den Herrn," Leopold Stein's German adaptation of Kol Nidre).

52. *Allgemeine Zeitung des Judenthums,* July 12, 1864, 447–48.
53. Ibid.
54. This and all references in this paragraph refer to Leeser, review of *Zemirot Yisrael, Occident,* October 1, 1863, 330.
55. Preface to the second edition of *Zemirot Yisrael.*
56. Fischer supplied the music to two German hymns written by Rev. Milton Weil, the religious leader of Temple Hesed in Scranton, Pennsylvania, at the dedication of its new building. "Dedication of the New Synagogue at Scranton, PA," *The Israelite,* April 19, 1867, 6; "Pittsburgh, PA," *The Israelite,* April 5, 1867, 3. Wilhelm Fischer, *Gesangschule, oder Anleitung zum gründlichen Studium des Gesanges den Gesangvereinen der Union gewidmet* (Philadelphia: Schäfer & Koradi, 1867).
57. Isaac Mayer Wise, "The Sængerfest," *The American Israelite,* June 20, 1879, 4.

3

BILDUNGSMUSIK

G. M. Cohen, B'nai B'rith, and the Voices of American Jewish Cultivation

IN NOVEMBER 1843, SEVERAL MEMBERS OF NEW YORK'S recently founded congregation Anshe Chesed, including the congregation's cantor Jonas Hecht, banded together to form their own fraternal organization, a *Bunde Brüder*. Created in the model of other fraternal orders less friendly to Jews, including the Masonic lodges and the International Order of Odd Fellows, the new group sought to merge Jewish values and history with contemporary culture, yet exist independently of the synagogue. The members, mainly merchants, developed their own orders and rituals based on Jewish symbols and laid claim in the process to their emerging status as American gentlemen. As the founding chapter of what would soon be called the International Order of B'nai B'rith, the first group matured rapidly into a series of chapters that, in historian Cornelia Wilhelm's words, "became the central vehicle for a conceptual transfer of the goals of a progressive German Judaism to the social and religious reality of America."[1]

The following June, about four months after B'nai B'rith's second ("Zion") lodge was founded, Gustave M. Cohen came to New York.[2] Existing accounts place Cohen's birth around 1820 in the Thüringian city of Walldorf (Sachsen-Meiningen). Raised during a time of rapid change in emancipation-era Bavaria, he took an educational path largely dictated by government regulations: in 1828, Sachsen-Meiningen required all aspiring teachers, including Jewish religious leaders, to attend its state training institution (*Lehrerseminar*) in Hildburghausen. Cohen likely entered the school in the late 1830s, embarking on an integrated curriculum that balanced modern Western intellectualism, practical voice lessons, organ and

Figure 3.1. Portrait of G. M. Cohen (*Cleveland Plain Dealer*, March 24, 1900, 5).

music theory training, with a specific track covering Jewish liturgy and related subjects.[3] Educated with aspiring teachers from other denominations, Cohen gained a level of cultural fluency as part of his credential and emerged as an exemplar of the new Jewish scholar/musician.

Shortly after Cohen's arrival in the United States, the members of a recently formed, reform-minded, German Jewish *Cultus-Verein* (Culture Society/congregation) elected him to the role of hazan—a position that required facile service reading and, possibly, music coordination.[4] Cohen also joined several members of the new congregation, such as minister Leo Merzbacher, in gaining admission to the new Zion Lodge.[5] He thus effectively linked the world of religious observance with the lodges' motto of "Benevolence, Brotherly Love, and Harmony" that inveigled Jews in the universal value system of a progressive age.[6]

Cohen's life and work illuminates the sometimes contentious relationship between the *Bildung*-based ideas of B'nai B'rith and the religious progressivism promoted by proponents of moderate Jewish Reform. Neil Levin, in the most extensive discussion of Cohen's life to date, evaluates Cohen's major published work *The Sacred Harp of Judah* in the context of "great" traditions of Jewish music, such as the compositions of Salomon Sulzer, Samuel Naumbourg, and other prominent cantors—a comparison in which Cohen inevitably comes up short.[7] This chapter, in contrast, reframes Cohen's labors along a completely different and, in my view, more fruitful, axis: exploring the ways that musical activity factored into and complicated mid-nineteenth-century efforts to create coherence between religious ritual, private life, and the public square. Variously used as a tool for community identity, a symbol of liturgical reform, a barometer of cultural advancement, and a means of American acculturation, music—choral or solo, with or without accompaniment—could fill several overlapping roles in communal expression, depending on time, location, and intention. Wilhelm Fischer, described in chapter 2, viewed progressivism as a platform through which he, as a religious outsider, could encourage Jews to develop their own musical idiom. Cohen, as a *Jewish* musical specialist, faced a somewhat different paradox in defining his portfolio. Like Fischer, Cohen pursued music's potential as a public and immediate manifestation of ideology, belonging and enfranchisement. Yet Cohen's insider role as an architect of both religious reform and *Bildung* led him to see music as part of a larger social program that integrated Jewish educational, religious, and cultural goals in the service of an enlightened American future. Cohen's story oscillated between careers in music and education, depending on community needs and employment opportunities. Rather than treat these two streams separately, however, I present them here as elements necessary for instilling music as a vehicle for community development.

Cohen's career also adds interesting layers to the complex boundaries between B'nai B'rith's civic mission and the aims of contemporary American synagogue reform, particularly when considering Cornelia Wilhelm's assertion that both movements used symbols of Jewish religious and cultural life to connect with each other, even as they ultimately served different (if related) ends.[8] Cohen's early membership in the brotherhood hardly counted as unique: contemporary cantors such as Ansel Leo (who served B'nai Jeshurun from 1840 to 1867), Leon Sternberger (Anshe Chesed/Beth-El, 1849–68), and later Samuel Welsch (Ahawath Chesed, 1865–80) would take leading roles in the organization—and specifically the second Zion Lodge—as a way to reinforce their own cultivated reputations. Cohen's contributions, however, have remained as unique as they are unknown: despite international renown in his time, his emphasis on educational activities and his preference for the German language during a time of transition to English stunted his lasting impact. His nearly forty years in various hazan positions at major congregations in New York, Chicago, Cincinnati, Cleveland, and (briefly) Milwaukee, however, facilitated meaningful contributions both to B'nai B'rith and to the formation of the Union of American Hebrew Congregations; and he worked closely with Leo Merzbacher and Isaac Mayer Wise (themselves key figures in B'nai B'rith's early development). Actively mediating between competing approaches on the connection between sacred and secular Jewish life, then, Cohen ultimately forged his own middle path that recognized American Jewry's cultural and religious diversity, while promoting *Bildung*, and especially its musical manifestations, as a less politically charged and more inclusive approach to a consistent and meaningful Jewish existence.

Music and the Harbinger of Modernity: At New York's Temple Emanu-El, 1845–52

Cohen's first professional American pulpit put him at the forefront of synagogue musical development. Around April 1845, when the *Cultus-Verein* effectively changed its name to Emanu-El, it offered equal salaries to its chosen minister Leo Merzbacher and to Cohen: $200 plus a small fee for each wedding performed.⁹ Cohen put his training to work, leading services for the new group while assembling a male choir that comprised "a few amateurs with training in choral singing."¹⁰ An account of an early Emanu-El service in the German *Allgemeine Zeitung des Judenthums* viewed the event as an American breakthrough, with the music providing an antidote to the "vulgar Polish singsong" of "the old rite," ushering in a new era of order and sophistication; yet a sly subtext, which highlighted the choir's "enthusiasm" as a sign of better music to come, emphasized the gulf between intention and reality.¹¹ Cohen, as cantor, retrospectively took credit for organizing the ensemble, although records indicate that his contribution soon shifted mainly to overseeing other choir directors, if that. As hinted through his initial contract negotiations, Cohen saw himself as a modern religious teacher with a strong musical presence. Whatever he added to musical worship mainly complemented his growing rabbinic and educational responsibilities.

Emanu-El's early minutes project tensions between promoting local/amateur music production and aspiring to "fine" music. As in other European congregations, Emanu-El's board expanded its musical forces for the Jewish New Year by hiring a second hazan for the less crucial parts of the liturgy (such as Yom Kippur morning services), while presumably relying on Cohen for the evening services and, perhaps, preparing the choir. Evidence, however, points to a ritual still in sonic development. In early November 1845, about a week after the holidays' end, the directors sought to impose new standards "to strengthen the choir."¹² And in the following months, congregation member and local merchant Selig Kling was appointed as volunteer choir leader, attempting to train both old and new singers through systematic oral instruction.¹³ In June 1846, the synagogue took steps to improve its High Holiday ritual further, setting aside $10 to pay a "Shacharis [Morning Service] Chasan," and appointing a committee to send to Munich for a copy of its recent musical liturgy, created specifically to coordinate choral singing, congregational responses, and cantorial recitative ("Hazanut").¹⁴ While Merzbacher factored centrally into these discussions, Cohen received no mention save an August report that he could not find a second cantor for the morning services (the board filled the position on its own shortly thereafter). Instead Cohen appeared more a part of the program than its director.¹⁵

As neighboring congregations opted for increased musical refinement, however, Emanu-El felt pressure to devote greater resources to its music.

Its directors could not specify the amount of money available for including a choir in its November 1846 Thanksgiving Day service, but early the next year, they included music prominently in the congregation's financial projections: a January budget listed salaries for the rabbi ($1,000) and two hazanim ($800 and $400), plus $500 for the choir (presumably to pay for music, singers, and a director's salary). The following month, a more conservative projection retained the choir's $500 allotment against the rabbi's $800 and the hazan's $400.[16] Good intentions, however, gave way to modest realities as the congregation's planned move to a repurposed church on Chrystie Street forced it to reduce its salaries and other expenses. By July 1847, Kling's frustrations with a dearth of willing choristers, a lack of written music, and existing members' poor knowledge, inconsistent attendance, and inattentiveness found their way to his supervisors. The directorate had recently decided to give child choristers a free suit for every six months of service; but in response to Kling, the directors organized a committee to keep track of the choir's needs, gave singers (all male) free membership, and offered free seats to the singers' wives.[17] Aesthetic aspirations also led the directors to search Europe for a more distinguished cantor (*Vorsänger*), and in October 1847, they asked Merzbacher to consider offering the position to an unnamed candidate in Hanau.[18] Congregational minutes never mentioned this request again, nor did they mention Cohen by name after 1846. Rather, Cohen appeared to continue occupying the cantorial position by default, with Kling and Merzbacher given the community's other musical responsibilities—such as the proposed compilation of a six-part songbook (*Liederbuch*) for the congregation.[19]

The congregation's increased attention to music brought quick improvements. Even before Emanu-El had settled into its new building on Chrystie Street, the choir was singing music from the Vienna and Munich rites. Around the same time, Cohen supervised the American premiere of Salomon Sulzer's wedding music during the marriage ceremony of prominent member (and B'nai B'rith brother) Dr. James Mitchels.[20] By 1848, the congregation had clarified Cohen's responsibilities as a hazan: cooperating with the choir, providing all of his own sheet music (or assuming the expense of making copies), helping to lead the synagogue's hoped-for elementary school, and if necessary, serving as the congregation's assistant secretary.[21] At this early stage, the congregation seemed musically omnivorous, looking additionally to the recent European publications of Naumbourg (Paris) and Josef Johlson (Frankfurt) for inspiration, and asking Merzbacher to publish a collection of German hymns for congregational use, presumably with organ accompaniment.[22] Cohen seemed to welcome these changes as a path to greater congregational enfranchisement, leading to his unanimous reelection as cantor in April 1849.[23] But he went further: when he learned in May that Isaac M. Wise's Albany congregation included girls in its choir, Cohen amplified the call, writing to the editor of New York journal *Israels Herold* that "I read with pleasure . . . that Israel's daughters participate in the chorus [in Albany] and it is everyone's wish to imitate this beautiful example here [in New York City]."[24]

Yet, 1849 also highlighted the changing value of the cantor to the congregation: while the leadership raised Merzbacher's salary to $600, Cohen received $350, a difference possibly denoting the extent to which musical responsibilities had diversified to a broader range of personnel, while intellectual leadership focused to a single figurehead.[25]

Cohen actively expanded his portfolio as an independent educator, possibly to make up for the financial difference.[26] In May 1849, he began to advertise a subscription to finance the publication of his pamphlet "Lessons in the Hebrew Language, through a simple and practical method."[27] The *Israels Herold* editor, Isidor Busch, welcomed the prospective work, adapted from Ollendorff's then-popular "write-read method" (*Schreib-lesemethode*) as a much-needed salve for "the always limited space for Hebrew instruction in Israelite schools everywhere."[28] After a brief, unsuccessful microfinancing campaign, Cohen simply moved forward, releasing it the following year with endorsements from Max Lilienthal, clergy partner Leo Merzbacher, and other prominent city rabbis.[29] Dedicated to "Congregation Imanu-El," the book included a brief "Theoretical Part" that introduced basic grammar and a progressive series of exercises. *Asmonean* editor Robert Lyon hailed the publication for filling a lacuna in Jewish education; but Isaac Leeser (who felt similarly) lamented what he saw as numerous errors and an unfortunate German-centric approach that posed problems for English-speaking pupils.[30] Whether Cohen's decision to discount the book from one dollar to fifty cents after its first months of publication indicated its popularity or the opposite, his attempts to teach Hebrew through real words and phrases acknowledged the scarcity of Hebrew teaching time for synagogue schools where the language was increasingly peripheral to Jewish identity.

The book's publication also afforded Cohen an opportunity to explain his progressive philosophy of Jewish education in an emancipated age. In an editorial to the *Asmonean* on February 22, 1850, Cohen raised the dilemma of fulfilling the obligation to pass down Jewish tradition "when the rising generation brings ignorance, repugnance, and contempt into public life, instead of love for, and adherence to religion."[31] Rather than give up, he instead sought "to know what the mind of our youth is entertaining; we must become acquainted with the whole manner of their moral and scientific education—with all its motives and results—with all the possible aberrations and dangers; we must . . . know in what manner this or that idea may influence their life—what is to be stimulated and what repressed, giving them either a material or an immaterial form, so we can ascertain *how* to speak to [them]."[32] Crafting education to the needs of young people rather than presenting them with a morally weighted repetition of the previous generation's needs, Cohen argued, offered the best route toward enfranchising them in Jewish religious and institutional life.

A few months later, the name G. M. Cohen appeared in the *New York Herald* advertising instruction in French, German, and singing, and seeking "a situation as teacher in a college or a private family . . . no objection to the country."[33] The synagogue officers likely warned Cohen to stay focused. By mid-1852, however, around the same time that they forcibly retired a fragile and ailing Merzbacher, the officers decided not to renew Cohen's contract and compelled him to leave his sheet music for his successor, Adolph Rubin.[34]

Independent Educator, 1852–56

Lacking a pulpit, Cohen pursued an education-based career over the next few years. To improve sales of his Hebrew text, he reduced the price further to 37½ cents.[35] His continued devotion to *Bildung* likely led him to produce an engraving of Moses Mendelssohn by January 1854, which the *Asmonean*'s editor promoted to its readers.[36] And in May 1855, Cohen opened an "Educational Institute & Boarding School for Girls and Boys," that taught Hebrew, English, German, and French; instructed students in "the tenets of the Israelitish Faith"; and offered courses in music and trade-based studies in addition to standard academic subjects.[37]

Cohen's continued interest in the future of synagogue music, however, likely helped him land his next pulpit job. In a special dispatch to Isaac Mayer Wise's German Jewish paper *Die Deborah* titled, "Synagogue Song: How It Is, and How It Should Be," he argued vehemently for a model of synagogue musicality that seamlessly integrated cantor, choir, and congregation into a single unit, while criticizing existing models that appeared to lack such coordination.³⁸ Although he kept his school running through summer 1856, he likely noticed the advertisement placed in *The Israelite* and other Jewish journals by the young Chicago congregation Kehilath Anshe Ma'ariv (KAM). Hoping to make a major move, KAM sought "a gentleman to take charge of the Hebrew school of the congregation, and qualified to teach the Hebrew, English and German branches, also to act as *Hazan* of the congregation, according to modern style, organizing and leading a choir."³⁹ The advertised salary of $1,200 far exceeded Cohen's Emanu-El income, not to mention his current earnings. He answered the ad; and upon receiving the synagogue's call to its pulpit, he ventured out to the burgeoning Midwest.

Building a Musical Program in Chicago: KAM and Ohabey Or

Cohen's two years in Chicago reflected both the rising status of music in discussions of American Jewish identity and the ambivalence associated with allowing musical leadership to take precedence over intellectual vigor. Serving as the minister of KAM from late 1856, Cohen presided over a congregation actively seeking to implement moderate reforms in the style of Wise, who with colleagues laid out a new agenda at a conference in Cleveland the previous year.⁴⁰ A vocal faction, including some of KAM's founding members, pressed for changes. Yet Cohen's efforts at negotiation came to an impasse, threatening his tenure.

On June 1, the congregation seemed ready to part with Cohen and sent out a call for new religious leadership. Although the want ads specified separate positions for preacher and teacher/choir director, the reduced funds offered ($800), combined with the one-year term, posed challenges for attracting good candidates, especially from Europe.⁴¹

Cohen helped to inaugurate the city's B'nai B'rith Ramah Lodge no. 33 two weeks later and served as its first president.⁴² At KAM, however, trouble brewed. In August, the reform faction organized into the Israelite Reform Society and named Cohen as its religious head. Samuel Straus, prominent lawyer and former KAM founding member, announced the Israelite Reform Society's separate High Holiday services, which built on Cohen's experience "in the style of Temple Emanu-El in New York. . . . A nice organ and a good organist are already provided."⁴³ By bringing their dissent into the public, the Israelite Reform Society successfully forced another round of discussion at KAM. The Society's members pushed through a slate of moderate reforms at the next congregational meeting, claiming victory over the objections of the synagogue president.[44]

KAM leadership had by that point succeeded in securing the commitment of a new rabbi and a hazan. Fearing deepening conflict, they decided to hold off on implementing reforms until their chosen rabbinical candidate, Mayer Mensor, could arrive from Dublin and address the matter. (The group also awaited the arrival of its new cantor, K. Marx, from Alsheim, Rheinhessen.) In the meantime, public portrayals of the dispute began to take on ethnic colors—the reformers as recent arrivals from "Rheinish Bavaria" versus a more traditionalist "Polish" faction.[45] Tensions simmered as the board energetically defended its wait-and-see approach.[46]

While caucusing with the reformers, Cohen sought other opportunities in more stable settings. His drive to promote Jewish cultural enlightenment led him to issue an (unauthorized) American printing of recently retired Hamburg rabbi Gotthold Salomon's 1829 biography of Moses Mendelssohn.[47] A month later, in February 1858, Cohen guest-led services in Isaac Mayer Wise's Lodge Street Synagogue in Cincinnati.[48] Not formally an audition, Cohen's weekend pulpit nonetheless gave him some familiarity with Wise's recently-published *Minhag America* and allowed him to further his credentials as an advocate of Jewish reform. He may have taken Wise's liturgy to Straus and the Israelite Reform Society. Ultimately, however, Chicago's reformers clashed with Mensor, left KAM, and established a new congregation (Ohabey Or) with a different minister: Reverend Isaac N. Cohen, who agreed to an extravagant four-year contract and $1,000 salary.[49] About a month later, KAM's anticipated cantor (K. Marx) backed out of his offer, and the synagogue's officers tried to lure Cohen back to its pulpit to join Mensor and his more gradual reforms.[50] Yet Cohen had other ideas in mind, approaching Isaac M. Wise with news of his availability. Immediately, the trustees of the Lodge Street Synagogue declared the position of hazan vacant. They held an election, and by May Cohen had supplanted Gustav S. Ensel as the Cincinnati congregation's hazan (see chap. 4).[51]

The short-lived Ohabey Or congregation began holding services in April using the *Minhag America* liturgy. One account of the ritual notes that the congregation began "with a hymn . . . followed by a [German] prayer" and that Hebrew prayers included "the intercantations of the choir, supported by a melodeon."[52] During its brief, several-week existence, the congregation followed the triennial cycle of Torah reading—spoken rather than chanted—and eliminated second days of holidays. Cohen, however, had moved on.

Cincinnati: Working with Wise, but Retaining German Valences

Joining Bene Yeshurun (KKBY) in July 1858 on a pro tem basis, Cohen spent the summer acclimating to Wise's expectations for the *Minhag America* liturgy, while preparing for the High Holidays. His efforts led the congregants to reelect him that September to a one-year term at $500, plus a $100 bonus for his honorable work over the past months.[53] Compared to Wise's $2,000 salary as a spiritual figurehead, Cohen's remuneration reflected the congregation's integrated model of Jewish community, with music contributing to a broader public march of social and civic cultivation. Indeed, the emphasis on music as a communal activity became even clearer the following year, when the congregation put Cohen up for reelection. Cohen requested a "fair salary," which the synagogue's board interpreted as an increase to $600; however, the following month the congregation rejected the board's decision and even briefly considered a salary as low as $300 before returning to $500 for the following year.[54] As part of the same meeting, the congregation entertained a request by two of its members "that the singing by the Hazan be abolished and that the prayers be read by him plainly and audibly."[55] Particularly during the High Holidays, the congregation recognized the importance of musical leadership. Yet in contrast with the fundamental role given to Wise's ideological and theological direction, music represented a more complicated and less easily quantifiable landscape throughout the rest of the year.

Given his previous experiences, Cohen may have recognized his congregational status as a musical facilitator of Jewish identity. But Cohen also came to Wise's pulpit during a period of political rancor within B'nai B'rith. In the late 1850s the interests of the order's First (New York–based) and Second (Cincinnati-based) Districts began to polarize, creating contrasting groups of "Germanizers"—proponents of radical reform, German language and *Wissenschaft*, who avoided affiliating with religious initiatives—and "Americanizers"—those who sought to ally with the order with religious movements and institutions.[56] Wise, the Second District president during this period, came down solidly as an Americanizer: he mightily resisted both the order's attempt to keep its central authority in New York and its new constitution. New York in turn rejected Wise's ideas to connect the order with a national Jewish college and congregational union. Cohen, in contrast, seemed thoroughly immersed in the Germanizing school, diverging from Wise's ideas and philosophies even while working with him to create an effective local ritual. Upon this premise, Cohen embarked on a unique portfolio of projects to promote *Bildung*, hoping to integrate synagogue, home and school activities into a coherent lifestyle.

First came KKBY's choir. Initially created by Wise as a volunteer group in 1847 to enhance communal prayer, KKBY's choir had faced a decade of challenges, from competent leadership to effective singing. By 1858, like many voluntary synagogue choirs of the time, it appeared to have a large number of women and few men, with the congregation resorting to hiring at least a professional or two to maintain balance and quality. Cohen attempted to moderate this matter in November 1858, when he presented KKBY with "a plan for the organization of a musical Society for the improvement of the Choir." To a city with a strong singing society culture (three Sängerfests had been recently organized under the synagogue's long-standing organist Carl Barus), Cohen proposed adding an ensemble of Jewish men.[57] The congregation looked into the request, appointing a committee "to have Mr. G. M. Cohen examined by competent musicians in respect to his musical qualifications"; the presumably positive response led Cohen to found the eighteen-member Allemania Society, a social institution soon described as "the rare *Art Union* of German sociability, Hebrew genius, and American sentiments."[58] While few clues exist about the singing group's extended tenure, this ensemble nonetheless forged a meaningful link between the synagogue and the public square, in this case cultivating a male choral culture that could contribute effectively across both sacred and civic musical settings. After the 1860 High Holidays, Isaac Mayer Wise's rapturous recollection of the music sung by the mixed choir hinted at the significance of Cohen's efforts, while welcoming the modern sound of his vocal style:

> Whoever did not hear, last New year's day, the choir in the Lodge Street Synagogue, K. K. Bene Yeshurun, missed a grand occasion to admire the force and beauty of Hebrew music. If Sulzer, Naumburg, Lachner and the other composers had heard their master works sung by twenty-two excellent singers and accompanied on the organ by Mr. Barus, they must have rejoiced in their own works. We have heard much in the branch of Church music; but we do not recollect to have heard a better choir, better trained and more powerful, for the place intended, than this is. The Hazan Rev. Mr. Cohen deserves particular

mention for his tasteful delivery without any of the antiquated chants. All the synagogues were crowded during these holy days, but none could be so overcrowded as ours; we have scarcely twenty seats more than we have members, so that the building of a new temple is an inevitable necessity.[59]

Cohen's November advertisement in *Die Deborah*, announcing receipt of the latest European synagogue music and offering reasonably priced copies for interested congregations and cantors, attested to his self-confidence as a national source of American Jewish musical cultivation.[60]

Cohen also set afoot a plan for a coeducational institution in the city's German Quarter (also known as Over-the-Rhine), parallel to offerings in the city's public schools. Responding to what he claimed to be "a great need and the wishes of many friends," he began his own school in September 1858 that taught regular subjects—English, German, geography, history, science, arithmetic, handwriting, art for boys, "wifely housework" for girls, and singing—but also included Hebrew and "religious instruction," with an emphasis on moral behavior.[61] Building on the Hebrew primer he created in New York, Cohen also produced an inexpensive math text in 1858 titled, "Progressive Slate Exercises or: The Child's First Book, in Arithmetic."[62] These materials emphasized social continuity between Jewish and American identities in Cincinnati, rather than exclusivity. By 1860, Cohen also worked as a language and music instructor for the younger classes of KKBY's Talmid Yelodim Institute and continued to model broad knowledge as a function of modern Jewish identity.[63]

Der Israelitische Volksfreund, 1858–59: Germanizing American Jewish Culture

The most complete manifestation of Cohen's *Bildung*-based agenda, however, appeared in the guise of his literary journal *Der Israelitische Volksfreund* (*The Israelite People's Friend*). Utterly independent from Wise's *The Israelite* and *Die Deborah*, with a title that played wittily off the names of the local papers (Cincinnati also had a German-language paper called *Volksfreund* at the time), the ad-free journal apparently had its first issues financed through an advance on Cohen's salary—with hopes that a subscription base could build and carry the costs from there.[64] In his preface to the first issue in December 1858, Cohen described the journal as a companion that "knocks every month on your door and asks to be let in" in order to "present to people the best and most beautiful, the most useful and most entertaining materials in the field of Jewish literature, in a suitable selection, made accessible in the easiest manner."⁶⁵ Completely eschewing news and largely avoiding politics, the journal offered many of the same departments as German literary magazines, but fashioned for Jewish families. Cohen described the journal's purpose whimsically: "It . . . tells you the most beautiful stories, fairy tales, parables; it declaims the most magnificent poems you've ever heard, and has a large supply of anecdotes, riddles and charades."⁶⁶ Its pages included reprintings, with permission, of novels, essays, and poems from a cadre of European German Jewish writers, such as Ludwig Philippson, Wilhelm Frey, and Leopold Stein, sometimes with Cohen's own commentaries reinforcing values of family, literary knowledge, and liberal German Jewish religious life.⁶⁷ Beginning with the second issue, Cohen introduced sections intended to appeal to local interests. A children's section—"*Der Israelitischer Kinderfreund*"—had its own serialized novel and poems promoting industriousness and learning; in the sixth and seventh issues (May and June 1859), Cohen presented profiles of Cincinnati's two liberal synagogues (Bene Yeshurun and B'nai Israel); and in June 1859, he announced an unrealized series of articles advertising that "one of the most thorough and important scholars in America" had been engaged to write a rigorous illustrated history of Jews in the United States that emphasized their rapid development and influence "in areas of religious, political, mercantile and creative life."⁶⁸ These features spoke most directly to a Jewish audience but also gave the journal an air of accessibility to the general Germanophone public as the record of a successful minority population.

Cohen made particular efforts in the journal to integrate Jewish religious and civic life into an internally consistent "ethnic" outlook. Nearly all the literary contributions evinced an intimate knowledge of Jewish history and liturgy. Two key musical and ritual aspects, however, showed more openly Cohen's attempts to bring religious life into the home and home life into the synagogue. Issue no. 1 (December 1858) included a series of three Sabbath table songs ("Zemiroth") and one Hanukkah song, adapted by Leopold Stein into versified German that shared the original rhythmic meter, thus allowing families to sing them (and understand them more effectively) at home.⁶⁹ Cohen also introduced an English adaptation of Stein's confirmation ceremony in the "Kinderfreund" section of the journal, presumably to allow young people to gain familiarity with the relatively recent synagogue practice in a language more comfortable to the rising generation.⁷⁰

While substantial in both purpose and heft, the journal's run ended abruptly in July 1859 after eight issues (about three hundred pages in total), likely from a lack of funds. Perhaps because of its overlap with Wise's journals (which also published novels and poems, although in much smaller numbers), it received only a few acknowledgments in *Die Deborah* and ran only brief advertisements for subscriptions.[71] Yet *Der Israelitische Volksfreund* also may have clashed with Wise's larger purposes, displaying a rather more neutral stance on specific religious reforms and favoring democratic growth over charismatic leadership. Regardless, the journal laid out an important road map for Cohen's philosophy, pursued in Cincinnati but ramped up still further in his next position.

Cleveland: A Congregation of His Own

On May 19, 1861, a month into the Civil War, Cleveland's Congregation Anshe Chesed hired Cohen "as Hazan, Teacher, and Leader of the choir" for five years at $1,000 per year, to begin on July 1.[72] In some ways, Cohen's arrival represented a success for Isaac Mayer Wise, who saw Cleveland as ripe for moderate reform. Six months earlier, in December 1860, Wise had given the inauguration address in the synagogue's renovated sanctuary, which included a new organ and choir space.[73] Yet, like many congregations of the time—especially Cleveland's sister congregation Tifereth Israel, which had caused a stir by instituting mixed seating—its major concerns lay less with the contents of its services than its ability to foster a cohesive relationship between Jewish and American identities in a time of war.[74] Three days before Cohen's election, for example, Anshe Chesed raised over the synagogue an American flag made by the congregation's young women. In a gathering that started with "a choir of young ladies singing 'the Star-Spangled Banner' in a very spirited manner," and ended with the same group singing "Columbia, the Gem of the Ocean," those assembled listened to synagogue president Simon Wolf connect America's battles for national unity with similar struggles in Italy. "As Americans—as Israelites—we contemplate with peculiar delight Feudalism and Priestcraft swept away," Wolf proclaimed, siding with the North, "and leaving in its stead Institutions evoked by the free and untrammeled choice of a Nation of Freemen."[75] The ritual, which affirmed the congregation's fealty to a united, progressive America, also evinced the symbolic importance of music to encapsulate and amplify its message.

At Anshe Chesed, Cohen pursued a vision of Jewish life that followed Cincinnati's institutional arrangement, while further integrating Judaism into civic musical life. Undoubtedly aware of the proliferating Singing School culture emerging across the nation, led by such figures as George F. Root in Chicago and Lowell Mason in Boston, Cohen found its grounding in Christian theology problematic for Jews. Consequently, Cohen attempted to fashion the synagogue's choir into its own singing society: harnessing the human voice's power for moral betterment and democratization. On Sunday, August 11, 1861, the choir sponsored an elaborate picnic on the shore of Lake Erie. After a generous lunch, Cohen "addressed the party in German, with the true elegance of an orator, showing the benefits of a choir in a church organization, and the influence exerted upon those who listen to their music—that all hearts, though differing in opinion on minor points, seem blended together as one common mind, elated by that beautiful music, the human voice."[76] Promoting singing as a way to smooth ideological edges, he then announced "a society to be formed and called the 'Israelitish Sacred Music Society,' whose object shall be the cultivation of this 'best gift from God to man given,' (singing) thereby strengthening those mutual ties of love so naturally existing between members of one common brotherhood."[77] Eight days later, on August 19, Cohen assumed the principalship of the congregation's school, renamed the Anshe Chesed Institute; it would eventually take over the school at neighboring Tifereth Israel.[78] By September, a correspondent for the Cincinnati *Israelite* reflected positively on the recent High Holiday services, noting, "The school is well organized, and divine service is beautiful. . . . The choir is excellent, the organ good and well played, and the Hazan a known artist. The additional prayers (Piutim) were considerably lessened in order to give ample time to the choir."[79] Rather than manifesting "reform" directly, these developments allowed Cohen to introduce music as a people's art, deeply integrated into the population's daily routines. This same philosophy would also extend to Cohen's founding of Cincinnati's Hebrew Benevolent Society.[80] Indeed, when Cohen celebrated his eightieth birthday many years later, a retrospective report that highlighted his humanistic approach to leadership described three conservative congregants' responses to Cohen's first Rosh Hashanah services: "We agree with you, if this is what you call reform."[81]

On March 5, 1852, Cohen's Israelitish Sacred Music Society came out to the public as the renamed the Zion Musical Society, performing its "First Grand Concert" in the city's one thousand–seat Melodeon Hall.[82] Despite somewhat disappointing attendance, the forty-person society performed a series of "sacred choruses," including what appear to be several Sulzer works and Vincenzo Pucitta's then-popular composition "Strike the Cymbal."[83] A *Cleveland Plain Dealer* reviewer wrote admiringly of the "twenty young ladies, dressed in white and brilliants, with the dark eyed beauty of the Orient, supported by a like number of gentlemen," while noting that the "solos and choruses were admirably sung, evincing superior musical taste."[84] Yet the group's use of liturgical music in concert raised coreligionists' eyebrows in Cincinnati. On one hand, the Zion Musical Society followed a relatively standard German singing society model, which many congregations promoted in creating and sustaining synagogue choirs. Preparing the choir as a specifically Jewish singing society, however, unnerved even Isaac Mayer Wise, who cautiously observed in reaction that "the object of sacred music is edification and not amusement."[85] Nonetheless, the *Israelite* reproduced the *Cleveland Plain Dealer*'s review of the concert without commentary in the following issue.

Cohen's program to create a civic-minded, active congregation continued apace. On June 5, 1862, he presided over Anshe Chesed's first confirmation exercises at the Eagle Street Synagogue, where a group of the congregation's teenagers and young adults completed a course of education and declared their devotion to Jewish life.[86] Nearly three weeks later, on June 25, Cohen took a prominent role in the Anshe Chesed Institute's annual picnic, where he "led the school in several national [i.e., American] songs."[87] The choir, too, became a staple of congregational life, performing at key synagogue rituals as well as prominent weddings, such as that of A. Abraham and Sarah Straus on Thursday, May 7, 1863.[88]

The Sacred Harp of Judah (1864): Music to Unify the Community

Cohen's ambition to create a musically literate and social-minded congregation reached a milestone in 1864, when Cleveland-based music publisher S. Brainard and Company published his collection *The Sacred Harp of Judah* (see fig. 3.2). Dedicated to Benjamin Franklin Peixotto, recently elected "Grand Saar" of the entire national order of B'nai B'rith and founder of Cleveland's Maimonides Lodge a decade earlier, the work's title and purpose clearly reflected B'nai B'rith's ideals of self-improvement, while promoting an organic model of Jewish life that traversed synagogue and home practice.

Inside its covers, *The Sacred Harp of Judah* combined the format of a Singing School manual with a musical blueprint for revising the dynamic (if not necessarily the contents) of liturgical presentation. Existing collections of new Jewish liturgical music, nearly all published in Europe, aimed largely for a specialized audience: written either for a cantor/musical leader or trained choristers. Even Wilhelm Fischer's 1863 *Zemirot Yisrael*, which built on the claim that it satisfied families' desire to learn synagogue music at home, could seem overly erudite and preoccupied with musical purification rather than encouraging group participation.[89] Hymnals intended for corporate worship, in contrast, only covered parts of the service. Cohen's work aimed to eliminate these differences by empowering congregants to join fully in the ritual, intentionally blurring the line between the sanctuary, the classroom, and everyday life in the process. He took his title from the Sacred Harp singing schools that taught religious music to the masses through shaped notes, and perhaps even more pointedly from L. O. Emerson's popular choral music book *The Harp of Judah*, which like many such manuals assumed a Protestant Christian audience. Cohen's *Sacred Harp*, in contrast, promised compatibility with Jewish beliefs.[90] And his subtitle—"for Synagogue, School, and Home"—followed the "Kirche, Schule, und Haus" formula used by popular religious songbooks of the time (and which Jewish music authorities would continue to use well into the twentieth century).[91]

In the style of Singing School manuals, Cohen opened his book with a preface that extolled "the human voice in strains of Music" as "the most precious gift from God to Man." The text that followed, however, appealed specifically to Jewish sensibilities. A brief historical narrative described "sacred music" as a mode "practiced since the days of King David down to the present time," and linked to the precision of the sciences: "As man has advanced in scientific resources in nearly every branch of wisdom," he noted, "music has kept pace on equal strides, and now seems to outrival its sister sciences."[92]

Then Cohen turned to the role of choral singing in Jewish worship. He claimed responsibility for organizing "the first [choir] on the American continent . . . over twenty years ago" and framed the change as "one of the great improvements in our Synagogues." Yet "this great improvement even does not seem to reach the true aim of worship," he rued, because congregants now "listen to the Choir as they would to the feat of concert singers." In the face of choirs, congregations had gone silent: "order and decorum is

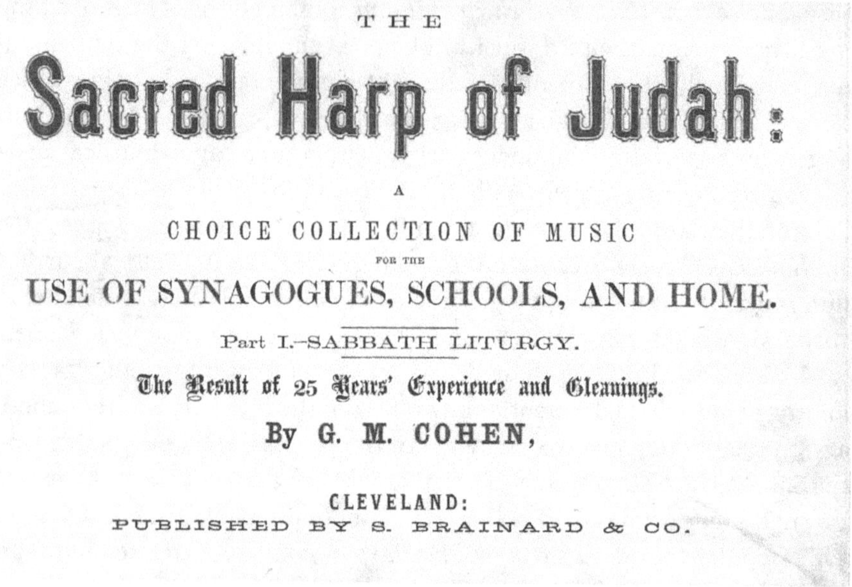

> # THE
> # Sacred Harp of Judah:
> A
> CHOICE COLLECTION OF MUSIC
> FOR THE
> ## USE OF SYNAGOGUES, SCHOOLS, AND HOME.
> Part I.—SABBATH LITURGY.
> The Result of 25 Years' Experience and Gleanings.
> By G. M. COHEN,
>
> CLEVELAND:
> PUBLISHED BY S. BRAINARD & CO.

Figure 3.2. G. M. Cohen, *The Sacred Harp of Judah*, title page (Brainard, 1864).

observed, but devoid of true devotion." Reinvigorating services, he asserted, required robust interaction between the choir, congregation, and minister, each of which professed its own musical form. "To the Congregation belongs properly the RESPONSE, to the Choir the SINGING. The Minister reads the prayer, and causes by the RECITATIVE either the Congregation to join by Responses, or the Choir by Singing."[93] Similar to the plan he facilitated in Cincinnati with Wise's *Minhag America*, *The Sacred Harp of Judah* offered itself, in Cohen's words, as the only "MUSICAL WORK, properly arranged for such a purpose": affordable, broadly accessible, and constructed to fill gaping lacunae in Jewish religious, educational, and home settings, just as other Singing School books had done in the Christian/secular world.[94]

In Singing School style, Cohen followed his preface with a concise pedagogical section on the "Elements of Vocal Music" —rhythm, melody, and dynamics—and then presented the Western staff system in fifty-six short, illustrated statements and two pages of scale and interval exercises.[95] While relatively comprehensive, Cohen's method differed from those of Root and Mason in its precision (perhaps assuming that students had musical training elsewhere) and its lack of catechism-like questions that the others used to reinforce students' knowledge.

Bildungsmusik | 95

Figure 3.3. Two options for the Call to Prayer ("Borechu") from *The Sacred Harp of Judah*.

Yet the contents of the fifty-page book proved the greatest difference from other Singing School publications. Taking after the compendia of Sulzer and Naumbourg, Cohen projected *The Sacred Harp of Judah* as the first of a three-volume collection covering the Jewish liturgical year. Volume 1, "Sabbath Liturgy," offered congregants a thorough illustration of their contributions to the Friday night and Saturday morning services, all original compositions presented in simple keys and clear notation—but also, as Neil Levin has noted, following a conservative liturgy that lacked the reforms of Wise or David Einhorn. The Friday evening service, comprising the first eleven selections, clearly denoted parts for "Reader," "Chorus," and "Congregation"; included alternative settings for the Barechu (call to prayer; see fig. 3.3) and "Mi Chamocha"; and ended with one German-language hymn, "Begrüßung des Sabbath" ("Welcoming the Sabbath"). The selections, all in C major or G major and using simple meters, clearly had broad participation in mind.

The selections for the Saturday morning service promoted a liturgical topography that peaked congregationally with the Torah-reading service and the closing hymns. The congregation's section commenced after the recitation of the morning psalms: it began with the "Kedusha," transitioned

Figure 3.4. "Sabbath Hymn" (solo song), words by American Jewish poet Gershom Lazarus. *The Sacred Harp of Judah*, no. 32.

into two songs for the New Month ("Hodu LeRosh Chodesh" and "Onno"), and then led into an extensive selection of music for the Torah service, including two options each for the processions with the Torah ("Lecho" and "Hodo"). Detailed coverage of the "Kedusha" starting the additional ("Mussaf") service led to a lacuna, implying either completion by the reader and chorus or (more likely) silent reading; the congregation resumed by singing the closing hymns with chorus and reader. Although these later sections were more involved and somewhat more harmonically varied—involving key signatures ranging to three sharps (A major) or flats (E-flat major) and occasional basic tonality shifts—the selections remained entirely in the major mode, retained their relative simplicity, and featured textbook voice-leading.

Four additional songs on Sabbath themes closed the volume. The first two set hymn texts from well-known Sephardic American poets Penina Moïse and Gershom Lazarus and appeared in popular parlor song style: the first as a duet and the second as a solo piece in $\frac{6}{8}$ time (see fig. 3.4). A pair of showy but harmonically safe psalm settings followed: a solo version of Psalm 150 ("Halleluyah") in English, and a four-part choral setting of Psalm

92 ("Mismor Shir LeYom HaShabbos") in Hebrew. In contrast to the vocals-only arrangements for the liturgical compositions (perhaps supplemented in services by an organist), Cohen provided a consumer-level keyboard accompaniment to the solo songs and duet. Practically speaking, these additions likely made the latter works accessible for use in amateur/family settings. Cohen's emotionally charged preface reinforced this perspective, as a way to enhance key moments of the Jewish life cycle: "Parents are delighted to hear their children sing and execute Waltzes, Polkas, and Marches on the Piano. But how would their hearts glow with rapture, as the holy Sabbath-day approaches, to hear them sing the songs of ancient Hebrew lore, as composed by the fondly remembered bard of Israel. Would it not prepare the heart of the business man for that time of devotion and praise, which he so justly owes to God? Or when the day draws nigh, to hear the children play and sing the songs appropriate for the festivals? Would it not keep in remembrance the protecting hand of the Almighty? Would it not prepare the parent as well to deeply impress the mind of the child with that solemnity or mirth, which is requisite upon these hallowed occasions?"[96]

Although the publisher, Brainard and Co., started a monthly magazine that promoted its own publications in 1864, extant issues include no mention of *The Sacred Harp of Judah*. Rather, the project had the air of a special, perhaps even vanity production for a focused audience; and the book's printing plates were forged in New York rather than Cleveland.[97] Aside from commentary in the local newspaper, moreover, copies appeared mainly to go to the Jewish press and major Judaica outlets across America. Lower east side New York bookseller S. M. Cohen, for example, printed advertisements for the book in the *Jewish Messenger*, which he sold at $1.50 each, or $15.00 per dozen.[98]

A Domestic, if Not Artistic, Success

Cleveland newspapers gave *The Sacred Harp of Judah* respectful praise, with emphasis on Cohen's status as a local clergyman. The *Daily Journal* mentioned the book as a way to lionize Cohen's accomplishments, largely summarizing his introduction in the process:

> Twenty years ago Mr. Cohen organized in New York the first Hebrew Choir on the American continent. Since that time choirs have been formed as an auxiliary to worship in nearly every synagogue in the land. This was a step in the right direction, but Mr. Cohen was not satisfied with this alone. He recognized

the truth that the congregation should partake of the musical worship, if it was to be real worship, and not merely display of professional skill, so after careful study and thought the present work was produced which is equally adapted for popular use in the synagoguge [sic], in the school room, or around the domestic hearth, where the family can "sing the songs of Zion."[99]

Jewish press outlets gave the work similarly respectful if uninformed reviews, perhaps due to the novelty of the music-based publication. New York's *Jewish Messenger* offered measured support, largely repeating Cohen's rationale while crediting him with doing "a public service by preparing this useful work."[100] Philadelphia's Isaac Leeser admitted in *The Occident* that he lacked the skills to evaluate the book fairly, but endorsed it nonetheless: "As we cannot read music we are not able to give any opinion of the work, but suppose that it has merit. . . . Every addition to this species of literature is . . . a welcome gift, and deserves encouragement from those who can profit by it."[101]

Even Isaac Mayer Wise, who engaged most deeply with the work, struggled to place it in his religious topography. From a liturgical perspective, Wise viewed Cohen's book as a means of modernization for communities whose members sought change but did not yet embrace reform. "[The volume] begins with *Lecko* [sic] *Dodi*," he wrote, highlighting differences from reform-focused liturgies. "It has music to *Wa'yehi binsoa-ho-aron*, to *En Kelohenu*, to *Yigdal*, with the personal Messiah doctrine in it, and is therefore the very thing which is wanted, as nobody ever thinks of publishing music for the so-called orthodox synagogues, and they are numerous especially if the half orthodox of Cleveland, Baltimore, Philadelphia, New York, Cincinnati, St. Louis, &c., are counted; they want something better than their antiquated chants. Therefore, we have no doubt the work of Mr. Cohen will meet with an extensive patronage."

At the same time, Wise differentiated the book's aims from the aims of reform-leaning congregations, which he implicitly saw as large, urban, wealthy, and constantly striving toward artistic elevation. In particular, he viewed the musical simplification required to encourage group singing as acceptable for resource-poor congregations, but inferior and impractical compared to the more desirable goal of creating majestic, meaningful music. "In the reform congregations light music will do no more," he noted. "But nobody cares for smaller [here contrasting with 'reform'] congregations, and 'The Harp of Judah' does. The object, as attempted by the book, to make the whole congregation chant, is laudable, but difficult to attain. It is all well in small congregations; but in a large one it is next to an impossibility."[102]

Cohen's compositions occupied the lower end of Wise's artistic hierarchy, particularly when compared with Sulzer's works and others' arrangements of "ancient" melodies, which Wise deemed more fitting for prayer texts. "Hebrew music of this century is of two kinds, original and arranged," he wrote. "Original music for the synagogue was first written by S. Sulzer, of Vienna.... Many besides Sulzer undertook the task of arranging ancient synagogal melodies into quartettes, *soli, tutti,* and *chori*.... We would wish to see those melodies collected, arranged, well-arranged and published; and we do hope that Mr. Cohen, in the forthcoming parts of his work, will pay more attention to original Hebrew melodies than to new compositions, which, in most cases, are at warfare with the text."[103] For Wise, who viewed music as a tool for supplementing and enhancing sacred text, Cohen's democratizing, *Bildung*-style methods seemed a half measure for congregations that chose not to go full Reform.

Little data exist on the number of copies *The Sacred Harp of Judah* sold or its broader patterns of usage; but given the public response, chances are its significance lay more in its existence than in its use.[104] Cohen, for his part, showed continued interest in balancing the broad needs of his congregants; following Benjamin Franklin Peixotto's lead, Cohen also ordered schoolbooks from Isaac Leeser, including twenty copies of his *Catechism for Jewish Children* at the start of 1865.[105] The congregation's reform-minded faction, however, saw him as a symbol of their struggle and began to use him as a bargaining chip in negotiations to defect to the city's openly liberal Tifereth Israel synagogue on Huron Street. Anshe Chesed, perhaps in retaliation, did not renew his contract, and Cohen moved to join the reformers at Tifereth Israel in mid-1866. The Huron Street congregation assumed that Cohen advocated Wise-style reform, based on his time in Cincinnati; in October, the synagogue officially introduced *Minhag America*, enthusiastically bringing Isaac Mayer Wise as a guest preacher for the inaugural weekend.[106] The match seemed to yield positive results for several months, reinforced by the congregation's surprise gift of an engraved gold watch to Cohen in January 1867.[107] Yet the strength of Cohen's musical facility seemed to be counterbalanced by his awkwardness in giving English-language sermons, posing challenges to the congregation's expectations.[108]

By May 1867, Cohen had auditioned for Milwaukee's expanding congregation B'ne Jeshurun, whose congregants seemed so enamored by his musical skills and experience that its board hired him on the spot with a "good full purse." Cohen promptly assembled a choir and prepared the congregation for a full musical complement as it moved to adopt the *Minhag America* liturgy. At its formal introduction, on Shavuot (the Feast of Weeks, June 9–10) 1867, a correspondent for *Die Deborah* was impressed by both the musical program and Cohen's "magnificent voice." Yet Cohen's attempt to give the sermon as well proved less successful: "The service with the choir would have been very beautiful and worshipful, if Mr. [Cohen] had not mutilated the sermon, which was illogical and hastily assembled," reported the correspondent, who hoped Cohen would limit himself to music from then on.[109] As with his time at Tifereth Israel, Cohen's efforts to embody the full complement of the "Reform" minister proved complicated.[110]

For Cleveland's not-quite-Reform Anshe Chesed, however, Cohen's skills remained an ideal package; by September, the congregation had re-engaged Cohen at a higher salary. He returned to Cleveland's Jewish landscape, perhaps chastened but with a clearer understanding of his strengths, and recommenced a campaign of balancing synagogue work with B'nai B'rith–based initiatives, musical activities with public civic engagement.[111] That fall, Cohen began to teach weekly music lessons at Cleveland's recently established Jewish Orphan Asylum—a prominent institution, spearheaded by Benjamin Franklin Peixotto and B'nai B'rith, that showed the Jewish population's compassion for the children of those fallen in the Civil War—and led the instrumental and choral parts of its first closing exercises the following July.[112] The next year, during Shavuot, Cohen conducted a public and well-received confirmation service at Anshe Chesed.[113] A few months later, he received the copyright to his publication *The Little Bible*, an English retelling with commentary that sought to appeal to the general public while proving friendly to Jewish readers; and he appears to have completed his own "Catechism for Jewish Children," perhaps with intent to replace Leeser's, which never saw publication.[114] In February 1870, Cohen formed the Young Ladies' Hebrew and Literary Society as an auxiliary to the city's Hebrew Literary Association, and presided over the forty-two-member group's first (nonmusical) entertainment on a stormy April evening.[115] These activities, supplemented by officiation at public events such as marriages—where organ and choir received approbation in the local papers—reintegrated Cohen into the community and likely shaped his continued work on *The Sacred Harp of Judah*.[116]

Jewish Music for America: *The Sacred Harp*, Volume Two

Cohen ambitions gained even more momentum with his participation in national Jewish initiatives. In 1870 and 1871, he participated in a series of meetings attended by a small number of prominent rabbis from reform-friendly congregations, all intent on establishing a union of progressive synagogues with a common liturgy and institutional structure: the group met first in Cleveland in mid-July 1870, in New York City in late October of the same year, and in Cincinnati the following June (a meeting that Cohen co-organized with Isaac Mayer Wise and Max Lilienthal).[117] During the second meeting, Cohen submitted his *Little Bible* and possibly *The Sacred Harp of Judah* for consideration as movement-wide materials. At the third meeting, the attendees approved *The Little Bible* for use by "schools . . . families and libraries." The group's Committee on Music and Liturgy, meanwhile, laid out an ambitious musical agenda to complement the anticipated publication of a new prayer book. Headed by Cohen and New York cantor Samuel Welsch, the committee sought to provide musical settings to the new texts "at the shortest time possible." To that end, the committee recommended Welsch's publication *Zimrath Yah* for liturgical accompaniment (see chap. 6) and Cohen's *The Sacred Harp of Judah* "for the introduction and use of Sabbath schools."[118] Cohen "promised," moreover, "to publish in the future . . . a collection of hymns, for two voices, which will fully meet the expectations and requirements of the Conference."[119] Combined with further ambitions to compile a "collection of German and English hymns," and to compose original music for "a selection of such psalms, which are well adapted for Divine worship," Cohen, Welsch, and the other members gave music a crucial role in the new era of American Judaism.[120] The two musicians also formalized the dichotomy between high art (Welsch) and people's music (Cohen) in the new era's sonic landscape.

A major sign of progress—likely motivated by his committee's 1871 report—emerged in early 1872, when Cohen released a self-published, original sacred chorus setting of Psalm 100. Cleveland Germania Orchestra conductor Alfred Arthur provided the vocal parts with a pianistic organ accompaniment featuring sixteenth-note runs. Rather than using the Hebrew text, moreover, Cohen opted for former Cleveland rabbi Isidor Kalisch's versified German and English adaptations. Clearly intended as a showpiece, perhaps to feature in synagogue dedication ceremonies, the composition slightly exceeded the most complex of the works in Cohen's 1864 volume:

a keyboard introduction in C major led into a four-part *maestoso* choral section; a tenor solo transitioned to an F major, unaccompanied chorale-like break in triple time; and then an abbreviated recapitulation of the first section (including the original key and time signature) ended in a chorale-like coda.[121] While adding interest, these changes remained well within the abilities of an amateur ensemble or singing society, especially with Cohen's straightforward vocal arrangement. Countering *Zimrath Yah*'s aspirations to high art music, Cohen's new work reinforced his devotion to the potential of popular music production: Isaac Mayer Wise, taking note, highlighted the work's "many happy points."[122]

Cohen also published Psalm 100 to announce the impending publication of *The Sacred Harp of Judah*'s second volume. The cover sheet arced the *Sacred Harp* title above "Psalm 100" and, after a quick note, listed the anticipated contents of "Part Second": fifty-five "original Pieces" ranging from "School Hymns" to German and English solos and duets, German-language works to help mark major Jewish holidays, and a new series of liturgical settings with a focus on the Torah service.[123]

Perhaps inspired to create a work for national consumption, Cohen sought input on the new volume from his synagogue music colleagues. He published announcements offering to send the full manuscript gratis to cantors and organists for their evaluation, "not only as a personal friendship, but as an obligation they owe to the author as well as to the public."[124] The manuscript itself, originally titled *Musical Relaxations for the Family Circle, for the School and Public Service/Selected, Arranged and Composed by G. M. Cohen*, continued to promote music's role in the tripartite model of communal unity. And its contents largely followed through on the promise of the Psalm 100 cover, including: "eight traditional melodies for German and English text, and 54 original compositions, [which] consist of: a) two-voice songs with English or German text, for the Sabbath School and the home, most with a light piano accompaniment; b) four-voice Hebrew, English and German songs, most with organ accompaniment and intended for public worship."[125] As with his first volume, Cohen set the music in simple meters and keys and included keyboard accompaniment for the large majority of pieces. But Cohen also used the guitar to set two German songs in his collection, likely in deference to the increased interest in guitar as a pedagogical instrument, especially in Cleveland, where African American composer and foundational guitar pedagogue Justin Holland had been using his method for nearly thirty years. Most notably, however, as if to clarify his own mission, respond to critics, and highlight his philosophical differences with *Zimrath Yah*, Cohen opened the book with an extended epigraph from Heinrich Heine that began, "Truly, one cannot honor enough those composers that give us melodies of the type that gain entry to the folk," and went on to criticize so-called art music composers who "are inwardly so spoiled, marshy and cranky that they can produce nothing pure, simple, in short nothing natural."[126] Heine had written these lines to praise Hamburg composer/conductor Albert Gottlieb Methfessel (1801–69), a champion of singing schools and contributor to Hamburg's Jewish hymnal. Cohen, subsequently, appeared to use the quote to place his work firmly in the Singing School tradition, while criticizing aesthetic movements to beautify religious ritual through increasingly complicated (and expensive) musical creation, as represented by *Zimrath Yah*.

Cohen's efforts soon took a detour, however. The rabbis who had approved *The Little Bible* for Sabbath schools in 1871 reversed themselves the following year at their Cincinnati convention.[127] Cohen resigned his position as Anshe Chesed's spiritual leader in 1873 and, lacking a pulpit, stopped attending meetings of the newly formed Union of American Hebrew Congregations. Instead he shifted to the private sector and devoted his energies to solving the perennial problem of musical page-turning for organists and choir directors. In July 1874, he and Bavarian-born clockmaker Gregor Dietz submitted their patent for a spring-loaded, automatic page turner, which the US Patent Office approved and published in its September 15 guide.[128] This object became a featured part of Cohen and Dietz's partnership, with contemporary directories through at least 1876 noting the leaf turner's availability in Dietz's watch and jewelry shop off the Cleveland Public Square.

Cohen likely returned to his *Sacred Harp* work in mid-1877, when the Union of American Hebrew Congregations announced a competition for "the best hymn-book for Sabbath-School purposes," with deadline of July 1 the following year.[129] Just weeks before the deadline, in June 1878, Cohen's second volume emerged in print—self-published and in a substantially different form than in 1872. Renamed *The Orpheus*, a term shared with singing societies across the United States (such as Cleveland), as well as the titles of other Singing School books, Cohen's compendium doubled down on its educational value (see fig. 3.5). While the book's preface restated Cohen's enthusiasm for democratic music making, its mission presented an important change: Cohen acknowledged "the numerous publications of

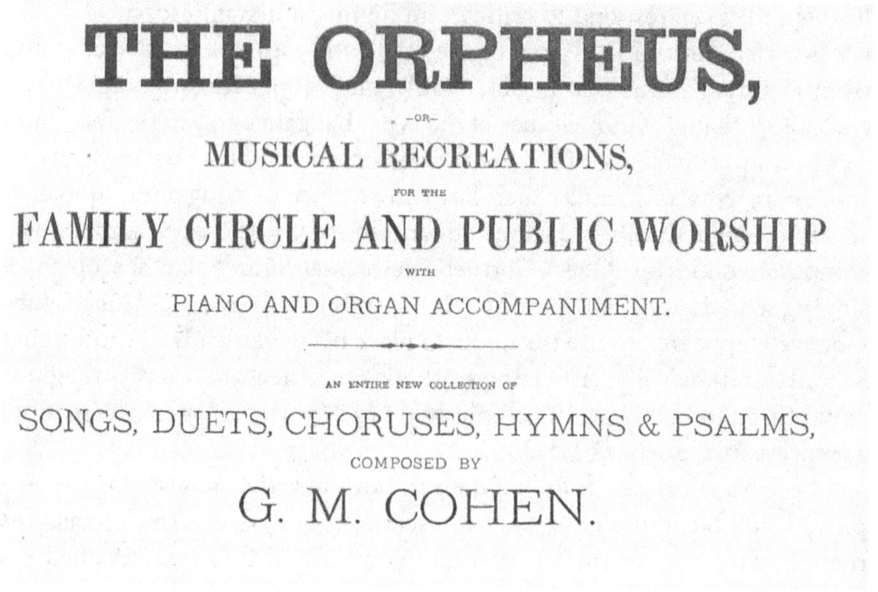

THE ORPHEUS,

—OR—

MUSICAL RECREATIONS,

FOR THE

FAMILY CIRCLE AND PUBLIC WORSHIP

WITH

PIANO AND ORGAN ACCOMPANIMENT.

AN ENTIRE NEW COLLECTION OF

SONGS, DUETS, CHORUSES, HYMNS & PSALMS,

COMPOSED BY

G. M. COHEN.

Figure 3.5. G. M. Cohen, title page, *The Orpheus* (1868).

new and excellent music" for the synagogue in his opening, but emphasized his own position alongside Mason, Root, Emerson, and others in presenting "a collection of songs for the *Family circle and the Church combined.*"[130] Dispensing with his 1872 Heine epigraph, he nonetheless declared his work "something that will give new life, and that will supersede the old songs and still retain their solemnity; songs, which by their simplicity and sweet sounding melody, will catch the popular ear."[131]

The contents of the oblong volume had changed substantially as well, perhaps due to his colleagues' criticisms of the 1872 manuscript, but also likely tempering the failure of his 1871 commitment to creating a separate book of hymns and psalm settings. Accordingly, *The Orpheus* omitted all the Hebrew prayer music and replaced it with popular psalm settings by Sulzer, Naumbourg, and Edward Weber (as well as Cohen's own Psalm 100). Cohen described the additions as works "of the most prominent composers of Hebrew melodies," yet in his continued drive to give these works a populist presentation, he actively adapted them to middlebrow American needs. He replaced the original Hebrew text with his own "English translation, which has never before been accomplished, and for the first time [makes them] the property of the musical world at large."[132] More subtly, Cohen

Figure 3.6. Sulzer, Psalm 113, arranged by G. M. Cohen in *The Orpheus* (first page).

consolidated staves, removed articulation markings, took out some chordal reinforcement, rearranged voices, cut some measures and repetitions, and (intuitively) modified rhythms to fit the new English words, all presumably to make them friendly to community groups. For his setting of Salomon Sulzer's Psalm 113, for example (Schir Zion I, no. 53), Cohen reduced Sulzer's original four-voice, three-staff arrangement with soprano and tenor clefs to a more hymn-like two-staff choral arrangement with treble and bass clef, removed one or two instances of vocal ornamentation, and replaced the Hebrew with an English text (see fig. 3.6). Cohen modified another work of Naumbourg's, "Darcho Eloheinu" (*Z'mirot Yisroel* no. 5), more drastically, reducing its original four-part Hebrew setting into an English duet titled, "Eternal Love Is Thine," that deleted the original's introduction and choral repetitions and eschewed counterpoint in favor of a predominantly homophonic texture of thirds and sixths.[133] While he retained the melody from his Psalm 100, moreover, Cohen gave it a markedly different arrangement from his earlier version. These adaptations invoked a compromise, acknowledging the ubiquity of some "art"-based compositions, while actively shaping these works into choral pieces made for "popular" performance "in which there are no technical difficulties to be overcome, so that the amateur may find it equally as easy as the practiced choir to sing them."[134]

The resulting collection (with guitar notation reverted to keyboard) offered users a repertoire that transitioned smoothly between synagogue and home, with a character that allowed them to share their music easily with their non-Jewish neighbors. Just as Welsch and others assembled the texts of major American liturgies in composing *Zimrath Yah*, Cohen continued in his second volume to bring together a variety of a texts that could speak meaningfully to contemporary Jewry. He drew liberally from Leopold Stein's 1840 *Gebete und Gesänge zum Gebrauche bei der öffentlichen-Andacht der Israeliten*, from the hymnal of Temple Beth Elohim in Charleston, South Carolina, and from Isaac Mayer Wise's recent collection *Hymns, Psalms, and Prayers*.[135] But he also included settings of poems by colleagues Max Lilienthal and Louis Aufrecht (the latter serving as director of the city's Jewish Orphan Asylum) and popular song texts with little direct connection to Jewish observance. Even though a number of these entries, such as "O Day of God" (a poetic adaptation of "Kol Nidre" rendered in German by Stein and translated into English by Wise), "New Year's Hymn," and a set of four confirmation songs, had liturgical functions, all appeared in English or German; the Hebrew that had pervaded the first volume completely disappeared in *The Orpheus*. Cohen maintained the dominance of the major mode in the second volume as well, although in step with other Jewish musical works coming out at the time, he included a limited number of works that began in a minor mode: two based on minor-mode "Traditional Melodies," one from an imported psalm setting (by Jacques Fromenthal Halévy, taken from a Naumbourg collection), and original settings of "Adon Olam" and the Day of Atonement text "What Is Man?" ("Mah Adam?").[136] These choices presented a friendly and popular musical method for normalizing American Jews' complicated and multifaceted lives in the public square, using accepted conventions for linking leisure and prayer.

The Orpheus again received appreciative, if brief, mentions in the appropriate outlets. The *Cleveland Plain Dealer* admiringly called it "a valuable acquisition to the musical publications of the day."[137] Isaac Mayer Wise recommended that "the book ought to be patronized by our teachers especially, and also our *Hazanim*, who might make good use of it."[138] In *Die Deborah*, a letter to the editor/advertisement by "Veritas" highlighted the book's value for the home and synagogue school, and its worth in preparing young people for congregational singing—even as the editor chided the title "which originates from the pagan world of gods."[139] Yet the volume had greater competition, such as the second edition of Simon Hecht's *Zemirot Yisrael* hymnal, with English and German hymns present in similar proportion (and no Hebrew).[140] And Cohen likely felt greater disappointment when the hymn book committee, at the July 1878 Union of American Hebrew Congregations meeting in Milwaukee, extended its competition for another year because "in their judgment, none of the works offered and examined is of such a character as to deserve the premium [i.e., the $50 prize]."[141] Disenfranchised by a body headed by his colleague Max Lilienthal, Cohen would publish no more music.

Final Years: A Commitment to Community Engagement

In the remaining twenty-four years of his life, Cohen continued to bridge Jewish identity and civic identity comfortably, particularly through his activity with B'nai B'rith's Solomon Lodge (no. 16). He cowrote public notices marking the deaths of notable B'nai B'rith members.[142] In 1882, he gave a set of lectures for the local Young Men's Hebrew Association that included a discussion of Moses Mendelssohn.[143] He weighed in on a controversial Hebrew spelling of a new engraving above Anshe Chesed's new windows in 1887.[144] And in 1888, he ran unsuccessfully for the Cleveland school board.[145] Throughout, however, the synagogues that Cohen had overseen in the 1860s and 1870s continued their largely successful musical practices. An 1880 report of Yom Kippur in Cleveland noted that both liberal synagogues had choirs, and admired Anshe Chesed's performance of Alois Kaiser's "Requiem" by "a double quartette, consisting of the best musical talent in the city" as "in itself one of the most beautiful ever listened to."[146] Limited evidence also exists that the *Sacred Harp* volumes enjoyed some sustained use in the years after publication, particularly among small congregations.[147]

Yet the strong currents of Wise's model of Jewish reform ultimately swept Cohen along. In 1900, when Cohen celebrated his eightieth birthday, an extended article in the local press paid tribute to him as an advocate of religious reform who energetically fought strong opposition in the name of progress.[148] This simplified narrative continued when Cleveland newspapers marked his death in 1902: remembering Cohen as a "Reformer," even while paying less attention to his name (misprinted several times as "Coehn").[149] The American Jewish press, by this point, largely treated him as a footnote. Cincinnati's *American Israelite* included only a notice of his passing in its "Jottings" section, far briefer than treatments of other recently deceased figures; and the account omitted his KKBY service, acknowledging only a short residence in Cincinnati.[150]

A Jewish Musical Culture for Emerging Americans

By the 1890s, as American liberal Jewish liturgies solidified behind the *Union Prayer Book* and *Union Hymnal*, as Eastern European cantors came to redefine the role of the prayer leader, and as German Jews turned their attention to the *Bildung* of their Eastern European brethren arriving on American soil, G. M. Cohen's work gradually came to seem provincial, an experiment cast aside to larger currents. When the members of New York's Temple Emanu-El publicly feted the congregation's fiftieth anniversary in the *American Hebrew* in 1895, a retrospective account of its cantors could only speculate about Cohen's whereabouts, forcing Cohen to write his former congregants from Cleveland's Sir Moses Montefiore Home for Aged and Infirm Israelites (established by the parallel Kesher Shel Barzel Lodge), and assure them of his continued vitality.[151]

But maybe Cohen's obscurity presents only part of the picture. While the aesthetics of Classical Reform continued to promote soaring music even after Isaac Mayer Wise's death in 1900, and cantors sought to consolidate their own identities by asserting their places in the pulpit, educators and scholars held on to German philosophical models of the singing congregation that emphasized a holistic cultural vision of Jewish life. The *Union Hymnal* described itself solely as an aid for worship from its 1897 publication; but those who wished to create alternative Jewish songbooks through the twentieth century, in attempts to enhance congregational participation, adopted the same formulation of "synagogue, school, and home" that Cohen used.[152] Smaller, heterogeneous, and exurban congregations likely faced similar musical concerns as earlier, often relying on the training of itinerant rabbis and the inconsistent musicality of its members.[153] Even twentieth-century orthodox groups such as Young Israel, again comprising small congregations, sought strategies for congregational leadership that included musical simplification and group singing. The desire for a musically facile congregation that could easily port its Jewish identity into and out of the sanctuary doors, in other words, remained strong even as more elaborate national projects sometimes gave the appearance of a shift away to more highbrow priorities.

Cohen, devoted to finding a Jewish life at the intersection of the synagogue and B'nai B'rith, presented a practical solution at a formative time in American Jewish organizational history. The bridge he constructed proved fragile in details but rich in concept—emphasizing music as part of a broad, sophisticated cultural knowledge that transformed both Jewish and secular symbols into an internally consistent system of identity. In the process, he modeled an alternate approach to musical leadership in the Jewish communal world that at least theoretically set discussions of liturgy and ideology aside, and let the voices of the people prevail.

Notes

1. Cornelia Wilhelm, *The Independent Orders of B'nai B'rith and True Sisters* (Detroit, MI: Wayne State University Press, 2009), 5.

2. Ibid., 29. Research on Gustave M. Cohen has been tricky in light of his relatively common family name, the frequency with which others misspelled it as *Kohn* or *Cohn*, and his tendency to use his first two initials (G. M.) in public. Cohen, moreover, shares his name with the British translator of Eduard Hanslick's *The Beautiful in Music* (trans. 1891), a nineteenth-century British Christian missionary who lectured as "a Prussian Jew," an early twentieth-century French Medieval drama scholar (1879–1958), and the mid-twentieth-century editor of the *Indiana Jewish Post and Opinion*.

3. "Rabbi Coehn [sic], Reformer, Dead," *The Cleveland Plain Dealer*, December 14, 1902, 5; "Rabbi Coehn [sic] at Rest," *The Cleveland Plain Dealer*, December 15, 1902, 5; Neil Levin, "Gustave M. Cohen, 1820–1902," Milken Archive of Jewish Music: The American Experience, http://www.milkenarchive.org/people/view/all/1109/Cohen,+Gustave. See also Irving H. Cohen, "Synagogue Music in the Early American Republic," *Gratz College Annual of Jewish Studies* 5 (1976): 20, 22–23; William Osborne, *Music in Ohio* (Kent, OH: Kent State University Press, 2004), 311–14; Geoffrey Goldberg, "The Training of *Hazzanim* in Nineteenth-Century Germany," *Yuval: Studies of the Jewish Music Research Center* 7 (2002): 330–31. At this point, I have been unable to find contemporary details of Cohen's early life and education, although the timing of Cohen's education suggests that he studied with Salomon Steinhard. He also appears to have started shortly after the departure of Hermann Ehrlich, who later edited *Der Liturgische Zeitschrift* (1850–59), an early periodical devoted to synagogue music and liturgy.

4. Hyman Grinstein, *Rise*, 354. Cohen's obituary in the *Cleveland Plain Dealer* states that he arrived on June 20, 1844; a search of Ancestry.com reveals a record of a Gustav Kohn arriving in New York from Rotterdam on the ship *Garonne* on June 5, 1844, although reporting a birth date of 1810 (which could well be an error).

5. Merzbacher had recently left the first B'nai B'rith lodge.

6. Wilhelm, *The Independent Orders*, 30.

7. Levin, "Gustave M. Cohen, 1820–1902." See also Cohen, "Synagogue Music in the Early American Republic."; Osborne, *Music in Ohio*, 311–14.

8. Wilhelm, *The Independent Orders*, 254.

9. Myer Stern, *The Rise and Progress of Reform Judaism: Embracing and History Made from the Official Records of Temple Emanu-El of New York* (New York: Myer Stern, 1895), 16, 19.

10. *Allgemeine Zeitung des Judenthums*, June 30, 1845, 407.

11. Ibid.

12. Temple Emanu-El Minutes Book, November 4, 1845. In possession of the Temple Emanu-El archives, New York City. I am grateful to Warren Klein for giving me access to this resource.

13. Temple Emanu-El Minutes Book, June 13, 1846. Item 8 specifically describes Kling's instruction as *"schriftlos"* (without written music).

14. Temple Emanu-El Minutes Book, June 13, 1846. Preface, *Vollständiger Jahrgang von Terzett- und Chorgesängen der Synagoge in München nebst sämmtlichen Chorresponsorien zu den alten Gesangweise der Vorsänger (Hazanut)* (Munich, 1839).

15. Temple Emanu-El Minutes Book, August 24, 1846, 26; September 13, 1846, 26.

16. Ibid., January 24, 1847, 153; February 16, 1847, 159.

17. Ibid., July 11, 1847, 36; May 30, 1847, 35.

18. Ibid., October 24, 1847, 42.

19. Grinstein, *Rise*, 356.

20. *Allgemeine Zeitung des Judenthums*, April 1, 1847, 22; *Israels Herold* 1, no. 12 (June 15, 1849), 94. Cohen corrected Isidor Busch's claim that Isaac Mayer Wise had premiered the music in Albany in May 1849 by noting that Mitchels had used the music two years earlier.

21. Grinstein, *Rise*, 484. See also "The Jews in America," *The New York Times*, December 18, 1870, 8.

22. Ibid.; Stern, *The Rise and Progress*, 30–31.

23. *Israels Herold* 1, no. 4 (April 20, 1849), 30.

24. G. M. Cohen, Letter to the Editor, *Israels Herold* 1, no. 12 (June 15, 1849), 94. Albany's Temple Beth-El in 1849 had a choir that included four girls, four boys, and "seventeen gentlemen" (*The Occident and American Jewish Advocate* 7, no. 8 [November 1849], 416–17).

25. Stern, *The Rise and Progress*, 29.

26. Cohen served on the committee charged with recommending publications to purchase for a joint library of all of B'nai B'rith's New York lodges. Wilhelm, *The Independent Orders*, 118–19, 290n19.

27. G. M. Cohen, "Unterricht in der hebräischen Sprache," *Israels Herold* 10 and 11 (June 1 and 15, 1849), 80, 88.

28. [Isidor Busch,] "Literarische Notiz," *Israels Herold* 10 (June 1, 1849), 74.

29. G. M. Cohen, "Prospectus for Publishing," *The Asmonean*, January 18, 1850, 104; [Robert Lyon,] Comment on Prospectuses, *The Asmonean*, April 29, 1850, 204; [Robert Lyon,] "New Books," *The Asmonean*, August 16, 1850, 132; Advertisement for G. M. Cohen's book, *The Asmonean*, September 22, 1850, 167; [Robert Lyon,] "New Books," *The Asmonean*, September 27, 1850, 180. The other two endorsing rabbis were Herman Felsenheld and M. I. Muhlfelder. Bruce Ruben notes that Lilienthal adopted the book (Bruce Ruben, *Max Lilienthal: The Making of the American Rabbinate* [Detroit, MI: Wayne State University Press, 2011], 97).

30. Isaac Leeser, "Literary Notices," *The Occident and American Jewish Advocate* 8, no. 8 (November 1850), 419–20.

31. G. M. Cohen, "Religious Instruction," *The Asmonean*, February 22, 1850, 141.

32. Ibid.

33. G. M. Cohen advertisement, *New York Herald*, June 1850. "Country" in this case may have referred to a location outside of the city.

34. Grinstein, *Rise*, 545n34.

35. *The Asmonean*, August 27, 1852, 172.

36. *The Asmonean*, January 20, 1854, 108, 112.

37. "G. M. Cohen's Educational Institute . . ." *The Israelite*, June 29, 1855, 407.

38. G. M. C., "Synagogen-Gesang: Wie er ist, und wie er sein sollte," *Die Deborah* 1 (September 21, 1855), 37–38.

39. "G. M. Cohen's Educational Institute . . ." *The Israelite*, January 26, 1856, 239; KAM ad, *The Israelite*, September 26, 1856, 95.

40. Cohen's predecessor at KAM, G. Schneidacher, left the congregational school in early November 1856 (*The Israelite* 3, no. 20 [November 21, 1857]). See also "Reformbewegung in der israelitischen Gemeinde zu Chicago," *Die Deborah*, February 27, 1857, 221–22.

41. *The Israelite*, June 26, 1857, 406.

42. Leonard J. Grossman, "B'nai B'rith," in *The Sentinel Presents 100 Years of Chicago's Jewish Life* (Chicago: Sentinel Publishing, 1948), 24; Letter to the Editor, *The Israelite*, July 10, 1857, 6.

43. *The Israelite*, August 21, 1857, 54. Reprints a letter dated August 5, 1857.

44. *The Israelite* 4, no. 13 (September 21, 1857), 102.

45. *The Israelite* 4, no. 15 (October 5, 1857), 118.

46. *The Israelite*, October 30, 1857, 133 [Letter dated October 18, 1857].

47. Die Deborah 3, 174 (January 15, 1858); Gotthold Salomon, *Moses Mendelssohn: Oder ein blick in ein schones, herrlich vollendetes menschenleben* (Chicago: G. M. Cohen, 1858).

48. *The Israelite*, February 5, 1858, 246.

49. Letter to the Editor, *The Israelite*, February 26, 1858, 270.

50. *The Israelite* 4, no. 24 (February 26, 1868), 270.

51. Minutes, Congregation Bnai Jeshurun, Cincinnati, March 28, April 18, and May 2, 1858. AJA MS-62, Box 3. Ensel's tenure with Bnai Jeshurun will be addressed in chapter 4.

52. "Affairs of the Synagogue," *The Israelite*, April 16, 1858.

53. *Die Deborah* 4, no. 7 (October 1, 1858), 52.

54. KKBY Minutes Book, September 6 and October 2, 1859.

55. KKBY Minutes Book, October 2, 1859.

56. Wilhelm, *The International Orders*, 83–88.

57. KKBY Minutes Book, November 7, 1858.

58. KKBY Minutes Book, November 14, 1858; "Domestic Record," *The Israelite*, December 9, 1859, 182; *Die Deborah*, December 9, 1859, 91; December 16, 1859, 95; January 13, 1860, 111; *The Israelite*, February 3, 1860, 242.

59. *The Israelite* 7, no. 42 (September 21, 1860), 94. Italics in original.

60. "Neue Synagogen-Gesänge," *Die Deborah* 6 (November 23, 1860), 84.

61. "Lehranstalt," *Die Deborah* 4, no. 4 (September 10, 1858), 31. The ad remained in the paper through October.

62. Advertisement, back cover, *Der Israelitische Volksfreund* (every issue).

63. *The Israelite* 6, no. 31 (February 3, 1860), 243.

64. KKBY Minutes, October 10, 1858. The minutes do not mention the reason Cohen asked for an advance, although the timing of the request strongly lends itself to the possibility that it was intended to finance his journal.

65. Vorrede, *Der Israelitische Volksfreund* 1, no. 1 (December 1858).
66. Ibid. A charade was an intricate word puzzle requiring readers to combine a series of one-syllable answers to a set of versified clues into a single solution word or phrase.
67. "Literarischer Wochenbericht," *Allgemeine Zeitung des Judenthums* 23, no. 17 (April 18, 1859), 246.
68. [G. M. Cohen,] "An die Leser," *Der Israelitische Volksfreund* 1, no. 7 (June 1859), 2.
69. "Zemiroth," *Der Israelitische Volksfreund* 1, no. 1 (December 1858), 19–22. The songs were "Begruesst das Fest," "Gezang am Sabbath nach der Malzeit" ("Sabbath Song after a Meal," or "Tsur Mishelo Achalnu"), "Abendlied zur Beendigung des Sabbaths" ("Evening Song for Sabbath's End," to the melody of "L'David Baruch"), and "Lied für das Chanukah-Fest" (to the tune of Maoz Tsur).
70. "Confirmation-Act," *Der Israelitische Volksfreund* 1, no. 4 (March 1859), 155–56; 1, no. 5 (April 1859), 196. Cohen attributed the original version to Stein's *Israelitische Volkslehrer*.
71. *Die Deborah* 4, no. 16 (December 3, 1858), 126; no. 19 (December 24, 1858), 157; no. 20 (December 31, 1858), 158; no. 29 (March 4, 1859), 227.
72. *Israelite* 7, no. 47 (May 24, 1861), 374; *Israelite* 7, no. 49 (June 7, 1861), 390; *Die Deborah* 7 (July 1861), 4.
73. Allan Peskin, *This Tempting Freedom: The Early Years of Cleveland Judaism and Anshe Chesed Congregation* (Cleveland, OH: Anshe Chesed, 1973), 22–23; "Rededication of the Eagle Street Synagogue—Imposing Ceremonies," *Cleveland Plain Dealer*, December 15, 1860, 3; Wise also printed excerpts of his sermon in *The Israelite* 7, no. 26 (December 28, 1860), 204, and *The Israelite* 7, no. 27 (January 4, 1861), 212.
74. "Radical Reform in Cleveland," *The Occident and American Jewish Advocate*, May 1861, 39.
75. "Raising a Flag on the Eagle Street Synagogue," *Cleveland Plain Dealer*, May 17, 1861, 3.
76. J. J. N., "Pic-Nic at Rocky River," *Cleveland Plain Dealer*, August 13, 1861, 3.
77. Ibid.
78. "Anshe Chesed Institute," *Daily Cleveland Herald*, April 10, 1862. Benjamin Franklin Peixotto reported a Hebrew school run by Cohen's predecessor, Elkan Herzman, in August 1860 with around 150 to 200 students ("Ohio," *Jewish Messenger*, August 3, 1860, 37). By April 1862, the school reportedly had 144 students, possibly due to the migration of students from the Tifereth Israel school ("Cleveland," *The Occident*, March 1862, 568). See also Nancy F. Schwartz and Stanley Laskey, "Jewish Cleveland before the Civil War," *American Jewish History* 82, nos. 1–4 (1994), 97–122.
79. *The Israelite* 8, no. 11 (September 13, 1861), 86.
80. "Resolutions of the Hebrew Benevolent Society of Cleveland, O.," *The Israelite*, October 12, 1866, 3.
81. "A Pioneer Rabbi of Cleveland," *Cleveland Plain Dealer*, March 24, 1900, 5.
82. "Grand Sacred Concert," *Daily Cleveland Herald*, February 21, 1862; "First Grand Concert," *Cleveland Plain Dealer*, February 28, 1862, 2; "Hebrew Sacred Concert," *Daily Cleveland Herald*, March 3, 1862. Listings of the concert program note that it was originally scheduled for February 27, but it shifted to March 5 around February 19. Claims that the Zion Musical Society was the first such ensemble in America are exaggerated. A "Hebrew Glee Club" was reported in Memphis in 1858, for example (*Memphis Daily Appeal*, April 25, 1858, 2).
83. A version of the program included in the *Daily Cleveland Herald* includes titles but no composers. Some titles, such as Psalm 114 and the Pucitta piece, are relatively easy to track

down; others are more difficult due to generic titles. In addition, in part due to the instrumental accompaniment that existed for at least part of the concert, the society may have performed pieces in arrangements that differed from the more common versions of liturgical pieces known at the time.

84. "The Sacred Concert Wednesday Evening," *The Israelite* 8, no. 37 (March 14, 1862), 294–95.

85. [I. M. Wise,] "Cleveland," *The Israelite* 8, no. 36 (March 7, 1862), 287.

86. "Hebrew Confirmation," *Daily Cleveland Herald*, June 10, 1862.

87. J. J. N., "Pic-Nic of the Anshe Chesed Institute," *Daily Cleveland Herald*, June 28, 1862.

88. "Hebrew Wedding," *Daily Cleveland Herald*, May 9, 1863.

89. Wilhelm Fischer, *Zemirot Yisrael: Auswahl Israelitisch religiöser Lieder in Musik gesetzt von Wilhelm Fischer* (Philadelphia: Schaefer and Koradi, 1863).

90. B. F. White and E. J. King (eds.), *The Sacred Harp: A Collection of Psalm and Hymn Tunes Odes and Anthems Selected from the Most Eminent Authors*, 2nd ed. ("New and Much Improved and Enlarged") (Philadelphia: S. C. Collins, 1860). The original version was published in 1844. See also L. O. Emerson, *The Harp of Judah: A Collection of Sacred Music for Choirs, Musical Conventions, Singing Schools, and the Home Circle* (Boston: Oliver Ditson, 1863).

91. See, among many examples, *Gesangbuch für Kirche, Schule und Haus* (Berlin: Hauptverein für christliche Erbauungsschriften, 1858).

92. G. M. Cohen, "Preface," *The Sacred Harp of Judah* (Cleveland, OH: S. Brainard, 1864), 2.

93. Ibid.

94. Ibid., 3.

95. Ibid., 4–8.

96. Ibid., 3.

97. Ibid., 3. The plates were made by "Henry Beyer, Electrotyper and Stereotyper, 538 Broadway, N. Y." This appears to be the only Brainard publication that used Beyer for layout and typesetting.

98. "Synagogue Music," *Jewish Messenger*, July 22, 1864, 22.

99. "Sacred Harp of Judah," *Cleveland Daily Journal*, June 28, 1864.

100. *Jewish Messenger*, July 15, 1864, 13 ("As the author suggests, its design is to occupy the same place for home devotion and for schools that is so admirable secured for trained choirs and professional singers by the more complicated musical works").

101. *The Occident and American Jewish Advocate*, October 1864, 330–31.

102. [Isaac Mayer Wise,] "Music for the Synagogue" [Review of *The Sacred Harp of Judah*], *The Israelite*, July 1, 1864, 4–5.

103. Ibid.

104. As of October 2018, WorldCat lists only three copies of *The Sacred Harp of Judah*, one at the British Library, one (or two) at Hebrew Union College, and one at the National Library of Israel. (*The Orpheus* only appears in the National Library of Israel.)

105. G. M. Cohen letter to Isaac Leeser, January 1, 1865, Gershwind-Bennett Isaac Leeser Project, http://leeser.library.upenn.edu/documentDisplay.php?id=LSDCBx2FF12_1.

106. *The Israelite*, October 19, 1866, 4.

107. *The Israelite*, January 25, 1867, 6.

108. "Cohen, Gustave M.," *Encyclopedia of Cleveland History* [online], https://ech.case.edu/cgi/article.pl?id=CGM.

109. Milwaukee, *Die Deborah*, June 11, 1867, 108.

110. B'ne Jeshurun Minute Book, Jewish Museum Milwaukee. I am grateful to Jay Hyland for his research assistance on Cohen's time in Milwaukee.

111. "Wedding at the Eagle Street Synagogue," *Daily Cleveland Herald*, September 12, 1867.

112. "The Cleveland Orphan Asylum," *Jewish Messenger*, January 22, 1869 (as "G. M. Cohn"); "The Orphans," *Daily Cleveland Herald*, February 10, 1870 ("G. M. Kohn"); "The Jewish Orphan Asylum," *Daily Cleveland Herald*, July 15, 1869 (as "Rev. S. M. Cohen"). See also Gary E. Polster, "'To Love Work and Dislike Being Idle': Origins and Aims of the Cleveland Jewish Orphan Asylum, 1868–1878," *American Jewish Archives* 39, no. 2 (November 1987), 127–56. Music and singing continued as subjects taught at the orphan asylum, suggesting that Cohen continued to offer his services; however, he is not mentioned by name in accounts of end-of-year exercises (see, for example, "Jewish Orphan Asylum," *Cleveland Morning Daily Herald*, July 11, 1872).

113. Americus, "At the Synagogue," *Cleveland Plain Dealer*, May 30, 1868, 3.

114. G. M. Cohen, *The Little Bible, or, The Instructor of Religion and Morals for Young and Old, Containing a Complete Extract of the Holy Writ, with Instructive Notes* (Cleveland, OH: Nevins, 1869); "U.S. Court—In Bankruptcy," *Cleveland Plain Dealer*, August 6, 1868, 3; "'The Little Bible,'" *Cleveland Plain Dealer*, February 24, 1869, 3. Cohen's choice of mainstream publisher Nevins rather than a Jewish publisher such as Cincinnati's Bloch underlined his intention to introduce the book as a work for the general public. This kind of book likely took after German models; see Ruth B. Bottigheimer, "Moses Mordechai Büdinger's *Kleine Bibel* (1823) and Vernacular Jewish Children's Bibles," *Jewish Social Studies* 1, no. 3 (1995), 83–98. On the "Catechism for Jewish Children," see *The Israelite*, December 6, 1867, 2.

115. "Retirement," Letter to the Editor, *The Israelite*, April 29, 1870, 7; "A Pleasant Entertainment," *Cleveland Plain Dealer*, April 21, 1870, 3. The Young Ladies' Hebrew and Literary Society required members to be aged sixteen and up.

116. "Local News/Jewish Wedding," *Daily Cleveland Herald*, February 17, 1870.

117. "The Next Conference," *The Israelite*, June 2, 1870, 8. By this point, Cohen viewed his work with Anshe Chesed as a march toward mainstream Reform and publicly took umbrage at a comment in *Die Deborah* describing the congregation as "half-Reform" in part because it did not yet use *Minhag America* or another accepted reform-minded prayer book (Cohen, Letter to the Editor, *Die Deborah* 16 [August 1870], 3).

118. "The Rabbis in Council," *Jewish Messenger*, October 28, 1870, 5; "The Rabbis in Council: Complete Report of Their Proceedings," *Jewish Messenger*, November 4, 1870, 4–5; "The Conference, Concluded," *The Israelite*, June 16, 1871, 8; "The Conference: Official Report of the Secretary. Conclusion," *The Israelite*, March 22, 1872, 9.

119. "The Conference," *The Israelite*, March 22, 1872, 9.

120. Cohen and Welsch were also appointed to the Committee for Sabbath Schools and Text Books (Welsch also became a member of the executive committee). They unsuccessfully opposed a decision by the group to read a selection of the week's Torah portion during the service; while speculative, there is a chance that this objection was musically motivated (seeking to chant rather than read the section, for example). "The Conference, Concluded," *The Israelite*, June 16, 1871, 8–9.

121. Isaac Mayer Wise, for example, featured Psalm 100 as the accompaniment for the first of seven circuits around the sanctuary to be dedicated, specifically indicating performance by the choir. See Isaac M. Wise et al., *Hymns, Psalms & Prayers in English and German* (Cincinnati, OH: Bloch, 1868), 238.

122. *The Israelite*, April 5, 1872, 8.
123. Cohen, "Psalm 100," cover page. Although the numbering goes to 64, it omits 45 to 53, likely in error.
124. Printed announcement accompanying G. M. Cohen, *Musical Relaxations for the Family Circle: For the School and Public Service: Selected, Arranged and Composed by G. M. Cohen*, American Jewish Archives, SC-2235.
125. Ibid.
126. Ibid.
127. E. Eppstein, Letter to the Editor, *The Israelite*, April 11, 1873, 5.
128. Cohen and Dietz received US patent no. 154945, submitted July 17, 1874.
129. *Proceedings of the Union of American Hebrew Congregations*, vol. 1 (Cincinnati: Bloch, [ca. 1880?]), 495.
130. Cohen, "Preface," *The Orpheus* (Cleveland, OH: G. M. Cohen, [1878]), 2. Italics in original.
131. Ibid.
132. Ibid.
133. "Eternal Love Is Thine," *The Orpheus*, 34–35.
134. Cohen, "Preface," *The Orpheus*, 2.
135. L. Stein, ed., *Gebete und Gesänge zum Gebrauche bei der öffentlichen-Andacht der Israeliten* (Erlangen, Germany: Ferdinand Enke, 1840); Congregation Beth Elohim, *Hymns for the Use of Hebrew Congregations*, 4th ed., revised and enlarged (Charleston, SC: Edward Perry, 1875); Isaac Mayer Wise, *Hymns, Psalms and Prayers* (Cincinnati, OH: Bloch, 1868).
136. The five pieces were "Oh Day of God" (a setting of "Kol Nidre"), "Adon Olam" (with English text), "Dich Gott Erheben" (based on a "Traditional Melody"), Psalm 118:5–25 (originally "Min HaMetzar" in Naumbourg's *Shirei Kodesh* [Paris, 1864]), and what appears to be an original setting of "What Is Man?" Notably, only two of these selections—"Adon Olam" and "Dich Gott Erheben"—ended in the minor mode; all others resolved to either the parallel or relative major.
137. "The Orpheus," *Cleveland Plain Dealer*, June 13, 1878, 140.
138. *The American Israelite*, June 14, 1878, 6.
139. "G. M. Cohn's Orpheus," *Die Deborah*, May 17, 1878, 2. The book's $2 price (ca. $46 in 2016 dollars) may have been off-putting as well.
140. Simon Hecht, *Zemirot Yisrael: Jewish Hymns for Sabbath Schools and Families* (Cincinnati, OH: Bloch, 1878). Hecht's preface is dated January 1878, although *The Israelite* appears to have advertised it only in May/June 1878.
141. *Proceedings of the Union of American Hebrew Congregations*, vol. 1 (Cincinnati, OH: Bloch, [ca. 1880?]), 527.
142. "Resolutions," *The American Israelite*, July 3, 1874, 6 [on Alexander Schwab]; "Resolutions of Respect," *Cleveland Plain Dealer*, November 19, 1879, 4 [on Abraham Aub].
143. "Personal Mention," *Cleveland Plain Dealer*, January 21, 1882, 8.
144. *Cleveland Plain Dealer*, June 30, 1887, 8.
145. "The City Election," *Cleveland Plain Dealer*, April 3, 1888, 1.
146. "Atonement Day," *Cleveland Herald*, September 16, 1880, 4. While the Cleveland Herald does not identify the "Requiem" piece specifically, Kaiser's publication of the piece in 1879 makes it the most likely option.

147. Observer, "Amsterdam, N.Y.," *The American Israelite*, April 24, 1890. The choir of Amsterdam's Temple of Israel sang Cohen's adaptation of Sulzer's Psalm 92 on the Friday evening service during Passover.

148. "A Pioneer Rabbi of Cleveland," *Cleveland Plain Dealer*, March 24, 1900, 5.

149. "Cleveland," *Jewish Messenger*, December 26, 1902, 10; "Rabbi Coehn [sic], Reformer, Dead," *Cleveland Plain Dealer*, December 14, 1902, 5; "Rabbi Coehn [sic] at Rest," *Cleveland Plain Dealer*, December 15, 1902, 5. Cohen apparently declined rapidly, as a report from the Montefiore Home for the Aged only notes his admission in the last quarter of 1902, shortly before his mid-December death ("Montefiore Home for the Aged," *The American Israelite*, January 15, 1903, 6).

150. *The American Israelite*, December 25, 1902, 7.

151. A. J. Dittenhoefer, "Early Recollections of Emanu-El," *The American Hebrew*, April 12, 1895, 683; "The Cantors of Emanu-El," *The American Hebrew*, April 19, 1895, 732. Cohen, in his response, noted that he had written an autobiography; as of this writing, however, the unpublished manuscript has not yet been found.

152. For Jewish songbooks that later used the same phrasing, see, inter alia, Isaac S. Moses, *The Sabbath-School Hymnal: A Collection of Songs, Services and Readings for the Synagogue, School and Home*, 6th ed., revised and enlarged (New York: Bloch, 1904); A. W. Binder, *The Jewish Year in Song: A Collection of Songs, Hymns, Prayers and Folk-Melodies in English, Hebrew and Yiddish for Synagogue, School, and Home* (New York: Schirmer, 1928); A. Z. Idelsohn, *Jewish Song Book for Synagogue, School and Home* (Cincinnati, OH: A. Z. Idelsohn, 1928); Sol Zim, *The Joy of Israel Songbook, for Synagogue, School and Home, with Chords* (Hollis Hills, NY: Zimray Productions, 1980). Note that the first edition of Moses's book had the less concise name *The Song Book for Jewish Worship: Adapted for Congregational Singing, as well as the Sabbath School and the Home* (Chicago: I. S. Moses, 1896).

153. Implied in Lee Shai Weissbach, *Jewish Life in Small-Town America: A History* (New Haven, CT: Yale University Press, 2005).

4

MUSICAL POPULISTS

G. S. Ensel, Simon Hecht, and the Quest for the Singing Congregation

ON MARCH 16, 1894, THE SMALL JEWISH POPULATION of Paducah, Kentucky, dedicated its new synagogue building, featuring the Moorish architecture fashionable for progressive synagogues of the time.[1] The well-attended affair reportedly involved "a choir consisting of twenty-four voices, selected from the best singers in the churches of our city," led by locally admired, sixty-six-year-old volunteer music director Gustav S. Ensel. An observer writing for Cincinnati's *American Israelite* complimented Ensel on his "profound knowledge of music" and lauded his efforts to adapt "the very choicest compositions from the [Classical] masters . . . Haydn and Mozart, Beethoven and Schubert, Mendelssohn, Gounod, and other luminaries of music . . . to the texts of a Jewish hymnal." Then, in perhaps an unexpected turn, the reporter added that Ensel "has always prided himself on the fact that he never composed a piece of music himself." Implicitly criticizing the high cultural strivings of a "Jewish chazzan educated in the school of Sulzer, Naumb[o]urg, and other shining lights of music," the reporter wrote that Ensel considered "Jewish" sound in a more populist frame, as "a style of music which is at once suitable to the modern tastes of our co-religionists."[2] The program of arrangements from works by Meyerbeer, Rossini, Mercadante, and Mozart, as if by illustration, appeared to deeply gratify the assembled ecumenical crowd.[3]

About a hundred and fifty miles away in Evansville, Indiana, Simon Hecht likely looked on appreciatively. Hecht (1824–1908) had himself become a local elder, respected among his coreligionists for his turn as leader of the town's congregation B'nai Israel in the late 1860s. As the compiler of an American Jewish hymnal in the 1870s, Hecht had carried on spirited public discussions with Ensel since their early years as synagogue leaders in Germany, arguing crucial details about the precentor's role in the nature and practice of synagogue song. But by the 1890s, although still a member of the local synagogue and B'nai B'rith lodge, Hecht's creative and professional efforts mainly focused on German American culture. Like Ensel, he devoted himself to public education, teaching German in the Evansville school system. In 1892, local musician J. Cintura had transformed his poem "Wo ist meine Heimath?" ("Where Is My Homeland?") into an anthem pitched as German Americans' counterpart to the German patriotic song "Was ist des deutschen Vaterland?" ("What Is the German Fatherland?").[4] Once invested in improving the lot of synagogue music, Hecht now pursued German-style education as a basis for elevating civic life.

As long-term residents of Ohio River Valley communities, Ensel and Hecht's activities provide insight into Jewish musical expression as it took root in America's Midwestern towns. Their debates about musical leadership might seem quaint in retrospect; as with G. M. Cohen in the last chapter, scholars who have considered the era largely efface perspectives like Hecht's and Ensel's in favor of a trajectory of increasingly sophisticated art music composition.[5] Their exchange, however, comprises a rich musical dialogue that contributed to the larger local aim of "building Jewish religious, social, and cultural institutions," ultimately developing middle-class norms that, in Amy Hill Shevitz's words, "helped build American pluralism at the same time that they transformed Judaism into an American way of life."[6] Both Ensel and Hecht came to their positions as synagogue readers, trained in Germany to integrate music and prayer through education. Yet they took different positions on how to energize their small but active congregations. Ensel produced the first substantial scholarly treatise on music in Judaism on American soil, significantly predating—and predicting—the currently accepted historiographic time line of Jewish musicology; Hecht, a lifetime pedagogue, strenuously sought respect for the cantor as a "people's preacher," whose ideal balance of education, musical knowledge, and religious leadership effectively served the needs of smaller communities. Both, moreover, lived their middle-class ideals: excepting a brief period during which he worked with Isaac Mayer Wise to introduce the *Minhag America* liturgy in Cincinnati, Ensel rendered his ecclesiastical services part-time while running small businesses; and Hecht's career as an educator far exceeded his five-year tenure (1866–71) in the pulpit of Evansville's B'nai Israel.

Their alternative model of American Jewish musical identity emphasized service over employment, so smaller, financially precarious communities could maintain viable musical programs amid the uncertain availability of resources. Rather than representing part of an illiterate and uninformed generation, in other words, the intertwined stories of Ensel and Hecht indicate a musical pragmatism necessary for a tiny Jewish minority to establish itself in the American church-based ecosystem, particularly in small towns. They relied heavily on cultivating open dialogue with other religious music reform movements such as the Germany-based Cecilia Societies, and Protestant groups of various stripes who experimented with different approaches to corporate singing. They also promoted a view of musical history compatible with broad-based scholarly discussions of ancient musical origins. And they offered practical options for meaningful worship in the rapidly changing communal landscape of mid- to late nineteenth-century Jewish American settlement.[7]

From Germany: A First Debate Over Synagogue Song

Ensel and Hecht grew up among a generation of Jewish teacher/leaders, educated via a patchwork of developing training institutions that connected regional universities with local Jewish academies. Gustav S. Ensel, born in the southern Bavarian town of Hechingen (Hohenzollern), Germany, on April 7, 1827, trained in choral, instrumental, and piano performance with local masters, likely in parallel to his religious training.[8] He took his first Jewish leadership post under Rabbi Bernhard Wechsler in the northern port city of Varel (Friesland) from 1846 to 1855 as a "teacher, cantor, and slaughterer."[9] Hecht, born 250 miles to the north in Nordheim in the mid-1820s, trained with his brother Emanuel in Würzburg during the 1840s, learned Jewish texts with Rabbi Seligman Bamburger, and completed teacher training at the city's university.[10] Ensel and Hecht began their service at a time of shifting Jewish identity, where local communities, including the nearby Jewish authority of Württemberg/Stuttgart, created songbooks and hymnals to promote a coherent, modern Jewish identity bridging synagogue, school, and home (see chap. 2).[11] Undoubtedly also aware of the trend toward new composition emerging since Salomon Sulzer's appointment to the pulpit of Vienna's Seitenstettengasse synagogue in the late 1820s, Ensel, Hecht, and their circle of community-based trained readers avoided such a complex (and expensive) path as unrealistic in the small populations they served. Instead, taking inspiration from such musical facilitators as Israel Jacobson of Seesen and Berlin, they advocated for congregational participation, including communal hymn-singing, to promote the religious spirit of the age.[12]

The combination of musical and religious skills that their one-man pulpits entailed, and their self-identified struggles to bring progressive views to their constituents, led Ensel, Hecht, and their contemporaries to begin envisioning a new professional role that some called the *Volkslehrer*, or "people's minister." In a series of letters to the *Allgemeine Zeitung des Judenthums* in 1849, several of the central players began offering perspectives on how such a leadership position might be framed both socially and historically.

Hecht, in his contributions, drew on his early experiences at congregations in Bavaria's Lower Franconia to describe a rigged educational system for teacher/rabbis that reeked of empty conservatism, because congregations, rather than the government, supported Jewish seminarians. A candidate might first charm a community with his ability to "make a beautiful operatic song to the *Lecho Dodi*, and here and there interweave a lively Schottische through the text of a Jewish prayer," but then, through rabbi Bamburger's influence, acquire a conservative "Jesuit-like" face and costume "as second nature."[13] The resulting scene, in Hecht's view, meant that anti-intellectual "Old Believers" could squelch emerging trends in choral singing by claiming that they too closely resembled Christian practices. His experiences with Sulzdorf's congregation, which dismissed him in 1848 "because [he] did not give the right emphasis to the [*Shochen Ad* prayer] and [thereby] handled Eve's apple," led him to urge progressive preachers to range outside of Bavaria to "find their sphere of influence."[14]

Two months later, writing from an apparently more accommodating position in Weimarschmieden, Hecht began to construct a two-step approach to synagogue song that could profitably translate the antiquated "traditional" (*traditionellen*) musical practices he attributed to an era of "choral director-hazanim," into what he saw as a much-improved contemporary (*zeitgemäßen*) practice of rabbinically supervised music.[15] His first step, echoing Sulzer on a more participatory level, involved a "choral revision" process that systematically excluded popular tunes and encouraged composers to turn artfully to traditional melodies as source material: shortening and simplifying them for mass singing and pairing them with appropriate prayer texts. The second step, a true contemporary musical canon, would occur "once the Israelites became increasingly used to this progress, and no longer found these improved old songs adequate."[16] Hecht suggested a set of guidelines for composing such music:

1. The melody and music must agree with the meaning of the text; it would therefore be a contradiction to put a Hallelujah in the minor style and a pleading prayer in the major.
2. The melody must be easy to harmonize and be uplifting.
3. The melody must be compatible with (average) human voices.
4. The song may be neither too slow nor too fast in order to evince a soulful character.
5. The song should contain nothing operatic or dancelike.
6. The song must avoid any trendy effect (*Knalleffekt*).[17]

Hecht's article spurred a lively conversation in the journal, to which Ensel added his voice on June 18, 1849.[18] In the wake of his recent work on the dedication of Varel's new sanctuary, Ensel laid out a practical philosophy of Jewish music that emphasized "refurbishing and simplifying the existing chants" to champion congregants' natural abilities. He criticized attempts by cantors to "strengthen their own power" by composing complex harmonic music, and he rebutted a previous writer's claim that laypeople could not carry a tune.[19] Recalling the Varel synagogue inauguration, Ensel described how he began about three months beforehand to hold music sessions with thirty congregants two to three times a week. Rather than focusing on creating sonorous harmonies, he introduced congregational melodies through "repeated playing on the violin." Ensel later reinforced these melodies by "providing rhythmic accompaniment on the piano" (likely indicating underlying harmonic changes) to give congregants a stronger structural context for their singing. By the July inauguration, he claimed, even those congregants who had not attended the training sessions felt comfortable singing along. People also added their own organic harmonies: some improvised a second voice, while others intoned "an extremely simple but proper bass." Ensel downplayed the constant demand for new music: "If, in many communities, cantors have been less successful in their attempts at reform, in my opinion that is not so much because of the lack of suitable music, as it is by the incorrect use of existing music."[20] He then concluded by outlining future steps for simplifying the liturgy, such as eliminating poetic hymns (*piyyutim*) that encouraged unnecessary musical complexity, and publishing an inexpensive monthly Jewish music journal—printed in a format "already used in so many choral and folksong books"—that could enhance congregational participation further. "And to those zealots who do not want to sacrifice their own harmonious singing," he gave as a parting shot, "we declare with [Ludwig] Uhland: 'Where's there's singing, settle down / Evil people have no songs.'"[21] The twenty-two-year-old thus articulated his support of synagogue music reform as a means of democratization, joining others who questioned the "artful" direction of Sulzer's followers. Even Ensel's most controversial assertion—that the "superficial yodeling" Hecht and others sought to strip from Jewish prayer actually contained much of those melodies' "character"—spoke to a preference for a populist folk-aesthetic over imposed (elite) artistic standards.[22]

These conversations led Herman Ehrlich, reader of Berkach (near Meiningen), to renew his call to establish a regular journal devoted to synagogue music. Hecht responded that he had his own synagogue chant publication project in the works but offered Ehrlich both his support and that of his brother Emanuel, by then a prolific theologian.[23] In 1851, Ehrlich published the first issue of *Der Israelitische Volkslehrer*, a periodical that sought to standardize the local preacher's musical portfolio through a combination of philosophical treatises, practical instruction, and music dissemination. Ensel, perhaps content with his own knowledge, did not contribute to the journal during its nine-year run (1851–60). Simon Hecht contributed occasionally, however, introducing its material to his congregation and once noting with pride that even churches used some of the journal's articles. His brother also provided frequent articles and musical selections.[24] While their 1849 conversation did not necessarily lead directly to the journal's appearance, it did crystallize the sentiment of the time, with Simon Hecht and Ensel contributing to a drive to endow local synagogue readers with a mantle of both musical and liturgical authority, as an alternative to the urban majesty of Sulzer's obercantor.

Ensel: Introducing Isaac Mayer Wise's *Minhag America*

In mid-1857, after a two-year tour as the religious leader of Bremen's young Jewish community, Ensel came to the United States. Perhaps with an eye toward working with Isaac Mayer Wise, he settled in Cincinnati and advertised his availability as a piano teacher.[25] By September, congregation Bene Yeshurun (KKBY) viewed his skills favorably, and hired him as "Chazan pro tem," at a prorated salary of $400 (paid $25 monthly).[26] The date of the hire, at the congregation's annual meeting between Rosh Hashanah and Yom Kippur, gave Ensel little time to prepare the musically intense

Day of Atonement services. But it also presaged a still more significant task: introducing Wise's hotly anticipated *Minhag America* liturgy, adopted by congregational vote in the same meeting.[27] Just the previous year, Wise had characterized the hazan as an unnecessary drain of resources on congregations thirsting instead for intellectual leadership, arguing, "Let the singing of the Minister be altogether abolished, all the singing and chanting ought to be done by the choir or congregation or by both jointly . . . and let the Minister preside over it and direct it so that his principal part may be the expounding of the Law."[28] The elaborate nature of the new liturgy, however, likely proved more than Wise could handle on his own. He backtracked for the sake of practicality, recognizing that choirs and congregational singing could not easily organize themselves.

Ensel inherited a well-appointed musical program with a recently expanded building, an ample choir loft, and an organ with a professional organist; he also took a position in the community's school, the Talmud Yelodim Institute (TYI), which had incorporated choral singing into the curriculum. Such an arrangement accelerated ongoing concerns about the choir's relative professionalism during services, the role of congregational singing, and the status of the service as a balance of beauty, knowledge, and ideological "progress." After the building's expansion and rededication ceremonies in 1855, for example, the synagogue board faced regular requests for payment from its "volunteer" congregational choristers and had to devise public (and low-cost) ways to honor member-singers while maintaining a budget for skilled outsiders (especially a "Tenorist").[29] It thus fell to Ensel to effect a balance between Wise's ideal of organic congregational musicality and the practical aesthetics required to achieve that ideal. Wise publicly affirmed Ensel's initial work after Yom Kippur, especially noting his "grand chorus" of the hymn "Hayom Haras Olam" ("Today Is the Birthday of the World")—which "speaks well for the musical talent of this young man, and shows his thorough knowledge of harmony."[30] Yet he likely knew that the new liturgy would require coordination of a different magnitude.

Wise appeared to approach *Minhag America* as a collaborative form that brought the congregation's musical forces, its progressive philosophy, and the TYI into a cohesive, mutually reinforcing system that satisfied all the community's demographic groups. Ensel, tasked with realizing Wise's plan, consequently had to rehearse both the largely volunteer choir and the TYI students to prepare the music-heavy premiere as an event that balanced religious and pedagogical functions. Such intricately orchestrated expectations, however, taxed Ensel to the point that Wise ultimately had to delay the liturgy's premiere from the first day of Sukkot (Friday night, October 2, 1857) to the first Friday after Sukkot (October 16) so that Ensel could prepare the choral forces more fully.[31] The week's delay seemed to pay off: Wise described afterward the complex interplay of choir, TYI students, and hazan as an interactive liturgical community, with each linguistic, artistic, or age-based cohort contributing in kind. When the hazan and the TYI students alternated lines of "the *Ashre*" (mainly Psalm 145, with introductory and conclusion verses from other psalms)—a prayer presumably taught in the school but unfamiliar to many parents—Wise described the experience as "intended for the whole congregation, who should become used to it in this way."[32] Ensel presented similarly coordinated moments throughout the Friday night and Saturday morning services, including a number of Sulzer compositions reconfigured to Wise's significantly altered liturgical text. Thus enacted, the weekend aimed to establish a seamless, relevant ritual that made the Sabbath a focal point for congregational unity. Music's centrality to the ritual's success became clearer still when Ensel placed an ad in *The Israelite* the following week, offering "to all congregations having introduced the MINHAG AMERICA, a complete copy of all the music, solos, choruses and recitations, as used in the Synagogue in Lodge Street." His announcement, which preceded the announced sale of the *Minhag America* text itself, remained in the paper for the next ten issues.[33]

Ensel's work with the congregation would be short-lived. While synagogue records show no open conflict with Bene Yeshurun's choir, congregation, or leadership, the ambitious agenda of the new liturgy and its music may have proven a less-than-perfect match with Ensel's own ideas—exemplified by his January 1858 editorial in *Die Deborah* cautioning against the trendy attractions of *"Bildung"* (culture/education) at the expense of a solid moral compass.[34] In March 1858, older and better-known Rabbi G. M. Cohen (1820–1902), who had proven his own musical and choral bona fides at New York's Temple Emanu-El from 1845 to 1852, indicated his availability for the Bene Yeshurun pulpit; two months later, the congregants voted Cohen into the position by a count of fifty to twenty-eight.[35] Ensel received a $50 severance payment and remained at least a few months longer in the city as one of Wise's recognized "professors of music" before departing westward.[36]

Ensel in St. Louis: Smaller Fields, Wider Visions

Ensel soon arrived in St. Louis, where he established a liquor shop with his father and brothers (who had also recently emigrated). With business appearing to satisfy his financial needs, Ensel continued his musical activities on a volunteer basis with the city's reform-minded B'nei El congregation. On July 8, 1859, Isaac Mayer Wise happily reported in *The Israelite* of Ensel's success in premiering the synagogue's first choir with organ accompaniment; the congregation showed its appreciation in the following months by presenting Ensel with honorary membership, materially represented by an inscribed ring.[37] Ensel continued as B'nei El's volunteer choir director through the 1860s—seeming to take permanent direction of the choir only in 1863—and received regular approbation for his work from Wise and other correspondents.[38] His participation in the cornerstone-laying and inauguration ceremonies for the city's new Shaare Emeth synagogue, in 1867 and 1869, respectively, led to particular praise.[39] Even though Ensel, who became a naturalized citizen in June 1866, appeared to publish little during this period, his method seemed mostly consistent with his 1849 editorial: empowering members of the choir to take charge of their own synagogue music, while presenting himself as an amateur with professional training. Ensel later pointed to this time as the start of his formal study of sacred music, perhaps in part because his switch to synagogue music as an avocation allowed him to participate more broadly in religious musical circles, thus whetting his intellectual appetite.[40]

Ensel had begun to split his time between St. Louis and Springfield, Illinois, as early as 1868, where he ran a liquor store with G. A. Mayer; and he appeared to take up full residence in Springfield by 1874.[41] Newspaper records show his involvement in several musical functions there, such as playing organ for a Baptist wedding and Catholic Easter service, and briefly serving as president of Springfield's Musical Union.[42] As in St. Louis, Ensel pushed to advance reforms, this time through the local synagogue B'rith Sholem—a congregation that, noted Isaac Mayer Wise, "though small in number, is not so in means."[43] Banding together with the congregation's well-off members, Ensel established a Sabbath School by 1875 and received credit for introducing the latest version of Baltimore rabbi Benjamin Szold's liberal-leaning *Avodat Yisrael* liturgy, released in a German-English edition by Philadelphia rabbi Marcus Jastrow in 1873. The following year, when the congregation dedicated its new building, Ensel played the organ and directed an amateur choir of Jewish and non-Jewish singers.[44] Music, regularly rendered in services alongside Ensel's own English-language sermons, thus became a preoccupation of the community and a way for the congregation to assert its national significance in the changing religious landscape.[45] Ensel's activity caused his stock to rise within the recently established Union of American Hebrew Congregations (UAHC) as well. As the congregation's regular service leader, he held the title of "reverend" in the Union's 1878 meeting proceedings, became a member of its national finance committee, and continued as the community's representative in successive national gatherings.[46]

Simon Hecht's Journey to Evansville, Indiana

In the same year that Ensel became an American citizen, Simon Hecht became the new religious leader of the Jewish community in Evansville, Indiana. During the 1850s and 1860s, Hecht had occupied spiritual and educational positions in Ritzebüttel (near Hamburg, 1852–53), Jever (1856), and Glan-Münchweiler (1857–60), among others. He continued to publish articles on both music and social conditions, while developing a strong advocacy for children's school-based singing pedagogy. In 1856, Hecht praised Magdeburg rabbi Ludwig Philippson's new hymnal for its artfulness and its quick tempi, and then launched into a request to include a children's section in a subsequent edition, followed by a general call to make "vocal instruction in the Jewish schools . . . a compulsory subject."[47] Two years later, Hecht expanded this call, deeming regular, school-based voice study a more effective investment than organ accompaniment in promoting congregational singing and Jewish identity.[48]

In his 1859 marriage to Regina Heimann, Hecht perhaps unintentionally set his future plans.[49] Heimann's brothers David and Isaac had migrated to Evansville, Indiana, in the 1850s, and become leaders in the town's Jewish community—a small but ambitious group that pushed moderate reforms, including the introduction of Salomon Sulzer's music by a mixed choir in 1860.[50] In May 1866, the population advertised for a new spiritual leader to accompany the opening of their new, large sanctuary, and to lead a choir and teach both German and Hebrew.[51] Hecht, whose beloved brother Emanuel's death in 1862 may have cut his strongest ties to Europe, applied and received the call from his in-laws. While he may have arrived in Evansville before the synagogue's early August consecration, Hecht's name did not appear in the main local account of the ceremony, perhaps overshadowed by both the appearance of Isaac Mayer Wise as the guest officiant, and the congregation's decision to adopt Wise's *Minhag America*. The choir received high marks, though, for its renditions of works by Sulzer and Sigmund Schlesinger.[52]

Over the next five years, his salary rising from $1,200 to $1,600 in 1867, Hecht worked to promote congregational singing in a manner consistent with his philosophies, aiming to give each boy and girl vocal training and ample performance opportunities. To serve his new country's Jewish youth further, he repackaged German rabbi Salomon Herxheimer's catechism-like textbook *Yesod HaTorah* into a confirmation guide for German Jewish American students, and appended his own musical selections.[53] Hecht reiterated his ideas in an 1870 editorial in *Die Deborah* in which he championed choral singing over opera-style, solo-based synagogue music; vigorously sought to distinguish true Jewish music from "the pompous music of the Catholic mass nor the sluggish protestant church singing" arbitrarily introduced by non-Jewish choral directors; dismissed works by Sulzer, Naumbourg, and their ilk as unsuited to American liturgy; and announced his intention to create a chorale book of adapted traditional tunes that would give the American synagogue a uniform repertoire and sound.[54] Such claims, which Hecht hoped would serve as an introduction to an unrealized series of articles in *Die Deborah*, made direct reference to his 1849 *Allgemeine Zeitung des Judenthums* article, affirming the continuation of his small-town project as he labored in his new American setting.

Positive reports from visitors to Evansville show Hecht's work paying off locally. An account in *The Israelite* in March 1871 faulted the organ for excessive volume during the synagogue ritual but noted how "the choir, composed of a number of young ladies and gentlemen of the congregation, some of whom sing remarkably well, does much toward making the services interesting and impressive."[55] Yet later that year, Hecht left his position to teach German in the public schools across the river in Henderson, Kentucky.[56] He would not return until 1876, as he continued to advocate for German culture and musical training on a broader, ecumenical social stage.

Forging the American Jewish Soundtrack for the New UAHC: A Contest and a Debate

In the late 1870s, the UAHC obliquely rekindled the thirty-year-old intellectual rivalry between Ensel and Hecht, in the process accelerating the former's scholarly interest in music. As a young organization seeking to address matters of common need among its varied congregations, the Union sought to improve the lot of its members' Sabbath Schools by creating a uniform set of educational materials. Music factored into this discussion from the start, though with some misgivings about its utility.[57] Consequently, at the Union's fourth meeting in 1877, President Moritz Loth included among the group's ambitions "to vote a liberal prize for the composition of hymns, to be sung at the opening and closing exercises of the Sabbath-school."[58] By the time the meeting closed, the idea of creating a musical repertoire had expanded into a contest for the best Sabbath School hymnal, with a $50 award and the prospect of national usage.[59] Only Hecht submitted a full entry over the following months: his work *Zemirot Yisrael*, containing forty-three English hymns and nine German hymns with texts from Isaac Mayer Wise, Missouri rabbi Isaac Schwab, and public school hymnal author G. B. Loomis, as well as patriotic and pedagogical songs from other sources (see fig. 4.1).[60] Hecht supplied about a quarter of the music for the book, which ranged from one to four voices in simple keys, and looked to local musicians for most of the rest (see fig. 4.2).[61] Likely due to the number of non-Jewish texts and composers, the judging committee of Max Lilienthal, James K. Gutheim, George Jacobs, Emil G. Hirsch, and Louis Naumburg did not find it worthy of the prize.[62]

Perhaps with an inside knowledge of the competition, Ensel joined the conversation through the columns of *Die Deborah*. In a September 20, 1878, article titled, "On Synagogue Music," he offered his own ideas on such a publication's scope and purpose.[63] Hailing the UAHC's competition as a remedy to a long-standing lack of attention to American Jewish music composition, he critiqued the existing options for their narrow focus and simplistic melodies. Instead, he laid out a far-reaching philosophy that went beyond the hymns' immediate pedagogical function, highlighting instead the need for such music to transform students over time into competent and devoted synagogue singers, able to read Hebrew and trained in effective versification. At the core of his argument, Ensel held in mind the needs of small congregations that comprised a majority of the Union's members:

> The works already published for the synagogue are not only very expensive for a large part of our congregations, but also offer songs which can only be mastered by such choirs, whose money and vocal means are unlimited. Here we have many communities with 20–40 members who are not able to salary professionally trained male and female singers as well as an organist who is famous as an artist. Most of the congregations recruit their chorus from their

זְמִרוֹת יִשְׂרָאֵל

JEWISH HYMNS

— FOR —

Sabbath-Schools and Families,

(ENGLISH AND GERMAN),

— BY —

REV. SIMON HECHT,

Evansville, Ind.

BLOCH & CO.,
Publishers and Printers, Cincinnati, O.

Figure 4.1. Simon Hecht, *Zemirot Yisrael* (Bloch, 1878), cover.

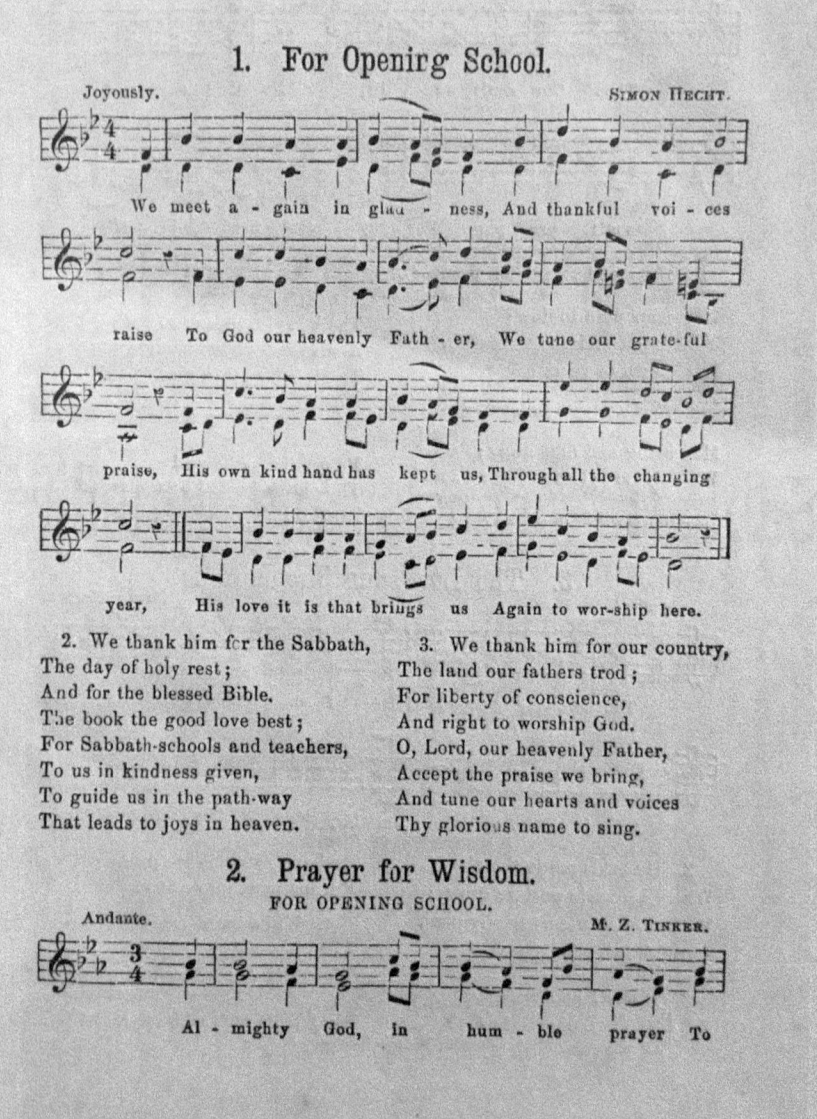

Figure 4.2. Opening songs in two parts from Hecht, *Zemirot Yisrael*. Music pedagogue M. Z. Tinker, author of song no. 2 ("Prayer for Wisdom") and six others in the hymnal, directed music education in Evansville's public schools. Hecht's hymnal also included original contributions from local musicians P. Esser, C. C. Genung, and Christian Mathias.

own midst, where singers and choir directors rarely rise above the simplest dilettantism. For them, a selection of the lighter compositions by our masters [Sulzer and Naumbourg, Welsch, and Kaiser] would be a most welcome gift, and, I am sure, would also be greeted by non-Jews *(Fremden)*.[64]

Continuing what he hoped would be the first of a series of articles, Ensel hailed the seventeenth-century Mantuan composer Salamone Rossi as another "master" recently rediscovered by Samuel Naumbourg. While presenting Rossi's work as usable material for a viable hymnal, Ensel also saw his achievements as a Jewish analogue to the lives of other "great" Renaissance composers supported by the church, such as Claude Goudimel, Orlando di Lasso, and Giovanni Palestrina, and hoped that Rossi could inspire similar musical support in the contemporary synagogue.

A few weeks later, Simon Hecht responded with a long and energetic defense of the Sabbath School hymnal, which he believed should focus on children alone.[65] Writing from his sick bed at the end of a months-long illness, Hecht categorically argued that no school hymnal could satisfy Ensel's overreaching program; he pointed to the parameters of the UAHC's contest, which pointed specifically to Sabbath School usage, as justification. Regardless of the contest committee's decision, however, Hecht spoke with pride about the success of his own work, *Zemirot Yisrael*, which had sold more than 1,500 copies and gained wide adoption in St. Louis, New York, and elsewhere across the country.[66] With some swagger, Hecht then claimed that should the committee adopt Ensel's proposed standards, he would quickly come out with a worthy "Kol bon" (*kolbo*; containing all things) to match them as well.[67]

Although Hecht's response vigorously rebutted Ensel's ideas on the hymnal, they sidestepped Ensel's historical disquisition. Ensel's proposed second article, titled, "What Specifically Is Jewish Music? What Is Its Source? And Is It Desirable to Preserve It for Modern Jewish Worship?" never materialized in *Die Deborah*. This line of thought, however, appeared to inspire Ensel to explore further a historical basis for his philosophy of synagogue music practice, particularly his interest in the relationship between Jewish music and the musical practices of their host societies.

G. S. Ensel as Jewish Music Scholar

Ensel's financial security as a small business owner gave him the latitude to develop a new identity as a recognized scholar of sacred music.

Two years after Springfield's new synagogue building opened, Ensel gave a pair of lectures on sacred music to general audiences: the first initially for the Springfield Literary Society and the second for the local Scientific Academy. Drawing on the work of contemporary music scholars, Ensel used these lectures to trace music's evolutionary history through intellectual developments in human society—in this case, starting with the civilization of the ancient Middle East/Orient and then tracking forward with increasing sophistication and complexity into modern Europe. In doing so, he attempted a corrective to the major European music historians up to that time, such as Giovanni Martini, Charles Burney, Johann Forkel, and François-Joseph Fétis, who only mentioned the ancient Hebrews early in their narratives.[68] As Bennett Zon notes, in a claim easily extendable from his discussion of British nineteenth-century musical scholarship, the motivations behind such historians' claims reflected a quietly ingrained tendency to characterize Jews as relevant to the development of Western music only in their position as precursors to Christianity.[69] While Jewish musician/scholars such as Emmanuel Hecht, Hermann Ehrlich, Samuel Naumbourg, Arnold Marksohn, and William Wolf had begun to respond to these narratives by the time of Ensel's lectures, their work had largely appeared in European Jewish publications with limited external readership.[70] Ensel, aware of these and other efforts, sought to craft a story that appealed to a broad American audience by addressing liturgical music as a joint development of the three major Abrahamic religions. His lectures thus offered a variant on the "ethnic genres" strategy that Ann Ostendorf deemed "a practical way [for nineteenth-century Americans] to consider the various and clearly identified cultural groups through exposure to what was *perceived* to be their music ways."[71] Ensel's communal history approach gave the sound of Jewish liturgical music a more comfortable middle ground in the Occidental-Oriental continuum (with Islam, rather than Judaism, epitomizing "the East"). Once released from the strict sonic East-West opposition of his predecessor scholars, a Jewish musical narrative could slowly forge its own path beyond the biblical period and claim developments parallel to the prevailing Christian-centered history. Ensel prepared live musical examples to supplement his text, hoping in the end "to instruct [his] hearers, by demonstrating, through *argument* and *vocal* illustrations combined, that the many analogies which exist between the liturgical music of the Synagogue, Church, and even the Mosque, point to one common origin."[72]

Ensel gave his initial lecture at Springfield's First Congregational Church on Wednesday night, November 27, 1878; poster illustrations provided visuals, and a mixed double quartet, accompanied by Ensel on the congregation's organ, offered musical examples.[73] Arranging his talk in a four-part chronological format, Ensel began by describing ancient musical practices from evidence found in European museums' instrument collections, and emphasized that Jews were the only group to bring these practices into the present day. He then addressed Gregorian chant in the early church and followed developments through the late Renaissance that transformed sacred music from a beautiful product of the elite—illustrated with a performance of Palestrina's 1561 "Improperia"—into the more democratizing Reformation that advocated group singing and brought popular tunes into religious life. Ensel's final section, on "modern" liturgical music styles, allowed the two soprano soloists to shine with performances of Luigi Luzzi's 1866 "Ave Maria" (Op. 80) and the "Inflammatus" from Rossini's 1841 *Stabat Mater*. The enthusiastic response to Ensel's lecture led him to reprise the presentation twice over the next two months, with the proceeds benefiting the city's indigent population.[74] Despite its steadfastly ecumenical content, Ensel's own Jewish identity influenced the lecture's reception both locally and nationally. Coverage in *The American Israelite*, for example, reprinted a local account of the talk under the title, "Hebrew Music," with a short editorial introduction clarifying that Ensel "feels a special attachment to Hebrew music, which, we expect[,] he will place in a proper light before intellectual friends of music."[75] Before a year had passed, Ensel had delivered a version of his talk in St. Louis's Shaare Emeth congregation, reinforcing the Jewish population's growing recognition of music as a topic for public erudition.[76]

In December 1879, in front of Springfield's Scientific Academy, Ensel offered a second lecture, critically comparing biblical music to standards of contemporary liturgical performance. Extravagant accounts of biblical performances, he claimed, inspired awe only in their own time and context. Modern congregations would find them inferior when considered in terms of standard present-day criteria such as pitch (ancient instruments had only one pitch, if any at all), notation (no notation existed, thus necessitating shorter, memorized melodies), and ability (today's musicians, identified by talent, far surpassed ancient caste-based musicians). To illustrate his larger point, Ensel humorously described how the short French folk tune "Malbrook," played in Egypt by Napoleon's army band in 1799, roused the locals as no other tune had done—before revealing that "further investigation developed the fact that this tune was brought 700 years before from the Orient by crusaders and troubadours, and after its migrations among European musicians came now back to its original soil."[77] That the tune remained a favorite in Euro-America as "We Won't Come Home Till Morning" (and later as "For He's a Jolly Good Fellow") emphasized Ensel's claim that the simple qualities of ancient music rendered it no better than a pop tune by the late 1870s.

Both lectures relied heavily and implicitly on the precedents of Martini, Forkel, Burney, Fétis, and others.[78] Yet by critiquing their ideas in an American setting, Ensel could open up a more robust conversation between Judaism and the hegemonic historical trajectory of Christianity. Ensel's access to and knowledge of the leading works of music history in at least three major scholarly languages affirmed his cosmopolitan outlook within Springfield's small but active center as a state capital and railroad hub.[79] Combined with positive attention from the proponents of American Jewish reform, who similarly tried to use a narrative of European development alongside Christianity to integrate Judaism into American religious life, the discussion generated by these lectures likely encouraged Ensel to begin formalizing his ideas on paper for a wider readership.

Ensel's developing philosophy on synagogue music took its first published form in a contrasting pair of music reviews for Jewish publications. In a glowing 1879 assessment of cantor/composer Alois Kaiser's "Requiem for the Day of Atonement" in *The American Israelite*, Ensel praised the work as a "valuable addition" to the "musical literature of the synagogue" and a meaningful update of the Yom Kippur afternoon Yizkor/Remembrance service.[80] Ensel commended Kaiser's decision to use a recent, integrated text by rabbis Benjamin Szold (Baltimore) and Marcus Jastrow (Philadelphia), which to him gave the ritual a flowing quality and improved upon "the disjointed hymns suggested by nearly all the modern prayerbooks of the Reform Temples."[81] Remaining consistent with his 1849 editorial, Ensel also gave high marks to Kaiser's artful and organic use of the "Kol Nidre" melody from Yom Kippur eve, comparing it to Giacomo Meyerbeer's interpolation of "A Mighty Fortress Is Our God"/"Ein feste Burg ist unser Gott" in his opera *Les Huguenots*, and Richard Wagner's use of his own Venus grotto and pilgrim's chorus music as leitmotifs in *Tannhäuser*: "the different phrases of Kol Nidre appear as so many flowers," Ensel mused, "artistically and judiciously interwoven with the green leaves of a wreath." Kaiser's "very successful attempt at utilizing our ancient traditional melodies into modern texts," moreover, not only gave the Yom Kippur liturgy a greater coherence by extending the sounds of "Kol Nidre" into the next day, but also established a precedent for other synagogue composers. "We ought to have a great many more of these old tunes, so arranged that they fit the texts of our modern prayer and hymn books," Ensel wrote. Taken together, these comments offered a more complex perspective on *piyyutim* than in earlier writings; to Ensel, new and appropriately written texts could serve as vessels for old melodies that might otherwise disappear. As he warned, "If this [new approach to composition] is not done, [traditional melodies] will soon be lost, as our present prayer books have abolished a number of Piutim and other texts, to which these beautiful melodies were adapted many centuries ago." Welcoming the potential of new art music compositions to the synagogue, even without direct congregational participation, Ensel steadfastly advocated for musical organicism and continuity.

For congregations, however, Ensel championed a different standard that justified the mindful use of melodies and texts from other religious communities. In an enthusiastic May 1880 review of the new *Hymn Book for Jewish Worship* by Rochester rabbi Max Landsberg and Sabbath School cofounder/lawyer Sol Wile, Ensel lauded the creators' ability to channel meaningful spiritual texts and melodies from Christian settings into the synagogue alongside Jewish traditional melodies.[82] "By denying their own individuality," he wrote of the compilers, "their collection contains more than a sufficient number of popular Church songs, whose texts are not only extremely suitable for the special Jewish consciousness, but also very favorable to the efforts of other writers in their practical arrangement and perfectly correct verse meter."[83] Ensel, defending the book, ridiculed calls for synagogues to use exclusively Jewish musical and prosodic content—the product of what he called "the narrow-minded fear of . . . the Ideas Association"—and instead cited a recent study of seventeenth-century Poland to contextualize Jewish musical borrowing within a centuries-long legacy of interreligious exchange.[84] After praising the hymnal's unique flip-book–style format, which gave organists the ability to mix and match texts and melodies, Ensel (rhetorically) called on the UAHC hymnal committee to award its prize to Landsberg and Wile, claiming that increased adoption and scale could cut its $1.00/copy price in half.[85] While a proponent of art music, in other words, Ensel maintained a staunch interest in Jewish musical syncretism as a long-standing congregational practice that deserved its own present-day platform.

In the meantime, Ensel continued to work on his manuscript, which benefited from the suggestions of fellow Central European émigré Kaufmann Kohler.[86] Kohler appeared to like the work but warned Ensel of numerous "Germanisms" that might alienate American readers. Ensel consequently gave his manuscript to "an American friend" for editing, later noting with satisfaction that his colleague's "scientific education enabled him fully in making the review text readable."[87]

Ensel originally planned to produce his work through the more standard lithographic (plate-based) method. The projected outlay for the copious illustrations he needed, however—which he estimated at $1,500–$1,800 (approximately $35,000–$42,000 in 2017 dollars)—forced him to resort to a substantially lower cost hectograph process.[88] This relatively recent publishing technique, requiring the author to write the original manuscript with a special ink that could transfer onto a gelatin surface, allowed for intricate illustrations while circumventing the high price of producing wooden or stone plates. Because the gelatin could store only a limited amount of ink, however, copy quality degraded quickly, and resulted in small print runs. Ensel's (typical) case yielded about twenty usable copies, which he had professionally bound.[89]

Inside *Ancient Liturgical Music*

The final work—with the idiomatically grandiose title, *Ancient Liturgical Music: A Comparative and Historical Essay on the Origin and Development of Sacred Music from the Earliest Times, with Illustrations of the Music Employed in the Worship of the Synagogue, Church & Mosque* (herein *ALM*)— presented Ensel's musical philosophy in its fullest form (see fig. 4.3).[90] He emulated the approaches of prevailing treatises from both musicologists and composer/cantors, sometimes even incorporating passages directly into his own text (usually but not always cited). Yet his ideas went far beyond those works, aiming to correct the "exceedingly inadequate and in many cases inaccurate" claims of non-Jewish writers, while expanding the brief offerings of "unquestionable authorities" on Jewish music into a substantial contribution to general discourse.[91] Sixty-eight images of ancient instruments accompanied Ensel's arguments, as did numerous meticulously copied musical examples illustrating the history of musical notation, from chant, to tablature, to conventional staff notation ("modern notes"). He also made an effort to present his musical material, particularly melodies he saw as ancient, in an idiomatic manner that contemporary general audiences could understand.

Figure 4.3. G. S. Ensel, *Ancient Liturgical Music*, title page.

Drawing from previous experience, he surmised that providing these melodies with an "imaginary and modern" harmonic accompaniment could fulfill nineteenth-century readers' expectations, while helping lead them through phrasings and contours they might otherwise find foreign. These elements added up to an inquisitively transgressive approach to liturgical music, which Ensel bemusedly described on more than one occasion as equivalent to "the boy who broke his drum in order to see what made the noise."[92]

Ensel began by describing music as an organic outgrowth of human intellect, an important vessel of emotion (in the style of philosopher

H. R. Haweis's popular 1871 book *Music and Morals*), and therefore "the most important auxiliary to the Ritual of a Church."[93] This premise allowed him to promote the idea of music as "neither the invention of one person, nor of one people, nor yet of one period, but the gradual development of an inherent gift which grows up, under favorable conditions, from very small beginnings, like a seed corn to a mighty and stately tree, bearing on its branches the ripening fruit."[94] Although the prolonged evolutionary time scale invoked a common strategy for tracking musical development, Ensel's use of the phrase "under favorable conditions" opened an opportunity for Jews to enter the narrative via an alternate pathway. He set up this narrative by dutifully describing the most ancient Israelite music as an inheritance from Egyptian culture during the biblical slavery period, illustrated through a setting of "Miriam's Song on the Red Sea" (see fig. 4.4).[95] This transitional moment symbolized to him the emergence of an autonomous Jewish culture, and served to launch a millennia-long retelling of the Jewish musical story.

The first half of *ALM* presented a thoroughly researched summary of existing literature on the music of the ancient world, punctuated by short sections of more original commentary intended to connect with current-day liberal Jewish practices. A long chapter on organology, with credited images reproduced from contemporary compendia and a significant bibliography, rehearsed the prevailing biblical taxonomy of strings-based, winds-based, and percussion instruments before tracing these instruments' linguistic and evolutionary morphology across the ancient world (which also extended to China and "The Hindoos").[96] One part of Ensel's discussion followed the ancient ram's horn as—in his view—it gradually developed into the modern family of brass instruments that contemporary liberal Jews used for the same purpose: "In many Synagogues (Temples) of the Reformed Jewish Congregations," he observed, "a quartet of our improved brass instruments is added to the Shofar, the effect of which is augmented by a well-trained chorus of singers, whose voices blend harmoniously with the sonorous tones of the Cornet, Trumpet and Trombone" (see fig. 4.5).[97] A similar conversation about reed instruments repeated a well-circulated claim connecting the biblical *magrepha* to the contemporary pipe organ, with Ensel again noting "that the reformed wing of the present Synagogue—redeemed from the fetters of rabbinical mediaeval observances in the Liturgy, have adopted the Organ as the musical instrument of the modern Jewish Temple, as it has been for centuries that of the Church."[98] More than just histories, these accounts naturalized liberal Jewish musical choices as both religiously

Figure 4.4. "Miriam's Song," from *Ancient Liturgical Music*.

Continued

Figure 4.4. *continued*

It may be here stated that in many Synagogues (Temples) of the Reformed Jewish Congregations, a quartet of our improved brass instruments is added to the Shofar, the effect of which is augmented by a well trained chorus of singers, whose voices blend harmoniously with the sonorous tones of the Cornet, Trumpet and Trombone.

The Shofar is sometimes mentioned in the Bible synonimously with the Keren קרן, or Keren Jobel קרן יבל. Rabbinical commentators translate "Jobel" by the word ram[*], but it is probable that it means "triumphant" or rejoicing; the English word "Jubilee" is a derivation of the Hebrew Jobel. The Keren was perhaps a horn of larger dimensions, than the Shofar, or more curved, which

would naturally change the pitch, if not the quality of tone. The Oliphant, used during the middle ages, was made from the tusk of an Elephant; hence its name. It was essentially the same instrument as that, used by the Ashantees, a people of Africa. Some commentators are of the opinion, that the Keren was made of brass and

[*] S. Herxheimer, Com. to Joshua, VI v. 4. 5.

Figure 4.5. Illustrated discussion of ram's horns from *Ancient Liturgical Music*.

Continued

31

very much curved, similar to the Karna of the Babylonians, the Keras of the Greek, and the cornu of the Romans.

The Chatsotsrah, חֲצֹצְרָה, so frequently mentioned in Scripture, was, beyond the least doubt, the straight metal trumpet with a "bell" or "pavillon" at the end. Assyrian and Egyptian bas reliefs show trumpets of various sizes.

Roman Cornu.   Egyptian Melekta.   Hebrew Trumpets.

The only representations known of ancient Hebrew trumpets, are seen on the Triumphal Arch of Titus in Rome, and on some ancient coins. These trumpets hardly differ from those of other nations of antiquity, and they were probably made after the pattern of the two silver trumpets, mentioned in Numbers X v. 2.

The trumpet was chiefly an instrument of martial music, as is testified by many scriptural passages; however, we know also from II Chron. V v. 12.13 that in the solemn Temple liturgy of King Salomon,

Figure 4.5. continued

specific and deeply continuous with the larger (inherently Christian) religious landscape.

Ensel addressed vocal practices similarly, normalizing exotic sounds by highlighting their evolution into modern usage. In discussing a detail of an ancient Assyrian bas-relief in which "one of the women holds her hand to the throat," for example, he made a direct parallel to what "the Arab and Persian women still do, when they make those shrill sounds, peculiar to Eastern vocal music."[99] That view became the basis of a less-than-complimentary commentary on Eastern European Jewish prayer leaders, with Ensel noting that "a similar custom is still prevailing among the cantors or Precentors of the Eastern and Polish synagogues."[100] Advocates of synagogue reform had connected new practices with biblical precedents before to minimize a seeming "break" from tradition. Ensel, in presenting this material for a broad American audience, appeared mainly concerned with opening new pathways of connection between ancient and modern, as befitted a Jewish story—but he also subtly added an idiosyncratic, yet persistent, overlay of orientalism to the conversation, as a distinguishing quality needing careful control.

In his next chapter, "The Character of Ancient Music," Ensel repeated the assertions of his second Springfield lecture—that "glowing descriptions . . . [of] the magnificence of the musical performances in the Temples and other public places" could not compare to music's modern standards—by explaining that ancient performances were "mainly directed to the awakening of sacred emotions during worship . . . to restore a deranged mind to its normal healthy condition."[101] Supporting his position by describing the general "unnatural" design of art and architecture from that time and claiming the inferiority of the period's instrument construction, Ensel's primitivist portrait of music set the stage for a discussion of the next thousand years, when harmony and notation would harness "sacred emotions" in ever more sophisticated and varied forms.

As with his chapter on musical instruments, Ensel's subsequent discussion of notation largely followed the parameters of existing scholarship but shifted to focus on the Jewish narrative. He began by critiquing Greek semiography (letter-based notation) as a system whose unwieldy rationalism strangled musical spontaneity and variability, with its (alleged) 1,620 symbols "secur[ing] the immobility of every note in a scale series, thus fixing pitch" (see fig. 4.6).[102] In contrast, Ensel turned to "Oriental" practices of scriptural recitation, exemplified by Hebrew cantillation. As opposed to is copied from Forkel, vol. I. in original characters; and the Hymn to Apollo in modern notes by Emil Naumann. (Musikgeschichte 131.) If the interpretation of these two specimens be authentic, then we may wonder at the poor achievements of an art which — according to Mythology, had enabled Orpheus to subdue Cerberus at the gate of Tartarus.

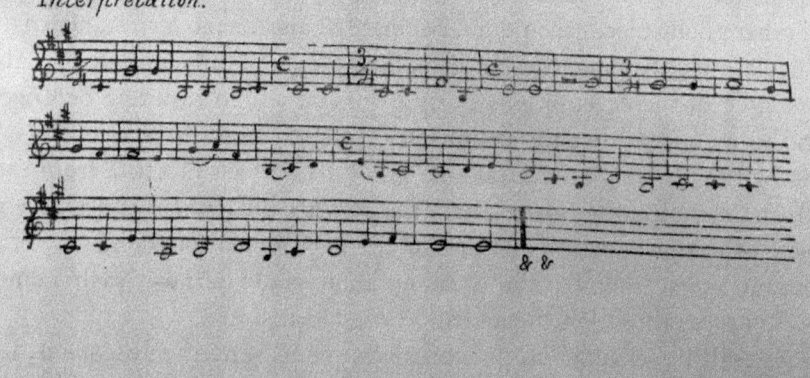

Figure 4.6. Illustration of Greek semiography notation from *Ancient Liturgical Music*.

Continued

Of the various interpretations which we possess of the following "Hymn of Pindar", two are here selected, to enable the reader to form an idea of the character of Greek music. Both the version of Burney and of Naumann must convince us, that this music held the middle between declamation and modulation, perhaps best compared with our modern "recitative". The employment of only four notes of the scale, (Tetrachord) with an occasional step above or below, invests the melody with a certain dignity and solemnity, which is also reflected in the Gregorian chant, as another chapter of this book will show. The "Hymnos" is composed for Solo, sung by the Coryphéus κορυφαῖος or leader, followed by a chorus of singers χορὸς εἰς κιθάρον, accompanied by one or more kitharas in unison or octave.

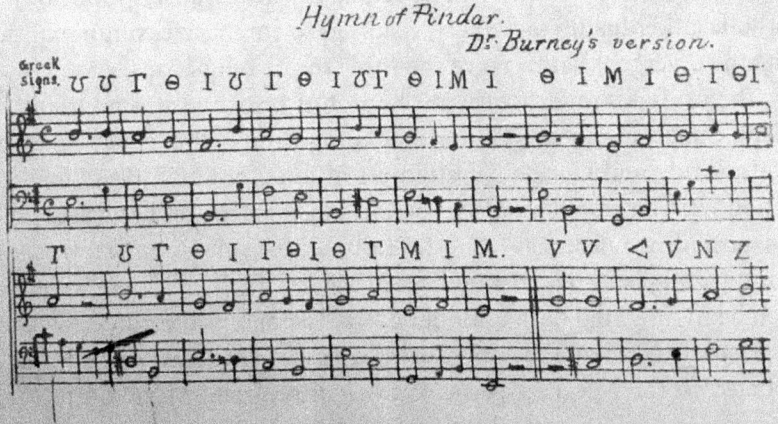

Figure 4.6. *continued*

the Greek (here read as proto-Western) system, Ensel claimed, "Oriental music is characterized by a slight melodic framework, around which profuse and extraneous ornamentations are clustering."[103] Used by "not only the Jews, but the Mahomedans, Parseis, Hindoos, and the Eastern Church," this more flexible form promoted emotional expression, as "a sort of irregular cantillation, often combined with a lively gesticulation and movement of the whole body."[104] Citing a lecture by recently appointed Hebrew Union College professor rabbi Moses Mielziner, Ensel assailed what he saw as intentionally misleading attempts by non-Jewish scholars to attribute primitive harmonic and rhythmic characteristics to the Hebrew cantillation signs.[105] He then laid out the system symbol by symbol with accompanying Western notation, and claimed that Jewish cantillation actually represented a forward-thinking musical practice with the flexibility to diversify as different religious systems developed. In this context, he viewed Hebrew cantillation's matrix of melodic fragments as the building blocks of Gregorian chant (and consequently, of Western music tradition), because its "ornate phrases, called 'melismatica' . . . probably point to an early Oriental origin."[106] Ensel followed by juxtaposing musical transcriptions of Jewish, Catholic, and Muslim sacred text readings to emphasize commonalities despite the divergent pathways of the three major religions.[107]

The psalms similarly became a point of transition from Orient to Occident, this time as a conduit for new compositions that could balance Oriental melody and Occidental attempts at fixed notation. Ensel began this section with an extensive discussion of music in the first and second Temples, providing references from the Talmud that imagined in retrospect the training and performance practices of the Levitical musicians and choir.[108] Then he highlighted both antiphonal singing and psalm tunes as examples of Oriental-Occidental balance, using a Jewish rendition of Psalm 144 that he dated to the Middle Ages as similar in self-determination to the later Lutheran hymn "Ein feste Burg ist unser Gott."[109] This comparison allowed Ensel to make a historical pivot from Jewish chant to Christian hymn singing through the oft-stated claim that "the first Christians . . . were mostly converted Jews, in whose religious assemblies Psalms and Hymns were sung."[110] Rejecting Greek and Roman music as too secular, Ensel cited a passage in Martini's eighteenth-century *Storia della Musica* to claim that newly converted Christians used the music of their birth religion to recruit other Jews.[111] These melodies subsequently became the bases for innovations that transitioned from the Syriac chant of the "Eastern Church" to

"Metrical Music" through the innovations of St. Ambrose and Pope Gregory VIII, Hucbald, Guido d'Arezzo, and subsequent champions of complex harmonic notation.[112] In each case, Ensel implied, the psalms illustrated how Oriental and Occidental influences balanced each other out in the church through the actions of talented individuals.

Once Christianity had absorbed their liturgical musical traditions, Ensel claimed, Jews found themselves pariahs, with constant persecution devastating the continuation of musical accompaniment and disrupting any further innovation. Using the axiom that persecuted peoples resisted adopting their oppressors' music, Ensel suggested that Jews subsequently looked inward, to the synagogue, as their only place of refuge: "Henceforth, the Sanctuary became the inexhaustible fountain, from which they drew the refreshing new pure waters of spiritual culture," Ensel wrote, in a nod to Jewish historian Leopold Zunz.[113] Jews of various communities, Ensel continued, turned to *piyyutim* and liturgy as a source of creativity well into the Middle Ages. In addition to compiling extensive bodies of text that ushered in the modern prayer book, they developed a broad range of musical materials that selectively incorporated the melodic and rhythmic forms around them. Cantors, in Ensel's view, became more prominent during this time as both communal leaders and as keepers of this new body of material.[114]

Ensel also used ideas of musical heterogeneity and exchange to rebut simplistic contemporary claims linking Jews' musical developments with their general level of acceptance or oppression in host societies, focusing instead on music as the product of multifaceted cultural interaction. To Ensel, the medieval era of Jewish dispersion allowed different communities to absorb the music of their respective neighbors in different ways, with East and West meeting through both common heritage and forced events such as the Crusades; folk (i.e., nonsacred) song regularly entered into the service during this time via settings for new hymns, for example. Ensel rebutted in particular what he (mis)interpreted as Naumbourg's claim that Sephardic Jews' tendency toward major tonalities resulted from their good relationship with the Moors, while the minor tunes of the Ashkenazic Jews reflected the sorrow of German Jewish persecution.[115] Instead, Ensel saw music emerging from more complex, localized interplay among different ethnic groups, emphasizing each community's agency in making its own musical choices. "It may be safely asserted," he claimed, "without fear of contradiction from unbiased critics, that the minor

[mode] chants of the Synagogue originated more from *ethnical* causes, than from *sentimental* motives—or, in other words, the Synagogue, like the Church, has *adopted* secular tunes and *adapted* them to its liturgical texts."[116] The musical conventions of the surrounding societies, he felt, held greater sway on the development of Jewish religious musical forms than previously acknowledged.

The significance of Jewish musical self-fashioning continued to develop as Ensel moved into the Reformation, the emergence of Protestantism, the reassertion of congregational choral singing, and then into the Jewish emancipation period of the nineteenth century. Recounting the career of Vienna's Salomon Sulzer as the Jewish analogue to Palestrina (ca. 1525–94), who removed "the dross, which centuries had accumulated" on synagogue music, Ensel welcomed the reintroduction of choirs and organs into Jewish worship and celebrated Naumbourg's rediscovery of early seventeenth-century Jewish liturgical music composer Salamone Rossi.[117] Placed alongside similar accounts of Palestrina and hymn singing in the Catholic and Protestant churches, respectively, Ensel thus orchestrated Judaism's return to a meaningful place in liturgical music. He emphasized this claim in his conclusion: rather than attributing musical ideas to one group or another, Ensel asserted that liturgical music derived from a wide spectrum of processes, based on a combination of self-determination, musical cultivation, and the specific character of each group. The source for such musical activity lay not in the hermetic space of the sanctuary alone, he argued, but in a fluid interaction with all aspects of musical life. "Both the Synagogue and the Church," Ensel asserted, "have at no time been reluctant in absorbing to their liturgies the music originally composed for other purposes than sacred."[118] Even gleanings from popular culture could have a home in the modern synagogue, church, or mosque, so long as they were tastefully chosen.

His ideas thus conceived, Ensel ended his book by presenting the "Trisagion" (Kadosh/Sanctus with preceding poetic verses) in notated versions for the synagogue (in his own arrangement; see fig. 4.7), Catholic Church (fig. 4.8), and Protestant Church (fig. 4.9). Noting that "no other tune, perhaps, can convey the vivid and ornate style of the Orient; massive and dignified chant of Rome; and the simple musical recitation of Wittenberg, Geneva, and Westminster," his closing example highlighted the textual parallels between three key faith groups, and their ability to stand together as related, and even interwoven, traditions.[119]

Figure 4.7. The Hebrew Trisagion from *Ancient Liturgical Music*.

Continued

Figure 4.7. *continued*

Figure 4.7. *continued*

Figure 4.8. The Catholic "Preface to the Roman Sanctus" from *Ancient Liturgical Music*.

Continued

Figure 4.8. *continued*

Figure 4.9. The Protestant Trisagion from *Ancient Liturgical Music*.

Continued

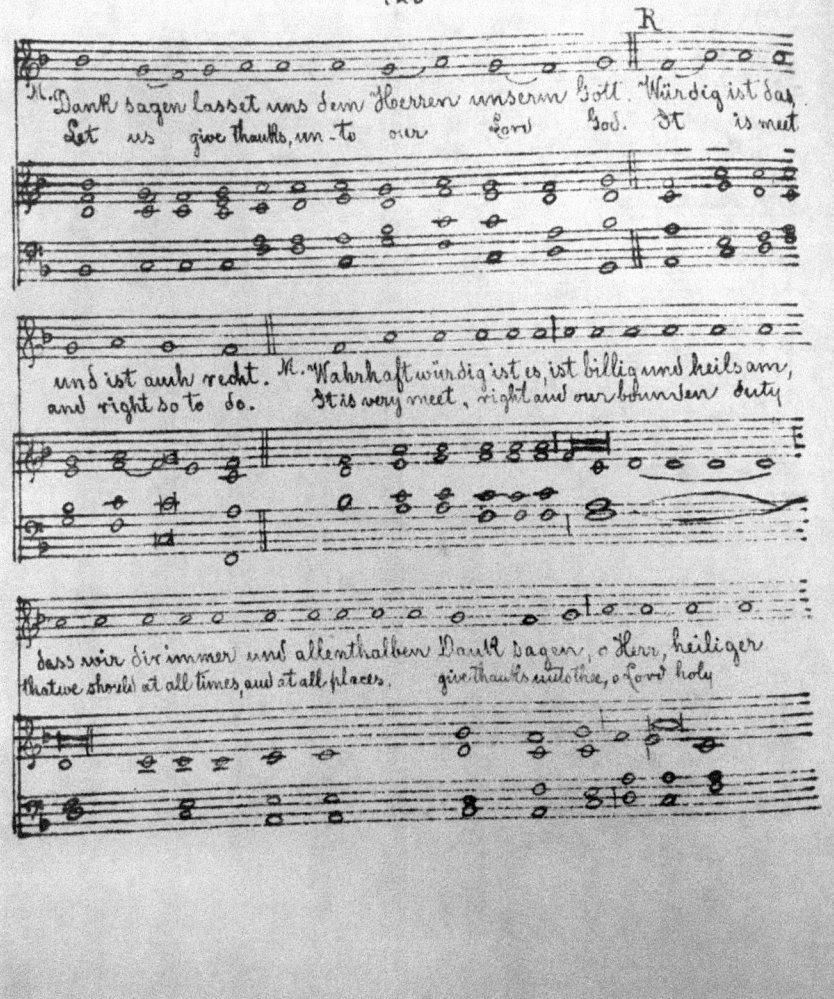

Figure 4.9. continued

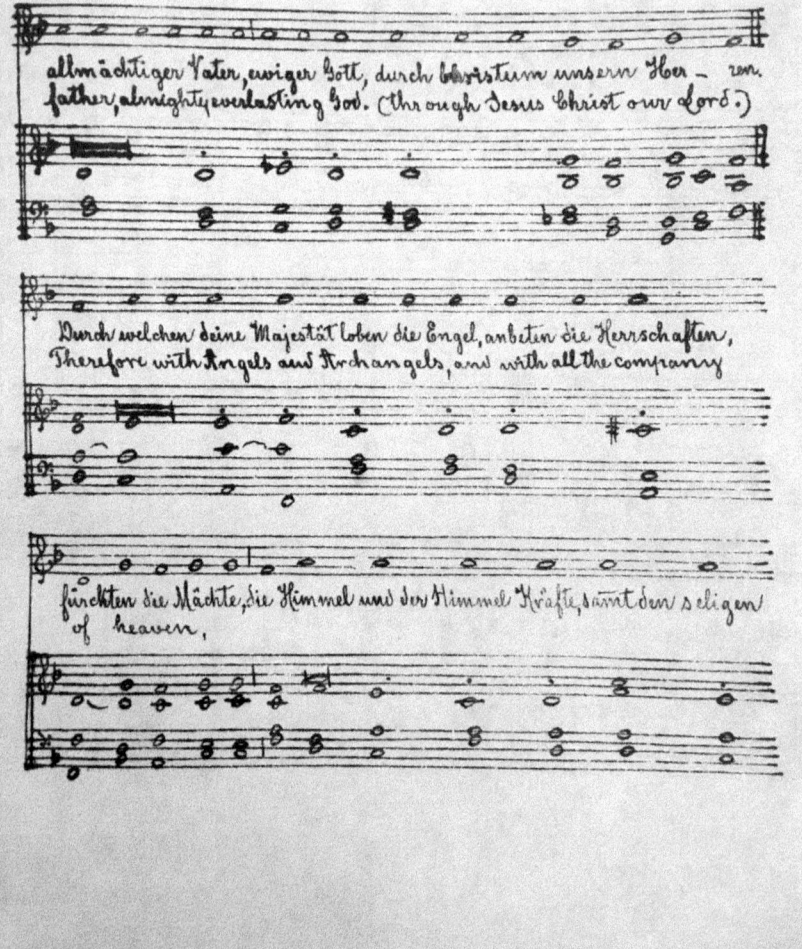

Figure 4.9. *continued*

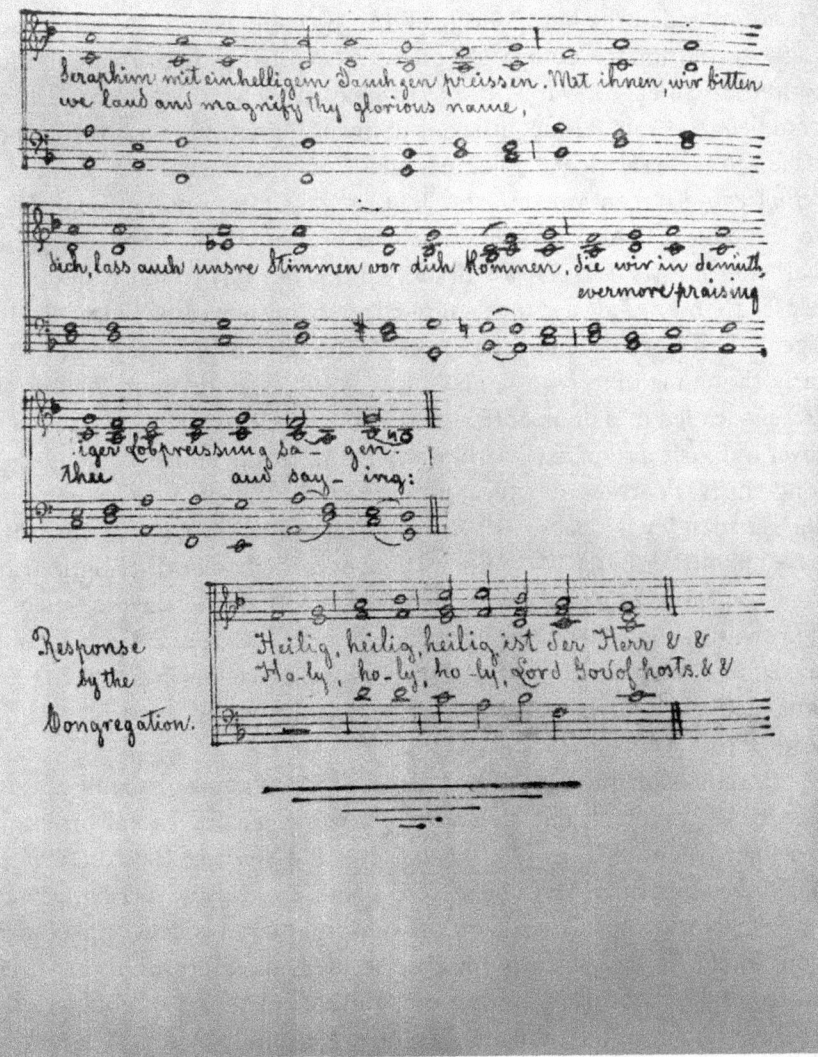

Figure 4.9. *continued*

Jewish Music on the National Stage

Contemporary reviews of *ALM*, while few, were strongly positive. Reviewers commended the book's accessibility, its copious images, and its seemingly revolutionary comparative treatment of the three major faiths. A writer for Chicago's *Daily Inter Ocean* hailed the work as "one of the most complete and valuable acquisitions to musical literature that has been published for several years."[120] Short-lived Chicago journal the *Musical Bulletin* (1879–83) mentioned the book in late 1881, after Ensel provided a copy to the editor.[121] And a reviewer in the prominent St. Louis–based journal *Kunkel's Musical Review* described the work as "remarkable in more senses than one," deserving "study not only of musicians but of the intelligent clergy of all denominations."[122] The Jewish press responded similarly, though with its own slant: Chicago's correspondent for *The American Israelite* called it "a book of the greatest interest to every historian, to every lover of music and of art and to every rabbi," while affirming its place as a long-elusive "correct, reliable, and unprejudiced history of Jewish music"; the German Jewish paper *Die Zeitgeist* responded similarly.[123] Cincinnati-based publisher Bloch & Company took over the book's distribution, and a copy was donated to the young Hebrew Union College; the extremely limited printing, however, severely curtailed the book's spread, even among its specialized readership.[124] Mainstream music educators' journal *The Étude* lamented the study's scarcity in an 1885 article aptly titled, "An Unpublished Work."[125]

Ensel, meanwhile, continued his work with Paducah's small congregation Bene Yeshurum and its young but well-regarded choral program.[126] During his tenure from 1881 to 1886, the first years of the congregation's membership in the UAHC, he served in both musical and clerical capacities while teaching music lessons on the side and making occasional contributions to *The Étude*.[127] One of his articles, likely drawn from his experience, mused on the difficulties of improving liturgical choral singing in a small town with its own religious politics: "The few good voices which may happen to be found in the place are distributed in the various denominations. The fine soprano is an Episcopalian, and would, of course, give the benefit of her voice to her own church. The alto, being a Baptist, would not accept the invitation to sing in the Presbyterian church; and the only good tenor in town does not like church music, nor attend church. Hence, another disappointment in the music teacher's experience in a small city."[128]

In July 1887, just after leaving his pulpit, Ensel returned to the speaking dais at the eleventh annual meeting of the Music Teachers National Association (MTNA) in Indianapolis, appearing in a panel session titled, "The True Style and Type for Congregation and Choir."[129] Standing before 1,800 music educators, Ensel represented Judaism alongside two major Christian American musical figures with contrasting approaches to congregational singing. Episcopal minister Rev. William H. Cooke (1837–89), of lower Manhattan's St. John's Chapel, had founded the Church Music Association in 1874, and had served as president of the Oratorio Society of New York since 1876—both organizations dedicated to elevating the aesthetics of amateur choral singing. Catholic priest Alfred Young (1831–1900) advocated tirelessly for "congregational singing" from the pews; he had edited *The Catholic Hymnal* in 1884 to achieve this end and wrote numerous articles supporting the practice in both Catholic and mainstream journals.[130] While all three speakers addressed historical matters, the session emphasized pragmatic steps that music teachers could take to empower voices well beyond the sanctuary, under the continued assumption of liturgical music's status as a progenitor of the art music tradition.

Ensel's message, developed within an ecumenical environment, found particular depth when juxtaposed with his colleagues' presentations. All three offered idiomatic accounts of music in their respective religious traditions, paying special attention to the congregation's role in affirming an appropriate level of spirituality; and each pointedly criticized efforts to enhance the sound of worship through elite musical artistry. Young, in the style of the Saint Cecilia Society reformers, marked the Renaissance and its turn to "art for art's sake" as a turning point toward musical degradation in the Catholic Church. Claudio Monteverdi's popularization of the leading tone in particular, he claimed, opened an era of indulgently complex harmony that took away from the corporate spirit of prayer.[131] He advocated returning to mass chanting in the Gregorian style, which would give congregants greater claim on the service and present a more direct harmonic and rhythmic connection to the text.[132] Cooke, in contrast, framed the Reformation as a period of harmonic elaboration that established a healthy balance between the corporate expression of choral arrangements and the devotional nature of basic chant and chorales, reflecting different levels of musical ability.[133] In the United States, however, the balance tilted away from the congregation, with choirs attempting pieces that exceeded their capabilities and obscured the text. "The choir," Cooke noted, "should never forget that in the devotional act the people have their proper place and function."¹³⁴

Ensel's speech, in sharp contrast, characterized Jewish chant as a creative stream that ran in counterpoint to its Christian analogues: focusing on Jews' preservation of Oriental Egyptian/Chaldean chant, their music's stunted development in the era of Christian efflorescence, and its reinvigoration under the still-alive Sulzer. This history, particularly in its orientalist angle, superseded the other speakers' concerns about balancing art music and congregational chant, because Jewish identity in Ensel's view lacked the same tensions. Although Ensel discussed Orthodox rejection of harmony and instrumentation during prayer, he represented the act as based on a lack of musical sophistication and justified its perceived "sadness" as a mirror image of the "spirit of the powerful [Catholic] church." The music of such a "lachrymose" Jewish worldview, while continuing in areas where Jews remained under persecution, ended in America, where Jews "have no cause to lament over the victories of Vespasian, Titus and Hadrian." Ensel ended his talk by describing the tune of the "Kol Nidre" prayer as an entity that today bridged ancient and modern, Orthodox and "Reformed," Occidental and Oriental—and, remarkably, represented a case where the music itself took precedence over the words, which were "nothing but the merest and driest of Talmudic casuistry."¹³⁵ Taken as a whole, Ensel's emphasis on historical description, and his much milder series of moral prescriptions compared to his colleagues', likely made sense to an audience that viewed Jewish music as an ancient practice of uncertain significance. Included as one of the three major faiths in the MTNA forum, his paper brought Judaism greater exposure in the Western musical narrative, especially as delivered by an active Jewish music practitioner and specialist.

The MTNA's journal, *The Voice*, published Ensel's talk afterward alongside those of his co-panelists Cooke and Young. *The American Israelite*, meanwhile, published his speech in a longer and seemingly less invasive edit that included cues for live vocal demonstration by local singer Dora Messing. In this second, Jewish setting, which lacked the context of Cooke's and Young's talks, Ensel's message shifted noticeably. Emphasizing Jewish primacy where *The Voice* implied confluence, the article expanded on the principle developed in *ALM* that sui generis musical innovation could only happen during periods of national self-determination.¹³⁶ While the ancient Hebrews included the musical style of their Egyptian oppressors in their earliest liturgical music, noted the *Israelite* version, only after "the peaceful possession of the promised land . . . could the leaders of the Hebrew people begin to mould whatever they had adopted from others, into such a type, as would become distinct from the parent stock." Referring to the musical liturgy developed by "Samuel, and after him David and Solomon," Ensel asserted in the *Israelite* version that the musical style developed during the Second Temple period comprised "the true type, the only true style of church music everywhere." While both versions of the talk noted that "the primitive church, following the advice of the apostles . . . intonated the Psalms in exactly the same manner [as the Israelites]," the *Israelite* article reinforced the Jewish narrative by adding, "And there is no doubt that they were chanted to Hebrew music."

Similarly, Catholic oppression of Jews during the medieval period led to the practice of pairing folk tunes with a growing body of *piyyutim*, leading Ensel to claim in the *Israelite* version that "it is to the synagogue, and later to the Protestant church, to which the musical world owes a debt of gratitude" for this process. Moreover, while composer/cantor Salomon Sulzer, in *The Voice*, received a tacit place in the European compositional tradition continuous with church music, the *Israelite* version noted how Sulzer's "polyphonous anthem style" appealed specifically to Jews, "in contradistinction to the Gregorian plainchant, and the Lutheran Choral, the introduction of which, having been tried, never could captivate a Jewish ear." Somewhat genteelly blunted in *The Voice*, Ensel's (original?) perspective in *The American Israelite* represented a more openly Judeo-centric revision of liturgical music's time line, placing Jewish creativity at the forefront of religious musical development, and citing Jews' history of oppression as a springboard for, rather than as an inhibitor to, such change.

Rather more subtly, the *Israelite* version of Ensel's address adhered to the ideological underpinnings of American Jewish reformers. While the article in *The Voice* noted that "it is to the Israelites to whom we have to look for authentic information in regard to ancient music," the version in the *Israelite* employed the more openly ethnic term "*Hebrew* people," possibly reflecting the contemporary Reform Jewish nomenclature used in, for example, the recently founded Union of American Hebrew Congregations (UAHC, 1873) and its associated seminary, Hebrew Union College (1875).[137] And where Ensel in *The Voice* described the introduction of "the organ and a choir of trained singers" into Jewish life as an innovation from "about forty years ago," the *Israelite* version added "after a lapse of nearly 2,000 years," fulfilling a Reform Jewish approach to theology that emphasized

Jews as a biblical (rather than talmudic, or law-based) people. Ensel's use of talmudic passages to describe ancient performance practices affirmed the Talmud's place as a historical document in the reformers' spiritual topography. Yet he openly criticized contemporary adherence to Talmud-based religious practice, specifically noting Orthodox Judaism's rejection of organ and mixed choir in worship because "the rabbis of the Talmud held that no other place in God's wide world is fit to cultivate the old temple music but Zion." This comment also affirmed Reform Judaism's rejection of a Jewish state at the time and added a new dimension to Ensel's concluding critique in *The Voice* of the dry talmudic text of the "Kol Nidre."

The differences between these two printed versions of Ensel's address highlighted the divergent interests that Ensel's two key constituencies took in his work, and the lens through which each saw its relevance: adding a living Jewish voice for music educators, and championing musical reform among liberal Jews who sought to create a comfortable place for themselves in the United States. While at least one more conservative voice in the Jewish press (probably Henry S. Morais of Philadelphia's *Jewish Exponent*) offered his own critique of Ensel's ideas, that author nonetheless acknowledged that "the history of Jewish music is surely an interesting study," and affirmed Ensel's "commendable acquaintance with that subject."[138] The increased exposure of such comments continued to expand music's role as both a distinct element of Jewish history and an active part of musical scholarship.

An Effaced Legacy

For the remainder of his life, Ensel appeared to look to music education as his primary outlet for finding professional peers and presenting his research. Speaking at the 1889 MTNA meeting in Philadelphia, Ensel repeated his story about the origins of "Malbrook" ("We Won't Come Home Till Morning"), leading local and national media outlets to retell it for years afterward.[139] Although he no longer served as a full-time synagogue musician—indeed, one account described him as late in life "inclined to have no particular religious views"—Ensel remained a member of the synagogue. He also continued to participate in select Jewish events that called for large-scale musical leadership, as he did at the March 1894 consecration of Paducah's new synagogue building described at the start of this chapter.[140] Mostly, however, Ensel continued to give private music lessons in Paducah and write anecdotes for *The Étude*.[141]

Ensel's work influenced the historiography of Jewish music in the United States; however, his writings and compositions were increasingly overshadowed by students of Sulzer who had come to the United States starting in the mid-to-late 1860s, especially Alois Kaiser and Morris Goldstein. Cantorial voices and the concept of the professional musician—in the form of the cantor—began to dominate American conversations about synagogue music, while interest in importing popular melodies faced wavering support. Ensel's arrangements of Rossini tunes and other "traditional" airs retained some popularity through the 1880s: his arrangements of two Portuguese/Sephardic melodies and two "traditional" holiday tunes with hymn texts by Gustav Gottheil appeared in a prominent 1887 collection of contrafact melodies by New York Temple Emanu-El organist A. J. Davis.[142] Yet American cantors' emphasis on musical content as a basis for authenticity discouraged the use of music written by non-Jews, instead seeking an opportunity for Jewish identity to assert itself by reintroducing "traditional" melodies and elaborate new compositions into the service. By the 1890s, cantors had formed professional organizations that aimed to enforce musical standards, argue for the legitimacy of the profession, and assume control of congregational music responsibilities. Paraprofessionals such as Ensel, G. M. Cohen, and Simon Hecht soon found themselves eclipsed on the national stage. When the Central Conference of American Rabbis sought a musical companion for its new Union Prayerbook in the early 1890s, they looked to Alois Kaiser and the Cantors Association, who emphasized original tunes by Jewish composers and largely shut both Ensel and Hecht out (see chap. 7).[143]

Aesthetic changes in cantors' framing of "Jewish" music also affected the staying power of Ensel's work, promoting radical sonic (and historical) dissociation from Christian musical forms where Ensel emphasized integration.[144] Kaiser and William Sparger's 1893 *A Collection of the Principal Melodies of the Synagogue from the Earliest Times to the Present* (described more fully in chap. 7) characteristically combed contemporary melodies for surviving indicators of Jewish ancientness, reversing Ensel's philosophy.[145] In 1899, British rabbi Francis L. Cohen described choral music as a recent phenomenon in Judaism and lauded the new trend toward monophonic chant and modal theory—a commentary that *Werner's Magazine* (the successor journal to *The Voice*) found odd, especially when placed in direct dialogue with Ensel's 1887 MTNA talk.[146] By 1929, Abraham Z. Idelsohn's *Jewish Music in Its Historical Development* gave only a dismissive nod to

Ensel's major work, as "an attempt to explain the *Ancient Liturgical Music*," and gave Hecht's hymnal a short, compulsory mention.[147] Out of vogue, with few extant copies, Ensel's work largely disappeared from the scholarly landscape. Hecht's work disappeared as well, save his setting of "We Meet Again in Gladness"—fittingly, a rare surviving musical adaptation of a common American pedagogical hymn text.[148]

Ultimately, Ensel and Hecht offered practical pathways for America's Jews to create a religious-musical continuum in the second half of the nineteenth century. Rather than opting for monumentalism and new composition that emphasized a sense of Jewish uniqueness, Ensel advised Jews to use the music around them as their guide, while Hecht emphasized vocal instruction and choral singing as the key to American Jewish self-actualization. Closer attention to music history, Ensel claimed, revealed a much more fluid idea of musical tradition than had previously been considered—one that emphasized a sense of common origin, frequent interaction, and parallel if not always equitable development. At the same time, he made sure that Judaism (re)claimed a part in that story, standing alongside Catholicism and Protestantism (and Islam) as both progenitor and protagonist, significant for its role and influence even if stunted in the comparative size of its population. Hecht, more focused on teaching than scholarship, framed musical training as a moral good for the entire community, and helped each polity realize itself as a meaningful part of an American pluralistic outlook. Within a Midwestern landscape of small congregations that needed to ration their musical resources, and working within a general era of progressive optimism, Ensel and Hecht put their comparative worldviews into action, prioritizing facilitation over composition, and balancing the value of civic unity with Jewish musical identity.

While the content of Ensel and Hecht's work may be forgotten, the philosophy it espoused remains relevant. Large congregations still often set the landscape of Jewish musical paradigms, publicly justifying, with the backing of cantorial schools and movement-based institutions, the financial expense of a cantor, the production of high-quality synagogue music, and the broader sonic values of Jewish spirituality. Yet music remains an important part of the small society as well, where cantors can be scarce and prohibitively expensive, rabbis fleeting, volunteers central to day-to-day spiritual leadership, and music (perhaps) more openly connected to contemporary popular styles. In this framework, both Ensel and Hecht bridged tenets of Jewish reform with the pedagogy of a singing community, highlighting music's place in a broad social discourse that filtered beyond the synagogue, proved compatible with other religious groups, and engaged openly with local cultural practices and norms. In some ways, then, the erasure of these two names from the historical record of music scholarship may, intentionally or otherwise, have proven their significance: since, as musical facilitators, they encouraged the people to create Jewish music in their own image.

Notes

I am grateful to Curtis Mann, manager of the Sangamon Valley Collection at the Lincoln Library in Springfield, Illinois, for locating information about Ensel in the local historical papers. All translations from German sources are the author's.

1. Negrononte, "Paducah, KY: Particulars of the Dedication of the New Temple," *The American Israelite*, April 5, 1894, 5.

2. Ibid. While the correspondent's claim about Ensel's lack of original compositions may not be completely correct (it appears that he wrote a few works while in Cincinnati ca. 1857), it reflects a more general perception of Ensel as a musical facilitator rather than a bona fide composer. For a record of Ensel's works, see Sharona Wachs, *American Jewish Liturgies* (Cincinnati, OH: Hebrew Union College Press, 1997), nos. 175 and 279.

3. "New Temple Dedicated at Paducah, Ky.," *The American Israelite*, March 29, 1894, 7.

4. J. Cintura and S. Hecht, "Wo ist meine Heimath?/Where Is My Home?" (English trans. May Cintura) (Evansville, IN, 1892); Gustav Reichardt and Ernst Moritz Arndt, "Was ist des deutschen Vaterland?" (1825); "Eine patrotische Komposition," *Taglicher Evansville Demokrat*, March 8, 1892, 5. Hecht and Cintura's anthem appeared as sheet music in a solo voice with piano arrangement but was also performed in an arrangement for orchestra and men's choir in late April 1892 ("Das Philharmonia Musikfest," *Taglicher Evansville Demokrat*, April 28, 1892, 5).

5. See, for example, Neil Levin, "Gustave M. Cohen, 1820–1902," Milken Archive of Jewish Music: The American Experience, http://www.milkenarchive.org/people/view/all/1109/Cohen,+Gustave; John Baron, "Frederick Emil Kitziger of New Orleans: A Nineteenth Century Composer of Synagogue Music," *Musica Judaica* 5 (1983): 20–33.

6. Amy Hill Shevitz, *Jewish Communities on the Ohio River: A History* (Lexington: University Press of Kentucky, 2007), 4.

7. Ann L. Silverberg, "Cecilian Reform in Baltimore, 1868–1903," in *Renewal and Resistance: Catholic Church Music from the 1850s to Vatican II*, ed. Paul Collins (New York: Peter Lang, 2010), 171–88; Paul Westermeyer, "The Evolution of the Music of German American Protestants in Their Hymnody: A Case Study from an American Perspective," and Otto Holzapfel, "Singing from the Right Songbook: Ethnic Identity and Language Transformation in German American Hymnals," in *Music in American Religious Experience*, ed. Philip V. Bohlman, Edith L. Blumhofer, and Maria M. Chow (New York: Oxford University Press, 2005); John Ogasapian, *Church Music in America, 1620–2000* (Macon, GA: Mercer University Press, 2007).

8. Ensel mentioned three musical mentors in his ad as a piano teacher posted in *Die Deborah* in July/August 1857 (vol. 2, 400, 408, 416): choral director Thomas Täglischbeck

(1799–1867; in Hechingen from 1827–48), a Bremen concertmaster named Schmidt, and a Hamburg pianist named Friedrich. The last two may have been later teachers.

9. "Varel: Zur Geschichte der jüdischen Gemeinde," *Alemannia Judaica* (http://www.alemannia-judaica.de/varel_synagoge.htm#Varel). Ensel's dates come from his gravestone at the Temple Israel cemetery, Paducah, Kentucky.

10. "Professor Simon Hecht," *Biographical Cyclopedia of Vanderburgh County* (Evansville, IN: Keller, 1897), 130. The Hechts studied with traditionalist rabbi Seligman Bamberger while separately attending the city's general Lehrerseminar—an existing arrangement—before Bamberger created the Israelitische Lehrerbildungs-Anstalt in 1864, which offered a combined program (Goldberg, "The Training of Hazzanim," 318–19).

11. The Württemberg/Stuttgart Jewish authority (Ober-Kirchen-Behörde) produced a major revision of its hymnal in 1836, aiming to integrate home, school, and synagogue: *Sefer Zemirot Yisrael. Gesang-Buch, zum Gebrauch beidem Unterichte in der mosaischen Religion und zur öffentlichen und häuslichen Gottesverehrung der Israeliten* (Stuttgart: Hallberger, 1836).

12. Geoffrey Goldberg attempts to give these efforts at congregational singing some context, particularly entering the second half of the nineteenth century. See Geoffrey Goldberg, "An Overview of Congregational Song in the German Synagogue Up to the Shoah," *Journal of Synagogue Music* 30, no. 1 (2005), 13–53.

13. Simon Hecht, letter, *Allgemeine Zeitung des Judenthums*, January 15, 1849, 36–37.

14. Ibid.; *Allgemeine Zeitung des Judenthums*, January 15, 1849, 36–37; April 23, 1849, 228–30; May 7, 1849, 252; July 5, 1849, 252; September 17, 1849, 536–37.

15. Simon Hecht, "Ueber Synagogengesang," *Allgemeine Zeitung des Judenthums*, April 23, 1849, 228–30. (Letter dated March 28, 1849.)

16. Ibid.

17. Ibid, 229–30.

18. For other responses, many of which offered opinions similar to Hecht's, see *Allgemeine Zeitung des Judenthums*, May 21, 281 (K. Kohl, of Flicken); June 25, 356–58 (Marx Hildesheimer, of Speyer); July 2, 373 (Simon Alexander, of Strelitz); July 30, 435–36 (Herman Ehrlich, of Berkach), and September 3, 513–15 (Schlesinger, of Anklam; an anonymous correspondent from Munich; and Rosenthal, from Meiningen).

19. Gustav S. Ensel, "Noch etwas über Synagogengesang," *Allgemeine Zeitung des Judenthums* 13, no. 25 (June 18, 1849), 339.

20. Ibid., 338–39.

21. Ibid., 340.

22. See Simon Alexander's response to Ensel: "Synagogengesang," *Allgemeine Zeitung des Judenthums* 13, no. 27 (July 2, 1849), 373. Ruth HaCohen notes that non-Jews, such as Richard Wagner, used the German term *gejodel* to comment negatively on the aesthetics of Jewish vocalizing (Ruth HaCohen, "Between Noise and Harmony: The Oratorical Moment in the Musical Entanglements of Jews and Christians," *Critical Inquiry* 32, no. 2 [2006]: 258). Geoffrey Goldberg also discusses this exchange in the context of the cantorial fantasia form (Geoffrey Goldberg, "The Cantorial *Fantasia* Revisited: New Perspectives on an Ashkenazic Musical Genre," *Musica Judaica* 17 [2003/4], 65–67).

23. Herman Ehrlich, "Synagogengesang," *Allgemeine Zeitung des Judenthums*, July 30, 1849, 435–36; Simon Hecht, letter, *Allgemeine Zeitung des Judenthums*, September 17, 1849, 536–37. Simon Hecht's collection of synagogue chants does not appear to have been published.

24. *Der israelitische Volkslehrer*, February 1852, 48; November 1853, 282.

25. Max Markreich, *Geschichte der Juden in Bremen und Umgegend* (Bremen: Edition Temmen, 2003), 81; Ensel, advertisement, *Die Deborah* 2 (July–August 1858), 400, 408, 416. Markreich describes Ensel as coming from Berne (Oldenburg) and credits him with creating the Bremen Jewish community's official seal.

26. Minute book of Bnai Jeshurun congregation, Cincinnati, meeting of September 20, 1857 and Congregational Meeting of September 24, 1857. American Jewish Archives, MS62, Box 3. It appears that Ensel moved with his family near Morganfield, Kentucky, in the early 1850s, although his activities during these early years are as yet undocumented. See "Adolph Ensel," in Joseph Wallace, *Past and Present of the City of Springfield and Sangamon County Illinois* (Chicago: S. J. Clarke, 1904), 481–82. (Adolph, who appears to be G. S.'s brother, is listed here as a member of the Episcopal Church.)

27. "Annual Report of the Officers of K. K. Bene Yeshurun," *The Israelite*, September 17, 1858, 86.

28. I. M. Wise, *The Israelite*, September 12, 1856, 76.

29. Minute book of Bnai Jeshurun congregation, Cincinnati, 1855–59. American Jewish Archives, MS 62, Box 3. Wise's own account of this period, which essentially focuses on the hiring of non-Jewish choristers, greatly oversimplifies the situation (Isaac M. Wise, *The History of the K. K. Bene Yeshurun, of Cincinnati, Ohio* [Cincinnati, OH: n.p., 1892], chap. 2).

30. [Isaac M. Wise,] "Cincinnati," *The Israelite*, October 2, 1857, 102. Wise's comment comprises the only reference to an original composition by Ensel; the sheet music has not been found.

31. *The Israelite*, October 2, 1857, 100; *The Israelite*, October 9, 1857, 110.

32. "The New Prayer Book *Minhag America*," *The Israelite*, October 23, 1857, 124.

33. *The Israelite*, October 23, 1857, 126.

34. G. Ensel, "Bildung," *Die Deborah* 3, no. 24 (January 29, 1858), 186–87.

35. *The Israelite*, May 2, 1858.

36. Ibid., June 18, 1858, 396.

37. Isaac Mayer Wise, "Choir and Organ in the Synagogue of St. Louis," *The Israelite*, July 22, 1859, 20; H. Kuttner, letter to the editor, *Die Deborah* 5, no. 8 (August 26, 1859), 31; J. Mass, letter to the editor, *Die Deborah* 5, no. 16 (October 21, 1859), 63.

38. See, for example, *Die Deborah*, August 27, 1869, 31.

39. R., letter to the editor, *The Israelite*, August 8, 1862, 45; B., letter to the editor, *The Israelite*, May 29, 1863, 370; "Domestic Record: St. Louis," *The Israelite*, June 28, 1867, 6; [Isaac Mayer Wise,] "Laying of the Corner Stone to the Temple of St. Louis," *The Israelite*, July 5, 1867, 4; Amicus, "Dedication of the Temple of St. Louis, August 27," *The Israelite*, September 3, 1869, 11. See also a letter of dedication in *Sinai* 4, no. 11, 360.

40. Charles Wessolowsky, letter to Rabbi Edward B. M. Browne, October 23, 1879, in Louis Schmier, ed., *Reflections on Southern Jewry: The Letters of Charles Wesselowsky, 1878–1879* (Macon, GA: Mercer University Press, 1982), 149–51. Other direct communications with Ensel in the late 1870s indicate a decade-long process of research and writing.

41. *Holland's Springfield City Directory, for 1868–1869* (Chicago: Western Publishing, 1868), 84 (listing the firm of Ensel & Mayer, and listing Ensel separately as a resident of St. Louis); email communication with Curtis Mann, January 21, 2016. Ensel's name appears in the city directories of Springfield, Illinois, in 1872, 1874, and 1875. He seems to have

returned to St. Louis (or commuted back and forth) between 1872 and 1874 but returned to Springfield in 1874 and opened a shoe business, which he ran for the rest of the decade.

42. "Easter," April 10, 1871, 4; "A Happy Event," *Illinois State Journal*, October 10, 1871, 4; "Musical Union," *Illinois State Journal*, March 14, 1874, 4.

43. [Isaac Mayer Wise,] *The Israelite*, February 16, 1872.

44. Letter to the editor, *The Israelite*, September 15, 1876.

45. "Jewish Holy Days," *Illinois State Journal*, September 20, 1876, 4; "Religious," *Illinois State Journal*, September 15, 1877, 4.

46. *Proceedings of the Union of American Hebrew Congregations*, vol. 1 (1873–79) (Cincinnati, OH: Bloch, [1879]), 405, 525, 734.

47. Simon Hecht, "Ein Wort über den Gebrauch den kleinen israelitischen Gesangbuchs von Dr. Phillipson," *Allgemeine Zeitung des Judenthums*, January 1, 1856, 7–8; Hecht referred to Ludwig Philippson, *Kleines israelitisches Gesangbuch: enthaltend deutsche Lieder und Melodieen, zu den hohen Festen, zur Totenfeier, Confirmation, Trauung, Synagogenweihe und zu vaterländischen Festen* (Leipzig: Baumgärtner, 1855).

48. *Allgemeine Zeitung des Judenthums*, August 16, 1858, 461–63. (The article reports to be from the pages of the *Israelitische Lehrer*.)

49. "Professor Simon Hecht," 1897.

50. *Die Deborah*, June 22, 1860, 202. This report notes that the forty-to-fifty-member congregation comprised mainly French (?) Jews, held services led by a "Mr. Leon" (perhaps Leon Leopold) in a rented hall, and had unusually high membership dues.

51. *Die Deborah*, June 8, 1866, 196 (the advertisement, which had been posted since May 18, also appeared in the *Allgemeine Zeitung des Judenthums*).

52. *Wochentlicher Evansville Demokrat*, August 3, 1866, 3. Wise, who recommended Schlesinger's works for publication in his account of the consecration, also noted the presence of a "Hazan from Memphis—he having been formerly the minister of this congregation": possibly he referred to Isaac Ritterman who served on and off in Memphis at the time (see chap. 1). See *Evansville Daily Journal*, August 13, 1866, 8.

53. *Die Deborah*, June 21, 1867, 199; Salomon Herxheimer and Simon Hecht, *Der israelitische Confirmand, oder, Glaubens- und Pflichtenlehre für den Schul- und Privatgebrauch in Reformgemeinden* (Evansville, IN: Simon Hecht, 1868).

54. Simon Hecht, "Ein Wort über Synagogen-Gesang," *Die Deborah*, February 18, 1870, 2.

55. *The Israelite*, March 31, 1871, 7.

56. "Gratulieren," *Taglicher Evansville Demokrat*, July 11, 1871, 2.

57. Ibid., 87, 153.

58. *Proceedings of the Union of American Hebrew Congregations*, vol. 1, 285.

59. Ibid., 368–69, 483–84, 486–87.

60. Simon Hecht, ed. *Zemirot Yisrael: Jewish Hymns for Sabbath Schools and Families* (Cincinnati: Bloch, 1878). Although listed as the second edition, I have thus far not been able to locate a first edition.

61. Among the local composers were M. Z. Tinker, Ed. Drewes, C. C. Genung, and Chr. Mathias, at least some of whom lived in Evansville.

62. *Proceedings of the Union of American Hebrew Congregations*, vol. 1, 526–27.

63. This and all references to Ensel's article come from Ensel, "Ueber Synagogen-Musik," *Die Deborah*, September 20, 1878, 2.

64. Ibid.

65. Simon Hecht, "Hymnenbuch für Sabbatschulen," *Die Deborah*, October 18, 1878, 2; October 25, 1878, 2.

66. See advertisement for H. Sakolski that notes Hecht's hymnal as "Adopted in all the Hebrew Free Schools of New York," in *The Year Book of Education for 1879* (New York: E. Steiger, 1879), 397. Here, the publication is listed as "Part I."

67. Ibid.

68. Giovanni Batista Martini, *Storia della Musica* (Bologna, 1757–81); Charles Burney, *A General History of Music from the Earliest Ages to the Present Period* (London, 1776); Johann Nicolaus Forkel, *Allgemeine Geschichte der Musik*, vol. 1 (Leipzig: Schwickertschen, 1788); François-Joseph Fétis, *Histoire générale de musique depuis les temps les plus anciens jusqu'a nos jours*, vol. 1 (Paris: Didot Frères Fils, 1869).

69. Bennet Zon, "Victorian Anti-Semitism and the Origin of Gregorian Chant," in *Renewal and Resistance: Catholic Church Music from the 1850s to Vatican II*, ed. Paul Collins (New York: Peter Lang, 2010), 99–119.

70. See Emmanuel Hecht and Hermann Ehrlich's numerous essays in the *Liturgische Zeitschrift zur Veredelung des Synagogengesangs mit Berücksichtigung des ganzen Synagogenwesens* (ca. 1851–59); Samuel Naumbourg, *Agudath Shirim: Receuil de chants religieux et populaires des Israélites* (Paris: S. Naumbourg, 1874); Arnold Marksohn and William Wolf, *Auswahl alter hebraïscher Synagogal-Melodien* (Leipzig: Breitkopf and Härtel, 1875).

71. Ann Ostendorf, *Sounds American: National Identity and the Music Cultures of the Lower Mississippi Valley, 1800–1860* (Atlanta: University of Georgia Press, 2011), 9. Emphasis in original.

72. Gustav S. Ensel, *Ancient Liturgical Music* (Paducah, KY: G. Ensel, 1880), preface. Emphasis in original.

73. "An Intellectual Treat," *Illinois State Journal*, November 28, 1878, 4. Reprinted as "Hebrew Music," *The American Israelite*, December 6, 1878, 6. All references to the talk in this paragraph come from this source unless otherwise noted.

74. "Relief and Aid," *Illinois State Journal*, December 21, 1878, 4; "Historical Concert," *Illinois State Journal*, January 14, 1879, 4.

75. "Hebrew Music," *The American Israelite*, December 6, 1878, 6.

76. *Die Deborah* 33, no. 17 (October 24, 1879), 3.

77. This and all other references to the Scientific Academy lecture come from "The Music of the Ancients," *The American Israelite*, December 26, 1879, 5. Malbrook has various spellings, including "Malbrouk" and "Malbrouch."

78. While Ensel did not credit these works in his lectures, the numerous reported illustrations, à la Fétis, the similarity of his cited examples, and Ensel's crediting of these and other histories in his 1880 published work, suggest that he consulted them nonetheless.

79. Springfield's population of twenty thousand made it the 100th most populous American city in the 1880 census.

80. Alois Kaiser, "Requiem for the Day of Atonement" (Baltimore: Alois Kaiser, 1879).

81. Gustave H. [sic] Ensel, Review of "Requiem for the Day of Atonement," *The American Israelite*, August 15, 1879, 2. The text Ensel describes comes from Benjamin Szold, "The Memory of the Dead," in Szold and Jastrow (trans.), *Songs and Prayers and Meditations for Divine Services of Israelites* (Philadelphia: Marcus Jastrow, 1873), no. 129 (68–70) (erroneously mentioned as on p. 129 in the article).

82. Isaac Brickner, *The Jews of Rochester* (Rochester, NY: Historical Review Society, 1912), 13, 49.

83. G. S. Ensel, "Für die Deborah: Hymn Book for Jewish Worship, by M. Landsberg and Sol Wile, Rochester, NY," *Die Deborah*, May 14, 1880, 3.

84. Ibid.; Leopold Löw, *Beiträge zur jüdischen Alterthumskunde* (Szegedin: S. Burger, 1875).

85. Ensel, "Für die Deborah"; Ensel sought a goal price of no more than fifty cents per book.

86. Kohler emigrated from Germany in 1869 and had recently moved from Chicago's Temple Sinai to New York's Temple Beth-El when Ensel approached him.

87. Letter from Ensel to Edward Freiberger, June 15, 1881. Bound into the copy of Ensel, *Ancient Liturgical Music: A Comparative and Historical Essay*, at the Newberry Library, Chicago.

88. Letter from Ensel to Edward Freiberger, October 4, 1881. Bound into the copy of Ensel, *Ancient Liturgical Music: A Comparative and Historical Essay*, at the Newberry Library, Chicago.

89. "An Unpublished Work," *The Étude* 3, no. 11 (November 1885), 230. The hectograph method rarely produced more than fifty copies of any quality.

90. G. S. Ensel, *Ancient Liturgical Music: A Comparative and Historical Essay on the Origin and Development of Sacred Music from the Earliest Times, with Illustrations of the Music Employed in the Worship of the Synagogue, Church & Mosque* (Paducah, KY: self-published, 1880).

91. *ALM*, preface.

92. Letter from Ensel to Edward Freiberger, June 15, 1881. Bound into the copy of Ensel, *Ancient Liturgical Music: A Comparative and Historical Essay*, at the Newberry Library, Chicago.

93. *ALM*, 1. See also H. R. Haweis, *Music and Morals* (London: Longmans, Green, 1871).

94. *ALM*, 4.

95. *ALM*, 9–10. Aguilar and De Sola, *Ancient Melodies* (1857), 9 (music section), no. 12, described as "the most ancient [melody] whose origin is supposed to be prior to the settlement of the Jews in Spain" (12, introduction). Ensel used only the melody, which he reharmonized.

96. *ALM*, 17–48. Many of these illustrations were copied from Carl Engel, *The Music of the Most Ancient Nations* (London: Murray, 1864). The taxonomy highlighted in Ensel's book remains relevant in the twenty-first century. See Theodore W. Burgh, "The Music of Israel during the Iron Age," in *The Cambridge Companion to Jewish Music*, ed. Joshua S. Walden (New York: Cambridge University Press, 2015), 75–83.

97. *ALM*, 30.

98. *ALM*, 41. See, among many other precursors to this argument, Stössel, "Ein Orgel im alten Tempel zu Jerusalem," *Sinai* 7, no. 3 (April 1862), 121–23.

99. *ALM*, 24–25.

100. Ibid.

101. *ALM*, 52, 54.

102. *ALM*, 62.

103. Ibid.

104. *ALM*, 63.

105. *ALM*, 64–65. Ensel particularly singled out an example by Forkel ("Vierstimmige Harmonie, nach welcher in einigen Synagogen der deutschen Juden die hebräischen Accente

gesungen warden," *Allgemeine Geschichte* 1, 167) as the extent to which "the misrepresentation of this branch of Hebrew music is, indeed, equal to the malignity of a Richard Wagner" (65).

106. *ALM*, 71.
107. *ALM*, 72–80.
108. *ALM*, 81–89.
109. *ALM*, 90–94. Ensel's presentation of Psalm 144 reproduced an arrangement of a "Traditional Tune of the Ashkenas Ritual" by Samuel Naumbourg (90–91).
110. *ALM*, 95.
111. *ALM*, 95–97. Giovanni Martini, *Storia della Musica* (Bologna, 1757).
112. *ALM*, 95–130.
113. ALM, 136. Ensel cites Zunz, *Die gottesdienstlichen Vorträge der Juden historisch entwickelt: Ein Beitrag zur Altertumskunde und biblischen Kritik, zur Lieratur- und Religionsgeschichte* (Berlin: A. Asher, 1832), but does not identify specific passages aside from writing on p. 134 of *ALM* that "the author of this essay acknowledges that the greater part of this chapter, is copied from the work of Zunz." (The relevant material appears in chap. 21, 379ff, in the second edition of 1892; I believe that the pagination in the first edition is the same here.)
114. *ALM*, 131–39.
115. *ALM*, 163. Ensel's claim conveniently conflates and misremembers comments on pp. 32 and 35 of Naumbourg's introductory essay to *Agudath Shirim* (Naumbourg 1874). On p. 32, Naumbourg suggests that Sephardic cantillation is always in the *minor* mode ("reste toujours dans la gamme mineure"), while Ashkenazic chant alternates between minor and major ("il passe alternativement dans les tones majeurs et mineurs"). Three pages later, Naumbourg points out that the freedom Jews had under the Moors and Arabs led them to adopt aspects of the surrounding culture as their own, including melodies. Naumbourg makes these comments in the service of a larger agenda championing the authenticity of Ashkenazic chant, which he claims conserved tradition under Christian oppression, as opposed to Sephardic chant which was compromised in the openness of Moorish society. Ensel in contrast, sought to rebut Naumbourg by claiming that *everyone* borrowed tunes, such that no one tradition could claim to preserve ancient Jewish melodies more than another.
116. *ALM*, 164–65.
117. *ALM*, 192, 196. "The fact . . . that these compositions should have been permitted to lie hidden for more than two centuries, until accidently [sic] extricated from the dust of a library, bears sad testimony to the neglect of Jewish sacred music, when compared with the fostering care, which the Church bestowed upon the works of Rossi's contemporary Palestrina, among others."
118. *ALM*, 217.
119. *ALM*, 219.
120. "Music," *Daily Inter Ocean*, October 15, 1881, 13.
121. Letter from Ensel to Edward Freiberger, October 4, 1881. Bound into the copy of Ensel, *Ancient Liturgical Music: A Comparative and Historical Essay*, at the Newberry Library, Chicago.
122. "Book Review," *Kunkel's Musical Review* 5, no. 11 (September 1882), 436.
123. Eduardo, "Chicago," *The American Israelite*, October 10, 1881, 122. See also the review in *Der Zeitgeist: Israelitisches Familienblatt* 3, no. 4 (February 16, 1882), 56.
124. "New Publications," *The American Israelite*, October 28, 1881, 142; Jacob Ezekiel, "Hebrew Union College, Proceedings of the Board of Directors," *The American Israelite*, November 18, 1881, 166.

125. "An Unpublished Work," *The Étude* 3, no. 11 (November 1885), 230. See also a similar article in the "Musical Melange" section of the *Daily Inter Ocean*, November 7, 1886, 13; despite the *Inter Ocean*'s previous mention of the book in 1881, it offered a similar interpretation based on a copy that had come into the possession of F. Ziegfeld, president of Chicago's musical college.

126. Isaac W. Bernheim, *History of the Settlement of Jews in Paducah and the Lower Ohio Valley* (Paducah, KY: Isaac Bernheim, 1912), 67.

127. See G. S. Ensel, "An Interlude from the Life of Beethoven," *The Étude* 3, no. 4 (April 1, 1885), 6; G. S. Ensel, "Origin of the Tarantella," *The Étude* 4, no. 1 (January 1, 1886), 27; G. S. Ensel, "Individualizing," *The Étude* 5, no. 7 (July 1, 1887), 98; G. S. Ensel, "The Music Teacher in a Small Town," *The Étude* 5, no. 12 (December 1, 1887), 171, inter alia. Ensel also contributed short quotes and translations to the journal's regular "Wisdom of Many" and "Pupil's Department" columns.

128. G. S. Ensel, "The Music Teacher in a Small Town."

129. "The Musicians Entertained: Close of the National Convention with a Reception by the Governor," *Indianapolis News*, July 9, 1887, 1.

130. Alfred Young, ed., *The Catholic Hymnal* (New York: Catholic Publication Society, 1884). See, inter alia, Alfred Young, "How to Obtain Congregational Singing," *The Catholic World*, 47, no. 282 (September 1888), 721–38.

131. The leading tone, a crucial part of tonal harmony from the seventeenth century onward, refers to the tone one half-step below the fundamental note of the intended "arrival" chord (B if moving to a C major chord, for example); contemporary listeners have been conditioned to feel the leading tone's "natural momentum" toward musical resolution.

132. Alfred Young, "The Divine Idea of Church Song," *The Voice* 9, no. 7 (July 1887), 111–13 [Part I]; no. 8 (August 1887), 119–21 [Part II].

133. W. H. Cooke, "Church Music in the Episcopal Church," *The Voice* 9, no. 7 (July 1887), 101–3.

134. Ibid.

135. Ensel, "The Traditional Music of the Synagogue," *The Voice*.

136. Ensel, "The Traditional Music of the Synagogue," *The American Israelite*, July 22, 1887, 4–5; July 29, 1887, 3.

137. Emphasis in original. The *Israelite* newspaper (called *The American Israelite* from 1874), likely retained its name for brand recognition (rather than switching to *Hebrew*), even as it represented an earlier era. Notably, however, a New York newspaper called *The American Hebrew* began in 1879.

138. [Henry S. Morais,] editorial, *The Jewish Exponent*, July 29, 1887, 6. Morais, one of three editors of the *Exponent* at the time, seems the most likely author for this article because of his simultaneous editorship of the *Musical and Dramatic Standard*. It is not clear to which version of Ensel's talk the editorial responded.

139. See, for example, "Origin of 'We Won't Go Home,'" *Los Angeles Times*, July 28, 1889, 12 (itself reprinted from the *Louisville Journal*); "Historical," *Our Paper* 10, no. 50 (December 15, 1894), 799; "'We Won't Come Home 'Til Morning' as a Classic," *Musical Record* (Boston) 418 (December 1896), 9 (reprinted from the *Home Journal*). Ensel's account of the origin of this song lingered, appearing, for instance in S. V. Clevenger, *The Evolution of Man and His Mind* (Chicago: Evolution Publishing, 1903), 216.

140. "New Temple Dedicated at Paducah, Ky.," *The American Israelite*, March 29, 1894, 7; "A Learned Man: Prof. G. S. Ensel Dies after a Long Illness," *Paducah Sun*, November 15, 1901, 1.

141. G. S. Ensel, "An Old Teacher's Opinion" [and additional poem], *The Étude* 9 (1891), 53.

142. A. J. Davis, *Music to the Hymns and Anthems for Jewish Worship by G. Gottheil, Vol. 1* (New York: Kakeles, 1887). Isaac Mayer Wise also noted that Ensel's arrangement of a Rossini piece to "Lecho Adonoi" was performed at the January 1884 consecration of the new Memphis, Tennessee, synagogue.

143. Alois Kaiser et al. (eds.), *Anthems, Hymns, and Responses for the Union Prayerbook* (New York: n.p., 1894); Society for American Cantors, *Union Hymnal* (New York: Central Conference of American Rabbis, 1897). By the time Kaiser's first anthology was published, the Central Conference of American Rabbis had recalled the 1892 *Union Prayer Book* and replaced it with the edition of 1894–95.

144. See in particular Josef Singer, *Die Tonarten des traditionellen Synagogalegesangs: Ihr Verhältnis zu den Kirchentonarten und den Tonarten der vorchristlichen Musikperiode* (Vienna: E. M. Wetzler, 1886), which became a touchstone of Jewish music modal theory.

145. (Chicago: T. Rubovits, 1893).

146. Francis L. Cohen, "The Song of the Synagogue," *The Musical Times* 40, no. 678 (August 1, 1899), 518–21; "Music in the Synagogue," *Werner's Magazine* 24, no. 6 (February 1900), 655.

147. A. Z. Idelsohn, *Jewish Music in Its Historical Development* (New York: Bloch, 1929), 329–30, 350.

148. *The Union Hymnal*, 3rd ed., rev. and enl. (New Yok: Central Conference of American Rabbis, 1932), no. 255; Robert Segal and Sidney Guthman (eds.), *Sabbath Eve Services and Hymns* (New York: Hebrew Publishing, 1944), no. 21; Eric Werner, ed., *The Union Songster* (New York: Central Conference of American Rabbis, 1960), no. 1 (Werner erroneously attributed the text to Hecht). The text appears in American hymnals of multiple denominations going back to at least 1850 (https://www.hymnary.org/text/we_meet_again_in_gladness_and_thankful).

5

THE 1866 *SULZERFEIER*

The Viennese Model and the Grandeur of the Urban Worship

> To the Master in the art of sacred music and singing, Solomon Sulzer, presented by his colleagues, and admirers in the United States of North America, on his official jubilee, in the year 5,626 (1866).
>
> —Inscription on the medal of honor sent by a group of prominent American cantors to Salomon Sulzer on his fortieth year in the pulpit of Vienna's Seitenstettengasse synagogue, May 1866
>
> We have given the description of the handsome medal presented to the celebrated Chasan Sulzer, of Vienna in our German department already last week, as those who took an interest in behalf of the great master, were exclusively Germans.
>
> —Jonah Bondi, editor, *Hebrew Leader*, June 29, 1866

BY 1866, SIXTY-TWO-YEAR-OLD SALOMON SULZER ENJOYED A REPUTATION as the Western world's most prominent champion of synagogue music. Sulzer held the mantle as one of the few musical figures beloved across the spectrum of observance: artful in his compositional style, respectful of "tradition"-based Jewish musical practices, gifted with a celebrated bel canto voice, and conservative enough (partly through congregational fiat) to eschew the attractions of both the mainstream music industry and synagogue instrumental music. Selections from his 1840 publication *Schir Zion* and other works circulated among American synagogue personnel in print and manuscript, hailed by both traditionalists and reformers. Volume two of *Schir Zion*, published in 1865, burnished his reputation further; New York cantor Raphael Lasker, taking the role of an agent, sold the second volume "to Chasonim and Congregations" in America.[1] Cantors who credited Sulzer as their teacher could hang their shingles high in the United States, anticipating additional attention from prospective congregations. Expecting a salary of Sulzer's rank, which one New York paper described as the highest among Vienna's Jewish spiritual personnel (higher even than co-officiating rabbi Noah Mannheimer), was likely ambitious.[2] Yet music's value was on the rise, as American congregations offered salaries of $800 and up for an "educated Chasan" who could replicate Sulzer's successes in their own sanctuaries.[3]

Postbellum America supported a critical mass of Sulzer-trained and -inspired cantors. From Leon Sternberger's 1849 arrival to Samuel Welsch's emigration in 1865, well over a dozen skilled practitioners built reputations in synagogues from Baltimore to Boston. Synagogue music budgets swelled accordingly, and the addition of well-trained choirs, choral directors, and sometimes organs/melodeons generated both admiration and new controversies. Continuing Sulzer's work in an American setting required substantial musical aptitude and precision, often forcing growing urban economic centers of Baltimore, Philadelphia, Boston, and New York to look beyond the Jewish population for top choristers.[4] Helping prominent cantors produce refined music, however, became its own moral good, justifying such practices as a necessary to attain the new standard.

Musical refinement in the synagogue, moreover, supplemented Jews' growing participation in and cultivation of public musical culture.[5] American Jewish newspapers of the time—such as New York's conservative-leaning *Hebrew Leader* and *Jewish Messenger*, its centrist *Asmonean*, and Cincinnati's liberal *Die Deborah* and *The Israelite*—printed extensive entertainment sections highlighting the latest theater, opera, and music performances. Ads from piano manufacturers such as Steck and Steinway appeared beside extensive accounts of community-based entertainments conducted by major figures such as Theodore Thomas and Max Maretzek. As Sulzer cantors assumed the role of urban Jewish music specialists, therefore, they also gained status as an order of versatile artists active in the high cultural scene, and strengthened by their connections to formal music training.

Sulzer had been feted in 1851 for his twenty-fifth anniversary with the Vienna community. Only in 1866, however, did the United States have the musical infrastructure and personnel to join in the celebration. Sulzer held a long-term interest in America: in 1858, for example, rabbinical student Simon Tuska met Sulzer after attending services in Vienna's Stadttempel and reported that "Mr. Sulzer expressed himself gratified at having been listened to by an American; and still more so on my telling him that his melodies are gaining more and more ground in our western world."[6] When American Jewish musical personnel returned the favor in 1866, they joined their European brethren in retelling—and in the process reorienting—the narrative trajectory of synagogue music around Sulzer's biography. Their work brought new exposure to choral music and the "obercantor" as a legitimate American career, and emphasized the attractions of refinement amid an elite matrix of increasingly wealthy urban pulpits.

A Modern (Jewish) Musical Family

The Sulzer name resonated with Jews well beyond the pulpit. Throughout the nineteenth century, American religious figures passing through Vienna occasionally reported on their brushes with Sulzer, whether through meetings or attendance at his services. In New York, Jewish Americans saw Sulzer in broader dimensions as the patriarch of an internationally successful, artistically emancipated musical family.[7] Despite Sulzer's own stated avoidance of the public spotlight, his daughters Henrietta and Marie pursued careers in Italian-language opera.[8] His son Julius briefly served as a cantor and choir director before gaining accolades as a midgrade composer. His son Joseph studied at the Vienna Conservatory. And Sulzer's daughter Sophie moved with her husband, Jakob Altschul, to New York in the late 1860s.[9] Of all his children, however, Henrietta had the greatest New York presence. She gave more than eighty-five performances as an alto in Max Maretzek's Italian Opera Company between 1863 and 1865, including a fund-raiser to establish a Hebrew Asylum for the Aged and Infirm, and her 1864 wedding to bass and fellow company member Hannibal Biachi became a major society event solemnized by New York mayor Charles Gunther.[10] Knowing of Salomon Sulzer, in other words, included an implicit recognition of the generational transitions between the sacred and secular that other Central European Jewish families could understand—including the continuum between the synagogue and opera hall.

The decision in early 1866 of progressive newspaper the *Hebrew Leader* to serialize a translation of Viennese writer Leopold Kompert's 1865 novella *The Carbuncle* (*Der Karfunkel*) directly reflected these conversations.[11] A story about Cantor David Brod, who allows his daughter to train for the opera stage at the hands of the local count, the narrative treated the intergenerational synagogue/opera trope with complexity if not nuance. Brod begins the story preparing to present a melody he had acquired from a Polish Jew to his synagogue, but it fails to engage his congregants. The count, meanwhile, tells Brod's daughter, Bella, that despite her beautiful voice she looks like a carbuncle (boil); and he trains her to shed her Jewish identity for high society under the new name Brodini. Cantor Brod attends a performance of his daughter singing the role of Valentine in Meyerbeer's *Les Huguenots*. He can hardly recognize her until she sings a telltale Act IV air that supposedly comes from Jewish folk music.[12] Afterward, in a backstage meeting, Bella at first rejects her father, but soon relents, falls at her father's feet, and pleads in vain for him to take her back. Brod walks away but remembers the Act IV air and soon introduces it to his congregation with great acclaim. Later, at the moment of his death, Cantor Brod forgives his daughter. Bella, upon hearing of her father's passing, mysteriously disappears from the opera scene and secretly distributes money to Jewish causes each year, funneled through the cantor's dedicated bass/singing partner. Readers followed this fictional clash of cultures in each new front-page installment. A few pages in, however, a real story was taking shape as cantors began organizing a tribute for Brod's arguably true-to-life counterpart.

The American Cantors Prepare to Be Heard

Prominent Prague cantor and Sulzer acolyte Moritz Pereles set forth the call in December 1865, convincing *Hebrew Leader* editor and former Prague resident Jonas Bondi to publish an announcement (*Aufruf*) anticipating Sulzer's anniversary in his paper on January 12, 1866.[13] "Due to the spread of the synagogue choral song of Professor Sulzer in Vienna," stated the announcement, Americans were called on to recognize him and his music, "which has also found its way to the new world, and through which, in many new places of worship, the level of devotion has been especially elevated."[14] Four of the area's premier cantors—Leon Sternberger, Samuel Welsch, J. Wassermann, and Adolph Rubin—moved on the initiative, working with Bondi to give America a voice in the event. Two issues later, an adulatory "card" in the paper announced a planning meeting to honor "Our master, Sulzer, the originator of the new method of Synagogal Singing."[15] Their phrasing offered an important interpretation of Sulzer's contribution to synagogue music, avoiding potentially controversial narratives of musical innovation in favor of a novel "singing method"—implying timbral and harmonic enhancements that augmented existing musical materials. Bondi, in an accompanying article, expanded on this approach to Sulzer's accomplishments:

> Sulzer has the great merit, not of having created new and original choral melodies, adapted for the Jewish worship, but of having clothed in artistic harmony, the old, dearly beloved tunes of our ancestors, whose well-known chords for ages have found their answering echo in the hearts of our fathers.
>
> His art was not to create, but to ennoble, without destroying the origin and the characteristic. His system has been adopted in temples of reform as well as in almost all the larger synagogues of Europe, where the worship is conducted in the old, original manner; it has called into existence the most excellent choirs, facilitated their artistic development, and has added a feature of such interest to our worship, that one only thinks of appreciating the ceremonies.[16]

Over the next several months articles about Sulzer's upcoming festivities appeared relatively regularly in the German section of the paper, both as original accounts and as reprints from Jewish newspapers such as *Abendland* (Prague) and the *New Yorker Journal* (New York).[17] German American readers, on a standard two-to-three-week delay from events in Europe, learned of good wishes and commemorative objects honoring Sulzer as they arrived in Vienna from Altona, Hohenems, Voralberg, Amsterdam, Leipzig, Berlin, Frankfurt, Dresden, Pesth, Bremen, Brody, Lviv, Paris, Trieste, and elsewhere across Europe. In early April, after the *Sulzerfeier* had concluded but before accounts of the event came to America, Bondi provided addenda in the *Hebrew Leader* reminding readers to give liberally to the New York committee honoring Sulzer; a similar appeal went out in *Die Deborah*.[18] Such exhortations attempted to reinforce cultural continuity with Central Europe, while establishing America as a cultural center that could participate fully in the conversation, if from a distance.

These intermediate rounds of publicity around Sulzer's celebration also carried implications for professionalization. The *Deborah* article highlighted Sulzer's story as a way to emphasize the idea of the cantorate as a class—*Chasanimthum*—that had a role in the Jewish community's well-being. "Sulzer taught the community both how a Chasan should be, and how he should be treated," stated the article. "The itinerant Chasan-class has ended with Sulzer; there is no longer a place for the wandering hired Chasan, equipped with his abundant trills and profane songs, for which this old man deserves gratitude and appreciation, even more so from his professional colleagues."[19] Sulzer represented not just security but also respectability to the emerging profession of the "modern" cantorate, who were poised to benefit the pulpits they served through a deeper, more clergy-like knowledge of musical spirituality. The subscription list for Sulzer's gift showed the breadth of this claim. By mid-April, seven cantors from New York, Philadelphia, and Hartford, Connecticut, had donated $5 apiece, but additional supporters included synagogue presidents, at least one doctor, and Ahawath Chesed organist, Charles Karpeles, among others.[20]

An American Debate over Sulzer-Mania

During these same months, in the English-language press, the local Sulzer committee announcement kindled a level of restiveness about the rising resources devoted to music in the prayer service, and its implications for the individual congregant. *Jewish Messenger* editor S. M. Isaacs, in particular, printed a reader's response that ridiculed the cantor's abilities ("A friend suggests that it is derived from the word '*Cant-or*,' meaning 'cannot read or pray'") and questioned the cantor's own faith ("Does the phrase 'our master Sulzer' ignore their Master in Heaven?").[21] The conservative Isaacs, witnessing the proliferating number of choral synagogues in the area, used this cue as an opportunity to speak out against what he saw as the trendy and misguided co-opting of synagogue music by skilled professionals, the creep of choral music into ever-greater portions of the service, and concerns that congregations were sacrificing meaningful Jewish prayer in pursuit of aesthetic beauty:

> Why [cantors] term Sulzer their "master" we do not know; for sure we are that [Sulzer] is ashamed of many of his disciples. The fact is, synagogue singing by the music of Sulzer and some other "masters," has become quite a mania. Time was, when Israelites went to synagogue, to offer their own words of prayer and praise to Heaven; now they attend to listen to paid choristers, who sing their parts to satisfy the auditors, but whether such chaunting is instrumental in wafting the soul to Heaven, is very doubtful. We prophesy that the time will come when Israelites will insist on *congregational* singing, not on trained choristers alone. The mania has seized on orthodox and reform, and those that are opposed to it are accused of having no ears for music. We, for ourselves, are in favor of singing being an adjunct to prayer, but then the singers should be God-fearing Israelites, who, awed by the responsibility they owe to Heaven, will say their prayers, as well as sing their parts. We are advocates for the singers understanding their prayers as well as their "notes." We are

staunch adherents to the principle that Jews should be employed to lead and to chaunt the portions of the services allotted to them, but when this principle is departed from, and a mixed worship is instituted, it derogates from Judaism, and tarnishes our reputation as Israelites.[22]

Isaacs's article caught the attention of reform champion Isaac Mayer Wise in Cincinnati, who three weeks later responded caustically in *The Israelite*. Wise, in his self-fashioned role as the herald of Sulzer's music in the United States, dismissed Isaacs's response as "ignorance coupled with shameless arrogance."[23] Using an idiomatic and illuminating rhetorical strategy, Wise recast Isaacs's position as the regressive side of a battle of musical leaders that pitted "the old, run-out, used-up, hoarse Hazan [Isaacs] against the modern Cantor of the progressive school [Sulzer]." Wise attacked Isaacs's populist appeal to individual Jewish autonomy as naively optimistic, stating, "in that entire [*Jewish Messenger*] office there is not a man who can read Hebrew without the crutches of vowel points, not one man who ever read a Hebrew book besides 'his prayers,' with an English translation appended." Fine music in the Sulzerian school, Wise implied, elevated Jewish populations whose so-called literacy existed only in Isaacs's imagination. "The excellent Sulzer, whose name has a better sound than a few hundred old Hazanim can bring forth," represented to Wise a means to his own ideological goal of a forward-thinking, devoted, and liturgically active Jewish population.

The Cantors' Tribute

By mid-May, with about $145 collected (approximately $2,235 in 2017 dollars), the Sulzer committee decided to forge a solid gold medallion that would accompany an intricately inscribed statement of dedication. Produced by lower Manhattan metalsmiths Klotz and Tanner, the 2½-ounce, 2½-inch diameter, ⅛-inch-thick medallion visually embodied its commissioners' standing as American admirers of Sulzer's work—and perhaps their own status as interpreters of German Jewish liturgical music.[24] The front side featured a lyre surrounded by an oak wreath, a neoclassical image typically used to honor esteemed European musical figures. Around the edge, the smiths engraved Psalm 119:54, a rich and knowing choice that encapsulated the cantors' relationship with the composer: "Your songs are like laws to me, wherever I may dwell."[25] On the back, an embossed American eagle and flag accompanied the words *Dem Meister die Krone* (To the Master [goes] the Crown) along with the English dedication, "To the Master in the art of sacred music and singing, Solomon Sulzer, presented by his colleagues, and admirers in the United States of North America, on his official jubilee, in the year 5,626—1866."[26] Simultaneously conferring quasi-divine qualities on their intellectual progenitor—commensurate with veneration practices for other German intellectuals—and showing a deep knowledge of Jewish classical texts, the signatories offered Sulzer an idiomatic tribute in an American variation.

The carefully composed and ornately calligraphed address acted similarly, identifying the supplicants as "German men [*deutsche Männer*]" who dwelled "on the far shores of the ocean." Living and working in America, and administering to populations with strong connections to Central Europe, the signees deemed themselves "men of your profession" whose status was elevated by Sulzer's work.[27] Rhetorically framing themselves as participants in a musical diaspora, the donors thus extended Sulzer's cultural orbit and strengthened their ethnic and religious claims to Vienna, enhancing their own local authority as respected musical figures in the process.

America in the Sulzerian Orbit

Sulzer had shown interest in the United States before, but the gift brought America fully to his attention.[28] On October 15, 1866, Sulzer wrote to Sternberger and Welsch confirming receipt of the medallion, thanking them for their initiative and complimenting them as "the most eminent men of my faith and race in America."[29] Likely realizing the developing market that the United States represented, and the potential spread of his influence, Sulzer remained in touch. Three years later, when the same collection of cantors contributed to a "Jubilee Festival" sponsored by the local Zion Lodge of B'nai Brith, Sulzer composed an original setting of Psalm 133 for Welsch to sing with choir and organ/harmonium accompaniment; the text, "How glorious it is to meet as brothers," may well have carried a further symbolic meaning in deepening Sulzer's relationship with the American cantorate.[30] Welsch, in turn, dedicated his 1869 setting of Psalm 93 to Sulzer (see fig. 5.1). That same year, cantors further insinuated Sulzer's name into popular culture when New York's *Jewish Messenger* picked up on Cantor Jacob Kantrowitz's (likely spurious) claim that British drag singer William Lingard had appropriated Sulzer's 1865 *Kedusha* melody in his popular 1868 song "Walking Down Broadway."[31] Communications like these strengthened Sulzer's presence in the United States as figure whose influence could raise Jewish music, and its specialized practitioners, to a new level.

Figure 5.1. Samuel Welsch, *Psalm 93: Der Herr ist König* (New York: J. Schuberth, 1869), cover. With inscription from Welsch to Alois Kaiser dated October 1869. (Source: Klau Library, Hebrew Union College)

By the end of 1866, German American cantors' efforts to honor Salomon Sulzer had set an ambitious program for synagogue music that emphasized craft as a medium for accomplishment and religious devotion. Synagogues with choral programs and beautiful singing became increasingly attractive in a competitive marketplace. Rising salaries and other musical expenditures required an affluence that mainly prosperous urban environments could sustain, and businesslike operations to support ever more elaborate musical infrastructures. Those congregations that chose alternate approaches, whether because of a lack of funds, personnel, members, or ideological differences, developed their own ideas about the sounds of worship, as other chapters have shown. Yet Sulzer remained a symbol of the most visible of the musical developments in American Jewish life, embracing the German identity of its constituents, and the cultural status it entailed, in order to give beauty a controlling stake in American synagogue services.

Notes

1. "An Chasonim und Gemeinden," *Die Deborah*, December 22, 1865, 100.

2. "Vienna—The Communal Budget," *Jewish Messenger*, September 30, 1864, 98. Sulzer's 1863 salary was 2,383 florins (about $1,500 1863 US dollars according to http://www.historical statistics.org/Currencyconverter.html, or $29,180 in 2017 dollars). Rabbis Noah Mannheimer and Adolf Jellinek earned 2,205 and 2,021 florins, respectively.

3. This claim refines Kimmy Caplan's discussion of cantorial salaries in the late nineteenth century: their value hinged as much on provenance, often through connection to Salomon Sulzer, as it did on raw talent. See Kimmy Caplan, "In God We Trust: Salaries and Income of American Orthodox Rabbis, 1881–1924," *American Jewish History* 86, no. 1 (March 1998), 88–93, 102–5.

4. *Jewish Messenger* editor S. M. Isaacs noted with displeasure a Rochester, New York, synagogue's hiring of non-Jewish choristers in his editorial, "The Sad Effects of Change," *Jewish Messenger*, July 21, 1865, 20.

5. See Judah M. Cohen, "Dawning Sounds: Jews and Music in the Young Republic," in *By Dawn's Early Light: Jewish Contributions to American Culture from the Nation's Founding to the Civil War*, ed. Adam Mendelssohn and Dale Baumgarten (Princeton, NJ: Princeton University Library, 2016), 113–22.

6. *American Israelite*, January 7, 1858.

7. In 1854, for example, the *Asmonean* covered the betrothal of one of Sulzer's daughters "to a gentleman in Cincinnati"; highlighted another Sulzer daughter's success as a prima donna singer in Madrid "that yet refuses to Jews a residence in the country [but] applauds every evening the *cavatina* of a Jewess"; and noted the passing of Sulzer's mother. *Asmonean*, June 23, 1854, 79; August 4, 1854, 127.

8. "Oesterreich" [Letter from Prague, February 28, 1849], *Israels Herold*, June 1, 1849, 78.

9. "Vienna—the Gold Medal," *Jewish Messenger*, June 20, 1862, 186. Sophie's son Emil was born in 1864 in Vienna; her son Leo was born in 1870 in New York (http://www.hohenemsgenealogie.at/gen/familygroup.php?familyID=F9020&tree=Hohenems).

10. "Henrietta Sulzer," in *Music in Gotham* (http://www.musicingotham.org/person/747); Henrietta Sulzer performing at Hebrew Asylum benefit performance, November 17, 1863 (http://www.musicingotham.org/event/30179); marriage of Henrietta Sulzer and Hannibal Biachi (http://www.musicingotham.org/event/42378).

11. *The Carbuncle* appeared in Kompert's 1865 collection, *Geschichten einer Gasse* (Tales of a Street). Kompert's connection to Vienna's Jewish musical world could also be seen in his poem celebrating the opening of the city's "Zion" singing society (Hanoch Avenary, ed., *Kantor Salomon Sulzer und Seine Zeit: eine Dokumentation* [Sigmaringen: Jan Thorbecke Verlag, 1985], 124–26).

12. Optimistic but often dubious claims of hidden Jewish tunes or themes in Meyerbeer's operas continue to preoccupy both fiction and scholarship alike into the twenty-first century. See, for example, William Pencak, "Jewish Themes in the Operas of Giacomo Meyerbeer," *Shofar* 32, no. 1 (2013), 43–59.

13. See Jonathan D. Sarna, "The Touro Monument Controversy: Aniconism vs. Anti-Idolatry in a Mid-Nineteenth Century American Jewish Religious Dispute," in *Between Jewish Tradition and Modernity*, ed. Michael A. Meyer and David N. Myers (Detroit, MI: Wayne State University Press, 2014), 89. Bondi moved to the United States from Prague in 1858.

14. *Hebrew Leader* 7, no. 15 (January 12, 1866).

15. "A Card," *Hebrew Leader*, January 26, 1866, 4. This note was repeated in German in the same issue.

16. [J. Bondi], "Professor Sulzer of Vienna and His New Method of Synagogue Singing," *Hebrew Leader* 7, no. 18 (February 2, 1866), 2.

17. *Hebrew Leader* 7, no. 26 (March 30, 1866), 2.

18. *Hebrew Leader* 8, no. 1 (April 13, 1866), 3, 5; "Für Sulzer," *Die Deborah*, April 6, 1866, 159.

19. "Für Sulzer," *Die Deborah*, April 6, 1866, 159.

20. "Sulzerfeier," *Hebrew Leader* 8, no. 2 (April 20, 1866), 14.

21. "Answers to Correspondents," *Jewish Messenger*, February 2, 1866, 5.

22. Ibid.

23. [Isaac Mayer Wise], "The Hazan vs. the Cantor," *The Israelite*, February 23, 1866, 268.

24. "Bericht der Sulzer Committee," *Hebrew Leader* 8, no. 12 (June 29, 1866), 2.

25. "The Sulzer Medal," *Hebrew Leader* 8, no. 13 (July 6, 1866). The *Jewish Messenger* apparently misreported the verse on the medal ("The Sulzer Testimonial," *Jewish Messenger*, June 29, 1866, 4).

26. "Bericht der Sulzer Committee," *Hebrew Leader* 8, no. 12 (June 29, 1866), 2.

27. Ibid.

28. See Avenary, *Kantor Salomon Sulzer*, 253–55, and Simon Tuska's account of his meeting with Sulzer in *American Israelite*, January 7, 1858. Sulzer's interest in the United States thus dates to at least the early/mid-1850s.

29. "Sulzer's Entgegnung," *Die Deborah*, November 12, 1866.

30. "Zion Lodge," *Jewish Messenger*, January 15, 1869, 4; Avenary, *Kantor Salomon Sulzer*, 205, 285 (noting Sulzer's dedication to Welsch *and* Sternberger); the piece appears without attribution in the 1905 revision of *Schir Zion* (ed. Joseph Sulzer), vol. 3, no. 483. The same concert also featured Sulzer's 1866 setting of Psalm 42 (verses 6, 10, 11, and 12), "in honor of the Jewish soldiers killed in the late Prussian war."

31. "Rabbi Sulzer v. Lingard," *Jewish Messenger*, February 19, 1869, [4]; *Jewish Messenger*, February 26, 1869, [2]; William Lingard, "Walking Down Broadway" (New York: William A. Pond, 1868). This story was picked up by other newspapers as well: see, for example, *Daily Memphis Avalanche*, February 25, 1869, [1].

6

A NEW CANTOR, A NEW REPERTOIRE
Zimrath Yah

> We see every day that, in the present constitution of Jewish affairs in this country, we can expect no American Chazonim, no ministers born and trained here and understanding our ways. Our only resource has been to send to Europe and be contented with some third rate man, of but little character in his own country, and of little or no knowledge of our language. There are some noble exceptions; but we are pained to say, the generality of these foreign Chazonim are slovenly, and but little acquainted with Jewish lore. Perhaps we would persuade a better class to "cross the water," if we offered more liberal inducements. But stories reach Europe of the small salaries, and bad treatment that Chazonim receive in America, and induce the better class to stay at home, while those who have but little reputation in their own country and whose desires are fewer, and who are more contented with the poor salaries offered, apply for situations, and are accepted, generally by reason of their more limited desires.
>
> —"Wanted—A Chazan," *Jewish Messenger*, August 19, 1864

THE MID-1860S BROUGHT RENEWED ENERGY TO AMERICAN SYNAGOGUE music and its advocates. Salomon Sulzer, whose crossover bel canto voice and choral compositions became to many an exemplar of Central European Jewish progress, extended a standard of achievement and elegance across the Atlantic that captivated Jewish populations seeking to build respected synagogue music programs. While the above 1864 editorialist in New York's *Jewish Messenger* had disparaged the poor quality of European synagogue leadership in America, the end of the Civil War stirred optimism. America's participation in the 1866 *Sulzerfeier* clarified a standard for congregations and cantors to use as they cultivated their own musical activities. Sulzer's inspiration, however, affected different religious leaders in different ways. Isaac Mayer Wise and other musically literate rabbinical figures had introduced Sulzer's music in the 1840s and 1850s as part of a reforming philosophy that gave congregants the tools to take charge of their own cultural development. Other leaders, in contrast, saw in Sulzer a tantalizing vision of the musical specialist-liturgist, whose artistic refinement, reputation, and conspicuous expense could elevate Judaism's cultural capital in the American landscape. Synagogue boards that shared this philosophy consequently designated significant resources to music programs as early as the 1840s: in 1856, *Occident* editor Isaac Leeser noted that New York's Temple Emanu-El devoted such a large portion of its annual expenses to its choir—a sum equaling nearly half of the combined salaries of "the ministers, readers, secretaries and sextons"—that "the officers have a right to complain of inadequate compensation."[1] The next wave of cantors, embracing this second philosophy, grew that expense further, while marketing their own leadership skills as equivalent, or at least comparable, to that of the rabbi.

With the end of the Civil War, a new round of musical expansion began in American synagogues. And a new, trained generation of figures from Europe came to satisfy rising demand, embodying the Viennese model in ways that extended the portfolios of elder statesmen such as Leon Sternberger, Jacob Kantrowitz, and Adolph Kramer. The arrivals dived into national discussions about American liturgy, striving to provide a common musical repertoire of the highest order. They pushed for artistry and held up the cantorate as an attractive career for devoted musicians. Complemented by able choirs and powerful organs, they distanced themselves from teaching and slaughterer roles, which they deemed below their social rank. Instead, they promoted attractive and accessible worship, enhanced by their ability to provide new music and expert direction. Adopting progressive social norms, they established themselves as intellectuals who treated their trade with scientific rigor, while imbuing their profession with a deepening history and legacy. Job security followed, raising music's potential as a symbol of Jewish cultivation alongside rabbis' scholarly prominence, and empowering cantors to assume control over Jewish music as a "tradition"—with broad and far-reaching implications.

Among the music publications of this era, none proved as central or significant as *Zimrath Yah*, a four-volume compendium of Jewish liturgical music published from 1871 to 1886, edited and distributed chiefly by cantors Samuel Welsch (1835–1901) of New York City and Alois Kaiser (1840–1908) of

Baltimore, with the assistance of New York's Morris Goldstein (1840–1906) and pianist (later industrialist/polymath) Isaac Leopold Rice (1850–1915). *Zimrath Yah* reflected Sulzer cantors' sustained effort to forge a national synagogue-based repertoire in same wave of 1870s activity that led Isaac Mayer Wise to establish the key institutions of Reform Judaism. Its extensive engagement with both the creators and styles of European synagogue music, transformed to address the American liturgical landscape, established a durable model for American synagogue leadership that came to dominate the Jewish communal imagination, marking the cantor's emerging position as a guardian of a Jewish sonic heritage.

A New Generation Gathers

Just as New York's cantors celebrated the United States' 1866 "arrival" in the Sulzerian sphere, they also heralded a general push toward a more polished synagogue choral sound. Congregations valued Sulzer-trained cantors highly, but even without direct contact with Sulzer, cantors could advertise their European conservatory training as proof of accomplishment. Many New York congregations, in the midst of building expansion and modernization, took interest in these leaders and looked to trade up—regardless of their place on the ideological spectrum.

In tandem with these changes, technological developments in music printing reduced barriers to publication.[2] Before the 1860s, the era's two most significant musical compendia—the first volumes of Sulzer's *Schir Zion* (1840) and Naumbourg's *Zemiroth Yisrael* (1847/1852/1857)—appealed mainly to professionals because they were too expensive for mass consumption. Even those synagogues dedicated to establishing elaborate music programs rarely purchased more than one copy or relied on the cantor to bring his own; the large quarto format of compendia (in this case about 9.5 in. × 13 in.) made them unwieldy for individuals, and their publication in full score typically required a separate copyist to write out singers' parts in a usable form. As American Jewish rabbis and intellectuals introduced new American prayer books for mass consumption beginning in the 1850s, however, cantors and composers began to entertain the possibility of wider distribution. Local publications from Philadelphia organist Wilhelm Fischer in 1863 and Cleveland-based G. M. Cohen in 1864 gave America a voice, but a revised edition of Naumbourg's first volume (1864) and Sulzer's more sophisticated follow-up volume (1865) continued to showcase the artistic prominence of music from Europe.³ Growing interest in producing a specifically American form of Jewish worship became a coveted goal, and opened the door for both local and national innovation.

The expanding inventory of cantorial want ads in Jewish periodicals complemented a spate of new debates about the role of cantors, choirs, and instrumental accompaniment. One 1865 article titled, "The Sad Effects of Change," bemoaned the decision of synagogues to pay its choristers as competition for good voices increased.⁴ Others openly announced the lucrative contracts of their ministers: an 1866 announcement of Judah Kramer's $1,000 salary at B'nai Jeshurun led the *Jewish Messenger*'s editor to note with satisfaction that Orthodox synagogues cared also about the quality of their musical leaders.⁵ And the same journal applauded New York congregation Darech Amuno's hiring of Theodore Guinsburg in 1868 to pursue music with an all-male choir.⁶ While theological and liturgical differences increasingly marked distinctions between Orthodox and Reform, the idiomatic improvement of music in the public ritual remained a point of general interest.⁷

Zimrath Yah: Dramatis Personae

The émigré cantors who pursued this path in America, including *Zimrath Yah*'s editors came mainly from clerical families in Austro-Hungary. Attracted to the goings-on in Vienna and participating at least to some extent in Sulzer's international ambitions to define Jewish sound, they had trained simultaneously as teachers in the city's teaching academy (*Lehrerseminar*) and as musicians in local conservatories. Their careers progressed accordingly: and while achieving some prominence in Europe, many flourished after their calls to American pulpits, energetically fashioning a Jewish liturgical soundtrack that sought to match the grand plans of their rabbinical partners. Commanding salaries that bolstered their status as cocreators, they worked to adapt Sulzer's paradigm to American soil.

Samuel Welsch, after a childhood in Prague, likely gained his secular training in a Vienna *Realschul* (secondary school) while gaining a religious musical education with Salomon Sulzer; in the early 1860s, he returned Prague to begin his career (see fig. 6.1). This educational arrangement, which appeared to bridge the sanctuary and the concert hall, led Welsch to take a role in the local "Arion" singing society (*Singverein*) and continued as he took a proper cantor position at Prague's Meisel Synagogue in

Figure 6.1. Portrait of Samuel Welsch, probably 1860s. (Credit: Abraham Schwadron Collection at the National Library of Israel)

February 1863, presumably while promoting Sulzer's cantor/choir model.[8] In late 1864, Welsch apparently gave notice of his resignation, and, attracted to New York's Bohemian congregation Ahawath Chesed, he stepped onto American soil at the start of 1865 to commence a three-year contract that began at $1,750 and rose to $2,000 in the third year.[9] Additional accommodations from Ahawath Chesed, including the congregation's agreement to hire a series of "second" cantors for weekdays and holidays, emphasized expectations that Welsch channel his energies into musical excellence, and raise the synagogue's national profile.

Welsch's ambitions to expand the cantor's role in the United States seemed to match Ahawath Chesed's expectations. The congregation lacked a rabbi, so he began his term by assuming both musical and nonmusical capacities. That June, less than a month and a half after starting his position, Welsch officiated at his congregation's memorial service for Abraham Lincoln (part of a national day of fasting and prayer), "deliver[ing] an effective address before the 'Memorial of the Dead' [prayer], speaking of the virtues of the lamented President Lincoln, and the tragedy of his death."[10] Three months later, he and Ahawath Chesed's organist, Charles Korzeles, announced a short-lived school that taught cantorial arts among its various subjects.[11] By his first anniversary with Ahawath Chesed, Welsch had achieved remarkable success: visiting rabbi Isidor Kalisch commented positively on Welsch's effective training of the choir, and Welsch's musical presentation of the Sabbath service had come to generate such impressive attendance that the congregants gave him a gift of $1,000 "to refurnish his house."[12]

In 1866, Rabbi Adolph Huebsch came to Ahawath Chesed from Prague, giving the synagogue a true power team. When the congregation threw a party to mark Huebsch's short trip to Europe about a year into his contract, Welsch prepared a rich and meaningful musical program. Held in the house of synagogue president Ignatz Stein, the event included a short performance by the congregation's choir, comprising men and women, Jews and non-Jews; it ended with Felix Mendelssohn's choral setting of Ernst von Feuchtersleben's 1825 poem "Auf Wiesersehn." Huebsch thanked Welsch for his "many respective merits in improving the prayer service of the congregation, and," most significantly, "called him his friend and colleague" (*"Freund und College"*). His comments affirmed a clear productive division of power in the pulpit: "for the functions of the rabbi and the cantor are different, and only through friendly and collegial co-operation could a beneficial influence be exercised on the congregation and the worship."[13] This extraordinary acknowledgment of balance between intellectual and musical leadership of one of the country's leading synagogues highlighted Welsch's rapid rise as an American counterpart to Sulzer. And it continued in September, when Huebsch strenuously defended Ahawath Chesed's use of non-Jewish women in its choirs from attacks by *Jewish Messenger* editor S. M. Isaacs.[14] The effectiveness with which the pair maintained this balance likely led the congregation to give Huebsch permission to revise their existing liturgy in July 1868, probably with the implication that Welsch would write the music. As part of their joint leadership, the pair would also consecrate the synagogue's grand new building in 1872.[15]

Alois Kaiser arrived in New York as part of an 1866 competition for the cantorial pulpit of congregation Shaarei Shomayim, then on Rivington Street in New York. Born in Szobotist, Hungary, according to a later-in-life account, Kaiser's family gained permission to resettle in Vienna about six years later. By the mid-1850s, he sang regularly in Sulzer's choir—the same retrospective account described him as a star soloist—and in 1859, he began his ascent through musical pulpits, first as an assistant cantor in Vienna's up-and-coming Fünfhaus neighborhood synagogue (ca. 1859–63), and then in Prague's Neusynagoge (ca. 1864–66) during which time he attended the city's music conservatory.[16] Kaiser's journey to New York in July 1866, to answer Shaarei Shomayim's want ad for a cantor who could lead choral services, ended in disappointment. He quickly discovered that the post had gone provisionally to Ignatz Gerstel, another "Sulzer disciple" from Buchau (near Württemberg); Gerstel's reputation as a composer who could provide new settings for *Minhag America* likely enhanced his application.[17] Kaiser remained in the United States, however, receiving a commendation from the local *Hebrew Leader* newspaper for his musical ability, his demeanor, and his positive recommendations.[18] Ultimately, Baltimore's Oheb Shalom congregation gave him a hearing and hired him shortly thereafter to assume its "teacher"/*lehrer* position. There, Kaiser plied his musical responsibilities next to prominent rabbi Benjamin Szold, whose 1864 liturgy *Abodat Yisrael* had already become an important part of several American Germanophone congregations (see fig. 6.2).

Appearing frequently in Oheb Shalom's minutes, Kaiser's assertions about the importance of music generally received a sympathetic ear. In July 1867, the congregation granted Kaiser an extra $300 in recognition of his "talents" and contributions to the synagogue; by September, the

Figure 6.2. Portrait of Alois Kaiser and Benjamin Szold, 1868. (Credit: Jewish Museum of Maryland)

congregation had purchased a melodeon, presumably to help the choir rehearse, and retained a choral director in local musician Nicholas Tillman.[19] In December, the congregation granted Kaiser $30 to purchase Samuel Naumbourg's music for service use, and over the next years Kaiser advocated for an expanded choir.[20] His salary grew regularly as well; while the congregation paid Kaiser half of Szold's $3,000 salary in 1867, by 1872 the gap had narrowed to just $500 (Kaiser's $2,500 to Szold's $3,000), in addition to a $1,600 budget for the choir.[21]

Back in New York, congregation Anshe Chesed on Norfolk Street began taking steps to implement a similar musical program under a rabbi whose own reforms had created some upheaval. Although in 1865, the congregation had signed Cantor Leon Sternberger to a five-year, $2,000 contract, possible differences with recently imported Rabbi Moses Mielziner led Sternberger to depart about a year later for David Einhorn's Adas Jeshurun congregation on West Thirty-Fourth Street.[22] Mielziner's persistent, if controversial, reforming efforts riled his somewhat more conservative congregants; however, in 1868, he succeeded in rededicating the synagogue as a vessel for Isaac Mayer Wise's *Minhag America*, with a new organ and choir under the charge of cantor Morris Goldstein.[23] Born around 1840 to a family of cantors in Kecskemét, Hungary, Goldstein also likely studied in Vienna while gaining experience in Sulzer's choir. His older brother Josef (b. 1838) became cantor of Vienna's Leopoldstadt synagogue in 1857, likely overshadowing Morris's early career in the same city.[24] Goldstein nonetheless gained the notice of an Anshe Chesed board that sought a Sulzerian aesthetic, and the congregation successfully lured him to the United States. His work at the building's dedication appeared to affirm the board's decision, with his strong training and "clear and well-modulated tenor voice, exceedingly powerful in the high notes."[25] The *Jewish Messenger* noted shortly afterward that Goldstein continued to excite his congregants. "Receiving the chanting of a *Reader* with applause and 'Bravos' is somewhat unusual," the paper noted, "but Mr. Goldstein and the organ of the Norfolk Street synagogue had a better reception on Sunday last than many a tenor at the [Musical] Academy."[26]

All three cantors, along with a few other contemporaries, worked closely with prominent rabbis on the pulpit; and when those rabbis received permission to revise their congregations' liturgies the cantors assumed the responsibility of providing new music. Text alone, after all, only went so far in giving communities ownership over the synagogue service. In the spirit of Isaac Mayer Wise, who also planned to revise his own 1857 *Minhag America* for a national audience during this time, creators of new prayer books recognized music's role in reinforcing their texts' new outlook and feeling, while establishing a contrast with the previous form. New compositions from local musicians likely heightened the anticipation of these works as reflections of a contemporary American Jewish identity.

These new cantors commanded salaries and respect that brought them closer to their rabbinic counterparts. Welsch, however, established himself on top of the cantorial hierarchy as a prominent voice for synagogue music and the cantorate more broadly. His authority at Ahawath Chesed transformed into a role as a music critic for the *Hebrew Leader*.[27] And he appeared to become an agent for Naumbourg's compositions in America. Welsch also began to follow in Sulzer's footsteps as a composer of celebrated liturgical settings.[28] His 1869 choral setting of Psalm 93, "Der Herr ist König" (dedicated to Sulzer), received a rave review in the *Hebrew Leader*; and on November 13–14, the ideologically diverse trio of New York congregations B'nai Jeshurun, Anshe Chesed, and Shaarei Shomayim all included Welsch's psalm setting in their services, perhaps symbolically taking a step toward an "American" liturgical sound.[29] In a step beyond Sulzer, moreover, Welsch also performed in occasional public concerts, such as a benefit for the Maimonides Library Association and a widely advertised March 1867 benefit with Cantor Gerstel.[30] This latter concert "delighted the audience, many of whom had listened perhaps with awe to their intoning the sacred services of the Sabbath"—but also received a warning from the *Jewish Messenger* about sullying the sacred cantorial office.[31] Such a broad array of activities allowed Welsch to cross cultural, liturgical, and ideological borders, taking leadership beyond the boundaries of the synagogue sanctuary.

The rapid development of the American concert music scene at this time also benefited the new cantors' ambitions, cultivating connections that would come to fruition in *Zimrath Yah* through the early career of Isaac L. Rice. Born in Wachenheim, Bavaria, in 1850, Rice moved with his family to Philadelphia six years later. Fellow German émigré pianist Carl Wolfsohn, who had come to America in 1854, discovered the young Rice there and began to cultivate his talents as part of a broader agenda to develop American art music performance (which included alliances with orchestra pioneer Theodore Thomas). Under Wolfsohn's tutelage, the eleven-year-old Rice performed his first public concert on January 28, 1862, in Philadelphia's Music Fund Hall, opening appropriately by performing a piano duet with Wolfsohn of the Coronation March from Meyerbeer's opera *The Prophet*.[32] Yearly concerts followed, each featuring Rice with prominent local musicians.[33] Rice continued his studies in Europe at the Paris Conservatoire from 1866 to 1868 (where he also provided updates to the Philadelphia *Evening Bulletin*) and then followed up with a year of teaching in London and a concert tour of Germany.[34] In late 1869, Rice planned his return to the United States, reuniting with Wolfsohn to start a "Beethoven Society" in Philadelphia and arranging concerts in Philadelphia's Academy of Music (October) and at New York's Steinway Hall (December). He also exhibited his talent as a composer by premiering a new large-scale composition—a three-movement "fantasia in concerto form."[35] Welsch praised Rice's work in the *Hebrew Leader*, while fending off accusations from the *New York Herald*'s critic that the second movement borrowed too obviously from Beethoven's seventh symphony.[36] Rice, in turn, remained in New York to continue his piano instruction career and very likely struck up a friendship with the city's premier cantor.

Working within a vibrant Jewish population that participated in a wide array of musical activities across the religious and social spectrum, this quartet of liturgical music artists sought to give music its own identity in a national model of religious practice. Welsch and Goldstein's paths crossed regularly as fellow New York cantors; Welsch appeared to follow Rice's career avidly; and Welsch had sent a copy of his Psalm 93 to Kaiser in October 1869, though their connection may have begun earlier in Prague.[37] By banding together, they intended to make music a medium for unifying American Jewish religious observance, superseding the Jewish liturgical differences of their rabbinical brethren.

1870: Launching *Zimrath Yah*

The seed for *Zimrath Yah* germinated in 1870, when Isaac Mayer Wise held a meeting of rabbis in Cleveland, the first of what would be three gatherings to help him revise his *Minhag America* for a national audience. Following the first meeting, Wise publicly called on his colleagues to support his English-language work by supplying him with verses that could supersede the "German prayers and hymns, which in a few years will be obsolete in our midst."[38] Samuel Welsch, perhaps made aware of the project through Huebsch, sensed an opportunity and sent a letter to Wise offering "to convene a meeting of all *Hazanim* favorable to modern Synagogal music, to agree upon a selection of compositions for the American synagogue."[39] Wise published a warm response to Welsch in *The Israelite*, emphasizing music's value in his vision of the American Jewish future. "Important as it is for the American synagogue to have one common liturgy," he proclaimed,

> it is probably no less important, to establish also a uniformity of melodies and songs. Music, in numerous instances, is a more adequate expression of prayer, petition, supplication, thanksgiving, repentance, mourning, gladness, adoration, praise and glory, than words can do it. Any how, it impresses itself upon the heart deeper than words, gives soul, ideality and elevating pinions to the sacred poet's worshiping sounds. The spoken Psalm, however sublime and beautiful, is lifeless to the masses; the Psalm clad in sombre melody and rising upon the swelling harmony, imparts life, emotion, and lofty-sentiments to the worshiping masses. Few, if any, can resist the inspiring influence of grand choral music. The evidence to support this hypothesis is before us every Sabbath in the temple.[40]

Wise's gushing endorsement opened a space for American synagogue composition in his planned liturgy, which he justified in asserting a pivot from the "plentive [sic] melodies" of the past to a music that could better characterize America's "lofty temples of Israel, with that youthful, vigorous, and hopeful spirit." That music, moreover, needed a sound that Judaism could claim as its own. "Other music, other melodies, another harmony," he opined, "is required than those in imitation of Protestant worship." Viewing the task as both "sacred" and "divine," he outlined a possible path, building on the works of "Sulzer, Naumbourg and Weintraub," the efforts of "the organists in our various synagogues, whose composed or adopted music, will be found of eminent value," and the works of known Jewish composers such as Jacques Fromental Halévy.[41] Sensing the potential to gather the cantors to his cause, moreover, he invited Welsch and any other interested musicians to the second *Minhag America* meeting in New York on October 24.[42]

Welsch found his spotlight at that second meeting. On the second day of the rabbinical gathering, two attendees praised Welsch's composition "Der Herr ist König," and elicited promises from their colleagues to introduce it more broadly in American congregations. (And they followed through: Wise's congregation premiered the piece at the end of November, and in New Orleans, the Jewish Widows and Orphans Home included it in an anniversary celebration the following January.[43]) The rabbis also agreed on the penultimate day of the meeting "to appoint Cantor S. Welsch, in connection with two more experts [including G. M. Cohen], to prepare the music to the Hebrew portion of the new prayer-book."[44] By the time they dispersed, Welsch had earned the support to pursue a unified American musical liturgy and create a musical repertoire that could be beautiful, affordable, convenient, accessible, and quickly available.

Welsch's star continued to rise. By January 1871, a month after directing the music at the cornerstone-laying ceremony for his congregation's new building, he had teamed up with Goldstein, Kaiser, and Rice to publish a prospectus for *Zimrath Yah* in *Die Deborah*.[45] Symbolically responding to Wise's own "Synagogal Music" column, the four musicians asserted that "for all the excellence of the work published up until now in this field—Sulzer's, Naumbourg's, and others—it is nonetheless a fact that due to the reorganization of the Order of Prayer, which in the spirit of the times has abandoned the older prayers, the most excellent pieces from these works can no longer be applied."[46] This declaration placed progressive American Jewish liturgy ideologically ahead of European practices, and gave the writers license to scrutinize European musical works and edit them for inclusion into the new musical order: "The editors of *Zimrath Yah* will therefore make an effort to incorporate those masterpieces, as well as those traditional melodies that have become embedded in the hearts of the Jewish community, and even those worthy on their own musical merits, into the new and contemporary texts, thus preserving these treasures for public worship." They also promised to provide a new musical repertoire for these texts that included specific attention to standard keyboard usage, including "independent organ preludes, as well as organ accompaniment for each piece."[47]

Despite Wise's call for an all-English liturgy, Welsch and his colleagues chose to gear their work toward the full range of contemporary liberal-leaning prayer books, while making their work immediately relevant. "Careful selection of English and German anthems from the hymn books adopted in the American Progressive Communities," they noted, could "help to remedy a deficiency so far felt." Such a strategy also maximized their audience, crucial for making the project financially viable. To get off the ground quickly, they planned to issue their music as a subscription, in monthly twelve-page installments that would allow congregations to build up repertoire with little delay. The editors assured readers that "the price will be so cheap that the respective congregations will certainly prefer to provide their singers with printed copies, which will make the former costly and time-consuming system of voice copying unnecessary."[48] Scale, technology, and marketing savvy aimed to make *Zimrath Yah* a convenient solution, overcoming many of the perceived roadblocks to broad adoption.

The first issue, which the editors labeled a "Liturgic Song Book," arrived in March (see fig. 6.3).[49] Isaac Mayer Wise reviewed it with great fanfare, describing its multilingual settings as both effectively crafted and uniquely American; European compositions, after all, had "no hymn music, no organ accompaniment, no preludia," and thus inadequately addressed America's liturgical norms.[50] Two more issues appeared in the next three months, comprising in total eighteen compositions arranged for organ and choir, that took congregations through most of the Sabbath evening service. By the third and last *Minhag America* gathering in Cincinnati that June, Welsch, further empowered, led the conference service, successfully added sacred music instruction to the group's official education agenda, and joined the prospective Union's publication and executive committees.[51] Together with G. M. Cohen, moreover, he promoted *Zimrath Yah* for synagogues alongside Cohen's *Sacred Harp of Judah* for Sabbath schools, promising to continue his installments until the nation's cantors had achieved their musical vision of American liturgical independence.[52]

A torrent of rabbinical dissent ultimately derailed Wise's hope to turn *Minhag America* into America's synagogue prayer book.[53] Welsch's group, however, took a different strategy as they continued to build *Zimrath Yah*, contributing compositions that incorporated liturgical variations from the Wise (Cincinnati), Szold (Baltimore), Huebsch (New York), and Einhorn (Baltimore/New York) prayer books, even if that sometimes required multiple pieces to accommodate. Many selections offered liturgical text options in Hebrew, German, and English. Most notably, though, *Zimrath Yah* had an unprecedented level of musical flexibility. Each issue came fully arranged for mixed choir and organ, even adapting European materials to fit the American aesthetic; yet, the editors also appeared to be sensitive to congregations without organs by designating many accompaniments "*colla parte*" ("C.P.")—an indication that the organist simply play a composite of the vocal parts, thus rendering its role nonessential. Similarly significant was the work's royal octavo format (10 in. × 6.25 in., or 253 mm × 158 mm—half the size of European compendia), which followed conventions for choral materials and was promoted for its ease of use among organists, choristers, and choir directors. After the editors sent out the twelfth issue in February 1873, completing the Sabbath evening and morning services, they continued to sell the whole set as a single bound volume. In the introduction added to the full collection, the four editors felt "compelled by the belief that they are contributing toward maintaining the elevated character

Figure 6.3. *Zimrath Yah*, cover (1871). Courtesy Sotheby's.

of our service—toward propagating our peculiar sacred music on the American soil."[54]

Inside *Zimrath Yah*

The sixty-six selections in volume 1, separated into sections for Sabbath evening (nos. 1–24) and Sabbath morning (nos. 25–66), emphasized a particularly American stripe of utility and flexibility. The Friday evening service, for example, offered eight options for opening hymns and psalms, including original compositions by Welsch, Rice, and Kaiser; a setting of Psalm 92 by Goldstein; settings of Psalm 93 by Naumbourg (from the 1864 edition of *Zemirot Yisrael*) and Josef Fischhof (from the second volume of Sulzer's *Schir Zion*); and a prelude by Johann Christian Heinrich Rinck that was likely already popular in the area's houses of worship.[55] Prayer leaders could choose between call to prayer ("Barechu") settings by Morris Goldstein and Sulzer; and the Shema ("Hear, O Israel") featured a setting by Josef Goldstein (Morris's brother, a leading cantor in Vienna), in addition to Samuel Welsch's adaptation, from Naumbourg's music, of a German variant used in the Einhorn prayer book ("Ewige Wahrheit"). Four versions of "Mi Chamocha" ("Who Is Like You, O Lord") followed, one each by Welsch (for Huebsch's prayer book), Rice, and Sulzer (set to the Einhorn prayer book text), and a special Hanukkah-themed version set to the "traditional" tune "Ma'oz Tsur" ("Rock of Ages"). After original settings of "V'Shamru" (Exodus 31:16–17) by Welsch and Kaiser, the evening service concluded with five musical options for use during the service's final prayers—including Rice's "Prelude on a Traditional Theme" for solo organ, a setting of the Hebrew and German words of "Bayom HaHu" to music of G. F. Handel, and a hitherto unpublished Sulzer setting of "Adon Olam" that Goldstein adapted from a manuscript (see fig. 6.4).[56] Selections for the Sabbath morning service progressed similarly, with particular attention given to the central "Kedusha" ("Holiness") prayer. Recognizing that each American Jewish prayer book treated the Kedusha differently due to its proclamation of core Jewish tenets, the editors supplied seven musical options from six composers, marking specific versions for Szold's, Einhorn's, and Huebsch's texts. In all, *Zimrath Yah*'s first volume projected the vitality of American synagogue composition: the editors' compositions comprised about 70 percent of the volume's selections, and their arrangements of works by Sulzer, Naumbourg, and others to accommodate organ, mixed choir, and American texts

Figure 6.4. Salomon Sulzer, "Adon olam," from M. Goldstein manuscript. *Zimrath Yah I*, no. 24 (beginning).

Figure 6.5. Isaac L. Rice, "Prelude on a Traditional Theme," with organ settings. *Zimrath Yah I*, no. 21 (beginning).

comprised the other 30 percent. That all music except for Rice's "Prelude on a Traditional Theme" (see fig. 6.5) featured a major modality may have reflected Wise's call for a change from the "sad" melodies of the past. Just as likely, however, the sound of music in volume 1 provided its own take on the conventions of the era, which had only started to recognize a canon of "traditional" Jewish melodies.

The completion of *Zimrath Yah*'s first volume coincided with the end of post–Civil War prosperity. Ahawath Chesed opened its majestic, Moorish-design synagogue in 1872, with its massive three-manual pipe organ by George Jardine and Sons openly displaying its renewed commitment to high-level music.⁵⁷ Welsch, who also published a pair of choruses in Vienna in memory of his father in 1871, now held an international reputation, and his salary climbed commensurately to $3,500; the congregation additionally committed more than $3,000 to the choir and other musical expenses.⁵⁸ In September 1873, however, corporate failures from overstretched American railway speculation set off a global panic that continued through the end of the decade, wiping out vast amounts of wealth and spiking unemployment to 25 percent nationally. Throughout the country, congregations shifted resources to address the growing financial needs of its members, leaving music programs vulnerable. *Zimrath Yah*'s $6.50 cost per shipped bound volume (about $133.00 in 2017 dollars), reasonable in good financial times, became a significant expense for congregations under sudden financial stress. As Welsch and his coeditors continued in their path toward a complete American liturgy, therefore, they had to balance their desires to produce a musical legacy-work with changing fiscal realities.

The forty-five selections in volume 2 appeared in only three installments—in March and May 1874, and March 1875. Together they covered a wide variety of holidays, such as Passover (with a Hallel/Praise service), Shavuot (including hymns for the confirmation service that had become a staple of liberal Jewish life), Sukkot (including special hymns for Simchat Torah), Purim, Hanukkah, and American Thanksgiving.⁵⁹ Seemingly ignoring rising pressure in synagogues to reduce salaries and musical forces, however, the editors (now without Rice) ramped up their musical sophistication. Welsch, Goldstein, and Kaiser contributed thirty-four original compositions, including many elaborate multipart set pieces with independent organ accompaniments that far exceeded the *colla parte* emphasis of volume 1. European cantor/composers had little presence in the book beyond arrangements of "traditional" melodies: only Naumbourg's "Etz Chayim" ("It Is a Tree of Life"; no. 23) and a Thanksgiving hymn that Welsch adapted from a similar Sulzer composition (no. 42) stood out.⁶⁰ And once again, the major mode dominated; even the three works that began in minor—Welsch's supplication hymn "Onno" (no. 17), his "Min Ha metzar" ("Out of the Depths"; Psalm 98:5–26, no. 27), and Kaiser's Purim hymn (no. 44)—resolved to a major key by the end. Combined with the addition of numerous English texts and continued attention to serving all American liturgical guides, the volume firmly asserted its American identity, setting itself in parallel to Europe's Jewish musical monumentalism.

Only Welsch and Kaiser continued their editorial partnership into volume 3. Covering services of the High Holidays (Rosh Hashanah and Yom Kippur), this new collection maintained its focus on American composition while aiming to preserve, perhaps more than the first two volumes, the "traditional" character of the service. European works rarely appeared: of its eighty-nine selections, issued in three parts over nearly two years (August 1875 [nos. 1–17], May 1876 [nos. 18–41], and May 1877 [nos. 42–89]), Sulzer appeared as the author of only two short responses, and Naumbourg of only one traditional melody arrangement.[61] Most other selections came from the American cantorial brotherhood, with Leon Sternberger (1 selection), Adolph Rubin (1 selection), and Simon Hecht (1 selection) joining Welsch (32 selections), Kaiser (21 selections), Goldstein (6 selections), and Rice (2 selections). Chicago organist/choir director Otto Lob, whose forty-hymn collection *Israelitische Tempel-Gesänge* also appeared in 1876, contributed six original responses as well.[62] While the western and southern United States remained unrepresented in the collection, the expansion of authorship to other active synagogue music personnel suggested that the work had begun to generate a wider dialogue.

A review of the first part of volume 3 highlighted two of its key distinguishing characteristics: the artful weaving of "traditional" melodies into modern compositions and Welsch's use of "chasonuth" (cantorial chant) in modern recitatives (see fig. 6.6).[63] These qualities, which appeared rarely in the first two volumes, pervaded the new material. Fourteen selections (16 percent) carried a "Traditional" attribution—perhaps explained through the increased importance of holiday themes and composers' attempts to deepen their music by highlighting melodies symbolizing agelessness and prestige. Modally as well, the volume broke with its predecessors. Over a third of the pieces (31 of 89) included substantial minor-mode sections. While only seven of these, including the Aramaic and German versions of Kol Nidre/O Tag des Herrn, ended on a minor chord, the musical material overall hinted at a shift taking place in American Jewish music.

By the time the third volume of *Zimrath Yah* was completed in 1877, the economic landscape of American Jewish life had changed for the worse. As both bank and business failures accelerated past mid-decade, indigent members could no longer keep up with their dues, and synagogue boards had to tighten their belts. Music programs, once important status symbols of Jewish progress, went on the chopping block as synagogues shifted into survival mode. In 1877, Kaiser agreed to reduce his salary from $2,500 to $2,000;

Figure 6.6. Samuel Welsch, "W'Sim Loch Attoh & Jimloch." *Zimrath Yah III*, no. 15. Cantorial recitative (first page).

three years later, as the financial strain continued, his pay briefly bottomed out at $1,700.[64] Welsch (along with Huebsch) resisted Ahawath Chesed's request for a salary cut in 1877 but agreed to teach for free in the congregational school; he also agreed to train a choir comprising members' sons and daughters, thus allowing the congregation to lower its professional choir expenses by a third (from about $3,000 to about $2,000). The following year, however, when conditions did not improve, the congregation cut Welsch's salary to $2,500 anyway.[65] (Another star New York cantor, B'nai Jeshurun's

Edward Kartschmaroff, hired in 1876, kept his $3,000 salary even as the salary of the rabbi Henry S. Jacobs dipped from $5,000 to $4,500. Presumably to compensate, the board slashed the choir budget nearly in half, from more than $3,000 to about $1,600.[66]) Congregations sought to put as positive a face as possible on these moves, hoping that declarations of gratitude to their clergy might soften salary reductions, and describing the volunteer/youth choirs that supplanted trained voices as long-hoped-for opportunities to give congregants a greater role in the ritual. Amateur choirs indeed promoted greater buy-in among the financially stressed membership, especially as a bulwark against concerns of straying youth and as a solution to lingering concerns about hiring non-Jewish singers. And cantors received a great deal of credit for their efforts to train young choristers: in 1880, the *Jewish Messenger* singled out the success of Welsch, Sternberger, and Kaiser in their musical youth ensemble work, while calling for the area's cantors to create "a choral training school" in the style of a pre-rabbinic academy.[67] Despite these successes, however, the creative landscape for Welsch, Kaiser, and their ilk remained bleak. With fewer trained voices in their choirs, they could no longer hold the same expectations for high-level synagogue music; rather, they had to shift their agendas and compositions to accommodate substantially more meager musical conditions.

For Samuel Welsch, these changes proved too much. In March 1880, he announced his departure from Ahawath Chesed, with the intention to return to "private life" in Prague. Shortly before his departure in late May, the area's top cantors—including the old guard of Rubin, Sternberger, Joseph Leucht, and (in absentia) William Armhold, contemporaries Morris Goldstein and (also in absentia) Alois Kaiser, and recently arrived cantor Edward Kartschmaroff—gathered to celebrate his accomplishments. In a ceremony that rhetorically affirmed Welsch as an American champion of synagogue music, the cantors gave him an ornate album adorned with a silver harp and the Hebrew words "*Zamru L'Adonai B'Chinor*" ("Sing unto God with the Harp") on the cover, and inscribed a flowery tribute to his leadership inside:

> Enviously we admit to you that you were the best. How many thousands of troubled hearts have you, through your religious and heartfelt song, carried to the heavenly height, and into how many souls have you, through your artistically well-rounded and profound performances, sung our faith!
>
> But we do not lose in you only a master of song, but also an excellent collaborator in the field of worship. How beautifully you used the talent given to you by God, and created melodies for our worship which, friend, outlive you.

> Your musical poetry, which are in the "Zimrath Yah" that you founded in association with other colleagues, and which have found their way into all synagogues and temples, testify to the purity, the tenderness, and the pious penetration of your sentiment, and will be a lasting honorable memory to your name.[68]

As a leader of New York's Jewish liturgical music fraternity, Welsch's departure left a lacuna. His absence, however, did not end *Zimrath Yah*. Instead, the project and its distribution fell fully into the hands of Alois Kaiser, who continued to work on its final part while monitoring developments emerging in international discussions about "Jewish music" and its practitioners.

The Cantor Reborn as an Ancient Figure

The 1880s opened a new round in cantorial identity politics, as European synagogue singers banded together into professional organizations. Seeking to gain a greater part of the Jewish musical franchise, they began to build the case for an elite clerical status while campaigning for improved job security and social standing. To this end, cantors founded at least two journals—Bromburg's *Der jüdische Kantor* (*JK*, 1879–98) and Vienna's *Österreiche-ungarische Cantoren-Zeitung* (*OUCZ*, 1881–1903)—through which they promoted a new professional order, created a guild-like history, fostered a sense of communal empowerment, and attempted to parlay their work into a global movement.[69] Each paper served as the communication organ for a new cantorial organization: *Israelitischen deutschen Cantorenvereins*, covering Germany and West Prussia, and the Austro-Hungarian *Österreiche-ungarische Cantorenverein*, overseen by Sulzer's successor Josef Singer.[70] Together with the journals' editors, Abraham Blaustein (*JK*) and Jacob Bauer (*OUCZ*), Singer in Vienna and Eduard Birnbaum in Königsberg worked to expand their cities' respective networks of influence, while gathering each region's cantors into a cohesive and respectable class of "colleagues" (*College*). The pages of both journals celebrated accomplishments and created camaraderie by recasting Jewish music history as a function of cantorial development, with a unique modal character connecting biblical times to the present; offering long excurses on professional skills such as music theory, Jewish philosophy, and Torah reading; printing occasional vetted musical supplements to identify and disseminate model compositions; reporting on association meetings and developments; carefully decoupling the cantor's musical status from that of slaughterer and/or teacher; tirelessly seeking to use the cantor's legacy as the basis for controlling all musical aspects of the synagogue service; arguing for the establishment of cantorial institutions, especially a training academy; and reviewing and publicizing the growing number of synagogue music publications.[71] Contributors staked their integrity, moreover, on the greatness of unifying figures. The *OUCZ* elevated Salomon "Papa" Sulzer to near-immortal status: anointing him the "Nestor" of cantors and placing him at the moral, musical, and historical center of their identity. Singer in particular wrote extended, multipart histories of cantorial art ("Chasonus") and the development of synagogue song ("Ueber 'Entwicklung des Synagogen-Gesangs'"), both of which charged cantors to take control of the musical franchise and concluded with extensive praise of Sulzer's works. Another narrative article sought to deglamorize the choirboy (*meshorer*) culture prominent in Eastern Europe, presumably to influence cantors to endorse a Sulzer-inspired institution-based education model; and Cantor L. Stern, in another article, made an impassioned argument for naming the biblical King David as Sulzer's only worthy predecessor.[72] The *JK* similarly admired Sulzer but promoted as its unifying figure Berlin music director Louis Lewandowski, who regularly sent its membership encouraging messages through the journal's pages.[73] Occupied with giving Jewish music aesthetics a modicum of European "modernity," as musicologist Philip Bohlman has noted, these journals emphasized a union-like elitism that compiled, and then used, an insider corpus of musical knowledge to inspire collective identity and action.[74]

The forces that aimed to bring the cantorate into orbit around European centers of activity placed the United States in a dim light. Aside from the rare article celebrating American cantors' milestones as extensions of European cantorial tradition, the journals largely portrayed American Jewry as compromised, prone to attenuation, and harboring cantorial frauds and hucksters.[75] (Even later on in the 1890s, when Cantor Osias Hochgluck became both journals' American correspondent, his reports emphasized social conditions rather than musical developments.[76]) The most significant break in this downcast view appeared as an 1882 addendum to a list of famous cantors and composers ("Berühmte Cantoren und Compositeure") published in both journals, that appeared to supplement a group portrait assembled by Israel Wiesen. That portrait included images of "distant colleagues" G. M. Cohen, Alois Kaiser, and Samuel Welsch (the last of whom, the *JK* noted, had just returned to Prague) among sixty-eight Jewish musical luminaries, all oriented around a central image of Sulzer.[77] Such a brief acknowledgment only emphasized the growing gulf between America and Europe, coupled with Vienna's self-regard as a center of Jewish musical life. At the same time, perhaps backhandedly, the brief notice tacitly acknowledged the spread of Cohen's *Sacred Harp of Judah* and, just as prominently, of *Zimrath Yah*.

By the early 1880s, Kaiser (who subscribed at least to the *OUCZ*) could safely call himself America's leading Jewish liturgical composer. Alongside his educational melodies and hymns from the mid-1870s Kaiser published psalm settings and larger scale works through the end of the decade, most prominently his well-received, multimovement "Requiem for the Day of Atonement" in 1879.[78] When financial conditions improved in the early 1880s, therefore, he remained poised to resume *Zimrath Yah*. The others had moved on. Morris Goldstein accepted a pulpit at Cincinnati's Mound Street Temple (Bene Israel) in 1881, where he continued to compose in the same city as Wise and his nascent Hebrew Union College. Rice abandoned his music career in the late 1870s and enrolled in Columbia Law School. With Welsch in Prague, Kaiser moved forward alone with the last volume.

As early as September 1884, reports circulated about a completed manuscript for volume 4; yet the full work, comprising the High Holiday additional (Musaf), afternoon (Mincha), and concluding (Neilah; Yom Kippur only) services, did not see publication until nearly two years later in July 1886.[79] Its appearance completed a full American Jewish musical liturgy that connected the various prayer texts of American liberal Judaism with an idiomatic sound and style. Liberal Jewish newspapers gave the work effusive praise. A reviewer named Ludwig, writing in *The American Israelite*, saw the work as a coming of age for Kaiser and for American synagogue music more generally. Pointing out Kaiser's "intimate acquaintance" with the prayer texts, his artful use of "'Leitmotiv' from the beautiful treasures of our ancient synagogical melodies," and his pains to create a cohesive experience for a variety of languages and liturgical variants, the reviewer proclaimed that now "we are no longer depending for our temple music on foreign composers, who as yet seem to have no comprehension of what is needed here, but can safely rely upon men like Kaiser, Goldstein and others for perpetuating and developing the great work commenced by Sulzer, Naumburg [sic], Deutch [sic] and others."[80]

Where *Zimrath Yah* had begun as a collaborative project, the final volume clearly belonged to Kaiser. His original compositions comprised than two-thirds of the seventy-five pieces, and he provided additional arrangements of "Ancient Melodies" and "Traditional Melodies" that anchored the music in a palpable sense of Jewish tradition. Kaiser also gave necessary brief nods to Welsch (four short pieces), Sulzer (three arranged pieces plus a set piece [Se'u She'arim/Life Up Your Heads, O Gates!] right before the Neilah service), Weintraub (two short sections of the Aleinu prayer), and Naumbourg (an alternative to Sulzer's set piece). Musically, the work echoed volume 3: it included the same proportion of minor-mode works to "traditional" melodies, choral works to solo "Chazanut" passages for cantor and organ, and works of grandeur to those that projected spiritual intimacy. Just as significantly, Kaiser maintained the complexity of his compositions, thus continuing to rely on professional performers to produce a prayerful American sound.

Zimrath Yah's precise distribution and sphere of influence is not easy to gauge, even through synagogue records. Most likely, the editors' congregations purchased the books for their music personnel, and perhaps others followed their lead. Baltimore's Oheb Shalom used it at least through 1889, when an article in the *Baltimore Sun* noted Kaiser's use of *Zimrath Yah*'s Shavuot/confirmation service.[81] Yet chances are, the sixteen-year project occupying the top tier of American Jewish musical leaders enjoyed only a relatively brief period of significant usage at the best-endowed congregations, with a few pieces perhaps finding longer life. By the 1880s, as I describe in chapter 7, a turn toward congregational singing created a contentious dialogue between amateurs and professionals in American synagogues (and houses of worship more generally). The Union of American Hebrew Congregations, formed in 1875, reasserted what Zev Eleff calls "textualism" into the formation of a national synagogue network, centralizing liberal American Jewish discourse and eventually making a more effective push toward a shared American Jewish liturgy.[82] Combined, these factors upended *Zimrath Yah*'s pluralistic mission to unify a variety of coexisting American liturgical practices. The Union's boisterous pursuit of a single liturgy would eventually render the collection obsolete.

Nonetheless, *Zimrath Yah* chronicled a remarkable moment in American Jewish liturgy. Where Wise's efforts sowed discord, Welsch and his cohort found a moment of common cause, advancing a theological agenda that prioritized music and, by extension, its cantorial representatives. Viewed historically, moreover, the compendium offers evidence of a rich international musical dialogue, with Sulzer's émigré students providing their own reflections on a new land by building on the musical language they had internalized during their own training. While nearly forgotten today, *Zimrath Yah* established the United States as a full participant in the international flowering of synagogue music in the late nineteenth century.

Epilogue

Kaiser and Goldstein's American stories continue in chapter 7. But what of the others?

Upon returning to Prague, Welsch restored the *t* to his last name (Weltsch). At the urging of his brother Salomon, he initially spent two months in the pulpit at Prague's Klaus-Synagogue, leading the congregation in the wake of its cantor's sudden departure.[83] After this short stint, however, Welsch appears to have left the cantorate entirely—his name does not appear among the founders of the Bohemian branch of the Austro-Hungarian Cantors Association in January 1884.[84] Rather, he turned to a number of business pursuits, initially running a music publishing house and eventually becoming the Bohemian representative of the New York Life Insurance Company.[85] Welsch/Weltsch also remained closely connected to the Jewish population. By the 1890s, he had been named second vice-president of the city's Central Commission for Jewish Affairs (Centralverein zur Pflege jüdischer Angelegenheiten) and in this position gave occasional lectures, including a well-received 1895 talk on *"Die Juden in Amerika"* that traded at least a little on his personal experience.[86] As a prominent member of the local Committee for Regulating the Religious Service (Verein für geregelten Gottesdienst), he introduced parts of the American repertoire into Bohemian synagogue life while producing a few new compositions and partaking in central conversations about the sound of Jewish worship in the city.[87]

Isaac L. Rice went on to become a respected financier and executive, reorganizing several railroad firms after the 1873 panic, running a series of electric battery storage companies, and joining a wide range of intellectual societies, including at least three journals of scholarly inquiry. A passion for chess led him to advocate for an opening now known as the Rice Gambit, and he supported the sport with frequent donations to area chess clubs. He also maintained his interest in music, penning a book on the subject, and with his wife in the lead, advocating for environmental noise reduction laws in the increasingly industrial urban landscape. Liturgical music, however, ceased to factor among his numerous interests; notices of his 1915 death made no mention of his work with Welsch, Kaiser, and Goldstein.[88]

Zimrath Yah partly inspired at least one other publication—New Orleans organist/choir director Frederick Emil Kitziger's *Shire Yehudah*.[89] But ultimately, once new liturgies superseded the mid-nineteenth-century prayer books, scholars seeking ancient roots of Jewish music orphaned it. Abraham Zvi Idelsohn put the final nail in the coffin when he noted in 1929 that "German in melody and character, [*Zimrath Yah*] contains but few traditional elements."[90] In line with the writings of European cantorial journals, Idelsohn's reinvention of Jewish music in the 1920s accepted the works of Sulzer and Lewandowski as actively channeling authentic Eastern European Jewish melody; yet, he excluded *Zimrath Yah* as inconsistent, parochial, and most fatally, inauthentic. Eventually, this attitude led to skewed perceptions of the volumes as amateurish, causing them to slip out of the American Jewish historical narrative.

Notes

1. *The Occident and American Jewish Advocate* 14, no. 13 (June 1856), 148. According to the report, Emanu-El spent $1,386 on its choir, compared with $2,933 for the other officers' salaries combined.

2. *Allgemeine Zeitung des Judenthums* 4 (January 19, 1864), 52 (review of Lewandowski, *Deutsche Schullieder*); 29 (July 12, 1864), 447–48 (reviews of Fischer and Naumbourg).

3. Other less influential works, at least as mentioned in contemporary American Jewish periodicals, included Hirsch Weintraub's 1859 *Schire Beth Adonai* and Louis Lewandowski's 1864 *Deutsche Schullieder*.

4. "The Sad Effects of Change," *Jewish Messenger*, July 21, 1865, 20.

5. Kramer had come from Vilna in 1858 to assume the cantorial position at B'nai Jeshurun's pulpit (*Jewish Messenger*, August 27, 1858, 37); his $1,000 salary was announced on December 14, 1866. Kramer had instituted a choir ten months earlier (*Hebrew Leader*, February 2, 1866, 2).

6. *Jewish Messenger*, October 11, 1868; November 8; 1868; May 14, 1869; May 21, 1869; August 13, 1869.

7. See, among many other articles, "Orthodoxie und Reform in Amerika," *Hebrew Leader*, October 8, 1869, 3.

8. The website "Prague Concert Life, 1850–1881" notes that Welsch recited Schiller's poem "Der Tauscher" at an Arion concert on November 9, 1862, at which the correspondent for the November 11, *Prager Morgenpost* noted, "This speaker [Welsch] had a handsome powerful voice and he received much applause, which perhaps stemmed from several of the guests having already heard '*Taucher*' being given at the Konvikt Hall on the same day" (http://prague.cardiff.ac.uk/viewEvent.do?id=8512); and may have sung several lieder at a January 27, 1863, Mozart Festival concert sponsored by the singing society Aëde (http://prague.cardiff.ac.uk/viewEvent.do?id=10363, listed as "Wältsch"). In addition, Welsch (as Weltsch) sang Uhland's "Der Sängers Fluch" at a concert in early 1864 (*Blätter für Theater, Musik, u. Kunst*

10, no. 2 [January 5, 1864], 5 [Correspondence from Prague]). Regarding the Meisel Synagogue, see *Die Neuzeit*, February 13, 1863, 76.

9. The Meisel Synagogue advertised for a new cantor in December 1864, with visits by invited prospects to begin in February (*Allgemeine Zeitung des Judenthums*, December 23, 1864, 612); Ahawath Chesed Minutes, vol. 1, 28–29 (February 27, 1865); *The Messenger* reported on Welsch's election to cantor on April 28, 1865, [129]. Welsch arranged to be paid for the months of March and April 1865, before his arrival, based on a $1,750 annual salary (ca. $146/month).

10. *Jewish Messenger*, June 9, 1865, 179–80.

11. *Die Deborah*, September 8, 1865, 38, 39. See also *The Israelite*, April 15, 1864, 331 (announcement of Ahawath Chesed's new synagogue building dedication) and Eleff, *Who Rules the Synagogue? Religious Authority and the Formation of American Judaism* (New York: Oxford, 2016), 146.

12. *Die Deborah*, March 2, 1866, 139; Correspondence, *The Israelite*, June 1, 1866, 381.

13. *Die Neuzeit*, July 26, 1867, 354–55. Feuchtersleben's poem is better known as "Es ist bestimmt in Gottes Rat."

14. Judah M. Cohen, *Sounding Musical Tradition: The Music of Central Synagogue* (New York: Central Synagogue, 2011), 14–16.

15. *Jewish Messenger*, July 3, 1868, [5].

16. *Hebrew Leader*, July 22, 1866, 84.

17. *Allgemeine Zeitung des Judenthums*, March 6, 1866, 148; *Hebrew Leader*, May 11, 1866, 35; May 18, 1866, 51; July 22, 1866, 84; *Die Deborah*, August 7, 1867, 19. At one point, Gerstel prepared his compositions for publication, although the project never appears to have come to fruition (Isaac M. Wise, "Ho! For the East," *The Israelite*, August 9, 1867, 4).

18. *Hebrew Leader*, June 22, 1866, 84.

19. Temple Oheb Shalom Minutes, July 7, 1867; September 1, 1867; November 3, 1867 (MS-522, American Jewish Archives, Cincinnati, OH). Tillman later appears to have worked for congregation Oheb Israel; see *The Sun* (Baltimore), September 14, 1874, 4.

20. Oheb Shalom Minutes, December 1 and 8, 1867 (Kaiser noted that he could purchase Naumbourg's collection for a reduced price, from $40, received from New York, likely from Samuel Welsch [who advertised the volumes in the *Hebrew Leader* on October 29, 1869]).

21. Oheb Shalom Minutes, July 7, 1867; September 1, 1867; November 3, 1867; June 30, 1872. Szold's salary, however, rose to $4,000 shortly afterward, suggesting a persistent cantor/rabbi scale.

22. *Hebrew Leader*, July 27, 1866. The position also carried a $3,000 salary.

23. Eleff, *Who Rules the Synagogue?*, 137–39.

24. Contemporary periodicals highlight a Ferdinand Goldstein in Groß-Becskerek (now the Serbian town of Zrenaijnin): *Ben Chananja*, September 20, 1861 (vol. 4, no. 38), 330; *Die Neuzeit*, May 2, 1862, 208; September 22, 1865, 445–46; and an older cantor "M. Goldstein" appeared in Gross Kanicha in the 1820s.

25. *Jewish Messenger*, May 29, 1868, [6]; *New York Herald*, May 23, 1868, 7.

26. *Jewish Messenger*, June 26, 1886, [3]. Nearly a year later, a correspondent for the *Hebrew Leader* noted the congregation's continued satisfaction with Goldstein in the musical and liturgical helm (*Hebrew Leader*, September 17, 1869, 3).

27. "Jacques," "Letter from New York—No. 2," *The Israelite*, May 27, 1870, 10.

28. *Hebrew Leader*, May 4, 1866, 27; May 11, 1866, 38; May 25, 1866, 51.

29. *Hebrew Leader*, November 5, 1869, 3 (German) and 4 (English); November 19, 1869, 3.

30. Advertisement, *New Yorker Staats-Zeitung und Herold*, February 11, 1866; "The Rev. J. Gerstel's Concert," *Jewish Messenger*, March 15, 1867, [3]. See also reviews of the concert in the *New Yorker Staats-Zeitung und Herold*, March 14, 1867, 8, and *New Yorker Musik-Zeitung*, March 16, 1867, 505.

31. "The Rev. J. Gerstel's Concert," *Jewish Messenger*.

32. *Dwight's Journal of Music*, February 8, 1862, 358; *Musical Review and World*, February 15, 1862, 43.

33. *Dwight's Journal of Music*, March 21, 1863, 404; February 4, 1865, 390. Rice also published the "Summer Morning Waltz" in 1866 (*Philadelphia Evening Bulletin*, June 22, 1866, 4; the piece itself was published by William Boner).

34. Henry S. Morais, *The Jews of Philadelphia: Their History from the Earliest Settlements to the Present Time* (Philadelphia: Levytype, 1894), 341–42; "Mr. I. L. Rice's Concert at Steinway Hall," *Hebrew Leader*, December 3, 1869, 6. An example of Rice's musical criticism from Paris can be seen in Rice, "Letter from Paris: Offenbach's Robinson Crusoe," *Daily Evening Bulletin* (Philadelphia), February 1, 1868, 1. Rice signed his letter "Pupil of the Conservatoire."

35. *Daily Evening Bulletin* (Philadelphia), September 6, 1869, 4; October 22, 1869, 1; October 27, 1869, 1.

36. "Music and the Drama: Concert by Mr. I. L. Rice," *New York Tribune*, December 11, 1869, 7; "Mr. J. L. Rice," *Hebrew Leader*, December 17, 1869, 4.

37. The copy of Welsch's Psalm 93 (1869 edition) kept at Hebrew Union College, deposited from Kaiser's collection (see Conclusion), contains an inscription from Welsch to Kaiser dated October 1869.

38. Isaac Mayer Wise, "A Perfect Union," *The Israelite*, July 29, 1870, 8.

39. "Synagogal Music," *The Israelite* 17, no. 10 (September 2, 1870), 8.

40. Ibid.

41. Ibid.

42. Ibid.

43. Wise, "The Convention of Rabbis in New York," *The Israelite*, November 4, 1870, 8; December 2, 1870, 7 [Cincinnati]; *Jewish Messenger*, January 20, 1871, 2 [New Orleans].

44. Wise, "The Convention of Rabbis in New York," *The Israelite*, November 11, 1870, 8.

45. "On New York: The Laying of the Corner-Stone," *The Israelite*, December 23, 1870, 8; "Zimrath Yah," *Die Deborah*, January 27, 1871, 3.

46. "Zimrath Yah," *Die Deborah*, January 27, 1871, 3.

47. Ibid.

48. Ibid.

49. The relatively uncommon term *Liturgic Song Book* appeared to recall the subtitle of Salomon Sulzer's *Duda'im* (Vienna: n.p., 1860), a "Kleines Liturgische Gesangbuch." In contrast to Sulzer's work, however, which was intended for "schools, small congregations, and home devotion," *Zimrath Yah* had far greater ambitions.

50. Wise, "*Zimrath Yah*," *The Israelite* 17, no. 38 (March 17, 1871), 9.

51. "The Conference," *The Israelite*, June 9, 1871, 8–9; *The Israelite*, June 23, 1871, 10; "Zimrath Yah III," *The Israelite*, June 23, 1871, 11; "Resolutions," *The Israelite*, June 30, 1871, 10.

52. J. Wechsler, "The Conference: Conclusion," *The Israelite*, July 14, 1871, 9–10.

53. Eleff, *Who Rules the Synagogue?*, 185–87.

54. "Preface," *Zimrath Yah I* (New York: n.p., 1873).

55. Rinck (1770–1846) was known for his organ preludes and short instrumental keyboard works, and his compositions were included in popular organists' resources of the time, including Edward Rimbault's six-volume *Organist's Portfolio* (London: Chappell, 1865). In *Zimrath Yah*, he is listed as "Rink" in the table of contents.

56. I have been unable to locate the specific Handel work from which the *Zimrath Yah* version derives; however, its brevity (twelve measures) and homophonic choral sound hint at a secondary adaptation, perhaps from a contemporaneous popular book of choral responses.

57. For specifications of the 1872 organ, see http://www.nycago.org/Organs/NYC/html/CentralSyng.html#Jardine.

58. Samuel Welsch, "Todtenfeier: 2 Chöre für gemischte Stimmen und Soli" (Vienna: K. K. Hoflith & Steindr v. G. Wegelein, 1871); Cohen, *Sounding Musical Tradition*, 19–20.

59. Abraham Lincoln established the fourth Thursday in November as a national Thanksgiving in 1863, although other Thanksgiving celebrations took place in the United States throughout the nineteenth century and earlier.

60. Welsch adapted Sulzer's piece from *Schir Zion I*, no. 159 (pp. 211–14), a setting of Psalm 21:1–9 titled, "Am Geburtestage des Landesführen."

61. Sulzer, "V'Anachnu kor'im" (*Zimrath Yah III*, no. 40) and Bayom Hahu (no. 41); Naumbourg, "B'yodo Afkid Ruchi" (no. 48).

62. Otto Lob, *Israelitische Tempel-Gesänge: Hymnen für Sabbath und Festtage mit deutschem und englischem Text in Musik gesetzt* (Chicago: Rubovits, 1876).

63. M, "Review of Part 1 of Volume III of *Zimrath Yah*," *Die Deborah*, August 17, 1875, 2.

64. Oheb Shalom Minutes, 1877 (drop to $2,400 and then to $2,000 in October); and July 4, 1880 (drop to $1,700). Kaiser's salary began to rise again, first to $2,000 in October 1880 (Oheb Shalom Minutes, October 2, 1880). In comparison, Benjamin Szold's salary went down from $4,000 to $3,200 in the same interval.

65. Ahawath Chesed Minutes, General Meeting, April 8, 1877, II, 284; Financial Report, April 1877 to May 1878, II, 309; Trustees Report, April 20, 1879, II, 325.

66. B'nai Jeshurun annual reports, 1874–80. Born in Cherson, Russia, in the early/mid-1840s, Kartschmaroff (ca. 1843–1918) trained in Vienna like his two brothers, Leon and Jacob, and after occupying a series of cantorial positions in increasingly prominent synagogues in Hungary (Miskolcz, Szegedin) and then at the Prague Neusynagoge, he arrived in New York in mid-March 1873. Kartschmaroff announced his availability by leading a service in Welsch's congregation Ahawath Chesed and shortly thereafter signed with congregation Shaare Rachamim for three years. In 1876, B'nai Jeshurun called him to its pulpit, where he would officiate for the next four decades. Kartschmaroff passport application, National Archives and Records Administration (NARA), Washington, DC; NARA Series: *Passport Applications, 1795–1905*; Roll no.: 541; Volume no.: Roll 541—01 Mar 1900–12 Mar 1900; *American Jewish Year Book* 5 (1903–4), 68; Chajim David Lippe, *Ch. D. Lippe's Bibliographisches Lexicon der Gesammten Jüdischen Literatur der Gegenwart und Adress-Anzeiger* (Vienna: D. Löwy, 1881), 225–26.

67. "A Choral Training School," *Jewish Messenger*, June 25, 1880, 4.

68. *Die Deborah*, June 11, 1880, 2 (from a letter dated May 28, 1880).

69. Philip Bohlman, *Jewish Music and Modernity* (New York: Oxford University Press, 2008).

70. *OUCZ*, 1881, no. 1 (December 30, 1881), 1–2; no. 2 (January 7), 1–2.

71. Moritz Wallerstein, "Cantor und Schochet," *OUCZ*, July 21, 1882, 4; Emil Fränkel, "Schullehrer und Cantor," *OUCZ*, August 30, 1882, 4; *OUCZ*, December 30, 1881, 1–2.

72. Josef Singer, "Chasonus," *OUCZ* serial, 1883 (nos. 20, 21, 22, 24, 26, 28, 29, 31); Josef Singer, "Ueber 'Entwicklung des Synagogen-Gesanges,'" *OUCZ*, ongoing serial from 1884–85; L. Stern, "Wer is der Cantoren-Papa," *OUCZ*, August 18, 1884, 3.

73. See, inter alia, Louis Lewandowski, "Aufruf an die Herren Kantoren," *Der jüdische Kantor* 1, no. 26 (December 25, 1879), 97.

74. Bohlman, *Jewish Music and Modernity*, 96–99.

75. See, for example, *OUCZ*, December 21 and 29, 1883, 2–3 (in the celebration of Isadore Fränkel's seventy-fifth birthday in Philadelphia); August 16, 1883, 7 (on a colony of Russian Jews created in Oregon); November 19, 1883, 7 (criticizing a cantor's commercialization of High Holiday services in San Francisco).

76. *OUCZ*, December 21 and 29, 1883, 2–3; "San Francisco," *OUCZ*, November 19, 1883, 7; "New York," *OUCZ*, January 22, 1883, 2–3; "Der Reformrabbiner in Amerika," *OUCZ*, April 19, 1884, 7; *OUCZ*, November 21, 1896, 7 (from Osias Hochgluck).

77. "Gallerie berühmter und bekannter Kantoren und Komponisten [part III]," *JK* 4, no. 13 (April 1, 1882), 99; see also "Berühmte Cantoren und Compositeure," *OUCZ*, April 13, 1882, 4–5. A small image of the Wiesen's original group portrait can be seen in *Kehillat Ha-Kodesh: Creating the Sacred Community* (New York: The Library of the Jewish Theological Seminary of America 1997), 27. The *JK* cites Kaiser, Cohen, and Welsch as both skilled musicians and as "literary men." The list also includes "Grodzinski" in San Francisco—probably Israel Grodzinsky, who at one point served the city's Congregation Beth Israel (Ch. D. Lippe, *Bibliographisches Lexikon der gesammten jüdischen Literatur der Gegenwart* [Vienna: D. Löwy, 1881], 152).

78. Kaiser, "Tunes for the Israelitisch School" (Baltimore, 1873); Kaiser, *Shirai Chinooch: Confirmation Hymns* (Baltimore: Kaiser, 1875); Kaiser, *Requiem for the Day of Atonement* (Baltimore: Kaiser, 1879); Kaiser, *Psalm I, Verses 1, 2, and 3* (Baltimore: Otto Sutro, 1884). See Gustav Ensel's review of Kaiser's *Requiem* in chapter 4.

79. "Rev. Dr. Benjamin Szold Celebrates the Twenty-Fifth Anniversary of His Ministry in Oheb Shalom," *The Israelite*, September 19, 1884, 5; "New Temple Music," *The American Israelite*, July 30, 1886, 9.

80. Ludwig, "*Zimrath Yah*, Volume IV," *The American Israelite*, September 3, 1886, 2.

81. "The Feast of Weeks: Services in the Synagogue," *The Sun*, June 6, 1889, 6.

82. Eleff, *Who Rules the Synagogue?*, chapters 3 and 6.

83. *Prager Tagblatt* 262 (September 20, 1880), 5.

84. *OUCZ* 2 (January 14, 1884), 3–4.

85. *Adressář královského hlavního města Prahy a sousedních obcí Bubenče, Karlína, Smíchova, Kr. Vinohrad, Vršovic a Žižkova* (Prague, 1891), 453. Welsch stepped down in 1899 (*Prager Abendblatt*, August 24, 1899, [4]).

86. *Die Neuzeit*, December 20, 1895, 553–54. Welsch also gave a more general lecture in 1901 titled, "Die Grundpfeiler des Menschenthums—die des Judenthums" ("The Cornerstone of Humankind—That of Judaism") (*Bohemia* 201 [January 8, 1901], 2).

87. "Samuel Weltsch" death announcement, *Bohemia* 215 (August 6, 1901), 6. The Jewish Museum in Prague, which contains many of the committee's papers, shows a significant increase in American-composed music, in both print and manuscript, from the 1880s and 1890s. Archive and Jewish Museum Prague's collection of sheet music (no. 311, "Sbírka hudebnin [1835]–1947").

88. David B. Green, "This Day in Jewish History: 1850: A Jew Who Would Make Leonardo da Vinci Feel Inadequate Is Born," *Ha'aretz*, February 22, 2016 (http://www.haaretz.com/jewish/this-day-in-jewish-history/1.704563). Rice's book, *What Is Music?* (New York: Appleton, 1875) also appeared in a second edition (Appleton, 1883/1886).

89. Baron, "Frederick Emil Kitziger," 25, 28; Frederick E. Kitziger, *Shire Yehudah* vol. 1 (New Orleans: Frederick Kitziger, 1888).

90. Idelsohn, *Jewish Music in Its Historical Development* (New York: Henry Holt, 1929), 323.

7

THE PATH TO THE *UNION HYMNAL*

> For many years I have plowed the sea of our profession practically alone, and in fact we all have steered our little crafts regardless of each other's course. Imagine, therefore, the emotions that pervade me, at the sight of this assembly, at the realization of concerted action for the universal good. I can liken it to no other feeling than that of the tempest-tossed mariner, who after a long and lonesome voyage, beholds the encouraging outlines of the distant shore. The bars are crossed, the shore is reached.
>
> —**Alois Kaiser**, inaugural meeting of the Cantors' Association of America, New York City, October 18, 1892[1]

IN 1886, THE SAME YEAR THAT ALOIS KAISER released the fourth and final volume of *Zimrath Yah* in Baltimore, prominent Vienna cantor Josef Singer published his pamphlet *Die Tonarten des traditionellen Synagogengesanges*. Singer's thesis, which complemented a proliferation of scholarly musical tracts written by cantors, distilled Jewish chant into a set of musical modes (or *Steiger*), each with its own scale, idiomatic motifs, and emotional valences. Illustrated with extensive musical notations, Singer's arguments emphasized the extent to which cantors had become Jewish music specialists, parlaying their musical abilities into a nearly exclusive scientific field that could integrate with parallel studies in Christian chant and emerging ideas in the young discipline of musicology.[2] His work, and the prolific response to it, typified a shift in the status and content of music identified as "Jewish." From predominantly major modes and hymns before the 1860s, synagogue music publications began turning to ethnic sounds—augmented second intervals, for example, and experimental accidentals.[3]

Singer's work also indicated the growing self-perception of Vienna as a Jewish and intellectual hub of the Austro-Hungarian Empire, particularly in the final years of Sulzer's life. As president of the Austro-Hungarian

Society of Cantors, Singer's contributions helped to consolidate the region as a self-sustaining cantorial ecosystem, with its own society, its own journal (the *Österreiche-ungarische Cantoren-Zeitung* [OUCZ]) and ambitions toward a centralized, if not formalized, network of cantorial training, placement, and music publishing. "Papa" Sulzer, though weakened by age, remained a towering presence in this network, regularly inspiring and reinforcing Vienna's predominance through encouraging letters and frequent invocation.

Vienna's cantorial circle spent most of its efforts maintaining its own internal viability and international primacy. Where general European Jewish newspapers in the previous decades had regularly referenced events in the United States, for example, the *OUCZ* showed little interest in the American cantorial scene, even as its editor expected American cantors to subscribe.[4] Such insularity made sense considering Vienna's surging population, the result of internal urban migration, accompanied by a relative slowdown in Central European transatlantic immigration. The next major wave of European immigration westward would not gain momentum until the 1890s, momentarily weakening the need to maintain transatlantic ties.

At the same time, this period of internal nation-building hardly precluded the development of cantorial culture elsewhere.

England experienced its own notable developments. From April to July 1887, London's Jewish community featured music in the elaborate Anglo-Jewish Historical Exposition that it mounted at the Royal Albert Hall, affirming the richness of Anglo-Jewish history through a broad collection of manuscripts and art. Reverend Francis L. Cohen, a musically proficient rabbi recently appointed to London's Borough Synagogue, curated two shelves of the exhibit, which featured sixteen ram's horns and thirty examples of liturgical sheet music.[5] Although he had spoken on the subject of Jewish music four years earlier, Cohen's May 16 lecture-recital accompanied by the organist and choir from the West London Congregation established him as an English-language authority on the topic.[6] Combined with a variety of other lectures, displays, and objects, including occasional afternoon organ recitals of "Jewish music" by a Mr. Weil, the Exhibition imbued British Jewry with its own historical narrative, building a scaffolding that affirmed its own pride of place.

While American Jews remained aware of cantorial developments in London and Vienna, as well as other happenings in Prague and Odessa, they had by this point taken significant steps to establish their own musical foothold and consolidate their liturgical music across their own distinctive, interconnected national landscape.[7] *Zimrath Yah* had built that momentum, bringing music for the country's major liturgies together into a single collection. Over the next two decades, the nation's cantors would make another push to codify America's Jewish musical vocabulary. Working parallel to rabbinic efforts, their labors would eventually yield the *Union Hymnal*.

1880: The Revival of Congregational Singing

Fine choirs are very nice, Messrs. Trustees, but listening to fine choirs does not constitute worship. Let us have less performance and more participation; less choir and more congregational singing.

—Editorial, *The American Hebrew*, November 26, 1880

Jewish populations in America saw themselves coming of age in the late nineteenth century. Liberal Jewish reforms had become deeply invested in American culture. By 1880, a seminary, several liturgies, a Union that counted 118 out of America's 278 synagogues, and progress toward a common prayer book served as evidence of advancement and unification.[8] Numerous Jewish communities achieved the stability to build their own distinctive buildings, hire rabbinical authorities, set up congregational schools, and establish music programs, in many cases aiming to merge their efforts with the highest social ideals of the nation. Achieving these goals, however, generated as much ennui as accomplishment. Religious Jewish leaders asked publicly if their impressive accoutrements had actually suppressed the vitality of congregational life. A late 1870s census conducted by the Board of Delegates of American Israelites and the Union of American Hebrew Congregations estimated that 12,456 households belonged to synagogues, out of approximately 250,000 Jews. Although these statistics proved difficult to interpret definitively (how many Jews, after all, comprised a household?), they appeared to signal problems with communal commitment and synagogue attendance. Sanctuary services proved a particular focus of these concerns, with elaborate choirs and voice-focused cantors frequently blamed for rendering rituals lugubrious and congregational voices mute. Synagogues hardly faced this challenge alone: contemporary authorities on church singing such as John Curwen, Thomas DeWitt Talmadge, and John Young bemoaned similar concerns across Anglophone Christendom. As with these figures, Jews turned to their own sense of distinctiveness to find musical solutions that could draw on their unique view of history, identity, and culture.

Jewish newspapers from this time began to describe a turn to "congregational singing" movements emerging on both side of the Atlantic.[9] Appearing with greater frequency as the 1880s progressed, the concept gained particular force in urban, often well-off synagogues—the same group that had previously received national attention for their resource-rich music programs. As seen in earlier chapters, smaller, less affluent congregations, whether in urban or rural settings, tended toward congregational singing by default, as a more practical approach to synagogue music in the absence of ever more expensive paid professionals. Urban flagship congregations, however, presented as de facto leaders of their respective movements—often based on the stature of the religious figures officiating in their pulpits. Their theological and aesthetic choices tended to set the tone for synagogue pulpits around the country. When newspapers began to cover their efforts to empower congregational voices, then, the conversation took on significant implications—including the portfolio, and the very status, of the cantor.

Newspaper-based discussions often originated with concerns over the nature and spiritual topography of the prayer ritual. On one hand, the "congregational singing" of orthodox congregations was reported by one reader of *The American Hebrew* as "disjointed and inharmonious" by "well-meaning but loud-mouthed members" who should "restrain the exuberance of their devotion and sing in a tone which will permit the *Chazan* to be heard and to lead."[10] On the other hand, professional musicians hired to enhance reform synagogues swung the pendulum too far in the other direction. An editor of the same journal lamented a few months later, in an article titled, "Congregational Singing," that "the service has become a concert or recital, and the worshippers mere listeners, now with rapt attention, now with listless indifference."[11] Finding a good balance between these poles required a vision of the synagogue as a cohesive center of spiritual activity where all worked together in concert. Fixing the balance between pews and pulpit through congregational prayer, writers hoped, would strengthen the synagogue's power as a center of gravity for Jewish life.

New York City newspapers encouraged and applauded the efforts of individual synagogues toward this ideal, with *The American Hebrew* perhaps most vocal. Chronicling parallel efforts in both the London Jewish community and in local churches during the 1880s, the paper's editors wrote, "We foretell a grand triumph for the first Jewish congregation which will introduce congregational singing to enliven and solemnify the service."[12] One line of discussion, simmering on and off since the introduction of synagogue choirs, addressed the propriety of employing non-Jewish choral singers to lead worshipers in song, under the assumption that non-Jewish vocal production inherently mismatched a Jewish spiritual topography. New York City's Adath Israel, on Fifty-Seventh Street, employed this reasoning in mid-1883 when its cantor decided "to introduce congregational singing" jointly with the congregation's dismissal of non-Jewish singers. *The American Hebrew*, applauding this development, hoped that "other congregations will emulate [Adath Israel's] worthy example, to the end that the anomaly of having non-Jewish choristers as mediators for Jewish worshipers, may cease and nevermore desecrate a Jewish house of God."[13] In a different article in the same column, the editors mounted an "economic" argument for congregational singing as well, emphasizing that the savings realized from not having to pay as many choristers might sway congregants should "all other argument and appeal fall on dull ears."[14]

Different synagogues' efforts toward congregational participation took distinct shapes. In 1884, for example, the *Jewish Messenger* shared the progress of New York's Ahawath Chesed (later Central Synagogue), whose recently hired cantor Theodore Guinsburg had introduced a children's choir and relied on the attractiveness and sentimentality of their voices to "add to the interest of the Sabbath morning service, and the number of worshippers."[15] *The American Hebrew* offered details about the progress of congregation Shaarey Tefilah which hired a singing instructor to give weekly lessons to "the Young Ladies' Society of the congregation," and distributed "lithographed copies of the words and music" for the hymn "Ein Keloheinu" during services to test his effectiveness.[16] Sephardic congregation Shearith Israel joined the wave in 1885. Rather than starting their initiative with children or women, however, its representatives sought to prepare the entire congregation through regular Wednesday evening lessons.[17] By 1887, with London's Jews moving toward a general adoption of congregational singing, even as prominent a synagogue as New York's Temple Emanu-El had expressed its interest.[18] *The American Hebrew*, citing congregational singing's "little boom," predicted optimistically that if "a congregation that is as proverbially enthusiastic as Temple Emanuel, will succeed in setting the fashion . . . then *all* will follow."[19]

Leading synagogues produced new hymn books that aimed to make the new wave of congregational singing more broadly accessible. Morris

Goldstein, then cantor of Cincinnati's Mound Street Temple, published the hymnal *Kol Zimra* in 1885 for both choirs and congregational singing, "carefully selecting and arranging his texts from the collections of the Hamburg Temple, [Leopold] Stein, Temple Emanuel, Isaac M. Wise, and others [and] put[ting] to every one an original melody."[20] Cincinnati's Bloch Publishing Company, recognizing the emerging market in congregational singing materials, began to advertise a selection of hymnals (and synagogue music in general) from both Europe and the United States for American congregational consumption.[21] New York, however, produced the hymnals that embraced an American idiom most fully. Rev. Dr. Frederick de Sola Mendes of Shaarey Tefilah compiled a short book titled, *Synagogue and School*, explicitly addressing the role of children's education in fostering a harmonious sanctuary.[22] Temple Emanu-El rabbi Gustav Gottheil and his organist, A. J. Davis, produced in the same year a larger collection that placed religious hymns from Jewish and non-Jewish writers alongside hymns by prominent American poets such as John Greenleaf Whittier and Ralph Waldo Emerson.[23] The *Jewish Messenger*, presenting an illustration of Gottheil's efforts, reproduced the book's first hymn, "Early Will I Seek Thee," which was adapted from a poem by eleventh-century Jewish philosopher Solomon ibn Gabirol and set by Davis to American hymn composer Spencer Lane's 1875 tune "Penitence."[24] Reviewers in both Jewish and Christian publications recognized the Emanu-El hymnal as an important product of liberal Jewish culture, with the *American Hebrew* reviewer particularly praising "a volume which, in beauty and dignity of its lyric contents, as well as in mechanical execution, is a sumptuous evidence of the taste of refined American 'reform' Judaism."[25] While not necessarily adopted immediately across the country, Gottheil's work exemplified efforts at instituting congregational singing through a broad spectrum of American Jewish verse and attractive popular tunes.

Developments in New York swiftly spread as other congregations joined the congregational singing trend. In late 1887, Rev. Adolph Guttmann of Syracuse's Temple of Concord wrote in a letter to *The American Hebrew* that "I introduced congregational singing two years ago, and I am happy to say . . . that all, men and women, old and young, are only too willing to enter heartily into the worship by singing hymns unto the Lord."[26] However, as reports from other congregations similarly embraced congregational singing in Harlem, Albany, St. Louis, Baltimore, and beyond, the editor of Philadelphia's *Jewish Exponent* derided it as another fad by overendowed congregations that had pushed reform too far and sought to backtrack stylishly.[27]

By the late 1880s, the moral initiative to institute congregational singing had begun to sharpen its critique of choirs and cantors as sources of aesthetic obstruction and spiritual obfuscation, who monopolized the service rather than encouraging the congregation to lend its voice. Advocates of congregational singing disparaged professional choristers as mercenaries whose loyalty went only as far as their paychecks and whose unseen shenanigans in the choir loft belied their sacred labors.[28] When, in 1887, the first day of Shavuot fell on a Sunday morning, *The American Hebrew* editors called out choristers in Philadelphia who "after having sung the praises of the God of Israel in various synagogues, forthwith [were] obligated to seek a 'change of venue' and extol the trinity in the various churches."[29] In the choirs' place, two alternative models gained momentum (both of which had seen some use during the 1870s). Some newspaper editorials proposed that children's choirs replace paid choristers, claiming that a congregation's youth could inspire singing in the pews more effectively than trained singers.[30] Several congregations also began extended efforts to establish "choral societies," essentially volunteer choirs with an aura of sophistication aimed at engaging teens and young adults as central influencers of synagogue singing.[31] In many cases, cantors under pressure to reduce chanting and elaborate music in the sanctuary repositioned themselves as advocates for change, facilitating the desired choir programs and rhetorically supporting congregational song as a function of (rather than challenge to) their authority. Self-described orthodox and reform writers admitted that untrained voices complicated the idealism of congregational singing. But the practice continued to gain traction as a means of enlivening the service and democratizing American Jewish religious activity.[32]

The ideals of religious revival through congregational singing, however, met resistance, and often faltered after years of effort. The New York correspondent for *The American Israelite*, for example, described a chaotic clash of values that resulted in tensions between cantor and rabbi, choir and congregation, traditional melody and new composition:

> Where serious efforts have been made to introduce congregational singing, I have known, after the rubicon of the choir committee has been crossed, for the cantor to spoil all by insisting on singing in a pitch above the capacity of the congregation, or for the choir to be given such selections as prevented those present from joining in. There are some ministers who believe that the

"program" should be different each Sabbath, so as to avoid monotony, but if the congregation is to take part, it is asking entirely too much to expect that they be familiar enough with the different spiritual bills of fare to participate. Follow the old fashion and have certain familiar hymns weekly set to simple music that can be easily picked up, and you stand a fair chance of success.[33]

Writers held out hope for a meaningful balance, but they also faced the reality that as envisioned, congregational singing required a considerable time commitment for congregants, fundamental changes in ideas about appropriate worship music among congregational leaders, and a complicated calculus for cantors and synagogue readers seeking to retain their authority.

The Topography of Jewish Musical History

In parallel with congregational singing, new ways to think about Jewish musical history emerged. Especially Francis L. Cohen's extended work "The Rise and Development of Synagogue Music," derived from his 1887 speech at London's Anglo-Jewish Exposition, connected contemporary musical scholarship to synagogue music as a populist phenomenon. Four years earlier, in a presentation before the Jews' College Literary Society, Cohen had relied on the scholarship of Leopold Zunz, Carl Engel, Wilhelm Grimm, and (through personal correspondence) Eduard Birnbaum to establish contemporary Jewish chant as its own "national" music, unconnected to biblical music, separate in origin from Gregorian chant, and developed by Jewish populations over centuries through a folk-based "process of composition and improvement."[34] Cohen, who married the daughter of eminent British cantor Marcus Hast in late 1886, took a similar approach in his 1887 presentation, but this time he based his discussion on comments in a recently published English translation of Emil Naumann's *History of Music*.[35] Where Naumann credited nineteenth-century humanism as a source of Jewish emancipation and increased engagement with surrounding cultures, Cohen saw an opening to explore what he considered an inborn Jewish musical talent sustained over centuries of aniconism and material deprivation.[36] From such a premise, aided by the city's top synagogue musicians, he laid out a wide-ranging history of Jewish devotional music that spanned five successively narrowing eras (Biblical–70 CE; 70–ca. 900 CE; 9th–16th centuries; 16th–early 19th centuries; and the last fifty years). Cohen's narrative lecture privileged musical purity and synagogue reform, criticized "Polish Hazanuth," and derided what he considered virtuosic yet empty musicality. His polished live illustrations acknowledged but intentionally skipped over "old" cantorial styles—he declined to illustrate the hazan/singer/bass trio style because "you would probably not be edified with . . . these as illustrations"—and thus successfully brought the field of Jewish music to a well-heeled middle-class audience.[37] The intricate mode-based debates of his German-speaking cantorial colleagues, rather than taking center stage, fed into the broader historical narrative of musical development. And as with past histories, Cohen preferred to situate his story in current mainstream research—which he likely admired for its objectivity—rather than acknowledging a unique scholarly legacy of Jewish music study by Ensel (1880) and earlier contemporaries.

The lecture, publicized in the Anglophone Jewish press and published the year after the exposition, opened a new round of public discourse on "Jewish music," with the hybrid rabbi/cantor Cohen as its champion. Cohen continued to produce a number of scholarly mainstream publications, often based on the same opening paragraphs as his lecture. By the end of the decade, moreover, Cohen had further distinguished himself as the editor of the congregational singing manual *Shirei Keneset Yisrael*.[38] He would retain this leadership into the next century as the key contributor of topics on Jewish music history for the *Jewish Encyclopedia*, a major compendium of English-language German Jewish scholarship (1901–1906), and as the central editor of the *Voice of Prayer and Praise*, an expanded version of *Shirei Keneset Yisrael* that became the standard congregational singing manual for British Jewry.[39]

In the United States, meanwhile, similar developments complicated the roles of rabbi and hazan as authorities on synagogue music. Cantors and readers faced pressure to concede the musical authority that justified their salaries while struggling to claim the mantle of intellectualism, a trait more at home in the rabbi's portfolio. Initially, hazanim had followed a model similar to Francis L. Cohen's, combining the rabbi's philosophical erudition with the cantor's musical ability. Over time, however, a more musically exclusive cantor/musicologist also emerged. Both figures sought to capitalize on the development of musical science, or *Musikwissenschaft*, to transform their positions—for similar but distinct reasons.

Salomon Sulzer's death on January 17, 1890, may have played a part in these dynamics, serving as a catalyst for a continued continental drift among cantorial circles on either side of the Atlantic. British chief rabbi Nathan Marcus Adler's death four days later, however, appears to have eclipsed Sulzer in the news cycle, leading to relatively minimal coverage in the American press.[40] America's cantors, perhaps surprisingly, seemed otherwise occupied with their own work and remarkably offered little public comment.

In May 1891, *New York Herald* music critic Henry E. Krehbiel, fresh from a series of popular lectures on Richard Wagner, contributed an article on music to *The American Hebrew*'s special issue on "The Progress of the Jew."[41] Appearing alongside entries on art, literature, medicine, charity, and other areas of social accomplishment, Krehbiel's assessment of "The Jew in Music" held parallels to Wagner's notorious 1850/1869 screed "Judaism in Music." Like Wagner, Krehbiel assessed Jews' reentry into the nineteenth-century musical world as a matter of technical skill and patronage more than "creative ability"; like Wagner, he singled out Felix Mendelssohn as a creative force but primarily credited him with reintroducing Bach to the world; and like Wagner, he saw Jews' musical qualities as inherently racial, remaining vestigial during the eighteen centuries between the Roman conquest and European emancipation. Krehbiel attempted to counterbalance these comments, however, by praising music borne of religious sentiment, beginning with "the [ancient] grandeur of the Hebrew temple service." While lost at the time of the temple's destruction, such perceived grandeur led the way for "its evolution into the modern art," and therefore was "as little to be deplored from an artistic point of view as the loss of the music of the Greeks." Krehbiel encouraged Jewish composers to return to their ancient sources, celebrating them as a "manner in which the Jew can put an unmistakable impress upon the [musical] art." Such a premise allowed him to overlook contemporary mainstream Jewish composers and instead praise Sulzer, Naumbourg, and Löwenstamm for "utilizing traditional melodies in their settings of Hebrew services," in the hope that such activity "ought to stimulate composers who are not cantors to turn to this all-but-buried treasure for material to be otherwise applied."

Such a positive if race-based assessment of synagogue music gave cantors and choir leaders a welcome opening to assert their value as keepers of tradition. It also led to an ardent response from Hungarian-born religious leader William Sparger. Sparger, who served pulpits in Dortmund and Worms in 1881/82, allied with cantorial professionalizing efforts before his emigration to America. In June 1882, possibly as one of his last acts before leaving Europe, Sparger contributed an article to *Der jüdische Kantor* decrying the proliferation of subpar synagogue compositions sold by unqualified, fame-seeking composers.[42] In America, while flexibly shifting between liturgical roles—his first pulpit at Brooklyn congregation Beth Elohim described him as a "rabbi," but he moved to Manhattan's Temple Emanu-El to replace Cantor Adolph Rubin in January 1891—Sparger similarly appeared to cultivate a reputation as a figure who combined musicality with intellect.[43] Fifteen months into his Emanu-El position, he elaborated on his ideas in *The American Hebrew*, responding to Krehbiel's article with the essay, "Sing unto Us the Songs of Zion: A Plea for Jewish Music and for Congregational Singing of Jewish Hymns in Jewish Houses of Worship."[44]

In his article, Sparger promoted the importance of the cantor while filling in the 1,800 years that Krehbiel had characterized as a period of Jewish musical dormancy. During that time, he claimed, music ostensibly saved the Jewish people: "the combination of music with the liturgy" established the synagogue as "a source of inspiration, hope and comfort under oppression and demoralizing persecution." The music shared in the sanctuary thereby became a bulwark against forces of entropy. It supported not just the liturgical text, but also became the structure by which Jews maintained their home and community rituals. Music "kept alive and developed the poetic spark in the Jewish heart and . . . preserved the genius of the Jew from extinction." Sparger explained that the "meshorer," which he described as an itinerant minstrel, learned tunes from cantors and carried them from place to place, thus explaining the lack of available notation. While Jews' traditional melodies were today endangered by the tendency of reformers to replace them with popular tunes and hymns, Sparger noted, skilled synagogue composers were adapting them to new texts: "The Kol Nidre is gone [from the Reform service, for example,] but the melody was saved by its adaptation to [Leopold] Stein's 'O Tag des Herrn,' and by [Alois] Kaiser's and [Louis] Levandovsky's [sic] fitting it to the 130th psalm." On an analytical level, Sparger cited Josef Singer's 1886 treatise to "prove" that "there is such a thing as a [musical modal] system in synagogue music," which could be credited as a unique Jewish innovation with ancient origins. These arguments culminated in a final plea for congregational singing that engaged with contemporary politics of American Jewish reform. Anticipating the release of the *Union Prayer Book*, a liturgical guide intended by its creators to unify liberal-leaning congregations across the United States, Sparger continued to press the independent influence of music in American

Jewish religious life: "While we may have reasons to fear that many a year will pass before this prayerbook will be adopted by all our Jewish congregations and thus truly become a Union Prayer-book, there can be no earthly reason why our congregations should not unite on a Union Hymn-book for our synagogues and Sabbath-schools." Coming on the heels of Krehbiel's article, Sparger rearticulated the American cantor's position as both architect and curator of the American Jewish spirit, a recipient of longstanding tradition historically qualified to reawaken devotion and enliven the congregation's collective voice.

Sparger's call resonated with liberal Jewish intelligentsia in spirit if not in fact. Editors of *The American Hebrew* responded to Sparger with enthusiasm, embracing his mission as a champion of congregational singing even as they viewed his historical arguments with skepticism.[45] Prominent American Semitics scholar Cyrus Adler, in response, submitted the short music bibliography published by the Anglo-Jewish Exhibition to the same journal the following week as an encouraging place for expansion.[46] *The American Israelite*, meanwhile, reproduced Sparger's essay in full about three weeks later, on the page after Rabbi Isaac S. Moses's promise to release the *Union Prayer Book* by the end of the month.[47]

These articles established the terms for a complex and wide-ranging organizational dance that aimed to reconceive the role of music in the service, revive the cantor as a viable member of the clergy, and redefine the intellectual and musical boundaries of "Jewish music." Inserted amid various attempts by Jewish leaders to consolidate communities around common organizations and liturgies, these conversations gave cantors the opportunity to rebrand and reboot, affirming their reputation as the synagogue's musical experts. Complementary to the rabbi but ultimately separate from discordant theological arguments about the textual contents of a meaningful American Jewish liturgy, the new cantorate specialized in restoring music's ancient heritage to contemporary Jewry, a task that theoretically transcended denominationalism, promoted intellectual inquiry, and connected the cantor deeply to the people whom he served.

Cantors approached these goals through three interrelated projects: creating professional organizations, laying claim to a national hymnal, and intellectualizing the field of Jewish music. None proved a simple task, but each provided an important, if not existential, component of the cantorial portfolio as the twentieth century approached.

Who Writes the Soundtrack?

Under the somewhat contentious guidance of Isaac Mayer Wise, a succession of early meetings of American Jewish religious leaders from the 1850s through the late 1880s had generated a concerted desire for a common book of hymns. Despite optimism for producing such a volume, including at least one nationwide competition, a suitable candidate failed to appear. Disputes over language choice, repertoire, and the nature of congregational singing complicated the conversation, despite Wise's enthusiasm. By the time this clerical group rebranded itself as the Central Conference of American Rabbis (CCAR) in 1889, its publications wing had shifted its sights toward the more ambitious goal of a national prayer book. The limited number of competent musicians who joined them in their meetings, including G. M. Cohen, Samuel Welsch, William Sparger, and Alois Kaiser, worked to provide the service with a soundtrack nonetheless. And while Wise and others encouraged them to forge ahead before the rabbis had set the text, the earlier limited success of *Zimrath Yah* showed the complexity of such a strategy. Over the first half of the 1890s, a modest proposal for musical accompaniment thus transformed into a grandiose drama, firmly differentiating rabbis and cantors, pitting New York against the rest of the country, and stoking tensions of religious authority on the matter of congregational singing.

The discussion began in New York City, and involved two local clerical organizations. On November 3, 1891, a dozen city-based cantors founded the Cantors' Association of America (CAA), a body created "to elevate [the cantorial] standard, to promote brotherly feeling and harmony among its members, to further and encourage the composition of synagogal music, and to elevate that portion of the service which stands under the supervision of the cantor."[48] With the aim of uniting American cantors in a manner similar to that of the CCAR, the organization grew to more than forty members in the next several months, while extending to analogous groups in Bromberg, Germany, and Vienna, Austria.[49]

A few months later, New York's Board of Jewish Ministers invited the CAA to collaborate on a hymnal that could facilitate congregational singing. The cantors assented despite some reservations but then put the brakes on, acceding to the ministers' request to delay their plans until after the CCAR held its national meeting in New York in July 1892.[50] As promised, the CCAR endorsed the hymnal idea at that conference; yet rather than extending the cantors a true partnership, and over Sparger's objections, the rabbis took the task in-house and offered the Cantors' Association only an advisory role.[51]

Creating a Cantors' Agenda

Possibly in response, the CAA strengthened its hand by bringing in Alois Kaiser as its leader on the first Tuesday after Sukkot, October 18, 1892. Coming off a banquet held the previous night at the home of outgoing Association president and senior member Edward Kartschmaroff, Kaiser asserted the cantor's role as the primary champion of Jewish music in his inaugural address.[52] "It is needless to say," he announced, "that [the cantorate] is both a science and an art, a profession of honor and grave responsibilities."[53] He juxtaposed the cantor's specialty in music with the rabbi's specialty in liturgy and law: "we do not want to encroach upon any of their rights and privileges," he said of rabbis, "but simply to be humble co-workers in the vineyard of the Lord with a separate and distinct task before us, whose mission though not identical, is parallel with theirs." He also encouraged the CAA's members to work with rabbis to develop a common repertoire, even as cantors faced the new challenge of writing for a moving liturgical target. With a common prayer book still under discussion, Kaiser urged his colleagues to begin their task by "giv[ing] our attention to such texts that are common" to the existing prayer books and trusting that they would remain viable.

Kaiser hoped, through this approach, to create a national repertoire for congregational singing, analogous to what he saw as Christian church practice. That repertoire, in his view, could span the lifecycle from youth to old age. It needed to start with children's education at "Sabbath Schools." Youth well trained in congregational song could then replace the choir, whose professionalization had "condemned" the congregation "to utter silence." Synagogues could then return to what Kaiser described as the original unifying purpose of choral music, dispelling "the discord and disorder created by the irregular and haphazard responding of the worshipers to the chanting of the chazan." In this spirit, he charged his colleagues to make the hymnal "an eminently Jewish book in which every number will be a literary production of the highest order ... [and] adapted to exclusively Jewish melodies, arranged and harmonized by the best Jewish musical talent this land can command."⁵⁴ Undertaking this task, he felt, would consolidate the cantor's power, establish the history and theory of Jewish melodies as a scientific field of inquiry—here he credited Sparger's previous article incorporating the Jewish modes—and thereby rally composers to their side. "Let us take down the harps from off the willows, and attune once more the songs of Zion," he concluded triumphantly. By bringing the nation's cantors to common cause, Kaiser argued, music of the synagogue would regain its status as a true and lasting vessel of Jewish spirit.

The event brought cantors back into the middle of the hymnal discussion, setting off a round of public conversation about its contents that pitted Kaiser and Sparger against Scranton, Pennsylvania, cantor William Löwenberg. Sparger and Kaiser viewed their task as restorative, breathing new life into a trove of ancient national melodies. In contrast, Löwenberg, who received rabbinical ordination from Hebrew Union College in the early 1880s, advocated jettisoning all music that smacked of age in order to appeal to the next generation of Jews.⁵⁵ In a pair of editorials on the purpose of the hymnal, Löwenberg argued that "the everlastingly plaintive songs of the Polish or Russian chazan (who tolerates no other gods beside him) have certainly no attraction for the free-born American youth. The Hebrew songs of mediaevalism, pitched as they are with few exceptions in a minor key, are certainly not adapted to rouse young America to a new spirit of devotion."⁵⁶ In their place, Löwenberg called for "tunes which are at once melodious and inspiring" to American youth, and promoted the hymnal he compiled for his own congregation as an exemplar.⁵⁷ Sparger, in response, dismissed Löwenberg's musical practicality as a form of willing ignorance, similar to the approach of musically naïve rabbis hunting for novelty at the expense of deeper heritage. "Thousands of great musicians," over centuries, responded a snarky Sparger, had looked to long-held Jewish melodies for inspiration, testifying to their immense value.⁵⁸ Why should we seek such a superficial musical balm today?

Sparger gave his position further gravity by responding energetically to Cyrus Adler's call for a deeper well of Jewish music research materials. Over three successive issues of *The American Hebrew* in December 1892, Sparger produced "an attempt at a bibliography" on "Literature of the Music of the Jews," with more than 190 entries separated into scholarship and composition categories.⁵⁹ The scholarship category, with seventy-five entries, chronicled European writings about Jewish music chronologically between 1544 and 1891. "Musical Compositions" began with eighteen works between

1587 and about 1840, most of which appeared as short excerpts from larger books. Then, switching to an alphabetical arrangement, Sparger listed about a hundred works intended to represent the current era, from the first volume of Sulzer's *Schir Zion* to Alois Kaiser's publications.[60] Only eleven of these entries in total, all musical compositions, had American authors, implicitly laying forth the task for American cantors, and the historical precedent on which they could build.[61]

Kaiser sided with Sparger in advocating a revival of old melodies but chose to explain his reasoning patiently to Löwenberg and his rabbinical colleagues. Called to present on the topic before the CCAR's December 1892 meeting in Washington, DC, Kaiser offered the assembly "a word as to the merit of our Jewish traditional melodies and a plea for their reintroduction."[62] His presentation took a page out Sulzer's playbook, describing traditional melodies sentimentally, "as if a good old friend were whispering familiar words to us." Although Kaiser claimed that the "Polish chazan" corrupted these tunes "with [his] very indistinct notions of music and melody," in the right hands (implying the CAA) they could revitalize Jewish worship.[63] "It would only require some person well versed in modern music, as well as familiar with the ancient melodies, to properly select and arrange out of the multitude of traditional songs those best suited for the purpose in question."[64] Recast as "simple congregational songs"—he gave four harmonized examples—the tunes would not need to impinge on organ, professional choir, or any other aspect of the existing ritual to be effective. They would rather provide balance to an American Jewish population too often distracted by their aspirations to high art, as Kaiser described in an evocative gendered metaphor:

> I fear we have been making the mistake of embellishing our young and handsome daughter, American Judaism, with too much ornate finery, of looking too much to her external grace and beauty, instead of paying closer attention to the sounding of her health and heart.... Perhaps if wedded to this footsore wanderer of the distant East, who though gray in years still possesses much vigor of youth, she might be awakened to some grave and serious reflections. If only a portion of the attention were bestowed upon him that she has of late received, he might indeed soon be divested of his ancient appearance, and be gladly welcomed as an acceptable spouse. All he requires is a friendly hand to replace his tattered garments by more timely habiliments.[65]

Kaiser's focus on the role of ancient melodies in giving American Judaism a solid spiritual foundation became a central theme in arguments for the cantor's significance. As he and Sparger led the push for the right to create the new hymnal, the CCAR released its first *Union Prayer Book* to both applause and dissent. Despite adoption by several synagogues, most of which aligned with the moderate reforms of Isaac Mayer Wise, the book met with ideological disapproval by a vocal portion of the Conference looking for greater shifts away from such factors as messianism, Zionism, and the use of Hebrew. Within months, the CCAR had withdrawn the book and went back into negotiations. For cantors seeking to move forward, the target had moved again.

Kaiser and Sparger, looking for a more reliable platform, turned to the emerging and increasingly powerful network of Jewish women's organizations. Synagogue-based women's groups had provided significant support for orderly worship and congregational singing as facilitators of education and home life, suppliers of choir members, recipients of "proper" musical education, and self-appointed keepers of congregational order. More significantly, as part of the call to prepare for the Chicago Columbian Exhibition of 1893, a newly organized National Council of Jewish Women looked to music to symbolize their contributions to Jewish communal life. As member Emma Frank later recounted:

> That it is peculiarly [in the] women's sphere to introduce divine and sacred music into the household is self-evident; why should not we, then, deem it a duty to become familiar with the beautiful echoes of the past and the histories that surround them? . . . In our new and easy methods of teaching in the Sabbath School, it has been found unwise and unnecessary to bother the children with the study of Hebrew, but music, the language understood by young and old the world over, must not be buried.[66]

In March 1893, the committee of the Jewish Women's Branch of the World's Fair Religious Congress contracted Kaiser and Sparger to "compile and arrange the hymns" for a "Memorial Hymnal, to be at once a bibliography and a collection of traditional Jewish music."[67] Julia K. Simpson, "Jewess delegate to the world's congress of religions," followed up by noting, in preparations for the exhibition, that "Our committee are also endeavoring to make a collection of traditional Jewish synagogical music, beginning as far back as possible and containing notes relating to the authors of the hymns. We hope to make this a very interesting volume and think of publishing about 1,000 copies."[68] Their comments hinted at an approach that transcended denominationalism, and used longevity to craft a pluralistic vision that associated neither with the reform-leaning Union of American

Hebrew Congregations, nor the more conservative supporters of the Jewish Theological Seminary founded in 1886 (nor more religious independent orthodox congregations).

By June, Kaiser and Sparger had compiled a series of musical pieces prefaced by an extensive historical and analytical introduction, which would appear together as *A Collection of the Principal Melodies of the Synagogue from the Earliest Times to the Present* (see figure 7.1). Like Francis L. Cohen's work, their musical selections all carried an English-language text, presumably to ensure a wide appeal. At the same time, a clear mission came through, succinctly stated in the introduction: "Simplify the traditional chant, but preserve carefully its inherent characteristics and originality, and plant it again in the Synagogue and homes of our people in the only form in which this can be achieved now, namely, in the form of hymns."[69] Referencing Sparger's *American Hebrew* bibliography and drawing on Josef Singer's work on Jewish modes, the authors began by asserting a crucial distinction between "traditional melodies" and "ritual chant" in the service. The former, mainly German-based hymn tunes from the previous century, were "characterized by a childlike simplicity, and . . . mostly composed in the modern major key."[70] "Ritual chant," they claimed in contrast, showed a much older provenance and comprised a richer trove of source material.

The musical sections fleshed out the authors' arguments. A first part, "Traditional Melodies," presented about five dozen authorless tunes with English words, arranged by holiday and set for a variety of basic vocal and instrumental formats. These selections, including material that had previously appeared in the last two volumes of *Zimrath Yah*, contained what Kaiser and Sparger saw as "the most important melodies and chants of the Synagogue" due to their relative age (see Figure 7.2).[71] Almost every holiday's section began with an arrangement of an "ancient melody" for solo keyboard and then followed with a hymn-style choral arrangement of the same melody, often for four voices. Each entry also included titles in English and Hebrew, thus presenting a basic core knowledge for integrating each tune idiomatically into home and synagogue use.[72]

The back of the book included seventeen more complicated "Modern Compositions" by prominent European, British, and American liturgical composers, similarly fitted with English texts. Seven of these pieces, mostly by Europeans, featured "Traditional Themes" (although the editors left generally unidentified). Ten "Original" compositions, the book's most elaborate and technically involved, concluded the volume, exhibiting what

Figure 7.1. Title page, *A Collection of the Principal Melodies of the Synagogue from the Earliest Times to the Present*. Ed. Alois Kaiser and William Sparger (1893). Created by the Jewish Women's Congress for the World Parliament of Religions at the 1893 Chicago World's Fair.

the editors likely saw as an appropriate organic outgrowth of the ancient melodies. Of these final ten works, moreover, American émigré composers accounted for seven, hinting at Kaiser and Sparger's pride in their adopted country's energy, optimism, and adherence to tradition.

Commentary: A Glimpse at the Future of Jewish Music Study?

Cyrus Adler, who had taken a significant role in organizing exotic "villages" of peoples from Asia Minor and North Africa at the World's Fair's Midway Plaisance—many of which employed Jews to populate the exhibits—contributed a preface to Kaiser and Sparger's collection.[73] As a professor of Semitics and the fair's "commissioner . . . to Turkey, Paris, Egypt, Tunis, and Morocco," Adler chided the editors for their Ashkenazic bias, observing that their book was "written from the point of view of the Ashkenazic ritual. When referring to 'our' chants or melodies those employed by the

Figure 7.2. Comparison between *Zimrath Yah* and *A Collection of the Principal Melodies*.

a. "N'ila Hymn": Ancient melody arranged by Alois Kaiser. Four-part chorus with organ accompaniment *colla parte* (i.e., doubling the voices). *Zimrath Yah* IV, no. 66.

b. "The Sun Declines," from the "Traditional Melodies" section of *A Collection of the Principal Melodies*, no. 43. Identical to Figure 7.2a with organ accompaniment removed.

Continued

Figure 7.2. continued.

Ashkenazim are meant."[74] Noting the shortcomings of this approach as a method of scholarly inquiry, he presciently outlined a future project that might better present the ethnic Jewish musical landscape:

> There is still another field of investigation which while it offers many difficulties may be productive of some result—a collection of the chants of the scattered communities. The Jews of Damascus, of South Arabia, the Bene Israel of Bombay, the Falashas of Abyssinia and other scattered communities are quite independent of any European influence. The collection of the music of these people by means of a phonograph might furnish valuable material.... It is not impossible that the final upshot of the discussion, so far as Ashkenazim and Sephardim are concerned, will prove to be a belief that both cantilations are ancient, just as there is little question that both methods of pronouncing Hebrew are of ancient origin, and go back to a dialectic difference which existed in Palestine itself.[75]

Adler's advocacy of a non-Ashkenazic narrative would carry forward to his coeditorship of the music entries for the *Jewish Encyclopedia* with Francis L. Cohen a decade later. Shortly afterward, Abraham Z. Idelsohn would assume its mantle when he began his research among the "Oriental" Jewish populations in Palestine. In the context of Kaiser and Sparger's volume, Adler's concerns with the Eurocentrism of cantorial scholarship provided a potent footnote, even as he provisionally embraced the book's early efforts to bring greater scientific rigor to the topic.

Cantors' Continued Struggles

The efforts that the Jewish Women's Congress made to promote a new American Jewish musical vocabulary remained frustratingly isolated. In contrast, a series of scholarly lectures on Jews in the World's Parliament of Religions, organized jointly by (exclusively male) committees from the UAHC and the CCAR in September 1893, mentioned music only briefly, and never saw to address the matter in depth.[76] This strikingly gendered presentation reflected a broader shift that had been brewing for decades: women had taken greater ownership of the cultural aspects of Jewish communal life, while men maintained their grasp on text-based intellectualism (including their stewardship of new religious texts). Musical literacy, valued as a domestic skill and promoted as a key to synagogue participation, found itself caught in this complex social web, with cantors suspended accordingly.

As if to reinforce the matter, the CCAR delayed production on the hymnal further at its meeting in Chicago a week before Kaiser and

Sparger's hymn book officially premiered.⁷⁷ Rabbi Adolph Guttman, reporting as chair of the hymnal committee, noted that despite a national appeal for hymn texts, the committee had received only about seventy-five submissions, far below the two hundred to three hundred texts needed to constitute a viable hymnal.⁷⁸ The committee and the CAA had also begun to tussle over the creation process. Despite the low yield, the CCAR hymnal committee sent the cantors "fifty hymns, for which they were to find suitable melodies." The cantors, in turn, asked the rabbis to "officially adopt the texts, before they select or compose melodies."⁷⁹ Progress again stopped.

Facing a bureaucratic impasse and growing mistrust, the CAA decided to take matters into its own hands. A few months later, a committee of four leading New York cantors, plus Kaiser and Cincinnati's Morris Goldstein, resolved to "proceed at once to edit and publish a hymn book for Jewish houses of worship and for Jewish schools and religious instruction."⁸⁰ With a focus on "time-honored traditional melodies" and textual adaptations heavily weighted toward psalm texts, the group appropriated $500 to defray costs, and hoped to print five thousand copies of the final book for purchase at no more than twenty cents each. Again, the cantors situated themselves as vessels of song rather than advocates of a specific denomination, largely focusing on music and texts commonly used by all Jews.

The CCAR, however, about to release its revised *Union Prayer Book*, successfully countered in good faith that "the publication of another hymn book . . . would only complicate matters" and again convinced the CAA to hold off until after its next convention.⁸¹ Yet by early 1894, while the cantors remained patient, CCAR members in two cities had already announced forthcoming hymnals: one edited by Detroit's Louis Grossman and F. L. York, and the other by Chicago's Isaac S. Moses (who had also compiled the first *Union Prayer Book*).⁸² A representative of the CAA with "Copyrighted Advance Sheets" of Grossman and York's book publicly disparaged it in *The American Hebrew* that April. Despite Grossman's well-meaning premise that "there must be a self-born denominational music" for Jews as much as any other religious group, the cantor-reviewer faulted the collection for its lifted texts, poor syllabification, unnecessarily simplified harmonies, and overt rabbinic overreach.⁸³ The same cantor-reviewer had seen only the introduction of the Moses hymnal, but he ridiculed that work as well for what he saw as its ingenuous claim to be a "labor of love."⁸⁴ In a clever rhetorical snit, the reviewer evoked the spirit of Goethe, warning,

"As an American Jewish Rabbi thou wouldst have been utterly out of place. Why, thy excessive modesty might have even prevented thee from writing a new Prayer-book, or even from composing a new Hymn-book, which is the easiest thing in the world. What though thou hadst not enough musical knowledge to distinguish between the music-hall ditty and a symphony? No matter; there are very few things in this world which an American-Jewish Rabbi cannot undertake."[85] After the CCAR committee had delayed the cantors' work for years, these two independent solutions appeared to undercut their collaboration, straining trust.

Adolf Guttmann, chair of the CCAR hymnal committee, did not attend the conference's July 1894 meeting in Atlantic City, New Jersey. Implicitly abdicating his responsibility, he submitted no report. Instead, on the same day that the group approved the text of the High Holiday prayer book, two new overtures sought to engage the CAA.[86] Rabbi Kaufman Kohler introduced a unanimously adopted resolution "to seek the aid of the Cantors Association for appropriate music [for the new English-language prayer texts] . . . with a spirit of reverence for the past, and with regard to the earnestness of the service."[87] And after a discussion about the need for a hymn book, including Isaac Mayer Wise's suggestion that a small pamphlet might suffice rather than a large published collection, the conference heeded Sparger's argument that "we must have the means . . . of rousing our worshipers from the lethargy into which they fall from the moment they enter the synagogue till the end of the service."[88] A newly appointed hymnal committee promised greater transparency; and the editorial committee immediately committed to send its newly adopted texts to the cantors for musical setting. Yet on that Saturday morning, when the ministers prayed with an Atlantic City congregation that already "joined heartily in the responses and hymns," the service prompted optimism "that such a thing as congregational singing was a possibility, [and a new hymnal unneeded,] if the old melodies were used."[89] The cantors, seeking to use their musical expertise to show how indispensable they were, still had their work to do.

Given all of a month to complete the task, reported Alois Kaiser the following year, "the cantors reluctantly complied with the request, knowing full well that little of permanent value could be produced in so short a time."[90] Kaiser and Sparger, together with New York cantors Theodore Guinsburg (Ahawath Chesed) and Herman Goldstein (Shaar HaShomayim) consequently issued a seventy-two-page, photostatted musical companion

Figure 7.3. *Anthems, Hymns and Responses for the Union Prayer Book* (1894). Cover page.
(Credit: Klau Library, Hebrew Union College)

to the new *Union High Holiday Prayer Book* as a stop-gap measure (see fig. 7.3). In their preface, they noted their significant limitations:

> The Cantor's [sic] Association, to whom the preparation of the Music for the new Union Prayer-Book was intrusted, hoped to have the same ready for the fall holidays of this year. But, owing to the tardy appearance of the Prayer Book, this became impossible. At the urgent request of the Publication Committee of the Central Conference, however, it was decided to issue this pamphlet containing some forty English anthems and responses, and references to various well known musical works in which the music to the greater portion of the 2nd volume of the Prayerbook can be found. Under the circumstances, the Association craves the indulgence of the public for any shortcomings, and gives assurance that no effort will be spared to make the forthcoming volumes, which will contain new music for the entire Prayerbook satisfactory in every respect.[91]

Kaiser contributed twenty-two of the thirty-five new pieces in the book; Guinsburg, Goldstein, and Sparger contributed five, three, and four works, respectively; and Ahawath Chesed organist Gideon Froelich contributed one.[92] More significantly, the cantors supplemented these new works with a series of recommended musical selections from existing publications—notably volumes 3 and 4 of *Zimrath Yah*, Kaiser and Sparger's 1893 World's Fair volume, and A. J. Davis's music to the Emanu-El hymnal (1887)—to create a complete, 106-selection musical sequence for Rosh Hashanah (first day only) and Yom Kippur services tailored to the *Union Prayer Book* (see Figure 7.4).[93] Viewed as a whole, the pamphlet exhibited several strategies that the CAA used to model its members' expertise, including a deep knowledge of repertoire, skill in choosing meaningful music, and facility in shaping a large-scale liturgical experience. Likely presented in hopes of reclaiming the musical mantle of the service for cantors, the pamphlet publicly "met with great success" in the eyes of the CCAR, enjoying brisk sales and receiving "many letters from prominent rabbis" praising the work.[94] Hymnal editor Isaac S. Moses in particular reportedly sent a complimentary and politically astute response affirming that "by this feat, you have demonstrated the usefulness of the Cantors' Association."[95]

Such sterling rhetoric, however, hid a less rosy reality. The sophisticated music compendium, while useful for cantors and other music personnel, substantially exceeded the abilities or desires of a singing congregation. And while able cantors likely appreciated its concordance-like quality, they probably already held enough knowledge to program the

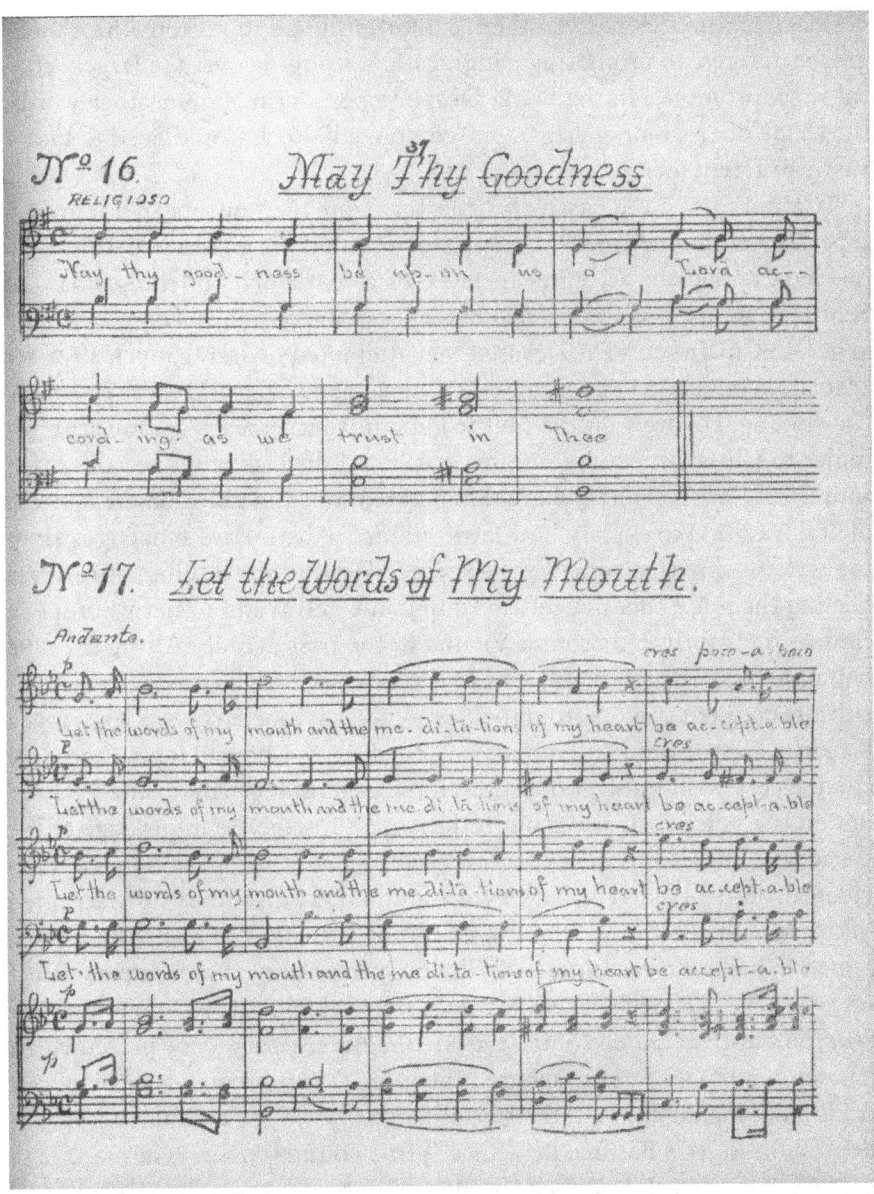

Figure 7.4. Nos. 16 and 17 from *Anthems, Hymns and Responses for the Union Pray Book*, no. 16 is a simple choral response; no. 17 is an elaborate choral piece with organ accompaniment doubling the voices. (Credit: Klau Library, Hebrew Union College)

holidays on their own. Even then, cantors still had to reckon with rabbis' greater interest in promoting congregational singing over the largely choral work promoted in the book. Despite open optimism, in other words, the shape of any more permanent "completed" work would need to take a vastly different form.

Cantors also faced passive belittlement from their European brethren—especially from the cantorial center of Vienna, which seemed simply to overlook American activities in favor of a markedly shifted agenda. On February 28, 1895, Vienna chief cantor Josef Singer published an extended article in Cincinnati's *Die Deborah* that attempted to draw a much stronger scholarly connection between biblical synagogue song and modern cantorial singing. He drew on the well-trod path from Israelite-era musical formulae to Christian neume singing, attributed the lack of medieval written sources of Jewish chant to Christian persecution, and relied on the concept of oral tradition to explain how Jews retained a distinctive synagogue singing style during that time. Yet here Singer's path took a different turn reflecting the more cohesive relationship that Central and Eastern European cantors had cultivated around Vienna in the past decades. Using his 1886 pamphlet on synagogue modes as an intellectual foundation, Singer specifically credited cantors from the East—"Kaschtan, Herschel, Kiew, Izegel, Kanarik, Davidl Brod and others"—as the figures who had most effectively channeled Jewish musical tradition in the generations before Sulzer: based not on the notes themselves but rather on an instinctive knowledge of the synagogue modes. This form, he argued, citing only European scholars, provided an authentic and unique Jewish sound that Sulzer only fully accepted in the second volume of *Schir Zion*.[96] While the editor of *Die Deborah* had hoped to include a rejoinder by William Sparger, illness prevented a direct response. Yet six weeks later, Sparger's musical analysis of Frank Van der Stucken's festival march "Shir Zion" in *The American Hebrew* presented an answer of sorts when he compared the march's interweaving of "six of our traditional melodies . . . in their original purity" to the architectural grandeur of St. Mark's Basilica in Venice.[97] In a country where (German) Jewish newspapers still described Yiddish as "jargon," and where the musical styles of Eastern European cantors appeared to remain marginal, Singer's plea for the primacy of Eastern European cantors worked at cross-purposes to current American initiatives.[98]

Meanwhile cantors' discontent with their poor treatment at the hands of the CCAR, even given the overtures of the previous year, opened internal divisions. Some, such as Alois Kaiser, continued to operate in concert with rabbinical agendas, evidenced by his full-throated advocacy of congregational singing in a sermon he delivered at New York's Temple Rodeph Sholom the following March.[99] By that time, however, major congregations across the country had begun to adopt Isaac S. Moses's *Sabbath School Hymnal*, including both of Cincinnati's progressive synagogues and New York's Shaarey Tefilah. Although geared toward children, the book catalyzed a rabbi-driven expansion of congregational singing, effectively stunting the cantors' efforts at instituting their own mediated approach.[100] On April 27, 1895, several defeated CAA members with weaker connections to the Union of American Hebrew Congregations reorganized under a new charter that reinforced the cantor's professional viability and scientific knowledge, and largely gave up on the hope of rabbinical partnership. Herman Goldstein, coeditor of the cantors' 1894 stopgap hymnal, became the organization's new president, leading a membership predominantly based in New York.[101] The recast charter emphasized the intellectual possibilities of Jewish music specialization, with a focus on "pursuit of the study of ancient Hebrew melodies, their origin and growth," and continued the group's aesthetic and social agenda, "provid[ing] for the methods to improve and beautify the [Synagogue] Service[,] and uphold[ing] and mutually assist[ing] the members of their profession."[102] By vote, however, the group "decided not to father the new hymn book," abandoning a fraught and frustrating collaboration.[103]

A sizable group of cantors, however, remained convinced that rabbinical collaboration offered the strongest way forward. On May 14, 1895, Kaiser and Sparger banded together in Baltimore with cantors representing Cincinnati (Morris Goldstein), Philadelphia (William Löwenberg), San Francisco (Edward Stark), New Orleans (J. Braunfeld), Manhattan (Sparger and David Cahn), and Brooklyn (Solomon Rappaport) to create the new Society of American Cantors (SAC).[104] Without mentioning the other group by name, inaugural president Kaiser laid out clear lines of contrast in his first address to the SAC, emphasizing a cantorial role that complemented and, at times, overlapped with the responsibilities of the rabbi. "Aside from musical attainments," Kaiser said, the cantor "must be a competent helpmate to the rabbi, not indeed by encroaching upon his province, but by aspiring to be his co-worker in all communal and religious work, and his substitute whenever the occasion may require."[105] Cantors' success, Kaiser argued, hinged on mutual respect and trust with rabbis, despite the challenges such a partnership might encounter along the way. Claiming that "the largest congregations [around the country] will testify that the cantor has again become a necessity in more than one way," Kaiser organized the new organization's agenda around encouraging congregational interaction, including "the raising of the standard of the synagogue music, the preservation of our traditional melodies, and the supply of proper hymns for congregational singing." The last of these claims implied a continued commitment to "revise, enlarge, and complete" the High Holiday music presented in the 1894 pamphlet, and consequently to bring the long-discussed hymnal to conclusion.[106] Such involvement, Kaiser and his colleagues seemed to suggest, would ensure the cantor's place as an essential occupant of the Union's synagogue pulpit.

The May 1895 appearance of volume 1 of the *Union Prayer Book* led to rapid adoption: by the CCAR's annual meeting in Rochester two months later, more than fifty congregations had embraced the book, purchasing over 5,200 copies.[107] Complementing the new book's strong reception, the Committee on the Union Hymn-Book brought report of a thriving partnership with Kaiser and the Society of American Cantors. Rather than seeking new verses, the committee reported compiling in short order a broad array of texts "from the existing Hymn-Books in present use in Jewish congregations, as well as from the translations of Psalms and other Biblical passages, put in meter and hymn-form by non-Jewish writers."[108] The Society of American Cantors, upon receiving this material, promptly "selected, arranged, and composed" melodies "to about a hundred of these hymns."[109] Both groups appeared to recognize that the spirit of this collaboration would give this book a different character from the High Holiday material of the 1894 pamphlet, emphasizing accessibility and ease of use. The cantors thus chose materials that they felt would have the widest appeal: an 1895 account of the musical service at Temple Emanu-El, which appeared to use an embryonic version of the hymnal, remarked upon the body of "time-honored traditional melodies" for liturgy being used.[110] New melodies were "directly composed for the text to which it is sung," superseding an earlier practice of using "arrangements from operas and Catholic masses."[111] A separate set of anthems (themed devotional songs) were "selected from the unlimited number of undenominational [sic] church compositions," with preference "given to the classical works of Beethoven, Handl [sic], Gluck, Haydn, Spohr, Mendelssohn, etc., almost to the entire exclusion of modern composers."[112] To these types of congregational song, the CCAR Hymn-Book Committee proposed to append a nonmusical section of prayer texts, containing a "considerable number of hymns, poems and anthems" that "do not lend themselves to congregational singing," and "may be used for private devotion and edification."[113] Emerging as a helpmate for individual worshipers, the book would emphasize comfort, familiarity, participation, and some choice. At the CCAR convention in July 1895, Isaac Mayer Wise proposed to limit the publication to twenty or so of the most common hymns (the rest presumably to come from local repertoires). CCAR meeting attendees, however, ultimately agreed to consider the full body of completed hymns before making a decision.[114]

Music for the new prayer book continued to pour forth in other forms as well. During the September High Holidays, Baltimore Hebrew Congregation premiered a *Union Prayer Book*–based series of services written by Cincinnati cantor Morris Goldstein. A report of the works emphasized their simplicity and familiarity, explaining that "Mr. Goldstein has followed the old traditional melodies as far as possible, and has confined his labors mainly to the arrangements."[115] Isaac S. Moses, chair of the CCAR publications committee, issued a new edition of his own *Sabbath School Hymnal*, with new contributions by Alois Kaiser and local Chicago musicians F. G. Rohner and P. C. Lutkin. Merely "offered as a temporary help for Jewish worship," and "not meant to anticipate the appearance of the Union Hymn-book," Moses nonetheless hoped that "the compilers of the Union Hymn-book will be able to draw valuable material" from it.[116] Kaiser himself, in a creative groove, premiered new *Union Prayer Book*–based music in his synagogue in February 1896. Around the same time, he received a commission from former American colleague Pinchas Minkowsky to compose a new setting of Psalm 21, to be performed at Odessa's Brody synagogue in commemoration Czar Nicholas II's May coronation.[117] With the *Union Prayer Book* fast becoming the standard, cantors and composers appeared to gain some confidence.

But the hymnal remained a sticking point. Temple Emanu-El rabbi Gustav Gottheil, in a friendly role, became the next authority to vet the hymnal texts, and released a completed compilation in May 1896; the CCAR hymnal committee then expanded Gottheil's collection to about 250 entries. At the CCAR's next meeting in July, however, internal theological differences continued to impede progress. Kaiser and Gottheil, working with the hymnal committee, prioritized artistry and emphasized the universal values that hymns could instill, possibly with a further (quiet) nod toward importing some repertoire from the general corpus of ecumenical popular sacred music works. Some rabbis had reservations about including non-Jewish elements in the book, whether authors, composers, or a sonic "nasal twang" possibly attributed to Appalachian-style Christian song, but they largely expressed confidence in Kaiser and Gottheil to produce a quality work.[118] Isaac S. Moses, defending his own hymnal, felt the new book was being "forced" on the conference. Isaac Mayer Wise, as president, continued to exhaust every avenue to sink the project, including a public attempt to void the original hymnal commission on procedural grounds.[119] Yet the rabbis, likely recognizing a shrinking window of opportunity, finally voted to move ahead with the publication.

And just in time. As the "congregational singing" debate began to wear thin, impatient groups began to act on their own. Throughout the mid-1890s, women's clubs across several cities had taken it upon themselves to establish "music sections," wherein (according to one club in Philadelphia) "old Jewish music is to be studied."[120] Synagogues, moreover, frequently adopted the *Union Prayer Book* with the intention of returning control of the service to the congregation. Kaiser's own Oheb Shalom congregation reduced its choir in November 1896 to "a single quartet of professional singers, assisted by a few volunteers from among the members of the congregation."[121] In January 1897, Shaarey Tefilah rabbi Frederick de Sola Mendes framed the adoption of the *Union Prayer Book* as a way to bypass the question of congregational singing without resolving it. He cited British Jewish writer and activist Oswald J. Simon, who described congregational singing in synagogues as a well-intentioned fiction ("I defy any musical person to accomplish the miracle of singing together with the average Jewish congregation").[122] De Sola Mendes, whose clergy partner cantor Charles L. Seiniger had become part of the cantorial organization that gave up on a Union hymnal, noted the still-independent spirit of American synagogues that advocated improvement through practice. He argued, however, that musical leadership "led by a trained choir" might be more effective than congregational singing alone.

The hymnal's long delays, combined with endless failed attempts at an effective model for congregational singing, soured community attitudes toward the cantor. In January 1897, the editors of *The American Hebrew* accused cantors of thwarting eager and willing congregations, claiming, "The average cantor finds in every suggestion to have congregational singing, a thrust at his official existence, and therefore opposes it, the while he pretends to favor it. This is blunt language, but it is the truth."[123] Oversimplifying the matter in deference to a populist call, the editors argued that "There is but one way to have congregational singing and that is—to have it."[124] The cantor's self-importance, in their view, rendered him a regressive figure in the face of American Jewish progress.

Incensed, William Sparger responded with a hyperbolic, sarcasm-laced editorial. Titled, "The Cantor Exposed and Congregational Singing Assured," Sparger took a false-congratulatory tone to the editors' exposé: "[The cantor's] power for evil is broken; his downfall is complete, and I—I rejoice in it."[125] Underneath the rhetoric, his response painted the cantor, and particularly Sparger's colleagues in the Society of American Cantors, as lifetime congregational servants of unimpeachable sincerity, and promoted the hymnal as a long-awaited product of their labors. His most colorful lines, however, brimmed with bitterness while savaging the previous editorial: "They have spent hundreds of dollars and sent delegates thousands of miles to Rabbinical conferences with the avowed purpose of advocating the speedy publication of a Union Hymn-book, while in reality they were opposing it with all the means at their command, knowing that its success would jeopardize their official existence. The hypocrites!" Sparger shifted blame to the resistance of "the organ-blower" (i.e., the organist) in preventing congregational singing, and assailed the *American Hebrew* editors' naïveté in their calls for congregations to take control of their own music by fiat. "The editor of *The American Hebrew* was fully aware of the well-nigh superhuman efforts that were made by both ministers and laymen for the last twenty-five years in this country, and lately also in England, to introduce congregational singing. Every possible and impossible means was resorted to, but without effect. And yet, all this while you were in the possession of the only true remedy without divulging it. . . . And what a glorious, wonder, sublime remedy it is. 'There is but one way to have congregational singing and that is—to have it.' Marvelous!" The forthcoming hymnal, Sparger argued, had deeper roots in the congregational singing movement, resulted from hard work and long-term negotiation, and in establishing a national body of common song, "can and will bring congregational singing into our synagogues and nothing else." As a vigorous defense of the cantor-as-mediator model, Sparger's letter bombastically set forth a path by which the cantor remained a crucial congregational team player, in marked contrast to the image of self-possessed cantors seen mainly as performers at the expense of congregational voices. Sympathetic responses in the paper pointed to Sparger's good work, and the need for patience in awaiting the hymnal's appearance, although one letter continued to fault cantors for usurping common chant by singing in inaccessible keys.[126]

On May 19, 1897, Kaiser and Löwenberg met in Philadelphia to complete what appear to be the final twenty-five selections of "a companion to the *Union Prayer Book*," called the *Union Hymnal*, having received the completed manuscript.[127] A report in the *Baltimore Sun* noted that Kaiser and the SAC continued to aim for a universal book, "for use in Orthodox and Reformed synagogues," that would "encourage the congregations to sing with the choirs" but also contain "solos, duets, trios and quartettes, besides the choruses."[128] Universal or not, however, the final phase of preparation had begun.

Finally, the *Union Hymnal*

On August 13, 1897, *The American Hebrew* joined other Jewish papers by announcing the hymnal's impending publication. Its description suggested that Kaiser and his group still wanted the book to serve all American Jewish synagogue needs, regardless of denomination, with contents "selected from the best choral works extant, and arranged in such a manner as to enable everyone to join in the singing of them."[129] An extended advertisement appeared in *The American Israelite*, again describing the book's final form as amenable for "making congregational singing a success" and apparently seeking to create a national repertoire that could be shared by Jews across the United States.[130] Just as importantly, notices advertised the book's aim to unify the shared domains of the home, the school, and the synagogue.[131] An elaborate notice in Philadelphia's *Jewish Exponent* claimed that the hymnal "will be valuable for its familiarizing of traditional melodies: for the possibility it affords for improved congregational singing and even for home devotions."[132]

As a herculean attempt to consolidate the entire complex and varied American Jewish musical landscape, however, the *Union Hymnal* burst at the musical seams (see fig. 7.5). The collection provided insight into the broad spectrum of ideas considered appropriate for Jewish worship music, from adapting generic American religious hymn repertoire to identifying and employing "traditional" Jewish melodies, to writing new compositions that reflected a growing body of cantorial scholarship, and to curating the broad array of work published for earlier liturgies.

UNION HYMNAL

TEXT EDITED BY THE
CENTRAL CONFERENCE OF
AMERICAN RABBIS

MUSIC SELECTED AND ARRANGED BY THE
SOCIETY OF AMERICAN CANTORS

Copyright, 1897
by
The Central Conference of American Rabbis

Figure 7.5. *Union Hymnal* (Central Conference of American Rabbis, 1897), title page.

Whereas a single volume of *Zimrath Yah* cost at least $6.50 in the 1870s, the new hymnal went for just fifty cents, achieving a long-sought-after economy of scale. As a function of its compilers' ambitions, moreover, the work brought to a head cantors' arguments for their legitimacy as essential Jewish clergy.

The first and largest of the book's four parts comprised 121 hymns, arranged into eight theme-based sections: five referencing divine relationships (Praise, Devotion, Supplication, Confidence and Trust, and Thanksgiving) and the other three providing works for key moments of the service ("Meditation") and the liturgical year ("Sabbath and Festivals," "Various Festivals"). Kaiser, who authored twenty-eight of these selections, seemed to arrange the pieces in each section to include an even balance of verifiably Jewish sources and popular hymns used more broadly in American civic and religious society. The "Sabbath and Festivals" section upped the "Jewish" percentage to two-thirds, with Kaiser incorporating more arrangements of "traditional" tunes in a format that encouraged congregational singing.[133] The "Thanksgiving" and "Meditation" sections, in contrast, contained only one Jewish source between them, highlighting their American character and their overlap with broader socioreligious norms.

Three appendices followed. Kaiser, following the order of the *Union Prayer Book*, added twenty Hebrew-language prayer settings: combining thirteen of his own compositions with popular alternate melodies by Sulzer, Lewandowski, Emanuel Kirschner (of Munich), and Israel M. Japhet (of Frankfurt).[134] A separate series of a dozen settings for religious schools covered group singing for students, framed within the larger context of a liberal Jewish musical life cycle that included generic popular hymns, three pieces by Jewish composers (two by Kaiser, one by Löwenberg), and two patriotic American songs ("The Star-Spangled Banner" and "Columbia, the Gem of the Ocean").

The last and most controversial section provided a list of options from the general market of available liturgical compositions that cantors, organists, and (presumably) rabbis could use as "anthems"—somewhat more elaborate musical settings of texts that reinforced the day's scriptural readings (see Figure 7.6). Sixty-three of these texts derived directly from Hebrew scripture, mostly the psalms and various prophetic writings (only three used texts from Genesis and Exodus). The remaining thirty-seven entries comprised a collection of well-regarded original hymns, some of

INDEX OF ANTHEMS.

No. of Anthem.	Scriptural Portion.	Verses.	Composer.	Title of Anthem or First Line.	Publisher.	Directions and Other Remarks.
1	Ps. vi.	4, 3, 9	A. J. Davis.	Turn Thee, O Lord.	Pond.	
2	Ps. xiii.	1, 6	J. Brahms. M. Greene. J. Clarke. Wm. Boyce.	Lord, how long wilt Thou forget?	Novello.	For female voices.
3	Ps. xvi.	1-8, 7, 8	Charles Salaman.	Preserve me, O Lord.	Novello.	
4	Ps. xxiii.	1-6	*L. Lewandowski. H. Smart. F. Schubert. A. R. Gaul. Wm. Greene. F. Schubert.	The Lord is my Shepherd.	Breitkopf & Haertl. Novello. " " Schirmer.	For female voices. For mixed quartette
5	Ps. xxv.	4-11 5-7	*L. Lewandowski. K. J. Pye.	Shew me Thy path. Lead me in Thy Truth.	Breitkopf & Haertl. Novello.	
6	Ps. xxvii.	1, 13, 14, 1, 14	A. J. Davis. X. Scharwenka.	The Lord is my light.	Ditson. Breitkopf & Haertl.	
7	Ps. xxx.	1, 2, 4, 5 4, 5	A. J. Davis. Charles Gounod.	I will extol Thee. Sing praises to the Lord.	Ditson. Novello.	.
8	Ps. xxxi.	10, 2, 18, 16	W. A. Mozart.	Have mercy, O Lord.	Novello.	
9	Ps. xxxi.	3, Ps. vi. 4	A. Attenhoffer. (Arr. by F.V.d.Stucken) F. H. Himmel.	Incline Thine ear.	The Arranger in Cincinnati. Novello.	
10	Ps. xxxvi.	5-11 5, 6, 10, 7 5, 6 5, 6, 7	*L. Lewandowski E. J. Hopkins. J. Barnby. F. A. Ouseley.	Thy mercy, O Lord.	Breitkopf & Haertl. Novello. "	
11	Ps. xxxvii.	7, 4, 5, 1	F. Mendelssohn.	O rest in the Lord.	Schirmer.	
12	Ps. xl.	1, 4	F. Mendelssohn	I waited for the Lord.	Novello.	
13	Ps. xlii.	1-7	A. J. Davis. Caryl Florio. A. Cortada. Ch. Gounod. *L. Lewandowski. L. Spohr.	As the hart pants.	Ditson. Schirmer. " Breitkopf & Haertl. Novello.	

Figure 7.6. "Index of Anthems" from *Union Hymnal*, first page.

which included additional psalm texts. Presented in a table format, the anthem list included purchase information—nearly all works came from major publishers Novello (London), Schirmer (New York), Ditson (Boston), and Breitkopf & Härtel (Leipzig), with some obtainable directly from Kaiser and other cantors—notable qualities of each work, and suggestions for needed modifications to make them usable in a Jewish setting. The chart noted, for example, when a composition called for an all-female choir, or when an English text could work as well as the existing Hebrew text. In several cases, a note instructed users to replace the "Gloria Patri" doxology that conventionally ended Christian church psalm settings with a repetition of the previous verse. Intended as a professional guide, the list's palette of sonic options for use during an artistic moment in the service showed the editors' interest in producing a book that maintained continuity with the broader musical landscape—both Jewish *and* American.

Despite the robust recent collaboration of the CCAR and the Society of American Cantors, the rabbis fell short of endorsing the *Union Hymnal* upon its publication. Instead, they opted to hold off on their decision until the following year's conference, while leaving it to the cantors—Kaiser specifically—to market and sell it in the meantime.[135] Isaac Mayer Wise's representative response in October 1897 mixed admiration and disappointment: "The rightful heirs of the most ancient and most solemn psalmodic literature might well wear their own uniform in their houses of worship. But this could not be accomplished just now, and we must be satisfied with the elegant hymn book and the appropriate music before us."[136] Revealing an internal controversy among rabbis, Frederick de Sola Mendes, reviewing the hymnal in *The American Hebrew*, praised the musical contributions but criticized the hymns' "slip-shod style of pigeon [sic] English [that] will not suffice this generation of College-bred Americans."[137] The long-in-preparation book, meant to establish the cantor and serve all congregations, landed with an awkward wobble.

In the style of the *Union Prayer Book*, the *Union Hymnal* magnified questions that swirled about the nature and content of synagogue music. About three dozen synagogues and Jewish orphanages adopted the hymnal in its first year of release, ranging from New York, Baltimore, and Philadelphia to Los Angeles and Stockton, California, to St. Louis and Houston, and including many congregations where members of the Society for American Cantors officiated. Publicity for the book highlighted its utility as an aid for congregational singing. In Richmond, Virginia, for example, Beth Ahaba Congregation's Isaac Held saw the hymnal ("compiled by cantors of some of the northern congregations") as an impetus to renew his call for a choral society to empower many of the synagogue's women.[138] New York's West End Synagogue, following Frederick de Sola Mendes's recommendation, introduced the *Union Hymnal* along with a cantor-trained "volunteer choir" that "shall aid, not displace, congregational singing."[139] A report at the July 1898 CCAR meeting noted that 4,663 of the initial 5,000-copy run had sold, at an average price of about thirty-five cents: a discount (from the retail price of fifty cents) suggesting that larger congregations purchased the hymnal in bulk.[140] While the Midwestern cities of Chicago, Milwaukee, and Cincinnati remained notably absent among the list of adopting institutions, the broader dissemination of the book portended some success.

The book's wide visibility also led to some critique. Jewish proponents of musical culture faulted Kaiser and his colleagues for promoting their own music, as the music reviewer of the *Jewish Messenger* noted, over "the infinitely superior music of [prominent composers such as] Mozart, Handel, . . . Schumann," Felix Mendelssohn, and Arthur Sullivan.[141] The same reviewer concluded by complaining that the editors needed only to look to nearby churches to assess musical quality: "The disproportion [of inferior music by Jewish composers] is the more incomprehensible when it was so easy to profit by the experience of our Gentile neighbors in this matter."

Isaac Mayer Wise, however, led a more contentious critique of the hymnal on grounds that it proved too permeable to music and songs from outside the core of Jewish tradition. Characterizing the effort as a desperate move to counter falling service attendance, Wise repeated a broader claim that only the psalms counted as a quintessential Jewish source of liturgical poetry through which Jews could contribute to American religious song.[142] An anonymous editorial in *The American Jewess* echoed this claim shortly afterward, noting of the hymnal: "We have the one hundred and fifty psalms which are our inheritance and the inheritance of Israel. The synagogue does not need to go to foreign and antagonistic sources for either words or music."[143] So stubbornly did Wise resist the hymnal that as president of the CCAR, he derailed the group's vote to adopt the hymnal project officially at the organization's July 1898 meeting.[144] In a dispute that stretched over three separate sessions in the first two days of the conference, Wise stymied his colleagues' initial vote to accept the book despite its faults. Reportedly opposing "anything in the synagogue that is foreign to it" as a pretense, Wise backpedaled from any commitment to the book and, as a consequence, from any institutional connection to the Society of American Cantors. His explanation painted the cantors' decision to adapt musical selections from the wider culture as counter to reform's progressive spirit:

> It was decided to have new Chazonuth [i.e., cantorial prayer chants] for our new Prayer Book. This work the Cantors did [in their 1894 *Anthems, Hymns, and Responses*. . .], and they did it well. Then the question of the Hymnal was broached. It simply provided that if at any time the Conference wished to adopt one, they could do so. But I was opposed to it as it was foreign to the synagogal spirit. We must not assume authorship of it. When we reform, it is not towards Christianity, but towards the age before us, and not towards the age behind us.[145]

In order to avoid any impression of disunity, the CCAR backtracked along with Wise and "decided that the publication of the Union Hymnal be determined upon by the Cantors' Association [i.e., the SAC]." Although the two organizations succeeded in appointing a six-member joint hymnal committee during the meeting to explore revisions, the book itself became a symbol of its conflicted origins: a product of the CCAR's members, but held at arm's length from the CCAR, and a document meant to bring rabbis and cantors together that ultimately reinforced their inequality.[146] While Kaiser tried to triage afterward, publicly describing the hymnal's progress, he went at it alone.[147]

In successive years, a hymnal committee comprising cantors Kaiser, Sparger, and Löwenberg continued to report positive sales and synagogue adoption rates. The CCAR, recognizing its expanded usage, approved an additional printing of two thousand copies in 1898 (accomplished in May 1899). From sixty-nine congregations using about 5,500 copies of the hymnal in 1898, according to Kaiser's testimony, usage increased to about a hundred congregations in 1900, leading the CCAR to authorize another two thousand copy print run.[148] By mid-1900, with more than 6,400 copies sold (compared with the *Union Prayer Book*'s nearly 42,500 copies), Kaiser touted the hymnal as a liturgical achievement and impending financial success.[149]

Kaiser's larger motive to unite cantors and rabbis together in common cause, however, lagged. The CCAR, which by 1900 still had not endorsed the hymnal, dogged Kaiser and his cohort with requests for a revised edition. Finally, at the 1901 CCAR conference—a year after Wise's death—Kaiser pushed back, describing the deleterious effects of such scrutiny: "The fact that every successive session of the Conference [since 1897] has discussed a revision of the book has greatly retarded its general introduction. It is the opinion of the [hymnal] Committee that, since the book has given satisfaction wherever it has been introduced, as well as for business reasons, it should be allowed to remain undisturbed at least a decade. A revised edition would not only entail a considerable outlay to the Conference but would also make the more than seven thousand copies that have so far been sold useless."[150] Even as he sought to assert the hymnal's significance on a par with the *Union Prayer Book*, Kaiser accepted suggestions for a future revision. At once seeking a common synagogue repertoire and a future for cantors as mediators of that repertoire, Kaiser sought to sell rabbis on the same level of flexibility they had afforded their own prayer book. Yet other factors pointed to his vulnerability. While Kaiser himself had become an honorary member of the CCAR by this point, only Löwenberg and Sparger, the other two cantor-members of the hymnal committee, retained their membership in the organization: and both were recognized as rabbis as well. Successive years continued to show hymnal sales of about a thousand copies per year, yielding a small profit. Kaiser highlighted these numbers as "good proof of the growing popularity of the Hymnal, which has already aided materially in the uniformity of the song service of the American synagogue."¹⁵¹ Despite conference president Joseph Silverstein's credit to both the prayer book and hymnal for "destroy[ing] the evils of rampant individualism by creating a uniform service," however, Kaiser publicly described "still a considerable number of congregations which have not yet given the book a trial."¹⁵² And the publication of complete services for the *Union Prayer Book* in these years by longtime choir directors/organists Sigmund Schlesinger of Mobile, Frederick Emil Kitziger of New Orleans, and Max Spicker of New York's Temple Emanu-El (with Sparger) merely underlined Kaiser's dilemma.¹⁵³ Ultimately, the CCAR's nonendorsement meant that the hymnal would remain a book apart, and the cantor a secondary figure in the congregation, whose musical efforts mainly benefited synagogues' other musical personnel.

The start of the twentieth century also saw music's expanding scholarly position in Jewish history and culture. William Löwenberg used the pages of *Die Deborah* to weigh in on a European debate over the survival of biblical-era Israelite music (Löwenberg, opposing Munich cantor Emanuel Kirchner's claims, sided with Emil Breslaur in viewing such survival claims as romanticized). Löwenberg also engaged with Philadelphia rabbi Henry Illowizi by insisting that the cantor's historic legacy made him compatible with congregational singing and the Reform movement more generally.¹⁵⁴ On a broader level, music factored meaningfully into the newly emerging *Jewish Encyclopedia*, a comprehensive American-led, multivolume state of the field, published between 1901 and 1906. Francis L. Cohen served as the work's chief liturgist, penning (or co-penning) ninety articles that covered parts of the religious ritual, devotional poetry, and significant musicians and musical personnel (including an article on his father-in-law Marcus Hast and another on the *sagerin*, or female precentor). Cohen's most significant entry, "Music, Synagogal," largely summarized his scholarship to date and became the latest word on the topic. Kaiser, comparatively identified as the primary American Jewish musical authority, wrote or contributed to substantive entries on Sulzer, Welsch, Josef Singer, Josef Goldstein, and Abraham Baer, among others, while expanding Cyrus Adler's article on the "Hazzan" with a sunny subentry on "Modern Times." These comparative contributions highlighted the Anglophone domination of the Jewish music world at this moment—Pinchas Minkowsky's Odessa-based, Yiddish-language scholarship had not yet received much attention in liberal intellectual circles—while acknowledging the United States as heir to one central stream of musical scholarship and practice.

In 1903, apparently seeking to strengthen their status, the Society of American Cantors "reorganized" and merged with their standout colleagues from the former Cantors' Association of America. Kaiser and Löwenberg retained leadership, while welcoming back New York cantors Edward Kartschmaroff (B'nai Jeshurun), Herman Goldstein (Shaar HaShomayim), Theodore Guinsburg (Ahawath Chesed), and David Cahn (Rodeph Sholom).[155] (Sparger, battling what may have been severe mental illness, attempted suicide twice in 1903, and then mysteriously disappeared.)[156] Kaiser's politic description of the group in the *Jewish Encyclopedia* highlighted its expanded, though not comprehensive, breadth, noting, "while its membership is open to all, it is in fact an association of cantors of both Conservative and Reform congregations."[157]

Shifting their focus to the Hebrew portion of the service, likely as a place of greatest agreement, the group convinced the CCAR to join them in honoring the centennial of Salomon Sulzer in March 1904, and publishing for the occasion a newly arranged booklet of Sulzer's music for American liberal synagogues' preferred organ/cantor/choir format.[158] Isaac S. Moses, now rabbi of New York congregation Ahawath Chesed and recently installed president of the CCAR, headlined the celebration and joined the Society's call to establish a school for cantors who could, as "religious functionar[ies]" alongside the rabbi, "rekindle the slumbering spark of devotion in the soul of the modern Jew."[159] That June at the CCAR conference, Kaiser reinforced the argument, highlighting "the desirability of more uniformity also in the music to the Hebrew responses." He continued, giving his argument a historical dimension: "The Conference should urge a more general use and adoption of the same [responses] among all congregations. This would enable an Israelite happening to visit any temple other than his own to join in the singing of [the prayers] Sh'ma, boruch adonoy, mi chomocho, kodosh, etc. In former times this was the case, and there is no reason why it should not so be now. Every denomination has some permanent tunes which link its devotees closer together. This suggestion is made at the request of the Society of American Cantors and is heartily concurred in by your Committee."[160]

Cantors' roles were changing again. At the CCAR's 1906 convention in Indianapolis, its members officially embarked on a revision of the *Union Hymnal*: rather than Kaiser at the helm, however, a committee comprised entirely of rabbis began the labor. Former hymnal committee chair Joseph

Stoltz, now serving as CCAR president, also formed a new, standing "Committee on Synagog Music," "with power to publish periodically, in bound form for a moderate price, dignified traditional settings of interpretations in the Jewish spirit, not only of our ritual responses but, especially, of our anthems intended for special occasions, holidays and the opening and closing of the weekly Sabbath services."[161] Kaiser and Löwenberg joined several rabbis on the new committee. Now late in years, they likely appreciated the new latitude to go beyond the bounds of congregational singing; however, as the only cantorial members of the conference, their influence had faded. Cantors continued to support themselves in autonomous organizations that struggled to serve a sense of "common good" in a changing Jewish population. Concerned more with the welfare of their profession, particularly in light of shifting populations and aesthetics, they began to promote music's perception as a "universal language," with a consequent specialized theory and vocabulary, as a central strategy for gaining status. The development of the international recording and concertizing industries, moreover, gave cantors the option of becoming artists in their own right, trading on music as a mode of direct public appeal. As new Jewish singers began to pour in from the East, American cantorial styles thus began to conform more to Josef Singer's "*Steiger*" model, valuing improvisation over set melodies as a marker of sophistication and authenticity. These developments helped a new population of self-defined cantors to distance themselves from the integrated practice of "synagogue, home, and school." Instead, standing at the threshold of a romantic "golden age," they found another calling for themselves as musical specialists who represented the rising voices of the Jewish spirit, amplified through phonographs that brought the synagogue into the parlor and the concert hall.

Notes

1. *The American Israelite*, November 10, 1892, 4.
2. Josef Singer, *Die Tonarten des Traditionellen Synagogengesanges (Steiger): ihr Verhältnis zu den Kirchentonarten und den Tonarten der Vorchristlichen Musikperiode* (Vienna: Em. Wetzler, 1886). See also Judah M. Cohen, "Modes of Tradition? Negotiating Jewishness and Modernity in the Synagogue Music of Isadore Freed and Frederick Piket," *Jewish Culture and History* 5, no. 2 (2002), 25–47.
3. The *OUCZ* gave *Die Tonarten* extensive coverage, including Singer's own discussion of his work, a detailed review, and responses by prominent cantors such as Moritz Deutsch and Eduard Birnbaum. *OUCZ*, April 7, 1886, 1 (Singer's own discussion); April 14, 5–6 (detailed re-

view); May 24 (Deutsch response); July 23, 2–3 (Birnbaum response); August 31, 3–4 (another Birnbaum response).

4. See, for example, the *OUCZ* editor's thanks to "Fr. in Philadelphia" while noting that he already sees more cantors in America taking out subscriptions. *OUCZ* 3, no. 10 (March 18, 1883), 7. The only clear mention of the United States in the journal's first three years was an accolade to "Papa Sulzer" from congregation Reim Ahuvim of Stockton, California (*OUCZ* 2, no. 8 [February 24, 1882], 4). Similarly, a rare reference to New York in the January 16, 1886, issue described a wedding, with no mention of the cantorate (2).

5. *Catalogue of Anglo-Jewish Historical Exhibition, 1887, Royal Albert Hall: And of Supplementary Exhibitions Held at the Public Record Office, British Museum, South Kensington Museum* (London: William Clowes and Sons, 1887), 97–99. The catalog includes a diagram of the exhibition's layout, clarifying the location of the music materials in a corner of the second room.

6. Francis L. Cohen, "The Rise and Development of Synagogue Music," in *Papers Read at the Anglo-Jewish Historical Exposition, Royal Albert Hall, London* (London: Jewish Chronicle, 1888), 80–135. The positive response to Cohen's lecture almost led to a reprise in Princes' Hall (Piccadilly). See "Report to the Members of the General Committee of the Anglo-Jewish Historical Exhibition," in *Papers Read*, 293, 297.

7. Prague had been in the Viennese cantorial circle of influence for decades; Ukraine's connections with Vienna appeared to begin formally around 1882, when Cherson cantor and developing musicologist Pinchas Minkowsky studied in Vienna for a year. Minkowsky sent a letter to the *OUCZ* in 1883 describing his experience in exuberant terms and promising to bring the message of the Vienna cantorial organization to Russian cantors as well. P[inhas] Minkowsky, letter to the editor, *OUCZ*, March 2, 1883, 5.

8. The number of congregations comes from Union of American Hebrew Congregations, "Statistics of the Jews of the United States" (Philadelphia: Edward Stern, 1880), preface, 57.

9. "Gemeinde-Gesang" in German. See, for example, B. Jacobsohn, *Der Israelitische Gemeinde-Gesang: fünf populäre Aufsätze als Beiträge zur Cultusfrage herausgaben von B. Jacobsohn, Cantor und Lehrer in Leipzig* (Leipzig, 1884). Jacobsohn followed a similar more-is-more philosophy when approaching congregational singing, particularly in his praise of Berlin choral director and composer Louis Lewandowski's elaborate work.

10. "Orthodoxy," *The American Hebrew*, October 1, 1880, 76.

11. "Congregational Singing," *The American Hebrew*, January 28, 1881, 122.

12. *The American Hebrew*, January 21, 1881, 109; August 18, 1882, 4; April 6, 1883, 85; "A Revival in Church Music," January 18, 1884, 124 (citing the *Christian Union*).

13. *The American Hebrew*, August 24, 1883, 13.

14. Ibid.

15. "Our City Synagogues," *Jewish Messenger*, February 1, 1884, 4; "Local News," August 29, 1884, 2.

16. *The American Hebrew*, February 8, 1884, 158.

17. "Nineteenth Street Synagogue," *The American Hebrew*, November 26, 1886, 40; "Cong. Shearith Israel," *Jewish Messenger*, November 26, 1886, 2; "Cong. Shearith Israel," *Jewish Messenger*, December 31, 1886, 2.

18. "Worshipers—Not Spectators," *The American Hebrew*, April 15, 1887, 146; "Congregational Singing," *The American Hebrew*, April 15, 1887, 155.

19. *The American Hebrew*, March 11, 1887, 66.

20. "Kol Zimra," *The American Israelite*, July 10, 1885, 2; *The American Hebrew*, July 17, 1885, 154.

21. "Temple Music," *The American Israelite*, August 21, 1885, 3.

22. Frederick de Sola Mendes (comp.), *Synagogue and School: Hymns, Songs, and Religious Memoranda for Jewish Congregations* (New York: Frederick de Sola Mendes, 1887).

23. Gustav Gottheil, ed., *Hymns and Anthems Adapted for Jewish Worship* (New York: G. P. Putnam's Sons, 1887). A. J. Davis produced a separate volume of music as *Music to Hymns and Anthems Adapted for Jewish Worship by G. Gottheil* (New York: Kakeles, 1887).

24. "From Rev. Dr. Gottheil's Hymn Book," *Jewish Messenger*, February 25, 1887, 9.

25. "Literary," *The American Hebrew*, February 4, 1887, 194. See also mention of Gottheil's book in the *Christian Intelligencer*, as noted in "The Jewish Revival," *The American Hebrew*, February 25, 1887, 37.

26. *The American Hebrew*, March 25, 1887, 97.

27. *The American Hebrew*, April 19, 1889, 170 ([St. Louis]); "Baltimore, MD," *The American Israelite*, August 8, 1889, 2; "Albany, NY," *The American Israelite*, December 19, 1889, 5 (instituting a congregational class).

28. *Jewish Messenger*, October 11, 1889, 4 (on misbehavior in the choir loft).

29. L., "Our Philadelphia Letter," *The American Hebrew*, June 3, 1887, 57; reproduced with further comment the following week as "Music in the Synagogue," *The American Hebrew*, June 10, 1887, 66.

30. *Jewish Exponent*, September 5, 1888, 4.

31. Philadelphia's Keneseth Israel, for example, began its efforts to start a choral society in 1889–90 (with varied success), with the term remaining in use in congregational minutes through at least 1897 (Keneseth Israel Records, MS-551, Box 4; American Jewish Archives, Cincinnati, OH).

32. *Jewish Exponent*, May 10, 1889, 4 (expressing concerns over untrained voices in Orthodox synagogues).

33. "New York," *The American Israelite*, March 22, 1894, 3.

34. Francis L. Cohen, "Synagogue Music, Its History and Character," *Jewish Chronicle*, August 17, 1883, 12. Reprinted in *The Musical World*, August 18 and 25, 1883, 516, 524 (see also *Jewish Chronicle*, February 22, 1884, 12); also translated in *OUCZ* (October 26, 1883, 3–4; November 11, 3–4; November 19, 4–5; November 27, 2–3; December 13, 3–4) as "Geschichte und Charakter der Synagogen-Musik."

35. Emil Naumann, *The History of Music*, trans. F. Praeger, special ed. (New York: Cassell, 1886), vol. 4, 994–96.

36. Cohen, "The Rise and Development of Synagogue Music," 81.

37. Ibid., 130.

38. F. L. Cohen, "A Synagogue Service," *Magazine of Music* 5, no. 10 and 11 (October and November 1888), 234–40, 255–57; Francis L. Cohen, "Ancient Musical Traditions of the Synagogue," *Proceedings of the Musical Association* 19 (1892/3): 135–58; Francis L. Cohen, ed., *Shire Knesset Yisrael: A Handbook of Synagogue Music for Congregational Singing* (London: Spottiswode, 1889).

39. Francis L. Cohen and David M. Davis (eds.), *Kol Rina Ve'Todah: The Voice of Prayer and Praise* (London: Greenberg, 1899). The second edition of the book, notably, was issued by congregational singing advocate John Curwen in 1914.

40. One significant exception is Benjamin Franklin Peixotto, "Salomon Sulzer: Remembrances from Vienna," *Menorah Journal* 8 (1890): 261.

41. H. E. Krehbiel, "The Jew in Music," *The American Hebrew*, May 22, 1891, 46ff. All quotations in this paragraph reference this article.
42. Wilhelm Sparger, "Etwas über die Kompositionswerth," *Der jüdische Kantor* 4, no. 23 (June 23, 1882), 181–82.
43. Howard M. Stahl, "William Sparger: Enigmatic Pioneer of the American Reform Cantorate," *American Jewish Archives Journal* 63, no. 1 (2011), 23–25.
44. William Sparger, "Sing unto Us the Songs of Zion," *The American Hebrew*, August 26, 1892, 534–39. All quotations in the following paragraph reference this source.
45. "Jewish Music" and "Jewish Singing," *The American Hebrew*, August 26, 1892, 532. See also Edward C. Calisch, "Communications: Then Sang Moses and the Children of Israel This Song," *The American Hebrew*, September 2, 1892, 571.
46. Cyrus Adler, "Important Literature on Jewish Music," *The American Hebrew*, September 4, 1892, 571.
47. William Sparger, "Sing unto Us the Songs of Zion," *The American Israelite*, September 15, 1892, 5.
48. "The Cantors' Association of America," *Jewish Messenger*, November 20, 1891, 3.
49. "The Cantors' Association," *Jewish Messenger*, August 5, 1892, 4; August 19, 1892, 2.
50. A Cantor, "More New Hymn Books," *The American Hebrew*, April 20, 1894, 765–68.
51. "Rabbis in Council," *Jewish Messenger*, July 15, 1892, 5.
52. "Jüdisches Leben in Amerika," *OUCZ* 12, no. 32 (November 21, 1892), 1.
53. Alois Kaiser, "The Sphere of the Cantor's Activity," *The American Israelite*, November 10, 1892, 4. All subsequent quotations from Kaiser's speech refer to this article.
54. Ibid.
55. The Frankfurt-born Löwenberg, son of Rabbi Ferdinand Löwenberg, came to the United States at age seventeen in 1872, and matriculated into Hebrew Union College as an indigent student in 1878 (Ancestry.com).
56. William Löwenberg, "A Jewish Hymnal," *Jewish Messenger*, November 4, 1892, 5.
57. Ibid.
58. W[illiam] S[parger], "Ancient Jewish Melodies," *Jewish Messenger*, November 11, 1892, 6; reprinted in *The American Hebrew*, November 18, 1892, 74.
59. William Sparger, "Literature on the Music of the Jews: An Attempt at a Bibliography," *The American Hebrew*, December 9, 1892, 197–99; December 16, 229; December 23, 265–66.
60. Sparger incorrectly dated Sulzer's first volume of *Schir Zion* to 1845.
61. Sparger included work by Kaiser, A. J. Davis, Simon Hecht, and Max Braun, as well as *Zimrath Yah*.
62. Alois Kaiser, "The New Hymnal, and Our Jewish Traditional Melodies," *Jewish Exponent*, January 5, 1893, 5.
63. Ibid.
64. Ibid.
65. Ibid.
66. Emma Frank, "Presentation of the Hymn Book," *Papers of the Jewish Women's Congress, Held at Chicago, September 4, 5, 6 and 7, 1893* (Philadelphia: Jewish Publication Society of America, 1894), 168–69.
67. "A Memorial Hymn-Book," *Jewish Exponent*, March 17, 1893, 7. See also Faith Rogow, *Gone to Another Meeting: The National Council of Jewish Women 1893–1993* (Tuscaloosa: University of Alabama Press, 1998), 13.

68. Fannie Fitzgerald, "Congress of Religions," *Atchison Daily Globe* (Kansas), June 7, 1893.

69. Alois Kaiser and William Sparger, *A Collection of the Principal Melodies of the Synagogue from the Earliest Times to the Present* (Chicago: T. Rubovits, 1893), xvi. Original in italics.

70. Ibid., ix.

71. Ibid., vii, xvii.

72. Kaiser and Sparger arranged these works in three frequently used formats—keyboard alone, keyboard and single voice (cantor/solo), and four-voice choral (probably with keyboard *colla parte*)—thus providing for versatile approaches to their use.

73. Barbara Kirshenblatt-Gimblett, "Exhibiting Jews," in *Destination Culture: Tourism, Museums, and Heritage* (Berkeley: University of California Press, 1998), 88–105.

74. Cyrus Adler, preface to *Principal Melodies*, v.

75. Ibid., v–vi.

76. *Judaism at the World's Parliament of Religions* (Cincinnati, OH: Robert Clarke, 1894).

77. Frank, "Presentation of the Hymn Book."

78. A Cantor, "More New Hymn Books."

79. *Yearbook of the Central Conference of American Rabbis*, 1893, 43.

80. A Cantor, "More New Hymn Books," 765.

81. Ibid., 767.

82. Louis Grossman and F. L. York (eds.), *Zemirot Yisrael: Responses, Psalms and Hymns for Worship in Jewish Congregations and Schools* (Detroit, MI: John F. Eby, 1894); Isaac S. Moses, *The Sabbath School Hymnal: A Collection of Songs, Services, and Responses for Jewish Sabbath Schools and Homes* (Chicago: I. S. Moses, 1894).

83. A Cantor, "More New Hymn Books," 767; "Detroit: Social," *The American Israelite*, May 10, 1894, 5.

84. A Cantor, "More New Hymn Books," 767.

85. Ibid.

86. Notably, the CCAR did not agree on the text for the Sabbath prayer book (officially volume 1) until the following year.

87. "Central Conference of American Rabbis," *The American Hebrew*, July 20, 1894, 362–63.

88. Ibid., 363.

89. Ibid.

90. *Year Book of the Central Conference of American Rabbis* 6 (1895), 32–33. The cantors received the text in mid-August and, according to Kaiser, needed to have the work "in the hands of the choirs by the 15th of September, at the latest, to enable them to rehearse the same."

91. Alois Kaiser et al., "Introductory Note," in *Anthems, Hymns, and Responses for the Union Prayer Book* (New York, 1894).

92. Ahawath Chesed organist Gideon Froelich contributed one piece as well.

93. The editors even suggested two selections from Isaac S. Moses's *Sabbath School Hymnal* as alternatives to two English Yom Kippur hymns, such as an arrangement of the *Kol Nidre* replacement "O Day of God."

94. *Year Book of the Central Conference of American Rabbis* 6 (1895), 33.

95. Ibid.

96. Josef Singer, "Synagogengesang," *Die Deborah*, February 28, 1895, 6–7. Reprinted without attribution in Aron Friedman, ed., *Dem Andenken Eduard Birnbaums* (Berlin: C. Boas, 1922), 54–61.

97. *Die Deborah*, February 28, 1895, 5; William Sparger, "'Shir Zion,' Festival March by F. Van Der Stucken. An Analysis by the Rev. Wm. Sparger," *The American Hebrew*, April 12, 1895, 672. Van der Stucken wrote "Shir Zion" for the fiftieth anniversary of Sparger's congregation, Temple Emanu-El.

98. Around this time, *Die Deborah* articles made references to a Yiddish newspaper as a "*Jargonblatt*."

99. "Congregational Singing," *The American Hebrew*, March 22, 1895, 581.

100. "The City: West End Synagogue," *The American Hebrew*, January 11, 1895, 302; "Sabbath School Hymnal," *The American Israelite*, November 22, 1894, 6.

101. Other members of the group included senior cantor Edward Kartschmaroff (B'nai Jeshurun), Charles L. Seiniger (Shaaray Tefillah), Gabriel Hirsh (Shaareh Berochoh), Herman Silverman (Beth El), and Bernhard Hast (Adath Israel).

102. *Musical Courier* 30, no. 20 (May 8, 1895), 15.

103. Ibid.

104. "Society of American Cantors," *The American Hebrew*, May 24, 1895, 73.

105. Ibid.

106. Ibid.

107. *Year Book of the Central Conference of American Rabbis* 6 (1895), 22–24.

108. Ibid., 31.

109. Ibid.

110. "The Musical Service of Emanu-El," *The American Hebrew*, April 12, 1895, 684D. This article implied that the musical practice at Emanu-El would serve as a musical incubator for the forthcoming national hymnal.

111. Ibid.

112. Ibid.

113. *Year Book of the Central Conference of American Rabbis* 6 (1895), 31, 33.

114. Ibid. The CCAR also nixed a motion to share proceeds of the book with the Society for American Cantors.

115. "A New Year Begins," *Baltimore Sun*, September 19, 1895, 8; "'Sabbath of Sabbaths,'" *Baltimore Sun*, September 28, 1895, 10. The service was used again the following year. By convention, the presentation of single-author services also included contributions by other composers outside of the central prayer settings, including a "Mah Tovu" by Samuel Naumbourg, S. Jadassohn's "Motette," hymns, and a sacred duet by Ambrose Thomas.

116. *Jewish Criterion* (Pittsburgh) 3, no. 19 (June 12, 1896), 8.

117. "Coronation of the Czar," *Baltimore Sun*, February 3, 1896, 10; "Rev. Alois Kaiser," *Baltimore Sun*, July 7, 1896, 8. Kaiser sent the work off in April, and its performance on May 26 was "greatly praised for its exalted feeling and melody."

118. "Rabbis at a Banquet," *Milwaukee Sentinel*, July 10, 1896, 4. Chicago rabbi Emil Hirsch, perhaps in jest, noted that he "did not know why some songs would have to be sung with the nasal twang, and said that the Jew had been functionally provided against such a thing by plenty of nasal room for air."

119. *CCAR Year Book*, 1896, 14–15; "Rabbis at a Banquet."

120. "Club of Jewish Women," *Milwaukee Journal*, October 15, 1895, 5.

121. "To Reduce the Choir," *Baltimore Sun*, October 22, 1896, 10.
122. Cited in Frederick de Sola Mendes, "As to Congregational Singing," *The American Hebrew*, January 15, 1897, 306.
123. *The American Hebrew*, January 2, 1897, 355.
124. Ibid.
125. William Sparger, "The Cantor Exposed and Congregational Singing Assured," *The American Hebrew*, February 12, 1897, 413–14.
126. *The American Hebrew*, February 19, 1897, 436, 439.
127. "The Forthcoming Union Hymnal," *The American Israelite*, May 27, 1897, 2.
128. "New Hymnal for Synagogues," *Baltimore Sun*, May 22, 1897, 10.
129. "Literary: Judaica," *The American Hebrew*, August 13, 1897, 439.
130. See also "Union Hymnal for Jewish Worship," *The American Israelite*, August 26, 1897, 5.
131. S[olomon]. R[appaport], "It Is and It Is Not," *The American Hebrew*, November 12, 1897, 39.
132. "Addition to Jewish Liturgy," *Jewish Exponent*, August 20, 1897, 4.
133. Ethan Goldberg, "In the Shadow of Sulzer: The Mixed Legacy of Cantor Alois Kaiser," BA thesis, Brandeis University (2012), 57–72. Remarkably, this thesis comprises the most significant analysis of Kaiser's work to date.
134. The only text for which Kaiser did not supply his own alternative was the very brief response "Kodosh"; in that case, Kaiser likely chose a Sulzer setting because of its ubiquity. The closing hymn "Ein Keloheinu" ("There Is None Like Our God") had four options: Kaiser, Lewandowski, Japhet (no. 23 from his 1856 *Shire Jeschurun*, arranged for four-part singing), and a "German" tune.
135. "Now Ready!! Union Hymnal for Jewish Worship," *Jewish Exponent*, August 20, 1897, 3. Wise criticized this arrangement ("Union Hymnal for Jewish Worship," *The American Israelite*, August 26, 1897, 5) but suggested instead a third-party seller.
136. [I. M. Wise,] editorial, *The American Israelite*, October 21, 1897, 4.
137. F[rederick]. de S[ola] M[endes], "Literary," *The American Hebrew*, December 3, 1897, 129. See also the response from "Not a Member of the Committee," *The American Hebrew*, December 17, 1897, 219.
138. Isaac Held, "Congregational Singing," *The Jewish South*, November 28, 1897, 11.
139. *The American Hebrew*, February 4, 1898, 423. Philadelphia congregation Beth Israel adopted the hymnal soon afterward (*Jewish Exponent*, March 4, 1898, 8).
140. "Central Conference of American Rabbis, Tenth Annual Conference," *The American Hebrew*, July 8, 1898, 281–82; *Year Book of the Central Conference of American Rabbis* 9 (5659), 34–35. The latter report noted 210 gratis copies and 4,453 copies sold "in quantities from 1 to 850 copies."
141. "Music," *Jewish Messenger*, March 11, 1898, 5.
142. See "A Jewish Hymnal," *Jewish Messenger*, October 21, 1892, 4.
143. *The American Jewess* 7, no. 4 (July/August 1898), 56.
144. "Central Conference of American Rabbis, Tenth Annual Conference," *The American Hebrew*, July 8, 1898, 282.
145. *Year Book of the Central Conference of American Rabbis* 9 (5659), 46; "Central Conference," *Jewish Messenger*, July 15, 1898, 5.
146. *Year Book of the Central Conference of American Rabbis* 9 (5659), 47.
147. Alois Kaiser, "The Union Hymnal," *The American Hebrew*, July 29, 1898, 369.

148. "Central Conference," *Jewish Messenger*, March 17, 1899, 6; *CCAR Year Book*, 1900, 35–38. Kaiser's CCAR reports contain detailed sales records, submitted for approval to an auditor.

149. *CCAR Year Book*, 1900, 28–29, 35–37.

150. *CCAR Year Book*, 1901, 51.

151. *CCAR Year Book*, 1904, 51–53.

152. *CCAR Year Book*, 1903, 20, 36.

153. William, Tuckman, "Sigmund and Jacob Schlesinger and Joseph Bloch: Civil War Composers and Musicians," *American Jewish Historical Quarterly* 53, no. 1 (1963): 70–71; Baron, "Frederick Emil Kitziger," 26, 32 (referring to *How Goodly Are Thy Tents, O Jacob* [Philadelphia: W. H. Kayser, 1897], *Memorial Service [Seelenfeier] for the Day of Atonement* [New Orleans, LA: Kitziger, 1897], and *Shire Yehudah* vol. 4 [New Orleans, LA: Kitziger, 1899]); Max Spicker and William Sparger, *The Synagogal Service* (New York: Schirmer, 1901).

154. "Ueber Tempelmusik," *Die Deborah*, January 4, 1899, 3 (reprinted from Berlin's *Die jüdische Presse*); William Löwenberg, "Alt hebraische Melodien," *Die Deborah*, January 19, 1899, 6; William Löwenberg, response to Henry Illowizi's "Historic Function of the Chasan," *The American Hebrew*, December 29, 1899.

155. American Jewish Year Book, 1904, 275–76.

156. Stahl, "William Sparger," 29–33. My own search on Ancestry.com and various digitized papers affirms Sparger's complete disappearance from public record after 1903.

157. Cyrus Adler and Alois Kaiser, "Society of American Cantors," *Jewish Encyclopedia*.

158. Salomon Sulzer and Society of American Cantors, *Shir Zion: A Friday Evening Service* (New York: Bloch, 1904).

159. Isaac S. Moses, "The Cantor as a Religious Functionary," in *Annual Report of the Society for American Cantors* (New York: n.p., 1904). This celebration was part of an international observance of the Sulzer centennial. See Tina Frühauf, *Salomon Sulzer*, 64–67.

160. *CCAR Year Book*, 1904, 53.

161. *CCAR Year Book*, 1906, 233.

CONCLUSION

Restoring the Soundtrack of Jewish Life in Nineteenth-Century America

IN HIS 1929 FIELD-DEFINING BOOK *JEWISH MUSIC IN Its Historical Development*, US émigré Abraham Z. Idelsohn largely dismissed the previous American century in a few presumptive sentences:

> The Jewish settlement in the United States is comparatively very young—all in all somewhat more than two centuries. During that period the settlers struggled hard to acclimatize themselves and adapt themselves to the new environment. This adjustment caused them to drop a great part of their inherited conceptions and to abandon manners to which they had been accustomed in their old dwelling places. Such a period of struggle immigrants and new settlers usually have to endure in the first few generations, until they root themselves in the soil of their adopted country. Thus, during the period of acclimatization and adjustment there was no possibility for spiritual creation. Yet, following that period of struggle, forecasts of creations of a new Jewish—we may say American Jewish—type are noticeable. It is from this point of view that the achievements in the field of Synagogue song in America have to be considered. And it is, therefore, not a history of achievements that we can offer here, but rather an insight into its first steps.[1]

Most of the key figures who had built the field of Jewish music in the nineteenth century had passed on. Leon Sternberger died in 1897. Gustav S. Ensel and Samuel Welsch died in 1901, in Paducah and Prague, respectively. G. M. Cohen and Louis Naumburg died in 1902. Francis L. Cohen left the field of musicology in 1905, when he earned his rabbinical degree and assumed the pulpit of Sydney, Australia's Great Synagogue. Morris Goldstein died in Cincinnati in 1906, outliving his Viennese brother Josef by seven years. When Jewish newspapers across the United States and Europe marked Alois Kaiser's 1908 death, Idelsohn was in Jerusalem with a portable phonograph machine, about a year into the fieldwork that would establish his career.

Josef Singer died in Vienna in 1912. And Pinchas Minkowsky, whose musical career and writings could have made him Idelsohn's most prominent intellectual foil, died weeks after his 1923 return to the United States to found a Boston-based cantorial school—a loss that likely changed the course of Jewish music scholarship.[2] Idelsohn, who had come to New York just months before Minkowsky, parlayed a short turn at Stephen S. Wise's Society for the Advancement of Judaism into a thriving intellectual career by taking advantage of the musical structures these forebears had established: connecting with Rabbi Jacob Singer, then head of the Central Conference of American Rabbis's Committee on Synagog Music; working closely with A. Irma Cohon, whose musical activities included a textbook written for the National Council of Jewish Women; and assuming a faculty position at Cincinnati's Hebrew Union College, where he trained rabbinical students in music and Hebrew far from centers of cantorial activity in Chicago and the east coast.[3] In essence, Idelsohn fulfilled the connection between rabbis and cantors that Kaiser and his colleagues had long sought, even as he left the pulpit to do so. Yet at the same time, Idelsohn only superficially acknowledged the labors that made his American career possible. He treated his adoptive nation as a fallow field, privileged the primacy of Europe, and following Cyrus Adler introduced the Middle East to Jewish music study as the basis of new ethnic-sounding "traditional melodies."

Whether he acknowledged it or not, Idelsohn correctly surmised that as the social and liturgical music landscape changed, so should the history of Jewish music. German Jewish culture ebbed in the United States after Isaac Mayer Wise's death in 1900. Where Cincinnati and the Midwest had been a central influence in Jewish ideology, New York began to dominate as the Jewish population's center of gravity shifted eastward. Local German Jewish newspapers persisted, but the national German-language paper *Die Deborah* folded in 1902. A heterogeneous range of Central European–focused religious practices had generally consolidated under the Reform movement and its Union of American Hebrew Congregations. New institutions, however, ensured a vibrant and changing marketplace. New York's Jewish Theological Seminary, under the presidency of Solomon Schechter, became a prime competitor, establishing the United Synagogue of America in 1913.[4] And the Orthodox Union (founded at Jewish Theological Seminary in 1897) emerged as the most prominent of a series of organizations devoted to Jewish orthodoxy that cultivated their own array of musical practices—from celebrated Eastern European cantors and choirs to the congregational singing of Young Israel. Most of these new groups viewed America through the eyes of recent arrivals, who treated American soil as a place to give their practices new roots. And so, in the context of a renewed search for musical relevance, the voluminous activity of the previous century faded.

Remnants of the Nineteenth Century

By his death in 1908, Alois Kaiser had become the doyen of his profession and his era. His compositions had characterized the changes in synagogue music since the 1860s, his writings sought to keep up with changing perceptions of music and Judaism, and his work on the *Union Hymnal* attempted to keep his labors relevant as the *Union Prayer Book* superseded regional liturgies. Over the course of his travels and activity, he had amassed a large collection of music. Just as he had sent copies of his work to colleagues in Europe and the United States, so did much of his music library reflect active exchange with his brothers in arms.

In his will, Kaiser left his music collection to his nephew, lawyer Hugo Steiner, who also sang in the Oheb Shalom choir.[5] Steiner held on to his uncle's materials for eleven years before Adolph Oko, director of the Hebrew Union College library, acquired the collection and brought it to Cincinnati.[6] Although Oko, in a contemporary account, noted about 600 items in Kaiser's library, the Hebrew Union College library's December 1919 accession books list only 124 entries.[7] Combined with the acquisition of the much larger Birnbaum Collection at around the same time, the Kaiser/Steiner materials represented a significant moment for Jewish music collection in the United States, in essence defining the field and placing Hebrew Union College at its forefront. "The subject of Jewish music had just begun to come into its own with musicologists and musicians," Oko recalled at the time, "and the material was not easy to gather—it was not represented even in our leading libraries." Still in the twenty-first century, these collections represent the large majority of musical materials available from before 1900.

The two collections, however, had diverging fates. Over the following decades, Birnbaum's much larger, manuscript-heavy European collection became a celebrated source for scholarly Jewish music study, facilitating the hires of both A. Z. Idelsohn and his successor Eric Werner. Kaiser's smaller, more publication-focused collection, in contrast, filtered into the library's general holdings, becoming a cryptic record of America's own contributions to the field. The active musical life that Kaiser had preserved thus became buried in the twentieth-century scholarly landscape.

Listening Again to the Nineteenth Century

Even though rabbis, cantors, scholars, and laypeople experienced music and sound in their everyday lives throughout the American nineteenth century, the era all too often seems mute when viewed through the pages of Jewish history. This book, I hope, turns up the volume at least a little, showing that amid the era's local synagogue discourses, sermonizing, and theological debate, music wove deeply in and around the conversation: serving as a central domain for expressing Jewish identity and practice, and even as an alternative philosophical entry point when ideological languages clashed. Musical leadership proved crucial for the development of American liturgy: rabbis needed to partner with composers to introduce new prayer books, empower a congregation, and connect with civic observances. Music also served as an important means of differentiating American Judaism from European Judaism, both indicating distance from a land of origin and affirming the ideological integrity of the émigré population. Musical personnel, in turn, developed their own rich vocabulary of negotiation that engaged with broad musical practices while seeking to understand the sounds that qualified as Judaism both locally and nationally. The sound of Jewish communal life that aimed to span the synagogue, school, and home, in other words, comprised a culture and understanding of its own. Readers and cantors stood on the musical front lines, directly shaping congregational involvement, and helping Jewish populations choose who, when, and what to sing, both in and out of the sanctuary. While such movements certainly took place in Europe as well, they took a unique contour and history in the United States, where musical figures became important liaisons to national conversations on Jewish liturgy, identity, and education.

Musicians knew, moreover, that music did not adhere to specific theologies as tightly as religious leaders would have wanted. Isaac Mayer Wise hoped music would elevate the community spirit of his *Minhag America* services, and he trumpeted in *The Israelite* every time a synagogue introduced organ and choir to its worship. The musicians who insinuated such changes, however, had their own things to say about music's purpose and function: epitomized by Wise's own struggle to find a clergy partner who could satisfy his mercurial musical philosophy. Instead, musical figures often shifted nimbly to accommodate structures of leadership, in both flagship and small congregations; they developed a range of strategies for bringing their musical abilities into mainstream religious discourse. Comforted by America's claims of church-state separation, religious musical leaders freed themselves from Central European regulations imposed on their training and qualifications and worked to produce a spirit of Jewish peoplehood with a distinctive sound. Sometimes they tried to establish themselves as men of letters, whose musical aptitude represented one facet of a larger skill set; sometimes they cast themselves as artists; and ultimately many campaigned to establish their own clerical class in the cantor. The works they produced during this time reflected music's significance for normalizing, historicizing, and socializing ideas across the ideological spectrum amid a constantly shifting and contested set of parameters for defining the future of American Jewry.

This book also shows that as synagogues developed during this period, two different musical approaches began to emerge. Smaller congregations tended toward unified communal models whose leaders had to handle both rabbinical and musical responsibilities. While these congregations formed choirs and included keyboard-based accompaniment, they relied heavily on the broader community for musical vitality, seeking to create a cohesive and multigenerational repertoire while often sharing musical resources with other churches and musical institutions. Lee Shai Weissbach points out that pragmatism proved to be the norm in this context, and I add that at least when it came to music, that pragmatism included intimate exchange across religious and civic lines.[8] The common association of Jewish "reform" with the local inclusion of choral and instrumental-based practices, in other words, both oversimplifies the wide-ranging religious landscape of the mid-nineteenth century and largely denies agency to orthodoxy's own fluid and modernizing musical creativity.[9]

Larger congregations, in contrast, increasingly sought specialized musical figures who could reflect a striving for high cultural norms, while explicitly connecting musical professionalization with the progressive values of "Reform Judaism." In this capacity, well-moneyed congregations provided fertile ground for the development of a musical figure—the cantor—who sought his own autonomy as a religious and intellectual authority fluent in the emerging field of "Jewish music." With these congregations as a base of operations, America saw a proliferation of sheet music, whose authors' lofty ambitions equaled those of their rabbinical colleagues and aimed to provide a normative model for communal pride and belonging. Smaller congregations received plaudits when they adopted these musical agendas, but more often, they admired these flagships from afar. The flagships, in turn, became the recognized voice, and sound, of American Judaism.

I have attempted to present the sound of mid-nineteenth century American Jewish life in its expansive, if sometimes messy fullness as a series of intersecting narratives and organic conversations. Details mattered. Should a choir have men only, men and boys, men and women, or women only? How many people could create a sufficient choral sound and in what vocal distribution? Should the choir's members come from the congregation or outside, and did religious preference matter when it came to encountering their (sometimes unseen) voices? Should the congregation grant singers benefits, salaries, or debts of gratitude, and how could they maintain hierarchies of ringers and volunteers in order to maintain a consistent or desired sound? Who could lead the choristers and/or train them and when? What music could they use? How did the choir function vis-à-vis the congregation and the reader/cantor/organist/rabbi? How did congregations weigh their choirs' quality versus their value? And how did congregations adjust as styles, populations, educational standards, and musical norms shifted in the new American environment?

Musical accompaniment faced a similar wide range of possibilities: Did a community feel comfortable using a parlor piano, a guitar, a melodeon, or a full-ranged instrument? How did populations acquire instruments, maintain them, and find people to play them? How did they determine when to play instruments, or when *not* to play them? And perhaps most importantly, how did these instruments relate to fluid or even seesawing theological norms? While the best endowed congregations could invest in conspicuous and pricey pipe organs, most congregations employed smaller, portable, relatively inexpensive instruments that came and went as ideas about music changed.

New compositions also abounded during this period. Many authorities sought to uphold the efforts of Sulzer and Naumbourg as paradigms of excellence. Others, however, saw them as unnecessarily elitist and out of touch with American realities, treating music instead as an educational medium for congregants to connect to their civic institutions as both Jews and Americans. Sulzer could inspire, but G. M. Cohen could get the masses to sing.

This era also opens a rich discussion on music and gender. At a time when men occupied nearly all pulpit positions, Jewish and otherwise, the domestic associations of musical training and performance in America as an agent of embourgeoisement ensured women a role in any attempt to improve the standing of worship. Indeed, the long business hours associated with the American work ethic meant that women typically outnumbered men in the pews and, where allowed, the choir. While the case of Julie Rosewald, the San Francisco–based cantor-soprano, has been held up as a notable anomaly, it may well have represented a practice that spread far more widely in the proverbial (and literal) choir loft.[10] Educational innovations, combined with the institution of the confirmation ceremony, showed ample evidence of a shift toward coeducation. Dovetailed with the significant integration of vocal training into educational curricula of the time, women could gain a foothold in musical leadership. In smaller communities, the congregation likely could see them plainly; but even when placed out of view with the rest of the choir, their voices had a clear presence in the liturgy. Synagogue women's groups, moreover, sometimes took responsibility for musical activities as the century came to a close, becoming stewards of practice as the field of Jewish music gained its own sense of history and legacy.

The still-larger question looms about the relationship between Europe and the United States. Indeed, even at the end of the nineteenth century, nearly every musical figure covered in this study migrated to the United States after training in Europe. To many, Europe remained a site of authenticity, or at least aesthetic entrenchment, that could define the idea of "tradition" more effectively in its existing precedents than in the relatively young American nation. Yet while Europe remained a place of ambivalence, America represented a land of opportunity. What America lacked in structure, hierarchy, and musical reverence, it gained in democratization, freedom, and the attractions of capitalism. Musical figures fluidly moved in and out of jobs, sometimes shifting between pulpit officiation and business, synagogue song and art song, rabbinical and cantorial responsibilities. Music publications faced a high but surmountable financial burden, receiving support from communities, individuals, and organizations. And in a number of cases, fame in America led to a European return, as Welsch did to Prague, Minkowsky did to Odessa, and Kaiser did through the wide circulation of his compositions.

This book hardly exhausts the topic. However, I hope it revitalizes the discussion beyond the occasional reference in American Jewish history accounts, and beyond Eurocentric perspectives that all too often see America through the lens of Salomon Sulzer or the Eastern European cantorate. Part of the issue here lies with the aesthetic standards of musicology, which largely established itself on the basis of musical sophistication and "greatness"—standards that Jewish music scholars have had little choice but to adopt since Richard Wagner's 1850 *Das Judenthum in der Musik* put Jews on the defensive.[11] America's related but fundamentally different view of Jewish community, culture, identity, and future found little place in this discourse. Yet rather than assuming that American Jews lived in a state of musical ignorance or naïveté, we can now see how Jewish musical figures in nineteenth-century America set the stage for what scholars tend to recognize as the "golden age" of American cantors to come: whether through scholarship, musical composition, institutionalization, or (perhaps most importantly) education. As subsequent waves of arrivals brought their own backgrounds and fresh eyes to American shores, they also stepped into a preexisting Jewish sonic infrastructure that would shape their musical aesthetics even as those who created it faded out of view.

A detailed trip to the nineteenth century can thus illuminate the way we see music in Jewish life during the first part of the twenty-first century. Jonathan Sarna points out in his 2004 history of American Judaism that like many religious groups, Jews have faced a constant set of "contradictory trends operating in their community, [of] assimilation and revitalization."[12] This study layers musical activity onto Sarna's paradigm, oscillating in this case between movements toward congregational singing and artistic veneration, universalism and particularism, innovation and tradition. And we can still see these concerns in action during our own era. To give but one example, the recent "conflict" between the cantor and the song leader that dominated the second half of the twentieth century here finds a remarkably similar precedent a century earlier—effected, moreover, by many of the same aesthetic values of education and group singing as we see today, alongside concerns about religious continuity and the commitment of young people.[13] Rather than seeing cantors as classic figures and "song leaders" as newcomers, we can now see them as complementary figures who have developed side by side for almost two hundred years, if not more. There still remains, in other words, much for us to learn by seeing ourselves as the product of those who came before.

I hope that this study helps establish more clearly the historical persistence of the musical dialogues and issues at play in America, while offering a stronger, more balanced view of where and how those dialogues took place. Too often, to paraphrase David Lowenthal, we allow the past to become a foreign country, claiming its fundamental difference even as we seek to preserve it as a site of heritage.[14] But by listening carefully, perhaps those echoes we once thought too distant to be heard can now gain proper recognition as the background to which we now harmonize our own voices.

Notes

1. Abraham Z. Idelsohn, "Synagogue Song in the United States of America," *Jewish Music in Its Historical Development* (New York: Henry Holt, 1929), 316.

2. Judah M. Cohen, "Embodying Musical Heritage in a New-Old Profession: American Jewish Cantorial Schools, 1904–1939," *Journal of the Society for American Music* 11, no. 1 (2016), 41-44.

3. Judah M. Cohen, "Rewriting the Grand Narrative of Jewish Music: A. Z. Idelsohn in the United States," *Jewish Quarterly Review* 100, no. 3, 417-53.

4. Michael R. Cohen, *The Birth of Conservative Judaism: Solomon Schechter's Disciples and the Creation of an American Religious Movement* (New York: Columbia University Press, 2012).

5. "Will of Alois Kaiser," *Baltimore Sun*, January 10, 1908, 8.

6. Adolph Oko, "Jewish Book Collections in the United States," *American Jewish Year Book* 45 (1919), 78.

7. Hebrew Union College accession books, December 1919, no. 28201-28325. Klau Library, Hebrew Union College, Cincinnati, OH. I am grateful to Noni Rudavsky for locating these records. It is possible that Oko's initial assessment of the collection included individual issues of cantorial journals, which the Accession Records grouped by year.

8. Lee Shai Weissbach, *Jewish Life in Small-Town America: A History* (New Haven: Yale University Press, 2005).

9. The study of American Jewish orthodoxy itself has been marginalized until only recently. See, among others, Jeffrey Gurock, *Orthodox Jews in America* (Bloomington: Indiana University Press, 2009), and Zev Eleff, *Modern Orthodox Judaism: A Documentary History* (Omaha: University of Nebraska Press, 2016).

10. Judith S. Pinnolis, "'Cantor Soprano' Julie Rosewald: The Musical Career of a Jewish American 'New Woman,'" *American Jewish Archives* 62, no. 2 (2010), 1–53.

11. See James Loeffler, "Richard Wagner's 'Jewish Music': Antisemitism and Aesthetics in Modern Jewish Culture," *Jewish Social Studies* 15, no. 2 (Winter 2009), 2–36; Ruth HaCohen, *The Music Libel against the Jews* (New Haven, CT: Yale University Press, 2011).

12. Jonathan Sarna, *American Judaism: A History* (New Haven, CT: Yale University Press, 2004), 374.

13. Cohen, *The Making of a Reform Jewish Cantor*, 218–21.

14. David Lowenthal, *The Past Is a Foreign Country—Revisited* (New York: Cambridge University Press, 2015), 3–4.

WORKS CITED

Online Sources

Alemannia Judaica (http://www.alemannia-judaica.de)
Ancestry.com
Gerschwind-Bennett Isaac Lesser Digital Repository of the Jesselson-Kaplan American Genizah Project, University of Pennsylvania Libraries, Philadelphia, Pennsylvania (http://leeser.library.upenn.edu/ilproject.php)
Hohenems Genealogy, Jewish Museum of Hohenems (http://hohenemsgenealogie.at)
Hymnary.org
Isaac Mayer Wise Digital Archive, American Jewish Archives (http://americanjewisharchives.org/collections/wise)
Jewish Encyclopedia (1901–1906) Online (http://jewishencyclopedia.com)
Milken Archive of Jewish Music (http://www.milkenarchive.com)
Music in Gotham (http://musicingotham.org)
New York City Chapter of the American Guild of Organists (www.nycago.org)
Prague Concert Life, 1850–81: An Annotated Database, School of Music, Cardiff University (http://prague.cardiff.ac.uk/about.jsp)

Archival Sources

Abraham Lincoln Presidential Library, Springfield, Illinois

Sangamon Valley Collection

American Jewish Archives, Cincinnati, Ohio

MS-62: Congregation Bene Yeshurun (Cincinnati, Ohio) Records. 1841–1968 (bulk 1900–60)
MS-517: Congregation Rodeph Shalom (Philadelphia, Pennsylvania) Records. 1802–1966
MS-522: Temple Oheb Shalom (Baltimore, Maryland) Records
MS-551: Reform Congregation Keneseth Israel (Elkins Park, Pennsylvania) Records. 1847–1952
SC-2235: *Musical Relaxations for the Family Circle, for the School and Public Service/ Selected, Arranged and Composed by G. M. Cohen*
SC-10634: United Hebrew Congregation, Minutes, 1841–59

Central Synagogue Archives, New York City

Ahawath Chesed Minute Books

Works Cited

Early New York Synagogue Archives, http://synagogues.cjh.org

Congregation B'nai Jeshurun, New York City

Board of Trustees Minute Books and Letter Books
B'nai Jeshurun Annual Reports, 1874–80
Congregational Meeting Minutes

Klau Library, Hebrew Union College, Cincinnati, Ohio

Eduard Birnbaum Collection
Hebrew Union College Accession Books

Jewish Museum, Prague, Czech Republic

Sheet Music Collection, no. 311, "Sbírka hudebnin [1835]–1947"

Jewish Museum, Milwaukee, Wisconsin

Synagogues Collection, Congregation Emanu-El B'ne Jeshurun materials

National Archives and Records Administration (NARA), Washington, DC

NARA Series: *Passport Applications, 1795–1905*

Temple Emanu-El, New York City

Minute Books for Temple Emanu-El and Anshe Chesed

Periodicals

Allgemeine illustrierte Zeitung (Stuttgart, 1858–1923)
Allgemeine musikalische Zeitung (Leipzig, 1798–1848, 1866–82)
American Jewish Year Book (Philadelphia, 1899–)
Atchison Daily Globe (Kansas, 1874–)
Baltimore Sun (1837–)
Ben Chananja (Szeged, Hungary, 1844, 1858–67)
Blätter für Theater, Musik, u. Kunst (Vienna, 1855–73)
Bohemia (Prague, 1828–1938)
Boston Almanac and Directory (1836–1904)
Boston Daily Advertiser (1813–1929)
Boston Evening Journal (1833–1917)
Chicago (Daily) Inter-Ocean (1865–1914)
Christian Intelligencer (New York, 1830–1920)
Cleveland Morning Daily Herald (1871–74)
Cleveland Plain Dealer (1842–)
Daily Alta California (San Francisco, 1847–91)

Daily Cleveland Herald (1853–74)
Daily Memphis Avalanche (1866–85)
Der Allgemeine Zeitung des Judenthums (Leipzig, 1837–90; Berlin 1890–1922)
Der Israelit (Mainz, 1860–1906)
Der israelitische Volksfreund (Cincinnati, 1858–59)
Der israelitische Volkslehrer (Frankfurt, 1851–60)
Der Jude (Altona, 1832–33)
Der jüdische Kantor (Bromberg, Germany, 1879–98)
Der Orient (Leipzig, 1840–51)
Der Zeitgeist: Israelitisches Familienblatt (Milwaukee/Chicago/Louisville, 1880–82)
Didaskalia (1823–1930)
Die Deborah (Cincinnati, 1855–1902)
Die Neuzeit (Vienna, 1861–1903)
Dwight's Journal of Music (Boston, 1852–81)
Evansville Daily Journal (Evansville, IN, 1834–1936)
Hebrew Leader (New York, 1858–82)
Illinois State Journal (Springfield, 1831–)
Indiana Jewish Post and Opinion (Indianapolis, 1935–)
Indianapolis News (1869–1999)
Israelitische Annalen (Frankfurt, 1839–41)
Israels Herold (New York, 1849)
Jewish Chronicle (London , 1841–)
Jewish Criterion (Pittsburgh, 1895–1902)
Jewish Exponent (Philadelphia, 1887–)
Jewish Messenger (New York, 1857–1903)
Kunkel's Musical Review (St. Louis)
Liturgische Zeitschrift zur Veredelung des Synagogengesangs mit Berücksichtigung des ganzen Synagogenwesens (Meiningen, 1850–59)
Los Angeles Times (1881–)
Magazine of Music (London, 1884–97)
Memphis Daily Appeal (1847–86)
Memphis Daily Avalanche (1858–66)
Milwaukee Journal (1882–)
Milwaukee Sentinel (1837–)
Monatschrift für Theater und Musik (Vienna, 1855–59)
Musical and Dramatic Standard (Philadelphia, 1884)
Musical Courier (New York, 1880–1962)
Musical Record (Boston, 1878–1900)
Musical Review and Musical World (New York, 1860–64)
Musical Times (London, 1836–)
Neue Zeitschrift der Musik (Leipzig, 1834–)
New York Daily Times (1851–1905)
New York Herald (1835–1924)
New York Times (1851–)
New-Yorker Musik-Zeitung (1865–79)
New-Yorker Staats-Zeitung und Herold (1834–)

Österreiches-Ungarisches Cantoren-Zeitung (Vienna, 1880–1901)
Paducah Sun (Kentucky 1896–)
Philadelphia (Daily) Evening Bulletin (1847–1982)
Prager Abendblatt (Prague, 1867–1982)
Prager Morgenpost (Prague, 1858–1860s)
Prager Tagblatt (Prague, 1876–1939)
Public Ledger (Memphis, 1865–93)
Sacramento Daily Union (1851–1994)
St. Louis Globe-Democrat (1852–1986)
Schwäbische Kronik (Stuttgart, 1785–1941)
Sinai (Baltimore, 1856–62)
Sunday Times (London, 1821–)
Taglicher Evansville Demokrat (Evansville, IN, 1864–1918)
The American Hebrew (New York, 1879–)
The American Israelite (Cincinnati, 1874–)
The American Jewess (New York, 1895–99)
The Asmonean (New York, 1849–58)
The Catholic World (New York, 1865–1996)
The Era (London, 1838–1939)
The Étude (Lynchburg, Philadelphia, 1883–1901)
The Israelite (Cincinnati, 1854–74)
The Jewish South (Richmond, VA, 1893–99)
The Occident and American Jewish Advocate (Philadelphia, 1841–69)
The Standard (London, 1827–)
The Voice (Albany, 1879–88)
Werner's Magazine (Chicago, 1889–)
Wochentlicher Evansville Demokrat (Evansville, IN, 1864–1916)
Yearbook of the Central Conference of American Rabbis (1889–)

Music Publications

Aguilar, Emanuel Abraham, and D. A. de Sola. *The Ancient Melodies of the Liturgy of the Spanish and Portuguese Jews*. London: Wessel, 1857.
Binder, A. W. *The Jewish Year in Song: A Collection of Songs, Hymns, Prayers and Folk-Melodies in English, Hebrew and Yiddish for Synagogue, School, and Home*. New York: Schirmer, 1928.
Büdinger, Moses. *Kol Zimra: oder, Gesänge zur Erweckung der Andacht und der religiösen Gefühls bei der israelitischen Jugend, mit drei- und vierstimmig Gesetzten Melodieen*. Cassel: n.p., 1832.
Central Conference of American Rabbis. *Union Prayer Book*. Chicago: Central Conference of American Rabbis, 1892.
———. *Union Prayer Book*, rev. ed. Cincinnati: Central Conference of American Rabbis, 1894–5.
———. *Union Hymnal*, 3rd ed., rev. and enl. New York: Central Conference of American Rabbis, 1932.

Cintura, J., and S. Hecht. "Wo ist meine Heimath?/Where Is My Home?" (English trans. by May Cintura). Evansville, IN, 1892.
Cohen, Francis L., ed. *Shire Knesset Yisrael: A Handbook of Synagogue Music for Congregational Singing.* London: Spottiswode, 1889.
Cohen, Francis L., and David M. Davis, eds. *Kol Rina Ve'Todah: The Voice of Prayer and Praise.* London: Greenberg, 1899.
Cohen, G. M. *Musical Relaxations for the Family Circle, For the School and Public Service/ Selected, Arranged and Composed by G. M. Cohen.* American Jewish Archives, SC-2235.
———. *The Orpheus.* Cleveland, OH: G. M. Cohen, [1878].
———. *The Sacred Harp of Judah.* Cleveland, OH: S. Brainard, 1864.
Congregation Beth Elohim. *Hymns for the Use of Hebrew Congregations*, 4th ed., rev. and enl. Charleston, SC: Edward Perry, 1875.
Davis, A. J. *Music to the Hymns and Anthems for Jewish Worship by G. Gottheil.* New York: Kakeles, 1887.
De Sola Mendes, Frederick, comp. *Synagogue and School: Hymns, Songs, and Religious Memoranda for Jewish Congregations.* New York: Frederick de Sola Mendes, 1887.
Emerson, L. O. *The Harp of Judah; a Collection of Sacred Music for Choirs, Musical Conventions, Singing Schools, and the Home Circle.* Boston: Oliver Ditson, 1863.
Ensel, Gustav S. *Ancient Liturgical Music: A Comparative and Historical Essay on the Origin and Development of Sacred Music from the Earliest Times, with Illustrations of the Music Employed in the Worship of the Synagogue, Church & Mosque.* Paducah, KY: Gustav S. Ensel, 1880.
Ephros, Gershon, ed. *The Cantorial Anthology of Traditional and Modern Music.* 6 vv. New York: Bloch, 1929-69.
Fischer, Wilhelm. *Gesänge für den öffentlichen jüdischen Gottesdienst: aus verschiedenen Liedersammlungen zusammengetragen.* Philadelphia: Stein & Jones, 1862.
———. "Preface." In *Zemirot Yisrael: Auswahl Israelitisch religiöser Lieder in Musik gesetzt von Wilhelm Fischer.* Philadelphia: Schaefer and Koradi, 1865.
———. *Zemirot Yisrael: Auswahl Israelitisch religiöser Lieder in Musik gesetzt von Wilhelm Fischer.* Philadelphia: Schaefer and Koradi, 1863.
Goldstein, Morris, Alois Kaiser, Isaac L. Rice, and Samuel Welsch, eds. *Zimrath Yah.* New York: Morris Goldstein, Alois Kaiser, Isaac L. Rice, and Samuel Welsch, 4 vols., 1871–86.
Gottheil, Gustav, ed. *Hymns and Anthems Adapted for Jewish Worship.* New York: G. P. Putnam's Sons, 1887.
Grossman, Louis, and F. L. York, eds. *Zemirot Yisrael: Responses, Psalms and Hymns for Worship in Jewish Congregations and Schools.* Detroit, MI: John F. Eby, 1894.
Hecht, Simon. *Zemirot Yisrael: Jewish Hymns for Sabbath Schools and Families.* 2nd ed. Cincinnati, OH: Bloch, 1878.
Heinemann, Jeremias. *Deutsches Andachtsbuch für Israeliten zur Erweckung und Belebung religiöser Gefühle. In Gesängen und Gebeten.* Berlin: Bureau für Literatur und Kunst, 1825.
———. *Religiöse Gesänge für Israeliten, insbesondere das weibliche Geschlecht und die Jugend.* Cassel, 1810.
———. *Religiöse Gesänge für Israeliten, insbesondere das weibliche Geschlecht und die Jugend.* Berlin, 1812, 1815, 1817.
———. *Religiöse Gesänge für Israeliten, insbesondere das weibliche Geschlecht und die Jugend,* 4th ed. Berlin: E. H. G. Christiani, 1821.

Hymns Written for the Service of the Hebrew Congregation, Beth Elohim, Charleston, S.C. Charleston, SC: Levin & Tavel, 1842.

Idelsohn, A. Z. *Jewish Song Book for Synagogue, School and Home.* Cincinnati, OH: A. Z. Idelsohn, 1928.

Jacobsohn, B. *Der Israelitische Gemeinde-Gesang: fünf populäre Aufsätze als Beiträge zur Cultusfrage herausgaben von B. Jacobsohn, Cantor und Lehrer in Leipzig.* Leipzig: Baumgärtner, 1884.

Japhet, J. M. *Shire Jeschurun: Gottesdienstliche Gesänge: Eingeführt in die Synagoge der israelitischen Religionsgesellschaft zu Frankfurt am Main.* Frankfurt: J. Kauffmann, 1856.

Johlson, Joseph, ed. *Deutsches Gesangbuch für Israeliten: Zur Beförderung öffentliche und häuslicher Andacht.* Frankfurt, 1816.

———. *Deutsches Gesangbuch für Israeliten: Zur Beförderung öffentliche und häuslicher Andacht*, 2nd ed. Frankfurt: Wilmans, 1819.

———. *Shire Yeshurun: Israelitisches Gesangbuch zur Andacht und zum Religionsunterricht*, 3rd ed. Frankfurt: Andreas, 1829.

———. *Shire Yeshurun: Israelitisches Gesangbuch zur Andacht und zum Religionsunterricht*, 4th ed. Frankfurt: Andreas, 1840.

Kaiser, Alois. *Psalm I, Verses 1, 2, and 3.* Baltimore: Otto Sutro, 1884.

———. *Requiem for the Day of Atonement.* Baltimore: Kaiser, 1879.

———. *Shirai Chinooch: Confirmation Hymns.* Baltimore: Kaiser, 1875.

———. "Tunes for the Israelitisch School." Baltimore: n.p., 1873.

Kaiser, Alois, et al., eds. *Anthems, Hymns, and Responses for the Union Prayerbook.* New York: n.p., 1894.

Kaiser, Alois, and William Sparger. *A Collection of the Principal Melodies of the Synagogue from the Earliest Times to the Present.* Chicago: T. Rubovits, 1893.

Kitziger, Frederick Emil. *How Goodly Are Thy Tents, O Jacob.* Philadelphia: W. H. Kayser, 1897.

———. *Memorial Service [Seelenfeier] for the Day of Atonement.* New Orleans, LA: Kitziger, 1897.

———. *Shire Yehudah*, vol. 4. New Orleans, LA: Kitziger, 1899.

Kley, Eduard, ed. *Hamburgisches Israelitisches Gesangbuch für hausliche und öffentliche Gottesverehung.* Hamburg, 1821.

———. *Israelitisches Gesangbuch für hausliche und öffentliche Gottesverehung.* Hamburg: Johann Philipp Erie, 1827/8.

———. *Religiöse Lieder und Gesänge für Israeliten zum häuslicher und öffentlicher Gottes-Verehrung.* Hamburg: Otto, 1818.

Kohn, Meir. *Vollständiger Jahrgang von Terzett- und Chorgesängen der Synagoge in München nebst sämmtlichen Chorresponsorien zu den alten Gesangweise der Vorsänger (Hazanut).* Munich: Palm, 1839.

Lewandowski, Louis. *Deutsche Schullieder.* Berlin: M. Poppelauer, 1864.

Lob, Otto. *Israelitische Tempel-Gesänge: Hymnen für Sabbath und Festtage mit deutschem und englischem Text in Musik gesetzt.* Chicago: Rubovits, 1876.

Marksohn, Arnold, and William Wolf. *Auswahl alter hebraïscher Synagogal-Melodien.* Leipzig: Breitkopf and Härtel, 1875.

Melodien zu J. Johlsons Deutschen Gesangbuch für Israelitische Schulen. [Frankfurt]: n.p., n.d.

Melodien zu J. Johlsons Israelitische Gesange, Zweite verbesserte und vermehrte Auflage, mit unterlegten Textworten. Frankfurt: Benjamin Krebs, 1842.

Moses, Isaac S. *The Sabbath-School Hymnal: A Collection of Songs, Services and Readings for the Synagogue, School and Home*, 6th ed., rev. and enl. New York: Bloch, 1904.

———. *The Sabbath School Hymnal: A Collection of Songs, Services, and Responses for Jewish Sabbath Schools and Homes*. Chicago: I. S. Moses, 1894.

———. *The Song Book for Jewish Worship: Adapted for Congregational Singing, as well as the Sabbath School and the Home*. Chicago: I. S. Moses, 1896.

Mühlhäuser, J. *Auswahl deutscher Gesänge im Tempel der Imanu-El Congregation in New York: nebst Anhang*. New York: Mühlhauser, 1848.

Naumbourg, Samuel. *Agudath Shirim: Receuil de chants religieux et populaires des Israélites*. Paris: S. Naumbourg, 1874.

———. *Zemiroth Yisrael: Chants Religieux des Israelites, contenant Les Hymns, Psaumes et la Liturgie complète de la Synagogue, des temps les plus reculés*. Paris: S. Naumbourg, 1847 [Vol. 1], 1852 [Vol. 2], 1857 [Vol. 3]

———. *Zemiroth Yisrael: Chants Religieux des Israelites, contenant Les Hymns, Psaumes et la Liturgie complète de la Synagogue, des temps les plus reculés*. Revised Edition of Vol. 1. Paris: S. Naumbourg, 1864.

Philippson, Ludwig. *Kleines israelitisches Gesangbuch: enthaltend deutsche Lieder und Melodieen, zu den hohen Festen, zur Totenfeier, Confirmation, Trauung, Synagogenweihe und zu vaterländischen Festen*. Leipzig: Baumgärtner, 1855.

Reichardt, Gustav, and Ernst Moritz Arndt. "Was ist des deutschen Vaterland?" Arnhem, Germany: Van der Wiel, 1825.

Segal, Robert, and Sidney Guthman, eds. *Sabbath Eve Services and Hymns*. New York: Hebrew Publishing, 1944.

Society for American Cantors. *Union Hymnal*. New York: Central Conference of American Rabbis, 1897.

Sparger, Wilhelm. "Etwas über die Kompositionswerth," *Der jüdische Kantor* 4, no. 23 (June 23, 1882): 181–82.

Spicker, Max, and William Sparger. *The Synagogal Service*. New York: Schirmer, 1901.

Stein, L., ed. *Gebete und Gesänge zum Gebrauche bei der öffentlichen-Andacht der Israeliten*. Erlangen, Germany: Ferdinand Enke, 1840.

Sulzer, Salomon. *Schir Zion: ein Cyklus religiöser Gesänge zum gottesdienstlichen Gebrauchen der Israeliten*. Vienna: Artaria, [1840].

———. *Schir Zion: gottesdienstliche Gesänge der Israeliten*. Vienna: Engel & Sohn, [1865].

———. *Shir Tsiyon: Gesänge für den israelitischen Gottesdienst*. Revised and edited by Joseph Sulzer. Leipzig: Kaufmann, 1905.

———. *"Shir Zion": A Friday Evening Service Arranged for Use in American Synagogues by the Society of American Cantors from the "Shir Zion" of Salomon Sulzer*. New York: Bloch, 1904.

Weintraub, Hirsch. *Schire Beth Adonai*. Leipzig: Breitkopf & Härtel, [1859].

Welsch, Samuel. "Todtenfeier: 2 Chöre für gemischte Stimmen und Soli." Vienna: K. K. Hoflith & Steindr v. G. Wegelein, 1871.

Werner, Eric, ed. *The Union Songster*. New York: Central Conference of American Rabbis, 1960.

Wise, Isaac M., et al. *Hymns, Psalms & Prayers in English and German*. Cincinnati, OH: Bloch, 1868.

Wohlwill, J. *Allgemeine israelitisches Gesangbuch eingeführt in dem Neuen Israelitischen Tempel zu Hamburg*. Hamburg: Perthes & Besser, 1833.

Württembergische, Königliche and Israelitische Oberkirchenbehörde. *Sefer Zemirot Yisrael. Gesang-Buch, zum Gebrauch beidem Unterichte in der mosaischen Religion und zur öffentlichen und häuslichen Gottesverehrung der Israeliten.* Stuttgart: Hallberger, 1836.

Young, Alfred, ed. *The Catholic Hymnal.* New York: Catholic Publication Society, 1884.

Related Nineteenth-Century Publications

Adler, Cyrus. "Preface." In Alois Kaiser and William Sparger, *A Collection of the Principal Melodies of the Synagogue from the Earliest Times to the Present,* v–vi. Chicago: T. Rubovits, 1893.

Benjamin, Israel J. *Drei Jahre in America, 1859–1862.* Hanover, Germany: Israel Benjamin, 1862.

Brickner, Isaac. *The Jews of Rochester.* Rochester, NY: Historical Review Society, 1912.

Burney, Charles. *A General History of Music from the Earliest Ages to the Present Period.* London: T. Becket, J. Robson, and G. Robinson, 1776.

Catalogue of Anglo-Jewish Historical Exhibition, 1887, Royal Albert Hall: And of Supplementary Exhibitions Held at the Public Record Office, British Museum, South Kensington Museum. London: William Clowes and Sons, 1887.

Cohen, Francis L. "Ancient Musical Traditions of the Synagogue." In *Proceedings of the Musical Association for the Investigation and Discussion of Subjects Connected with the Art and Science of Music, Nineteenth Session, 1892–93.* London: Novello, 1893.

———. "The Rise and Development of Synagogue Music." In *Papers Read at the Anglo-Jewish Historical Exhibition, Royal Albert Hall, London, 1887.* London: Jewish Chronicle, 1888.

Cohen, G. M. *The Little Bible, or, The Instructor of Religion and Morals for Young and Old, Containing a Complete Extract of the Holy Writ, with Instructive Notes.* Cleveland, OH: Nevins, 1869.

"Deutsche Republische Kampflieder." *Mittheilungen des Deutsch Pionier-Vereins in Philadelphia* 2 (1906).

Engel, Carl. *The Music of the Most Ancient Nations.* London: Murray, 1864.

Ensel, Gustav S. Letter from Ensel to Edward Freiberger, June 15, 1881. Bound into the copy of Gustav S. Ensel, *Ancient Liturgical Music: A Comparative and Historical Essay,* Newberry Library, Chicago.

———. Letter from Ensel to Edward Freiberger, October 4, 1881. Bound into the copy of Gustav S. Ensel, *Ancient Liturgical Music: A Comparative and Historical Essay,* Newberry Library, Chicago.

Fétis, François-Joseph. *Histoire générale de musique depuis les temps les plus anciens jusqu'a nos jours,* vol. 1. Paris: Didot Frères Fils, 1869.

Fischer, Wilhelm. *Gesangschule, oder Anleitung zum gründlichen Studium des Gesanges den Gesangvereinen der Union gewidmet.* Philadelphia: Schäfer and Koradi, 1867.

Forkel, Johann Nicolaus. *Allgemeine Geschichte der Musik,* vol. 1. Leipzig: Schwickertschen, 1788.

Frank, Emma. "Presentation of the Hymn Book." *Papers of the Jewish Women's Congress, Held at Chicago, September 4, 5, 6 and 7, 1893.* Philadelphia: Jewish Publication Society of America, 1894.

Furber, Daniel. "Choir-Singing Appropriately Jewish." In Austin Phelps, Edwards A. Park, and Daniel J. Furber, *Hymns and Choirs: or, the Matter and the Manner of the Service of Song in the House of the Lord.* Andover, MA: Warren F. Draper, 1860.

Goldstein, Morris, Alois Kaiser, Isaac L. Rice, and Samuel Welsch. "Preface." *Zimrath Yah* 1. New York: n.p., 1873.
Hauptverein für christliche Erbauungsschriften. *Gesangbuch für Kirche, Schule und Haus*. Berlin: Hauptverein für christliche Erbauungsschriften, 1858.
Haweis, H. R. *Music and Morals*. London: Longmans, Green, 1871.
Herxheimer, Salomon, and Simon Hecht. *Der israelitische Confirmand, oder, Glaubens- und Pflichtenlehre für den Schul- und Privatgebrauch in Reformgemeinden*. Evansville, IN: Simon Hecht, 1868.
Holland's Springfield City Directory, for 1868–1869. Chicago: Western Publishing, 1868.
Kiddle, Henry, and Alexander J. Schem. *The Year Book of Education for 1879*. New York: E. Steiger, 1879.
Kompert, Leopold. *Geschichten einer Gasse*. Berlin: Gerschel, 1865.
Lešer, Václav, and Obec Král. *Adressář královského hlavního města Prahy a sousedních obcí Bubenče, Karlína, Smíchova, Kr. Vinohrad, Vršovic a Žižkova*. Prague: Důchodci obce pražské, 1891.
Levitt, M. T., and Asher Isaac Myers. *Prayers for the Sabbath, Rosh-Hashanah, and Kippur: or, the Sabbath, the Beginning of the Year, and the Day of Atonements: With the Amidah and Musaph of the Moadim or Solemn Seasons according to the Order of the Spanish and Portuguese Jews*. Translated by Isaac Pinto. New York: John Holt, 1765/6.
Lewandowski, Louis. "Aufruf an die Herren Kantoren." *Der jüdische Kantor* 1, no. 26 (December 25, 1879): 97.
Lingard, William. "Walking Down Broadway." New York: William A. Pond, 1868.
Lippe, Chajim David. *Ch. D. Lippe's Bibliographisches Lexicon der Gesammten Jüdischen Literatur der Gegenwart und Adress-Anzeiger*. Vienna: D. Löwy, 1881.
Love, William DeLoss. *The Fast and Thanksgiving Days of New England*. New York: Houghton, Mifflin/Riverside Press, 1895.
Löw, Leopold. *Beiträge zur jüdischen Alterthumskunde*. Szeged, Hungary: S. Burger, 1875.
Martini, Giambattista. *Storia della Musica*. vol. 1. Bologna, 1757.
Morais, Henry S. *The Jews of Philadelphia: Their History from the Earliest Settlements to the Present Time*. Philadelphia: Levytype, 1894.
Naumann, Emil. *The History of Music*, special ed. Translated by F. Praeger. New York: Cassell, 1886.
Peixotto, Benjamin Franklin. "Salomon Sulzer: Remembrances from Vienna." *Menorah Journal* 8 (1890): 261.
Pinto, Joseph Yesurun. "The Form of Prayer which Was Performed at the Jews Synagogue in the City of New York on October 23, 1760." New York: W. Wyman, 1760.
"Professor Simon Hecht." *Biographical Cyclopedia of Vanderburgh County*. Evansville, IN: Keller, 1897.
Rice, Isaac L. *What Is Music?* New York: Appleton, 1875.
Rimbault, Edward. *Organist's Portfolio*. London: Chappell, 1865.
Salomon, Gotthold. *Moses Mendelssohn: Oder ein blick in ein schones, herrlich vollendetes menschenleben*. Chicago: G. M. Cohen, 1858.
Seixas, Gershom Mendes. "Discourse Delivered in the Synagogue in New-York, on the Ninth of May, 1798, Observed as a Day of Humiliation. Etc. etc. Conformably to a Recommendation of the President of the United State of America." New York: William A. Davis, 1798.

———. "Religious Discourse Delivered in the Synagogue in This City on Thursday the 26th November, 1789: Agreeable to the Proclamation of the President of the United States of America, to Be Observed as a Day of Public Thanksgiving and Prayer." New York: Archibald McLean, 1789.
Singer, Josef. *Die Tonarten des traditionellen Synagogalegesangs: Ihr Verhältnis zu den Kirchentonarten und den Tonarten der vorchristlichen Musikperiode.* Vienna: E. M. Wetzler, 1886.
Stern, Myer. *The Rise and Progress of Reform Judaism: Embracing and History Made from the Official Records of Temple Emanu-El of New York.* New York: Myer Stern, 1895.
Szold, Benjamin. "The Memory of the Dead." In *Songs and Prayers and Meditations for Divine Services of Israelites.* Translated by Benjamin Szold and Marcus Jastrow. Philadelphia: Marcus Jastrow, 1873.
The Metropolitan Ecclesiastical Directory. London: T. Hurst, 1835.
Union of American Hebrew Congregations. *Judaism at the World's Parliament of Religions.* Cincinnati, OH: Robert Clarke, 1894.
———. *Proceedings of the Union of American Hebrew Congregations*, vol. 1 (1873–79). Cincinnati, OH: Bloch, 1879.
———. "Statistics of the Jews of the United States." Philadelphia: Edward Stern, 1880.
Weigl, T. O. *Vollständiges Bucher-Lexicon*, vol. 3. Leipzig: Ludwig Schuman, 1835.
White, B. F., and E. J. King, eds. *The Sacred Harp: A Collection of Psalm and Hymn Tunes Odes and Anthems Selected from the Most Eminent Authors*, 2nd ed. Philadelphia: S. C. Collins, 1860.
Wise, Isaac M. *Reminiscences.* Translated by David Philipson. Cincinnati, OH: Leo Bloch, 1901.
———. *The History of the K. K. Bene Yeshurun, of Cincinnati, Ohio.* Cincinnati, OH: Bloch Printing, 1892.
Wolf, G. *Geschichte der Israelitischen Cultusgemeinde in Wien (1820–1860).* Vienna: Wilhelm & Braumüller, 1860.
Zunz, Leopold. *Die gottesdienstlichen Vorträge der Juden historisch entwickelt: Ein Beitrag zur Altertumskunde und biblischen Kritik, zur Lieratur- und Religionsgeschichte.* Berlin: A. Asher, 1832.

Secondary Sources

Ahlquist, Karen. "Musical Assimilation and 'the German Element' at the Cincinnati Sängerfest, 1879." *Musical Quarterly* 94, no. 3 (2011): 381–416.
Avenary, Hanoch. *Kantor Salomon Sulzer und seine Zeit: eine Dokumentation.* Sigmaringen, Germany: Jan Thornbeck, 1985.
Baader, Benjamin. *Gender, Judaism, and Bourgeois Culture in Germany, 1800–1870.* Bloomington: Indiana University Press, 2006.
Barnett, Arthur. *The Western Synagogue through Two Centuries (1761–1961).* London: Valentine Mitchell, 1961.
Baron, John. *Concert Life in Nineteenth Century New Orleans: A Comprehensive Reference.* Baton Rouge: Louisiana State University Press, 2013.
———. "Frederick Emil Kitziger of New Orleans: A Nineteenth Century Composer of Synagogue Music." *Musica Judaica* 5 (1983): 20–33.

Baumgarten, Elisheva. *Practicing Piety in Medieval Ashkenaz: Men, Women, and Everyday Religious Observance*. Philadelphia: University of Pennsylvania Press, 2014.
Bernheim, Isaac W. *History of the Settlement of Jews in Paducah and the Lower Ohio Valley*. Paducah, KY: Isaac Bernheim, 1912.
Biale, David. "Preface: Toward a Culture History of the Jews." In *The Cultures of the Jews: A History*, edited by David Biale, xvii–xxxiii. New York: Schocken, 2002.
Bohlman, Philip. "Ethnic Musics/Religious Identities: Toward an Historiography of German-American Sacred Music." In *Land without Nightingales: Music in the Making of German-America*, edited by Philip Bohlman and Otto Holzapfel, 127–58. Madison, WI: Max Kade Institute, 2002.
——. *Jewish Music and Modernity*. New York: Oxford University Press, 2008.
Bottigheimer, Ruth B. "Moses Mordechai Büdinger's *Kleine Bibel* (1823) and Vernacular Jewish Children's Bibles." *Jewish Social Studies* 1, no. 3 (1995): 83–98.
Brinkmann, Tobias. *Sundays at Sinai: A Jewish Congregation in Chicago*. Chicago: University of Chicago Press, 2012.
Burgh, Theodore W. "The Music of Israel during the Iron Age." In *The Cambridge Companion to Jewish Music*, edited by Joshua S. Walden, 75–83. New York: Cambridge University Press, 2015.
Caplan, Kimmy. "In God We Trust: Salaries and Income of American Orthodox Rabbis, 1881–1924." *American Jewish History* 86, no. 1 (1998): 77–106.
Carpenter, Audrey T. *Giovanna Sestini: An Italian Opera Singer in Eighteenth-Century London*. Leicester, UK: Troubador, 2017.
Clevenger, S. V. *The Evolution of Man and His Mind*. Chicago: Evolution Publishing, 1903.
Cohen, Francis L. "Sagerin." *Jewish Encyclopedia*. http://www.jewishencyclopedia.com/articles/12991-sagerin.
"Cohen, Gustave M." *Encyclopedia of Cleveland History*. https://ech.case.edu/cgi/article.pl?id=CGM.
Cohen, Irving H. "Synagogue Music in the Early American Republic." *Gratz College Annual of Jewish Studies* 5 (1976): 17–23.
Cohen, Judah M. "Becoming a Reform Jewish Cantor: A Study in Cultural Investment." PhD diss., Harvard University, 2002.
——. "Dawning Sounds: Jews and Music in the Young Republic." In *By Dawn's Early Light: Jewish Contributions to American Culture from the Nation's Founding to the Civil War*, edited by Adam Mendelsohn and Dale Baumgarten, 113–22. Princeton, NJ: Princeton University Library, 2016.
——. "Embodying Musical Heritage in a New-Old Profession: American Jewish Cantorial Schools, 1904–1939." *Journal of the Society for American Music* 11, no. 1 (February 2017): 25–52.
——. "Interwoven Voices of the Religious Landscape: G. S. Ensel and Musical Populism in the Nineteenth Century American Synagogue." *American Jewish Archives Journal* 69, no. 1 (2017): 1–40.
——. *The Making of a Reform Jewish Cantor: Musical Authority, Cultural Investment*. Bloomington: Indiana University Press, 2009.
——. "Modes of Tradition? Negotiating Jewishness and Modernity in the Synagogue Music of Isadore Freed and Frederick Piket." *Jewish Culture and History* 5, no. 2 (2002): 25–47.

———. "Rewriting the Grand Narrative of Jewish Music: A. Z. Idelsohn in the United States." *Jewish Quarterly Review* 100, no. 3 (2009): 417–53.
———. *Sounding Musical Tradition: The Music of Central Synagogue*. New York: Central Synagogue, 2011.
———. *Through the Sands of Time: A History of the Jewish Community of St. Thomas, US Virgin Islands*. Hanover, NH: Brandeis University Press, 2004.
———. "Whither Jewish Music? Jewish Studies, Music Scholarship, and the Tilt between Seminary and University." *AJS Review* 32, no. 1 (2008): 29–48.
Cohen, Michael R. *The Birth of Conservative Judaism: Solomon Schechter's Disciples and the Creation of an American Religious Movement*. New York: Columbia University Press, 2012.
Conway, David. *Jews in Music: Entry into the Profession from the Enlightenment to Richard Wagner*. Cambridge, UK: Cambridge University Press, 2012.
Crawford, Richard. *America's Musical Life: A History*. New York: Norton, 2001.
Eisenstein, J. D. "The History of the First Russian-American Jewish Congregation: The Beth HaMedrosh Hagodol." *Publications of the American Jewish Historical Society* 9 (1901): 72–74.
Eleff, Zev. *Modern Orthodox Judaism: A Documentary History*. Omaha: University of Nebraska Press, 2016.
———. *Who Rules the Synagogue? Religious Authority and the Formation of American Judaism*. New York: Oxford University Press, 2016.
Endelman, Todd M. "German-Jewish Settlement in Victorian England." In *Second Chance: Two Centuries of German-Speaking Jews in the United Kingdom*, edited by Werner E. Mosse et al., 37–56. Tübingen, Germany: J. C. B. Mohr [Paul Siebeck], 1991.
Finestein, Israel. *Anglo-Jewry in Changing Times: Studies in Diversity, 1840–1914*. London: Valentine Mitchell, 1999.
Friedman, Aron, ed. *Dem Andenken Eduard Birnbaums*. Berlin: C. Boas, 1922.
Frühauf, Tina. *German-Jewish Organ Music: An Anthology of Works from the 1820s to the 1960s*. Middleton, WI: A&R Editions, 2013.
———. *The Organ and Its Music in German-Jewish Culture*. New York: Oxford University Press, 2009.
———. *Salomon Sulzer: Composer, Cantor, Icon*. Jewish Miniatures vol. 133A. Berlin: Hentrich & Hentrich, 2012.
Goldberg, Ethan. "In the Shadow of Sulzer: The Mixed Legacy of Cantor Alois Kaiser." BA thesis, Brandeis University, 2012.
Goldberg, Geoffrey. "The Cantorial *Fantasia* Revisited: New Perspectives on an Ashkenazic Musical Genre." *Musica Judaica* 17 (2003/4): 32–85.
———. "Continuity and Change in Frankfurt Liturgical-Musical Customs: Text and Sub-Text in Salomon Geiger's 'Divrey Kehillot.'" In *Die Frankfurter Judengasse: jüdisches Leben in der frühen Neuzeit*, edited by Fritz Backhaus, 124–42. London: Valentine Mitchell, 2010.
———. "Mahzor ha-hayyim: Lifecycle Celebration in the Song of the Ashkenazic Synagogue." *AJS Review* 33, no. 2 (2009): 305–39.
———. "An Overview of Congregational Song in the German Synagogue Up to the Shoah." *Journal of Synagogue Music* 30, no. 1 (2005): 13–53.
———. "The Training of *Hazzanim* in Nineteenth Century Germany." *Yuval* 7 (2002): 299–367.

Goldman, Karla. *Beyond the Synagogue Gallery: Finding a Place for Women.* Cambridge, MA: Harvard University Press, 2000.
Goldstein, Israel. *A Century of Judaism in New York: B'nai Jeshurun 1825–1925, New York's Oldest Ashkenazic Congregation.* New York: Congregation B'nai Jeshurun, 1930.
Graziano, John, ed. *European Music and Musicians in New York City, 1840–1900.* Rochester, NY: University of Rochester Press, 2006.
Green, David B. "This Day in Jewish History: 1850: A Jew Who Would Make Leonardo da Vinci Feel Inadequate Is Born." *Ha'aretz*, February 22, 2016. http://www.haaretz.com/jewish/this-day-in-jewish-history/1.704563.
Grimes, Robert R. *How Shall We Sing in a Foreign Land? Music of Irish Catholic Immigrants in the Antebellum United States.* South Bend, IN: University of Notre Dame Press, 1996.
Grinstein, Hyman. *The Rise of the Jewish Community of New York, 1654–1860.* Philadelphia: Jewish Publication Society, 1954.
Grossman, Leonard J. "B'nai B'rith." In *The Sentinel Presents 100 Years of Chicago's Jewish Life*, 24. Chicago: Sentinel Publishing, 1948.
Gurock, Jeffrey. *Orthodox Jews in America.* Bloomington: Indiana University Press, 2009.
HaCohen, Ruth. "Between Noise and Harmony: The Oratorical Moment in the Musical Entanglements of Jews and Christians." *Critical Inquiry* 32, no. 2 (2006): 250–77.
———. *The Music Libel against the Jews.* New Haven, CT: Yale University Press, 2011.
Holzapfel, Otto. *Religiöse Identität und Gesangbuch: zur Ideologiegeschichte deutschsprachiger Einwanderer in den USA und die Auseinandersetzung um das "richtige" Gesangbuch.* New York: Peter Lang, 1998.
———. "Singing from the Right Songbook: Ethnic Identity and Language Transformation in German American Hymnals." In *Music in American Religious Experience*, edited by Philip V. Bohlman, Edith L. Blumhofer, and Maria M. Chow, 175–94. New York: Oxford University Press, 2005.
Idelsohn, Abraham Z. *Jewish Music in its Historical Development.* New York: Henry Holt, 1929.
Jaher, Frederic Cople. *The Jews and the Nation: Revolution, Emancipation, State Formation, and the Liberal Paradigm in America and France.* Princeton, NJ: Princeton University Press, 2009.
Janeczko, Jeff, curator. "Jewish Voices in the New World." Milken Archive of Jewish Music. http://www.milkenarchive.org/articles/virtual-exhibits/view/jewish-voices-new-world-sacred-music.
Kabakoff, Jacob. "The Use of Hebrew by American Jews during the Colonial Period." In *Hebrew and the Bible in America: The First Two Centuries*, edited by Shalom Goldman, 191–208. Hanover, NH: Brandeis University Press, 1993.
Kirshenblatt-Gimblett, Barbara. "Exhibiting Jews." In *Destination Culture: Tourism, Museums, and Heritage*, 79–128. Berkeley: University of California Press, 1998.
Landman, Leo. *The Cantor: An Historical Perspective.* New York: Yeshiva University, 1972.
Levine, Joseph A. "Introduction." *Journal of Synagogue Music* 32 (2007): 101.
Levine, Joseph A., and David B. Sislen, eds. "Nusach Wars." *Journal of Synagogue Music* 40, no. 1 (March 2015).
Levin, Neil W. "Gustave M. Cohen, 1820–1902." Milken Archive of Jewish Music. http://www.milkenarchive.org/people/view/all/1109/Cohen,+Gustave.
———. "Introduction to Vol. 1: Jewish Voices in the New World: The Song of Prayer in Colonial and 19th Century America." Milken Archive of Jewish Music. http://www.milkenarchive.org/articles/view/introduction-to-volume-1.

Lewis, Selma S. *A Biblical People in the Bible Belt: The Jewish Community of Memphis, Tennessee, 1840s–1960s*. Macon, GA: Mercer University Press, 1998.

Liberles, Robert. "Conflict Over Reforms: The Case of Congregation Beth Elohim, Charleston, South Carolina." In *The American Synagogue: A Sanctuary Transformed*, edited by Jack Wertheimer, 274–96. Hanover, NH: Brandeis University Press, 1995.

Loeffler, James. "Richard Wagner's 'Jewish Music': Antisemitism and Aesthetics in Modern Jewish Culture." *Jewish Social Studies* 15, no. 2 (2009): 2–36.

Lowenthal, David. *The Past Is a Foreign Country—Revisited*. New York: Cambridge University Press, 2015.

Lutz, Violet. Finding Aid for "Harmonie Singing Society Records," Ms. Coll. 54, PACSCL Finding Aids. http://dla.library.upenn.edu/dla/pacscl/ead.html?id=PACSCL_GSP_MsColl54&fq=top_repository_facet%3A%22German%20Society%20of%20Pennsylvania%22&#ref5.

Markreich, Max. *Geschichte der Juden in Bremen und Umgegend*. Bremen, Germany: Edition Temmen, 2003.

Marx, Dalia. "The Prayer for the State of Israel: Universalism and Particularism." In *All the Word: Universalism, Particularism, and the High Holy Days*, edited by Lawrence A. Hoffman, 50–54. Woodstock, VT: Jewish Lights Publishing, 2014.

Mendelsohn, Adam. "Great Britain, the Commonwealth, and Anglophone Jewry." In *The Cambridge History of Judaism, Volume 8, The Modern World, 1815–2000*, edited by Mitchell B. Hart and Tony Michels, 144–45. New York: Cambridge University Press, 2017.

Mintz, Sharon Liberman, Elliott Kahn, and Jewish Theological Seminary of America. *Kehillat Ha-Kodesh: Creating the Sacred Community*. New York: The Library of the Jewish Theological Seminary of America, 1997.

Morrow, Mary Sue. "Somewhere between Beer and Wagner: The Cultural and Musical Impact of German Männerchöre in New York and New Orleans." In *Music and Culture in America, 1861–1918*, edited by Michael Saffle, 79–109. New York: Garland, 1998.

Moses, Isaac S. "The Cantor as a Religious Functionary." In *Annual Report of the Society for American Cantors*. New York: n.p., 1904.

Nadel, Stanley. "Jewish Race and German Soul in Nineteenth-Century America." *American Jewish History* 77, no. 1 (1987): 6–26.

Nemtsov, Jascha, and Herman Simon. *Louis Lewandowski: "Love Makes the Melody Immortal."* Jewish Miniatures vol. 114A. Berlin: Hentrich & Hentrich, 2011.

Neusner, J. Jacob. "Anglo-Jewry and the Development of American Jewish Life, 1775–1850." *Transactions* (Jewish Historical Society of England) 18 (1953–55): 231–42.

Ogasapian, John. *Church Music in America, 1620–2000*. Macon, GA: Mercer University Press, 2007.

Ogburn, Christopher G. "Brews, Brotherhood and Beethoven: The 1865 New York City Sängerfest and the Fostering of German American Identity." *American Music* 33, no. 4 (2015): 405–40.

Osborne, William. *Music in Ohio*. Kent, OH: Kent State University Press, 2004.

Ostendorf, Ann. *Sounds American: National Identity and the Music Cultures of the Lower Mississippi Valley, 1800–1860*. Atlanta: University of Georgia Press, 2011.

Pencak, William. "Jewish Themes in the Operas of Giacomo Meyerbeer." *Shofar* 32, no. 1 (2013): 43–59.

Peskin, Allan. *This Tempting Freedom: The Early Years of Cleveland Judaism and Anshe Chesed Congregation.* Cleveland, OH: Anshe Chesed, 1973.

Pinnolis, Judith S. "'Cantor Soprano' Julie Rosewald: The Musical Career of a Jewish American 'New Woman.'" *American Jewish Archives* 62, no. 2 (2010): 1–53.

Polster, Gary E. "'To Love Work and Dislike Being Idle': Origins and Aims of the Cleveland Jewish Orphan Asylum, 1868–1878." *American Jewish Archives* 39, no. 2 (November 1987): 127–56.

Rabin, Shari. *Jews on the Frontier: Religion and Mobility in Nineteenth-Century America.* New York: New York University Press, 2017.

Rock, Howard. *Haven of Liberty: New York Jews in the New World, 1654–1865.* New York: New York University Press, 2012.

Rogow, Faith. *Gone to Another Meeting: The National Council of Jewish Women 1893–1993.* Tuscaloosa: University of Alabama Press, 1998.

Rosenbaum, Fred. *Cosmopolitans: A Social and Cultural History of Jews of the San Francisco Bay Area.* Berkeley: University of California Press, 2009.

Rosenberg, Shelley Kapneck. *Reform Congregation Keneseth Israel: 150 Years.* Philadelphia: Keneseth Israel, 1997.

Roskies, David. *The Jewish Search for a Usable Past.* Bloomington: Indiana University Press, 1999.

Rosman, Moshe. *How Jewish Is Jewish History?* Portland, OR: Littman Library, 2009.

Roth, Cecil. *Records of the Western Synagogue 1761–1932.* London: Edward Goldstone, 1932.

Rudolph, B. G. *From a Minyan to a Community: A History of the Jews of Syracuse.* Syracuse, NY: Syracuse University Press, 1970.

Sarna, Jonathan. *American Judaism: A History.* New Haven, CT: Yale University Press, 2004.

———. "The Touro Monument Controversy: Aniconism vs. Anti-Idolatry in a Mid-Nineteenth Century American Jewish Religious Dispute." In *Between Jewish Tradition and Modernity*, edited by Michael A. Meyer and David N. Myers, 80–95. Detroit, MI: Wayne State University Press, 2014.

Schappes, Morris. "Anti-Semitism and Reaction, 1795–1800." *Publications of the American Jewish Historical Society* 38, no. 2 (1948): 119–28.

Schleifer, Eliyahu. "Jewish Liturgical Music from the Bible to Hasidism." In *Sacred Sound and Social Change*, edited by Lawrence A. Hoffman and Janet Walton, 13–58. Notre Dame, IN: University of Notre Dame Press, 1992.

———. *Samuel Naumbourg: The Cantor of French Jewish Emancipation.* Jewish Miniatures vol. 136A. Berlin: Hentrich & Hentrich, 2012.

Schmidt, Axel W. O., ed. *One of the 999 About to Be Forgotten: Memoirs of Carl Barus 1865–1935.* New York: AWOS, 2005.

Schmier, Louis, ed. *Reflections on Southern Jewry: The Letters of Charles Wesselowsky, 1878–1879.* Macon, GA: Mercer University Press, 1982.

Schwartz, Nancy F., and Stanley Laskey. "Jewish Cleveland before the Civil War." *American Jewish History* 82, nos. 1–4 (1994): 97–122.

Seroussi, Edwin. "Liner Notes." With *Judeo-Caribbean Currents: Music of the Mikvé Israel-Emanuel Synagogue in Curaçao*, edited by Edwin Seroussi and Yuval Shaked. Anthology of Music Traditions in Israel 22. Jerusalem: Jewish Music Research Centre, Hebrew University of Jerusalem, 2009.

Shevitz, Amy Hill. *Jewish Communities on the Ohio River: A History.* Lexington: University Press of Kentucky, 2007.

Silverberg, Ann L. "Cecilian Reform in Baltimore, 1868–1903." In *Renewal and Resistance: Catholic Church Music from the 1850s to Vatican II*, edited by Paul Collins, 171-88. New York: Peter Lang, 2010.
Slobin, Mark. *Chosen Voices: The Story of the American Cantorate*. Urbana: University of Illinois Press, 2002.
Snyder, Suzanne G. "The Indianapolis Männerchor: Contributions to a New Musicality in Midwestern Life." In *Music and Culture in America, 1861–1918*, edited by Michael Saffle, 111–40. New York: Garland, 1998.
———. "The Männerchor Tradition in the United States: A Historical Analysis of Its Contribution to American Musical Culture." PhD diss., University of Iowa, 1991.
Sperber, Haim. "Rabbi Nathan Adler and the Chief Rabbinate in Britain, 1845–1890." *European Judaism: A Journal for the New Europe* 45, no. 2 (2012): 8–20.
Stahl, Howard M. "William Sparger: Enigmatic Pioneer of the American Reform Cantorate." *American Jewish Archives Journal* 63, no. 1 (2011): 23–25.
Stössel, "Ein Orgel im alten Tempel zu Jerusalem." *Sinai* 7, no. 3 (April 1862): 121–23.
Taitz, Emily. "Woman's Voices, Woman's Prayers: Women in the European Synagogues of the Middle Ages." In *Daughters of the King: Women and the Synagogue*, edited by Susan Grossman and Rivka Haut, 65–68. Philadelphia: Jewish Publication Society, 1992.
Trimble, Pamela Kordan. "Kol Ḥazzanit: Alternatives for Women Cantors to the Vocal Requirements and Expression of Traditional Hazzanut." *Journal of Synagogue Music* 32 (2007): 100–15.
Tripoli, David M. *Sing to the Lord a New Song: Choirs in the Worship and Culture of the Dutch Reformed Church in America, 1785–1860*. Grand Rapids, MI: Eerdmans, 2012.
Tuckman, William. "Sigmund and Jacob Schlesinger and Joseph Bloch: Civil War Composers and Musicians." *American Jewish Historical Quarterly* 53, no. 1 (September 1963): 70–71.
Wachs, Sharona. *American Jewish Liturgies*. Cincinnati, OH: Hebrew Union College Press, 1997.
Wallace, Joseph. *Past and Present of the City of Springfield and Sangamon County Illinois*. Chicago: S. J. Clarke, 1904.
Weissbach, Lee Shai. *Jewish Life in Small-Town America: A History*. New Haven, CT: Yale University Press, 2005.
Werner, Eric. *Mendelssohn: A New Image of the Composer and His Age*. Glencoe, IL: Free Press, 1963.
———. *The Sacred Bridge: The Interdependence of Music and Liturgy in Synagogue and Church during the First Millennium*. New York: Columbia University Press, 1959.
———. *A Voice Still Heard: The Sacred Songs of the Ashkenazic Jews*. University Park: Pennsylvania State University, 1976.
Westermeyer, Paul. "The Evolution of the Music of German American Protestants in Their Hymnody: A Case Study from an American Perspective." In *Music in American Religious Experience*, edited by Philip V. Bohlman, Edith L. Blumhofer, and Maria M. Chow, 155–71. New York: Oxford University Press, 2005.
Wiese, Christian. "Inventing a New Language of Jewish Scholarship." *Studia Rosenthaliana* 36 (2002–3): 273–304.
Wiese, Christian, and Cornelia Wilhelm, eds. *American Jewry: Transcending the European Experience?* New York: Bloomsbury, 2017.
Wilhelm, Cornelia. *The Independent Orders of B'nai B'rith and True Sisters: Pioneers of a New Jewish Identity, 1843–1914*. Detroit, MI: Wayne State University Press, 2011.

Wollenberg, Susan. "Charles Garland Verrinder and Music at the West London Synagogue, 1859–1904." In *Music and Performance Culture in Nineteenth-Century Britain: Essays in Honour of Nicholas Temperley*, edited by Bennett Zon, 59-82. New York: Ashgate, 2012.

Zim, Sol. *The Joy of Israel Songbook, for Synagogue, School and Home, with Chords*. Hollis Hills, NY: Zimray Productions, 1980.

Zola, Gary P. "The Ascendancy of Reform Judaism in the American South during the Nineteenth Century." In *Jewish Roots in Southern Soil*, edited by Marcie Cohen Ferris and Mark Greenberg, 156–91. Hanover, NH: University Press of New England, 2006.

Zon, Bennet. "Victorian Anti-Semitism and the Origin of Gregorian Chant." In *Renewal and Resistance: Catholic Church Music from the 1850s to Vatican II*, edited by Paul Collins, 99–120. New York: Peter Lang, 2010.

INDEX

Note: Italicized page numbers followed by 'f' indicate figures.

Abrahams, Simeon (1810–67), 19–20, 25, 27, 29, 49n37
Adas Jeshurun congregation (New York), 43, 193
Adath Israel congregation (New York), 221
Adler, Cyrus, 228, 231, 238, 257, 268
Adler, Nathan, 10, 25, 27, 225
"Adon Olam," 20–21, 22–23f, 31, 200, 201f
Ahawath Chesed congregation (New York): budgets for music programs, 204; efforts toward congregational participation, 221; Isaac Moses at, 258; new synagogue and pipe organ, 201–2; power team at, 190–91; Ritterman's refusal to invitation, 36; Welsch's tenure at, 205, 212n9
Ahlquist, Karen, 55
Allemania Society, 87
all-male choirs, 25, 28, 32–33, 56, 80, 87, 188
amateur *versus* refined music production, 71, 80–81, 101–3, 105–6, 232
American culture, 3–4
American Hebrew, The: on congregational singing, 219; criticism of cantors, 248–49; Emanu-El hymnal, 222; professional choristers, 223; response to Sparger's article, 228; solemnifying services, 220–21
American Israelite, The: on *Ancient Liturgical Music*, 158; coverage of Ensel's lecture on liturgical music, 133; Jewish creativity and musical development, 161; national repertoire in *Union Hymnal*, 250; praise for *Zimrath Yah*, 208; publication of Ensel's address at MTNA, 160–61; Sparger's article in, 228; title of, 172n137. *See also Israelite*
American Jewish culture: and American pluralism, 118; compared to European Judaism, 270; in enlightened American future, 78; European criticism of, 207; and lachrymose worldview, 160
American Jewish identity. *See* Jewish American identity
American national unity, spirit of, 13, 90
Ancient Liturgical Music (ALM) (Ensel), 135–57; biblical performances, 143; Catholic "Preface to the Roman Sanctus," 152–53f; discussion of ram's horns, 141–42f; elements of, 135–36; evolution of vocal practices, 143; historical knowledge of, 164; "Miriam's Song on the Red Sea," 138, 139–40f, 170n95; on musical innovation, 160; music as product of multifaceted cultural interaction, 147–48; music's evolution, 137–38; notation, 143–46, 144–45f; organology, 138; psalms, 146–47; publication of, 135, 137f; Reformation, Protestantism, and Jewish composers of the nineteenth century, 148; reviews of, 158; taxonomy in, 170n96; Trisagion, 148–57, 149–51f, 154–57f
ancient music and melodies, 133, 134–35, 209, 226, 231, 232–33, 234
Anglo-Jewish Historical Exposition (London, 1887), 218, 224, 260n5
Anshe Chesed congregation (New York): American liturgical sound, 194; attention to music program, 193; G. M. Cohen's tenure at, 90–92, 99, 100; founding of B'nai B'rith, 76; performance of Kaiser's "Requiem," 107, 115n146; Sternberger and Hecht at, 40–43
Anthems, Hymns, and Responses (1894), 240–42, 241f, 243f
anthems in *Union Hymnal*, 252–53, 253f
Arion singing society, 64, 188, 211n8
Armhold, William, 70–71

295

Arthur, Alfred, 101
art music: American trend toward, 8; cultivation of, 194; focus of scholars, 118; and people's music, 71, 80–81, 101–3, 105–6, 232
Ashkenazic melodies, 147, 171n115, 236–38
Aufrecht, Louis, 106
Austro-Hungarian Society of Cantors, 217–18
Avodat Yisrael liturgy, 125

Baltimore Hebrew congregation, 247, 264n115
Barechu (call to prayer) settings, 95, *95f*, 200
Barus, Carl (1823–1908), 57, 87
Bauer, Jacob, 206
Baumgarten, Elisheva, 14–15
"Bayom HaHu," 200
Beethoven Männerchor, 57
"Benevolence, Brotherly Love, and Harmony," 78
Bene Yeshurum congregation (Paducah, KY), 117, 158, 162
Bene Yeshurum congregation (KKBY, Cincinnati), 29–30, 44, 57, 85–86, 122–24, 158
Bertoni, Ferdinando (1725–1813), "*La verginella come la rosa*" ("Where, dear maid, should'st thou forsake me"), 22–23*f*, 47n6
Beth-El congregation (New York), 43, 106
Beth Elohim congregation (Brooklyn, NY), 227
Beth Elohim congregation (Charleston, South Carolina), 21, 24, 60, 73n21
Biachi, Hannibal, 176
biblical performances, 133, 143
Bildung (self-cultivation): and B'nai B'rith, 78; choral singing, vocal training, and, 164; G. M. Cohen's efforts to promote, 87–90; and cultural sophistication, 11; and moral compass, 124; through *Sacred Harp of Judah*, 92–99
Bildungsmusik. See *Bildung* (self-cultivation); Cohen, Gustave M.; communal unity, tripartite model of

Birnbaum collection, Hebrew Union College, 268
Blaustein, Abraham, 206
Bloch Publishing Company, 158, 222
B'nai B'rith. *See* International Order of B'nai B'rith
B'nai Israel congregation (Evansville, IN), 117, 118, 126–27
B'nai Jeshurun congregation (New York): American liturgical sound, 194; contract salaries, 188; feud with Shaarey Tefilah, 48n30; and Henry A. Henry, 29; hiring of Ansel Leo, 26–27; Kartschmaroff at, 214n66; purchase of organ, 33; requirements for cantor, 27, 32, 33, 48n28; use of all-male choir, 28
B'nei El congregation (St. Louis), 125
B'ne Jeshurun congregation (Milwaukee), 99–100
Board of Delegates of American Israelites, 219
Bohlman, Philip, 3, 74n45, 207
Bondi, Jonas, 177, 178
brass instruments, 138, *141–42f*
Braunfeld, J., 245
Breslaur, Emil, 70
Brinkmann, Tobias, 9
B'rith Sholem congregation (Springfield, IL), 125
British Jewish practices, 24–31, 218
British Jewry, 225
budgets for music programs: choral professionalism, 15, 36, 42, 74n38, 123, 179, 223; and cultural capital in America, 186, 211n1; and financial constraints, 81; organ purchases, 33, 38, 90, 193, 272; post-Civil War economy and, 201–2, 205; Sulzer cantors and urban centers, 12, 175, 186, 193
Busch, Isidor, 82, 110n20

CAA. *See* Cantors' Association of America (CAA)
Cahn, David, 245, 258
call to prayer settings ("Barechu"), 95, 200
cantillation: Hebrew cantillation, 143, 146; Sephardic cantillation, 171n105, 171n115

cantorial culture, 12, 18n27
cantorial journals, 206–8
cantorial singing, timbral shift in, 13
cantors and the cantorate: and American Jewish heritage, 13, 228; B'nai Jeshurun's requirements for, 32, 33; cantors' roles, 190–91, 272, 274; as embodiment of musical traditions, 5, 6; golden age of cantors, 274; group portrait of noted cantors, 207; move away from synagogue-school-home model, 259; musical authority of, 225, 228, 230, 242, 246, 252, 271; professionalization of, 45–46, 178–79, 186, 206–7; relationship with rabbis, 4, 8, 9, 245–46, 257, 268; salaries as symbols of value, 175, 183nn2–3, 185, 188, 194; soured attitudes toward, 248–49; status and European training, 187; use of terms, 16
Cantors' Association of America (CAA): founding of, 14, 229; merger with SAC, 258; musical authority of cantors, 242; rabbinical collaboration and hymnal, 229–30, 245; struggles with CCAR over hymnal, 238–40, 263n90
Caplan, Kimmy, 18n27
Catholic Hymnal, The, 159
Catholic "Preface to the Roman Sanctus," 152–53f
Central Conference of American Rabbis (CCAR): address on Jewish traditional music, 232; adoption and printing of *Union Hymnal*, 253–54, 255, 256, 257; control over *Union Hymnal* project, 229–30; disputes with CAA and hymnal delays, 238–40, 247–48, 263n90, 264n114; Moses's role in, 258; partnership with SAC, 246; praise for *Anthems, Hymns, and Responses*, 242; revision to *Union Hymnal*, 258–59
chanting and modal theory, 163
"chasonuth" (cantorial chant), 203
chaunting, 1
Chicago Columbian Exhibition (1893), 233
Children of Israel/Bene Israel congregation (Memphis), 35
children's and youth choirs, 37, 205, 221, 223

children's education, 222, 230, 273. *See also* Sabbath Schools
choirboy *(meshorer)* culture, 207
choirs: all-male choirs, 25, 28, 32–33, 56, 80, 87, 188; Anshe Chesed's choir, 42–43; in cantorial culture, 12–13; children's and youth choirs, 37, 221, 223; first Hebrew choir, 93, 97; makeup of, 272; protochoirs, 26; Sulzerian model of, 41–42; visibility of singers, 30
choral music and choral singing: adoption of English models of, 10; and American Jewish self-actualization, 164; and congregational participation, 93–94; and devotion, 159–60; exposure to through Sulzer's work, 176; in interactive liturgical community, 124; practices of, 4; and progressivism, 24; and psalm singing, 60; as reform measure, 21, 24; roles in community expression, 78. *See also* Naumburg, Louis; religious reform and choral singing; Ritterman, Isaac
choral societies, 223, 261n31
Christian hymnals, 67
Christianity: adoption of Jewish musical practices, 146–47; European developments and Judaism, 134; narrative of borrowing from, 11
Christian musical forms, dissociation from, 163
Church Music Association, 159
church participation, 219
Cincinnati, Jewish musical sphere of, 9, 268. *See also* Bene Yeshurun congregation (KKBY, Cincinnati); Cohen, Gustave M.; Ensel, Gustav S.; Goldstein, Morris; Hebrew Benevolent Society (Cincinnati); Mound Street congregation (Cincinnati); Sängerfests; Wise, Isaac Mayer
Cintura, J., 118
civic culture in American society, 11, 61
civic worship, conventions of, 2
classical reform, aesthetics of, 108
Cohen, Francis L.: career change of, 267; description of choral music, 163; on female singers, 45; *Jewish Encyclopedia*,

Cohen, Francis L. (*continued*)
　257; lecture at Anglo-Jewish Exposition, 218, 260n6; "Rise and Development of Synagogue Music" (1887), 224
Cohen, Gustave M. (c. 1820–1902), 76–116; overview of life and work, 11, 76–79, 77f, 109nn2–4; 1864 publications of, 187; at Ahshe Chesed, 90–92; at Bene Yeshurun, 86–88, 124; congregational participation, 272; death of, 267; *Der Israelitische Volksfreund*, 88–90, 111n64; at Emanu-El, 79–82; final years and impact of, 107–9, 116n149; impact of professionalization, 163; as independent educator, 82–84; *Little Bible*, 100, 101, 114n114; musical program in Chicago, 84–86; page turning device, 103, 115n128; portrait of famous cantors, 207; Psalm 100 setting, 101–2, 114n121; *Sacred Harp of Judah*, 12, 78, 92–100, 113n90, 113n97, 113n100, 198; *Sacred Harp of Judah*, second volume, 101–7, 115n136, 115n139; *Union Hymnal* efforts of, 229
Cohn, Levy, 42
Cohon, A. Irma, 268
colla parte accompaniment, keyboard, 198, 202
Collection of the Principal Melodies of the Synagogue from the Earliest Times to the Present, A (Kaiser and Sparger, 1893), 13–14, 163, 234–36, 235f, 262n55, 263n72
Committee for Regulating the Religious Service, 210, 215n87
communal unity, tripartite model of (synagogue-school-home), 7, 67, 86, 89, 92, 102, 103–4, 108–9. See also *Sacred Harp of Judah*
community building, 11, 12, 46, 57, 60, 63, 78–79
concert music in America, 194
congregational participation, 4, 8, 121–22, 219, 270
congregational singing: as adjunct to prayer, 179–80; aim of *Union Hymnal*, 245, 249–50, 254; national repertoire for, 230; panel at Music Teachers National Conference, 159; practices of, 4; preparing youth for, 106, 126; in Reform Judaism, 227; resistance to, 223–24; revival of, 219–24; in small communities, 120, 166n12; in *Union Hymnal*, 242–44. See also Ensel, Gustav S.; Hecht, Simon
congregational unity through *Minhag America*, 124
conservatism and emerging trends of choral singing, 120
Conway, David, 7
Cooke, William H. (1837–89), 159–60
cultural capital, 186
Cultus-Verein (Culture Society) congregation (New York). See Emanu-El congregation

Daily Inter Ocean, 158, 172n125
Darech Amuno congregation (New York), 188
Davis, A. J., 163, 222, 242
"Day of Public Humiliation" (May 9, 1798), 1, 2, 3
Die Deborah: about, 15; acknowledgement of Fischer's work, 70; appeals to honor Sulzer, 178; critique of *The Orpheus*, 106; demise of, 268; publication directed at women, 15; Singer article in, 244. See also Wise, Isaac Mayer
democratic worship, 61, 223, 273
Deutsch, Solomon, 39, 52n115
Dietz, Gregor, 103, 115n128

"Early Will I Seek" (Davis setting), 222
Eastern European cantors, primacy of, 244, 274
Eastern European Jewish musical culture: authenticity of, 244; bias in *Collection*, 236–38; criticism of practices, 39, 80, 143, 207, 224, 231; as endangered, 5; Idelsohn's promotion of, 211; role in American Judaism, 18n27, 231, 232; *sagerin* in, 45–46. See also Ashkenazic melodies; religious orthodoxy; Sulzer, Salomon; traditional Jewish melodies
economic impacts on music programs, 201–2, 203–4
Egyptian/Chaldean chants, 160
Ehrlich, Herman, 132; *Die israelitische Volkslehrer*, 122

Einhorn, David: choral music and progressivism, 24; and Louis Naumburg, 39; new congregation of, 43; *Olat Tamid*, 64–65, 71, 74n45, 74n51; relationship with Wilhelm Fischer, 11; sound of Jewish reform, 57
Eleff, Zev, 9, 209
Emanu-El congregation (formerly *Cultus-Verein*, New York): anniversary account of cantors, 108, 116n151; anniversary composition, 264n97; G. M. Cohen's tenure at, 78, 79–83; comments on emerging *Union Hymnal*, 246, 264n110; efforts toward congregational participation, 221, 222; hymnals of, 61, 242; music program budget, 186, 211n1; organist and composer for, 57; Sparger at, 227
Emerson, L. O., *The Harp of Judah*, 93
England, musical developments in, 10, 218
Ensel, Gustav S.: address at Music Teachers National Conference, 159, 160–61; approach to synagogue song, 121; background of, 118, 119, 165–66n8, 167nn25–26; Bene Yeshurum dedication, 117, 162; business and musical activities in Illinois, 125–26, 167–68nn40–41; as composer, 117, 123, 165n2, 167n30; death of, 267; introduction of congregations to *Minhag America*, 122–24; as Jewish music scholar, 131–36; lectures, 169n78; legacy of, 162–65, 172n127, 225; "Miriam's Song on the Red Sea," 170n95; musical philosophy of, 135; music reviews of, 134–35; "On Synagogue Music," 128, 131; origins of "Malbrook," 162; treatise on music in Judaism, 12; Varel synagogue dedication, 121
Ensel-Hecht debate on hymnals, 128, 131
ethnic sound in Jewish music, 13, 217, 268
ethnic tensions with Eastern Europeans and congregations, 85
Étude, The, 158, 162, 172n127
Eurocentric views of Jewish traditional music, 238, 274
Europe: primacy of traditions in musical culture, 3, 7; relationship with United States, 273

family singing, 7, 106
Fischer, Wilhelm: creation of hymnal *Zemirot Yisrael*, 11, 65–68; hiring of for Keneseth Israel congregation, 38; impact on American Jewish music, 57, 187; post-publication career activity, 71; progressive agenda of, 63–65, 78; reputation and positions held, 64, 74n37; singing method, 71, 75n56
Fischof, Josef, 200
folk aesthetic of music, 122, 166n22, 224
folk tunes paired with *piyyutim*, 161
Frank, Emma, 233
Frankel, Jacob, 64
Frey, Wilhelm, 89
Froelich, Gideon, 242, 263n92
Frohsinn society, 57, 62, 73n32
Frühauf, Tina, 3
Furber, Daniel, 61

Gabirol, Solomon ibn, 222
gender parity, 10, 273
German American culture, 55, 56, 118, 182–83
German era of American Jewish religious music, 9, 14. *See also* community building; hymn singing; Naumburg, Louis; Ritterman, Isaac; singing societies; Sternberger, Leon
German identity: hymn singing as part of, 56–57; through singing societies, 62
German immigration, 3
German Jewish culture, 70, 268
Gerstel, Ignatz, 191, 194, 212n17
Gesangverein. *See* singing societies
Goldberg, Geoffrey, 3, 166n12
Goldstein, Herman, 245, 258; *Anthems, Hymns, and Responses* (1894), 240–42, 241f
Goldstein, Morris (1840–1906): background of, 193, 212n26; death of, 267; *Kol Zimra*, 221–22; at Mound Street congregation (Bene Israel, Cincinnati), 208; music in *Zimrath Yah*, 13, 187, 200, 203; original compositions, 163, 200, 202; Society of American Cantors (SAC), 245; tribute to Welsch, 205–6; *Union Prayer Book*-based services, 247, 264n115
Gottheil, Gustav, 222, 247–48

Graziano, John, 4–5
Greek notation, 143, *144–45f*
Gregorian chants, 146, 159, 161
Grodzinsky, Israel, 215n77
Grossman, Louis, 239
Guinsburg, Theodore, 188, 221, 258; *Anthems, Hymns, and Responses* (1894), 240–42, *241f*
guitar, 102
Gunther, Charles, 176
Gutheim, James K., 29, 49n38, 128
Guttmann, Adolph, 222, 239

HaCohen, Ruth, 166n22
Halévy, Jacques Fromental, 196
Hamburg hymnal, 58, 59, 103
Hast, Bernhard, 264n101
Hast, Marcus, 224, 257
hazan. *See* cantors and the cantorate
Hebrew, use of term, 161, 172n137
Hebrew Benevolent Society (Cincinnati), 91
Hebrew cantillation, 143, 146, 171n105
Hebrew instruction, 82
Hebrew Leader, 176, 177, 178, 194
Hebrew Union College (1875), 13, 268
Hebrew Union College School of Sacred Music (New York), 5
Hecht, Jonas, 40–43, 76
Hecht, Simon: approach to synagogue song, 12, 120–21; background of, 119, 126, 166n10; at B'nai Israel congregation (Evansville, IN), 117–18; championing of choral music, 127; composed chants of, 122, 166n23; critique of conservatism, 120; focus of professional and creative efforts, 118; impact of professionalization, 163; music in *Zimrath Yah*, 203; overview of life and accomplishments, 118; submission to UAHC hymnal competition, 128–31, *129–30f*, 164; "We Meet Again in Gladness," 164, 173n148
Heimann, Regina, 126
Heine, Heinrich, 103
Heinemann, Jeremias, 59
Heinroth, J. A. G., 59
Henry, Henry A. (1800–79), 10, 25, 28–31, 32, 44, 49n44
Herxheimer, Salomon, *Yesod HaTorah*, 127

high art and people's music, tensions between, 71, 80–81, 101–3, 105–6, 232
Hirsch, Emil G., 128, 264n118
Hirsh, Gabriel, 264n101
historians' assessment of Jewish contributions to Western music, 132
Hochgluck, Osias, 207
holiday music, 202, 203, 208, 214n59, 242
Holland, Justin, 102
home. *See* communal unity, tripartite model of (synagogue-school-home)
Huebsch, Adolph, 190, 191
hymnals and singing societies, 55–71; early hymnals, 58–61; to enhance participation, 221–22; Ensel's philosophy regarding, 128; Fischer's role, 63–68; German identity and part singing, 55–57; Philippson's hymnal, 126; singing societies, 61–63; use of melodies from Christian settings, 135; *Zemirot Yisrael*, 65–71. See also *Sacred Harp of Judah, The*; *Union Hymnal*, evolution of; *Zimrath Yah*
Hymn Book for Jewish Worship (Landsberg and Wile), 135
hymns, educational, 7
hymn singing: in German populations, 11; in synagogue reform efforts, 56–57

Idelsohn, Abraham Z., 5, 6, 163, 211, 238, 267–68; *Jewish History in Its Historical Development* (1929), 46
improvisational style, 259
Independent German Congregation, 64
Independent Order of Patriarchs of Israel, 36
International Order of B'nai B'rith: cantors in leading roles in, 79; G. M. Cohen's activities with, 12, 100, 107, 110n26; founding of, 76; political rancor within, 86–87; Ramah Lodge, 84; Zion Lodge, 76, 78, 181
Isaacs, Samuel M., 27, 48n30, 179–80, 183n4, 191
Israelite: acknowledgement of Fischer's work, 70; on Anshe Chesed congregation's High Holiday services, 91; Ensel's article on Jewish music, 161–62; German language companion to, 15; report on B'nei El

congregation's first choir, 125; review of Zion Musical Society performance, 92; title of, 172n137. *See also American Israelite, The;* Wise, Isaac Mayer
Israelite Reform Society, 84–85
Israelitischen deutschen Cantorenvereins, 206
Der Israelitische Volksfreund (ed. G. M. Cohen), 88–90, 111n64
Italian Opera Company, 176

Jacobs, George, 128
Jacobs, M. N., 30
Jacobson, Israel, 58, 59, 120
Jastrow, Marcus, 125, 134
Jefferson, Thomas, 1, 2
Jewish American identity: asserted in *Zimrath Yah*, 202; and civic unity, 107, 164; and early American musical practice, 2; Idelsohn's comments on, 267; music as domain for expressing, 270; reflected in *Union Hymnal*, 253; role of music and worship in, 6, 7, 9, 20; and self-cultivation, 165; service to small communities, 119; through authentic Jewish compositions, 163; through singing societies, 62; and Western music history, 5; in worship, 88
Jewish and American identities, fostering cohesive relationship, 90
Jewish chant, 224, 234. *See also* Ashkenazic melodies; cantillation; traditional Jewish melodies
Jewish culture: historical emergence of, 138; progressivism and cultural advancement, 11; women's role in, 238
Jewish education, 82–83
Jewish Encyclopedia, 225, 238, 257
Jewish Exponent, 222–23
Jewish Messenger, 179, 184n25, 185; on Morris Goldstein, 193
Jewish music: adoption of European musical heritage, 5–6; Anglophone domination of, 257; assumptions about, 2, 4; authenticity in, 71, 244; contradictory trends in, 274; idea of, 3, 5; role in American Judaism, 20, 101; scholarship and literature, 231–32; tonality in, 13, 217, 268; in Western

musical narrative, 160. *See also* communal unity, tripartite model of; Ensel, Gustav S.; Hecht, Simon; hymnals and singing societies; religious reform and choral singing; Sulzer, Salomon; synagogue music; *Union Hymnal*, evolution of; Wise, Isaac Mayer; *Zemirot Yisrael*; *Zimrath Yah*
Jewish Music in Its Historical Development (Idelsohn, 1929), 163–64
Jewish oppression and creativity, 160–61
Jewish Orphan Asylum, 100, 106, 114n112
Jewish population in the United States, 3
Jewish reforms: criticism of, 19–20; solidified in American culture, 219. *See also* Cohen, Gustave M.; Ensel, Gustav S.; Hecht, Simon; progressivism; Reform Judaism; religious reform and choral singing; Wise, Isaac Mayer
Jewish Theological Seminary, 234, 268
Jewish Women's Congress, 238
Jewish worship, American forms of, 188
Johlson, Josef, 59, 81
"Die Juden in Amerika" (Welsch), 210
Das Judenthum in der Musik (Judaism in Music, Wagner), 226, 274
Der jüdische Kantor (1879–98), 206–7
Junkerman, G. F, 44

Kadosh/Sanctus. *See* Trisagion
Kaiser, Alois (1840–1908): advocacy of congregational singing, 245; *Anthems, Hymns, and Responses* (1894), 240–42, 241f, 263nn92–93; attention to Hebrew portion of service, 258; background of, 191; *Collection of the Principal Melodies*, 13–14, 163; contributions to *Jewish Encyclopedia*, 257; death of, 267–68; leadership in cantors' associations, 219, 230, 245, 258; music in *Zimrath Yah*, 13, 200, 203; at Oheb Shalom congregation, 191–93, 192f, 203–4, 214n64; original compositions, 107, 115n146, 134–35, 200, 202, 208; portrait of famous cantors, 207; premiere of Union Prayer Book–based music, 247; summary of accomplishments and music collection, 268–69, 275n7; tribute to Welsch, 205–6; *Union Hymnal* efforts of, 229, 230–36,

Kaiser, Alois (1840–1908) (*continued*) 239, 247–48, 250; *Union Hymnal* contents, 252–53, 265n134; *Union Hymnal* revisions, 256, 259. See also *Zimrath Yah*
Kalisch, Isidor, 101, 190
Kantrowitz, Jacob, 181, 186
Kartschmaroff, Edward, 205, 214n66, 230, 258, 264n101
Kedusha ("Holiness"), 95–96, 200
Kehilath Anshe Ma'ariv (KAM) congregation (Chicago), 84–86
Keneseth Israel congregation (Philadelphia): cantorial search, 52n102, 52n115; choral society, 261n31; first notated Jewish hymnal, 11; hiring of William Fischer, 64; hymnal compilation for, 65; Naumburg's tenure at, 37–39; William Armhold, 70
Kitziger, Frederick Emil, *Shire Yehudah*, 211
KKBY. See Bene Yeshurun congregation
Kley, Eduard, 59
Kling, Selig, 80, 81, 110n13
Klotz and Tanner, 180
Knesses Shalom congregation (Syracuse, NY), 30, 31–32, 222
Kohler, Kaufman, 43, 135, 170n86, 240
"Kol Nidre," 134, 160, 162, 203, 227
Kompert, Leopold, *The Carbuncle (Der Karfunkel)*, 176, 184n11
Konservatorium der Gesellschaft der Musikfreunde (Vienna), 50nn53–54
Korzeles, Charles, 190
Kramer, Adolph, 186, 211n5
Kramer, Judah (Julius), 33, 188
Krehbiel, Henry E., 226, 227
Kunkel's Musical Review, 158
Kuttner, Henry, 36

Landman, Leo, 46
Landsberg, Max, 135
Lane, Spencer, 222
Lasker, Raphael, 174–75
Lazarus, Gershom, 96, 96f
leading tones, 159, 172n131
Leeser, Isaac: adoption of regulations regarding choirs, 25; budgets for music, 186; call and response singing, 49n34; on G. M. Cohen's Hebrew lessons pamphlet, 82; comment on Temple Knesses Shalom building, 32; criticism of reforms, 19–20; critique of *Zemirot Yisrael*, 70; endorsement of *Sacred Harp of Judah*, 98; on Fischer, 64; and Henry A. Henry, 49n44; and S. M. Isaacs, 48n30. See also *Occident and American Jewish Advocate, The* (Leeser, ed.), setting of "Adon Olam"
Leo, Ansel (c. 1806–78): background of, 25–26, 48n21; in B'nai B'rith, 79; at B'nai Jeshurun, 26–28, 32, 33, 48n27; death of, 49n35; role in American Jewish music history, 10, 30–31, 44
Leo, Louis, 26, 28
Leo, Simon (c.1767–1837), 26
"Lessons in the Hebrew Language" (G. M. Cohen, 1850), 82, 110n29
Leucht, Joseph, 205
Levin, Neil, 2, 78, 96
Lewandowski, Louis (Berlin, 1821–94), 7, 8, 207, 260n9
Liedertafel, 64
Lilienthal, Max: advice on hazan position, 42; Cincinnati Sängerfest committee president, 56; endorsement for G. M. Cohen publication, 82; "Lessons on the Hebrew language," 110n29; poems of, 106; on singing societies, 71; Union of American Hebrew Congregations, 107, 128; use of Sulzer's *Schir Zion*, 44
Lincoln, Abraham, memorial service for, 190
Lingard, William, "Walking Down Broadway," 181
"Literature of the Music of the Jews" (Sparger), 231–32
liturgical music. See sacred music; synagogue music
Lob, Otto, 203
Lodge Street congregation (Cincinnati). See Bene Yeshurun congregation (KKBY)
London: Jewish musical authority in, 24–26; Western Synagogue, 25, 26, 28, 29
Loth, Moritz, 128
Löwenberg, William: background of, 262n55; in CCAR, 256; leadership in cantors' associations, 245, 258; on music in Jewish history and culture, 257; role in creating

Union Hymnal, 230–36; work on *Union Hymnal*, 250, 259
Löwenstamm, Max G., 226
Lowenthal, David, 275
Lyon, Robert, 82

magrepha, 138
major/minor tonality in *Zimrath Yah*, 201, 202, 203, 209
"Malbrook" ("We Won't Come Home Till Morning"), 134–35, 162, 169n77, 172n139
Männerchor, 56
Mannheimer, Isaac Noah, 71
"Mannheimer Kinder," 26
"Ma'oz Tsur" ("Rock of Ages"), 200
Maretzek, Max, 176
Markreich, Max, 167n25
Marks, David Woolf, 25
Marksohn, Arnold, 132
Martini, *Storia della Musica*, 146
Mason, Lowell, 91
medallion with dedication to Sulzer, 180–81, 184n25
Mendelssohn, Felix, 5, 226
Mendelssohn, Moses, 83, 85, 107
Merzbacher, Leo, 79, 80, 81–82, 83, 109n5
meshorerim, 26, 29
Messing, Dora, 160
Methfessel, Albert Gottlieb, 103
Meyerbeer Giacomo, operas of, 177, 184n12, 195
"Mi Chamocha" ("Who Is Like You, O Lord"), 200
middle class ideals, 118
Mielziner, Moses, 43, 146, 193
Mikve Israel congregation (Philadelphia), 20, 21
Minhag America (Wise): G. M. Cohen's familiarity with, 85; as collaborative form, 123; congregations' adoption of, 39, 99–100, 122–24, 193; dissent concerning, 198; and religious reform, 114n117; revision to, 194, 195–97; success of, 10; and synagogue-school-home model, 7
Minkowsky, Pinchas, 247, 257, 260n7, 268
Mishkan Israel congregation (Boston), 36
Mitchels, James, 81, 110n20

modernity, Sulzer's musical work as sign of, 45
Moïse, Penina, 96
Monteverdi, Claudio, and spirit of prayer, 159
Moses, Isaac S., 239, 242, 245, 247, 248, 258, 263n93
Mound Street congregation (Cincinnati), 222
music: as communal activity, 86; as people's art, 91; as product of multifaceted cultural interaction, 147–48
musical accompaniment, 272. *See also* guitar; organs in synagogues
Musical Bulletin (1879–83), 158
musical culture, cultivation of, 175, 178
musical literacy, 7–8, 238
musical populism and populists, 117–19, 179–80, 224. *See also* Ensel, Gustav S.; Hecht, Simon
musical prayer leader, use of term, 16
musical refinement and high art, 186
musical syncretism, 135
music education, community responsibility for, 12
Music Teachers National Association (MTNA) meetings, 159, 162

Nadel, Stanley, 56
National Council of Jewish Women, 233, 268
Naumann, Emil, *History of Music*, 224
Naumbourg, Samuel (1817–80): American agent for, 194; discovery of Rossi, 131, 148; "Etz Chayim" ("It Is a Tree of Life"), 202; history of Jewish and Western music, 132; hymnal, 65; musical compositions, 43; music in *Zimrath Yah*, 200, 203, 209; as paradigm of excellence, 8, 272; psalm settings, 104, 105, 171n109; publications of, 81; relationship to Louis Naumburg, 37; Sephardic compared to Ashkenazic chant, 171n115; status in Jewish music traditions, 7, 78; use of traditional melodies, 226
Naumburg, Louis (Lazarus) (1813–1902): death of, 267; Fischer's German hymns, 71; judge for UAHC hymnal contest, 128; at Keneseth Israel congregation, 37–39, 64; at Rodef Shalom congregation (Pittsburgh),

Naumburg, Louis (*continued*)
39–40, 52n121; role in American Jewish music history, 10, 45
New York, Jewish musical sphere of, 9, 229, 268. *See also* Adas Jeshurun congregation (New York); Adath Israel congregation (New York); Ahawath Chesed congregation (New York); Anshe Chesed congregation (New York); Beth-El congregation (New York); B'nai Jeshurun congregation (New York); Darech Amuno congregation (New York); Emanu-El congregation (formerly *Cultus-Verein*, New York); Hebrew Union College (1875); Jewish Theological Seminary; Ritterman, Isaac; Shaarei Shomayim congregation (New York); Shaarey Tefilah congregation (New York); Shearith Israel congregation (New York); Welsch, Samuel
Nicolai, Philipp, 69
non-Jewish musicians and choristers: advocate of, 191; budgets for, 123, 167n29; concerns about, 35, 63, 127, 183n4, 205, 221; for musical quality, 13. *See also* Fischer, Wilhelm
notation, evolution of, 143–46

Occident and American Jewish Advocate, The (Leeser, ed.), setting of "Adon Olam," 20–21
Ohabey Or congregation (Chicago), 85–86
Oheb Shalom congregation (Baltimore), 191–93, 209, 248. *See also* Jastrow, Marcus; Kaiser, Alois; Szold, Benjamin
Oko, Adolph, 268, 275n7
opera, 176–77
Oratorio Society of New York, 159
organology, 138, 272
organ preludes, 197, 200, 214n55
organs in synagogues: to advance cultural excellence, 12; Ensel's welcoming of, 148; historical precedents for, 138; and music's centrality in worship, 21, 24; opposition to, 35, 162; pipe organ at Ahawath Chesed, 202; purchase at B'nai Jeshurun, 33; Wise's support for, 44, 202, 270
orientalism in Ensel's work, 143, 146–47, 160

Oriental-Occidental balance, 146–47
Orpheus, The (G. M. Cohen, 1878), 103–7, *104f*, *105f*, 115n136, 115n139
Orthodox Union, 268
orthodoxy. *See* religious orthodoxy
Ostendorf, Ann, 132
Österreiche-ungarische Cantorenverein, 206
Österreichische-ungarische Cantoren-Zeitung (*OUCZ*, 1881–1903): on *Die Tonarten*, 259n3; interest in American cantors, 218, 260n4; purposes of, 206–7

page turner (device), 103, 115n128
Palestrina, Giovanni da, 148, 171n117
Peixotto, Benjamin Franklin, 92, 100
"people's minister," 120
Pereles, Moritz, 177
Philippson, Ludwig, 67, 89, 126
Phillips, Henry, 26
phonographs and recording, 259
poetic hymns (*piyyutim*), 121, 135, 147, 161
Poznanski, Gustavus, 24
pragmatism, 119, 271
professionalization: of cantors, 45–46, 178–79, 186, 206–7; of choirs, 123, 223, 230, 272; and congregational singing, 220; European developments toward, 21; of musicians, 8, 9, 15, 163, 271. *See also* congregational singing
progressivism: compared to European practices, 197; and German culture, 56; music professionalization and, 271; progressive synagogues, 114n117; union of progressive synagogues, 101. *See also* Sulzer, Salomon; Wise, Isaac Mayer
Protestant hymn traditions, 63
Protestant Trisagion, *154–57f*
protochoirs, 26, 27
psalm chanting: in dedication of B'nai Jeshurun's new synagogue building, 28; Jewish musical practice in 1700s, 1–2, 17n3. *See also* traditional Jewish melodies
psalms, Wise's view of, 255
psalm settings: example of Oriental-Occidental balance, 146, 171n109; by Goldstein and Naumbourg, 200; in

The Orpheus, 104–5; by Sulzer, 181, 184n30; by Welsch, *182f*, 194, 200, 202

rabbi, use of term, 16
rabbinic training and practice, 5, 9, 15, 20, 25, 30
Rabin, Shari, 9
ram's horns, 138, *141–42f*
Rappaport, Solomon, 245
Reformation, 159
Reform Judaism, 161–62, 227, 268, 271. *See also* Central Conference of American Rabbis; Hebrew Union College; Union of American Hebrew Congregations; Wise, Isaac Mayer
religious orthodoxy, 24, 30, 33, 35, 98, 162, 188, 275n9. *See also* United Hebrew Congregation (St. Louis)
religious reform and choral singing, 19–54; overview of, 19–24; adoption of British practices, 24–31; choral singing as political symbol, 43; as evidence of cultural advancement, 11; gendering of, 46; hymn singing in, 57, 58; Naumburg's work, 37–40; professionalization of cantorate, 45–46; Ritterman's work, 24–37; Sternberger and the Sulzer cantors, 40–43; Wise and synagogue choir, 43–45
religious reform and gender parity, 10, 45–46
Renaissance and spirit of prayer, 159
Rice, Isaac L. (1850–1915): background of, 194–95; career change, 210–11; contributor to *Zimrath Yah*, 13, 187, 200, 203; new career of, 208; "Prelude on a Traditional Theme," 200, *201f*
Rinck, Johann Christian Heinrich, 200, 214n55
Ritterman, Isaac (Ignatz) (c.1820–1890): biographical details, 31, 37, 50n52; at B'nai Jeshurun, 28, 32–33; at Memphis's Children of Israel congregation, 35, 51n87, 168n52; role in American Jewish music history, 10, 44–45; at Temple Knesses Shalom, 31–32, 50n63; training and early career, 31, 50n59; at United Hebrew Congregation, 33–36

Rodef Shalom congregation (Pittsburgh), 39–40, 52n121
Rodeph Shalom congregation (New York), 30, 245
Rodeph Shalom congregation (Philadelphia), 21, 63, 64, 74n38
Roget, Edward, 20, 21
Root, George F., 91
Rosenfeld, Jacob, 30
Rosenthal, Louis N., 65
Rosewald, Julie, 273
Rossi, Salamone, 131, 148, 171n117
Rubin, Adolph, 43, 83, 177, 203, 205

Sabbath School Hymnal (Moses), 245, 247, 263n93
Sabbath Schools: education in congregational singing, 230, 233; hymnbook competition for, 103, 128, 131. *See also* Cohen, Gustave M.; *Sabbath School Hymnal*; *Sacred Harp of Judah, The*
sacred emotions, awakening of, 143
Sacred Harp of Judah, The (G. M. Cohen, 1864), 92–100; contents of, 94–97, *95f*, *96f*; European acknowledgement of, 208; goals in, 11–12; origin of name, 93, *94f*; printing plate manufacture, 113n97; as reflection of B'nai B'rith ideals, 92; success of, 97–99, 107, 113n100; volume two of, 102–7
sacred music: lectures on, 132–34; MTNA panel on, 159
sagerin, 10, 45–46
Salinger, Julius, 64, 70
Salomon, Gotthold, 85
Sängerfests, 55, 57, 62–63, 87
Sarna, Jonathan, 274
S. Brainard and Company, 92, 97, 113n97
Schaefer & Koradi, 65
Schechter, Solomon, 268
Schir Zion (Sulzer, 1840), 174–75, 187–88, 232, 244
Schlesinger, Sigmund (1835–1906), 36, 57, 127, 168n52
Seiniger, Charles L., 248, 264n101
Seixas, Gershom, 1–2
self-cultivation. *See Bildung* (self-cultivation)

Sephardic *hazzanim*, 2
Sephardic tonalities, 147, 171n115
Sha'arai Shomayim congregation (Mobile, AL), 57
Shaare Emeth congregation (St. Louis), 133
Shaarei Shomayim congregation (New York), 191; 7, 194
Shaarey Tefilah congregation (New York), 27, 48n30, 49n35, 221, 222
Shearith Israel congregation (New York), 1–2, 221
Shema ("Hear, O Israel"), 200
Sherith Israel congregation (San Francisco), 30
Shevitz, Amy HIll, 118
Shirei Keneset Yisrael, 223, 225, 261n39
Silverman, Herman, 264n101
Silverstein, Joseph, 257
Simon, Oswald J., 248
Simpson, Julia K., 233
Singer, Josef: and cantorial art, 207, 259; death of, 268; Jewish traditional music, 217, 244; overseer of cantorial organization, 206; *Die Tonarten*, 259n3; treatise on musical modes, 227
singing in harmony, 12. *See also* Cohen, Gustave M.; congregational singing; Ensel, Gustav S.; Fischer, Wilhelm; Hecht, Simon
singing methods, 178
Singing Schools, 91, 103. *See also Sacred Harp of Judah*
singing societies, 61–63; in German culture, 11, 55–57; progressivism of William Fischer, 63–65; and synagogue music, 71; Zion singing society, 62, 73n33, 91, 112–13nn82–83
"Sing Unto Us the Songs of Zion" (Sparger in *The American Hebrew*), 227–28
Slobin, Mark, 6, 16
small congregations, 119, 128, 158, 164, 198, 271
Society for the Advancement of Judaism, 268
Society of American Cantors (SAC), 245, 246, 255, 258
Sofge, Henry, 29
Sola Mendes, Frederick de, 222, 248, 254
solo chanting, practices of, 4
source-based approach to study, 8–9
Sparger, William: *Anthems, Hymns, and Responses* (1894), 240–42, 241f; in CCAR, 256; disappearance of, 258, 266n156; importance of cantor, 226–28; review of Van der Stucken's "Schir Zion," 244; Society of American Cantors (SAC), 245; on subpar compositions, 226–27; "The Cantor Exposed and Congregational Singing Assured," 249–50; *Union Hymnal* efforts of, 229, 230–36. *See also Collection of the Principal Melodies of the Synagogue from the Earliest Times to the Present*
Spicker, Max (1858–1912), 57
Stark, Edward, 245
Stein, Leopold, 59, 89, 106
Steiner, Hugo, 268
Sternberger, Leon (1819–97): at Anshe Chesed, 193; background of, 40, 53n125, 53n127, 175; in B'nai B'rith, 79; death of, 267; effect of financial hardships, 205; impact as Sulzer cantor, 40–43; music in *Zimrath Yah*, 203; role in American Jewish music history, 10, 45; Sulzer letter to, 181; tribute to Welsch, 205–6; Viennese model and, 186; in Warsaw, 40
Stoltz, Joseph, 258–59
Straus, Samuel, 84
Sulzer, Henrietta, 176, 183nn9–10
Sulzer, Julius, 62, 176
Sulzer, Salomon (Vienna, 1804–1890): 1866 *Sulzerfeier*, 175–81, 180–81; "Adon Olam," 201f; in American Jewish worship, 10, 78; celebration of, 13, 258, 266n159; critique of, 73n33; death of, 225–26; family accomplishments, 176–77, 183nn9–10; interest in the United States, 176, 181, 184n28; as Jewish Palestrina, 148; Kedusha melody in popular tune, 181; musical place in services, 272; music in *Zimrath Yah*, 200, 202, 203, 209, 214n60; original music for the synagogue, 98; place in liturgical music, 161; premier of wedding music in US, 81; Psalm 42, 184n30; psalm settings, 104, 105, 105f; reform and, 7; reinvigoration of chanting,

160; Ritterman's relationship to, 31; role in American Jewish music history, 8, 21, 174–75, 207, 208; *Schir Zion*, 62; status among cantorial trainers, 218; training of American cantors, 12; use of traditional melodies, 226; at Vienna's Konservatorium der Gesellschaft, 31, 50n54

Sulzer cantors, 40–43, 122, 163, 175, 209–10. *See also* Goldstein, Morris; Pereles, Moritz; Ritterman, Isaac; Sternberger, Leon; Welsch, Samuel

Sulzerfeier of 1866: dedicatory medallion, 180–81; planning and fund-raising, 177–79; resources to honor Sulzer, 175–76; and standards to aim toward, 185

synagogue music: balance with spiritual core, 220; champion of, 174–75; chants, 166n23; debate over Sulzer mania, 179–80; debates on practice of, 118; and democratization of services, 122; emphasis on craft, 182; Ensel's music reviews, 134–35; great composers of, 78; Hecht's guidelines to composing song settings, 121; importance to American Jewish future, 196; model of musicality for, 83–84; pluralistic vision of, 233; purity in heritage of, 26; race-based assessment, 226; reconfiguration of by cantors, 13; rising value in American congregational worship, 175, 182–83; role in Jewish survival, 227; and spirituality, 164. *See also* congregational singing; Jewish music; traditional Jewish melodies

synagogue-school-home model: aim of *Union Hymnal*, 250; in American Judaism, 270; description of, 7; and ideals of B'nai B'rith, 92; promoted by G. M. Cohen, 89, 102, 103–4; promoted by hymnal and songbook creators, 108, 119, 166n11. See also *Sacred Harp of Judah*

synagogue services: beautification efforts, 41; full participation in, 93; liturgical contributions by congregations, 96; mechanisms for introducing choral music to, 62; participation by the congregation, 97–98; schedule of, 37–38

"Synagogue Song: How It Is, and How It Should Be" (G. M. Cohen), 83–84

Szold, Benjamin, 125, 134, 191, *192f*, 212n21, 214n64

Talmud as historical document, 162
Talmud Yelodim Institute (TYI), 123–24
tempi of hymns, 67, 68
Temple Society of Concord. *See* Knesses Shalom congregation (Syracuse, NY)
Tifereth Israel congregation (Cleveland), 90, 91, 99
Tillman, Nicholas, 193, 212n19
Die Tonarten des traditionellen Synagogengesanges (Singer, 1886), 217, 259n3
traditional Jewish melodies, 201, 203, 209, 226, 231–32, 234, 250, 268
Trisagion, 148–57, *149–51f*, *154–57f*

UAHC. *See* Union of American Hebrew Congregations
Union Hymnal, evolution of, 217–59; cantorial agenda for, 230–36; contents, 252–53; Eurocentric bias in, 236–38; liberal liturgies solidified behind, 108; publication of, 250–52, *251f*; reception to, 253–55, 265n139, 265n140; revision of, 256, 258–59; revival of congregational singing, 219–24; struggle for editorial control of, 229–38; struggles and delays in completion, 238–50, 263n90; views of Jewish musical history and, 224–28
Union of American Hebrew Congregations (UAHC, 1873): G. M. Cohen's contributions to formation, 79, 103; consolidation of Central European practices, 268; creation of uniform educational materials, 128; Ensel's stature in, 126; founding of, 13; hymnal competition, 107, 128–31, 135; pluralistic visions and, 233–34; synagogue membership, 219; unified liturgy, 209
Union Prayer Book, 14, 108, 227–28, 233, 239, 246, 248, 257
United Hebrew Congregation (St. Louis), 33–35, 36

urban congregations, 12–13, 175, 182–83, 220, 271

Van der Stucken, Frank, "Schir Zion," 244, 264n97
Vienna as Jewish and intellectual hub, 217–18, 260n7
Viennese model in America, 188. *See also* Goldstein, Morris; Kaiser, Alois; Sternberger, Leon; Sulzer, Salomon; Sulzer cantors
vocal talent: availability of, 158, 175; competition for, 188; effect of financial hardships, 205
vocal training, 127, 164, 273
Voice, The, 160, 161, 163
Voice of Prayer and Praise, 225
Volkslehrer ("people's minister"), 120
"V'Shamru" (Exodus 31:16–17), 200

Wagner, Richard, 166n22, 171n105, 226; *Der Judenthum in der Musik,* 226, 274
Wasserman, J., 177
Weber, Edward, 104
Weintraub, Hirsch (Königsberg, 1811–81), 7, 209
Weissbach, Lee Shai, 271
Welsch, Samuel (1835–1901): American counterpart to Sulzer, 191; background of, 188–90, 189f, 211–12n8; in B'nai B'rith, 79; death of, 267; effect of financial hardships, 204–5; and Kaiser, 195, 213n37; later career in Prague, 210; launching of *Zimrath Yah,* 195–97; leadership positions, 114n120; original compositions, 200, 202, 204f; portrait of famous cantors, 207; Psalm 93 ("Der Herr Ist König"), 181, 182f, 194, 196, 213n37; reputation of, 43, 202; tribute to, 205–6; *Union Hymnal* efforts of, 229; work with fellow cantors, 195; and *Zimrath Yah,* 13, 101, 106, 198, 200, 203, 209. See also *Zimrath Yah*
Werner, Eric, 5, 6, 268
Werner's Magazine, 163
Wiese, Christian, 64
Wiesen, Israel, 207
Wile, Sol, 135
Wilhelm, Cornelia, 9, 76, 79

Wise, Isaac Mayer: in B'nai B'rith political dispute, 86–87; choral music and progressivism, 24, 32, 43–44, 56, 82, 107; on G. M. Cohen's Psalm 100, 102, 114n121; community model of worship and music, 7; critique of *Union Hymnal,* 255; *Die Deborah,* 90; Ensel's work with, 118, 125; as guest preacher, 99; on hazan singing, 123; *Hymns, Psalms, and Prayers,* 106; *Israelite,* 90; on KKBY choir, 87–88; music's importance in Judaism, 9–10, 71, 270–71; on *The Orpheus,* 106; reform of synagogue choir, 43–45; response to Zion Musical Society, 92; on Rodef Shalom, 39; role in American Jewish music history, 45; on *Sacred Harp of Judah,* 98–99; on the Sängerbund, 55; support of Sulzer's music, 179–80; *Union Hymnal* efforts, 229, 248, 253–54, 265n135; use of Sulzer's music, 186; work with G. M. Cohen, 79; and *Zemirot Yisrael,* 70; and *Zimrath Yah,* 195–96, 198. See also *Minhag America*
Wise, Stephen S., 268
Wohlwill, J., 58, 60–61
"Wo ist meine Heimath?" ("Where Is My Homeland?," Cintura and Hecht), 118, 165n4
Wolf, William, 132
Wolfsohn, Carl, 194–95
women: in choirs, 35, 39, 42, 51n86; as liturgical leaders, 45–46, 54n158; roles of in synagogues and Jewish musical practices, 10, 14–15, 273; in singing societies, 61
women's organizations, 233, 247–48, 273
World's Fair (Chicago), spirit of, 14
worship, organic mode of, 67–68
Württemberg hymnal (1836), 59–60, 65, 119, 166n11
Württemberg Sängerfest, 61

Yom Kippur liturgy, 134–35
York, F. L., 239
Young, Alfred (1831–1900), 159, 160

Die Zeitgeist, 158
Zemirot Yisrael (Fischer, 1863): contents of, 68–69; creation and publication of, 65–67,

66f; critiques of, 69–71; "Du meine Seele schwinge," 69f; incorporation of German hymn conventions in, 57, 69; learning synagogue music at home, 93; as related to Sulzer's and Naumbourg's works, 67; representing German Gesangverein culture, 63; success of, 71

Zemirot Yisrael (Hecht hymnal), 128–31, *129–30f*, 168n61

Zemirot Yisrael (Naumbourg, 1847, 1852, 1857), 187–88

Zimrath Yah (Welsch, Kaiser, Goldstein, and Rice, 1871–86): cantors responsible for, 188–95; comparison to *A Collection of the Principal Melodies*, 236–37f; context for, 185–86, 187–88; European acknowledgement of, 208; historical significance of, 13, 186–87, 209–10, 211; launch of, 195–200, *199f*; praise for, 208; recommended works from for *Union Hymnal*, 242; use of, 209; volume 1, 200–202; volume 2, 202; volume 3, 203–4; volume 4 (final), 206, 208–9

Zion Musical Society (formerly, Israelitish Sacred Music Society), 91–92, 112–13nn82–83

Zon, Bennett, 132

Zunz, Leopold, 147, 171n113

JUDAH M. COHEN is the Lou and Sybil Mervis Professor of Jewish Culture and Associate Professor of Musicology at Indiana University Bloomington. He is author of *The Making of a Reform Jewish Cantor: Musical Authority, Cultural Investment* and *Through the Sands of Time: A History of the Jewish Community of St. Thomas, US Virgin Islands.*

www.ingramcontent.com/pod-product-compliance
Lightning Source LLC
Chambersburg PA
CBHW071401300426
44114CB00016B/2137